SHE MADE FRIENDS
AND KEPT THEM

Also by Fleur Cowles

In collaboration with Robert Vavra:

As a contributor:

Fleur Cowles as she was drawn by Rene Bouche in 1959.

Fleur Cowles

SHE MADE
FRIENDS
AND
KEPT THEM

AN ANECDOTAL MEMOIR

with an Introduction by
CARLOS FUENTES

HarperCollins*Publishers*

Endpaper photographs courtesy of The Hulton Getty Collection, Popperfoto.

This book was originally published in Great Britain in 1996 by HarperCollins Publishers.

HarperCollins books may be purchased for educational, business, or sales promotional use. For information please write: Special Markets Department, Harper-Collins Publishers, Inc., 10 East 53rd Street, New York, NY 10022.

FIRST U.S. EDITION

ISBN 0-06-018713-1

96 97 98 99 00 ❖/HC 10 9 8 7 6 5 4 3 2 1

To Tom

AS ALWAYS

CONTENTS

LIST OF ILLUSTRATIONS

xiii

Fleur Cowles with Prince Abdorreza Pahlavi of Iran and his wife and son

Fleur Cowles and her new husband Tom Montague Meyer at Heathrow airport

between pages 232 and 233

HM Queen Elizabeth the Queen Mother at an International World Wildlife Fund exhibition at Glasgow's Museum of Art

Peter (Lord) Carrington in Sarajevo (Sygma)

George Marshall, his wife and Fleur Cowles at the Coronation of HM Queen Elizabeth

Pierre Mendes-France, his wife, Lily and Fleur Cowles skiing in the Alps

Marilyn Monroe and Bertha Stafford Vester

Ramon Magsaysay with Fleur Cowles

Jacqueline Auriole with Fleur Cowles

Prince Rainier and Princess Grace of Monaco.

Sir Stafford and Lady Cripps at an exhibition of 'Paintings by Famous Amateurs' in New York

Salvador Dali stepping off the train in London in the late 1950s, greeting Fleur Cowles

Bernard Baruch with Fleur Cowles

Jung Chang and Fleur Cowles at dinner in London

Mamie Eisenhower with Fleur Cowles

Fleur Cowles in Panmunjon during the Korean war

The Shah of Persia with Fleur Cowles

Vivien Leigh and Fleur Cowles at *Look* magazine

Prince Juan Carlos of Spain, Gina Bachauer and Fleur Cowles after the wedding of Crown Prince Constantine of Greece to Princess Anne-Marie of Denmark

Cary Grant with Fleur Cowles in London

Maurice Chevalier

George Bush and Russell Train with Fleur Cowles

General Omar Bradley

Governor Chris Patten with John Major at Government House in Hong Kong in March 1996 (Popperfoto)

Fleur Cowles photographed at her desk as the lady editor at *Look, Quick,* and *Flair* magazines in the 1950s

ACKNOWLEDGEMENTS

Thank you: to my editor, John Boothe, who enhanced this book by his relentless scrutiny, erudition and care. To Arabella Quin, warm thanks for her superb assistance in the final handling of the book. To Liza Lapsley, my secretary, who transformed colourfully illegible handwriting into a computerized manuscript. And to Eddie Bell, who so firmly and finely marshalled this book on its way to publication. My grateful thanks.

THE LITERARY MEDALLIONS
OF FLEUR COWLES

THE NIGHT BEFORE I started reading Fleur Cowles's admiring and admirable coupling of memory and friendship, I saw Peter Hall's no less admiring and admirable version of *Hamlet* in London at the end of 1994. When I began reading the loose sheets of Fleur's manuscript the next morning, both premises of her book – memory and friendship – were firmly planted in my mind.

Hamlet swears to remember his father: 'Remember thee!' he exclaims, and promises the Ghost the gift of memory as long as 'memory holds a seat / In this distracted globe'.

Polonius, in the famous counsel to the departing Laertes, recommends to his son that friends be grappled 'to thy soul with hoops of steel'.

Yet both doomed men – the Prince and the Courtier – forget to leaven their actions with Dr Johnson's practical, everyday wisdom: keep your friendships in daily repair.

Fleur Cowles titles her book *She Made Friends – and Kept Them* – that is, she practised Dr Johnson's wise and worldly wisdom. But friendships in real life are one thing; they are, to be sure, self-sustaining, self-nourishing, as long as we attend to them, keep them 'in constant repair'. But writing about our friends is quite another matter. We can be unjust, partial, unfair, mawkish, maudlin, self-serving . . . and forgetful. Fleur Cowles avoids all of these pitfalls by exercising a loving memory, a discriminating remembrance which keeps the bonds of affection from overwhelming the clarity of perception. She can wield a mean rapier here and there, but her victims are generally deserving. She can have a liking for people I detest (Ronald Reagan for example, tied for ever to the Iran-Contra Scandal and his brutal interventions in my part of the world, Latin America). But both she and I are entitled to our sympathies and differences. What comes under scrutiny when we write about people we have known is not only their always-debatable relationship to good and evil, but the quality of the writer's memory, her or his capacity to draw a verbal portrait that may be as flattering as a Winterhalter court portrait, or as damning as a Goya rendition of a royal family grouping.

From Homer to Shakespeare to Proust, memory is in the telling. Homer tells the tale already known by all, and all who hear it know this. Shakespeare compares memory to a table from which, selectively, we can wipe away all trivial records, retaining only the essential. Proust sees in memory a way of freeing sensibility from the tyrannies of time and space. But in the telling, all three adhere to Coleridge's wonderful vision of memory as liberation; remembrance as a creative renewal.

Fleur Cowles is an American. Or, if you prefer – since the United States has kidnapped the name of a whole hemisphere – a Gringa, a Yankee, no longer a *norteamericana* since NAFTA now includes Canada and Mexico, and not a Unitedstater, as we sometimes call the citizens of that great country which, more than a nation, as Tocqueville foresaw, is a universe unto itself. Fleur is a cosmopolitan.

Yet she understands that to bring that universe of the land mass between the Great Lakes and the Rio Grande, between the Pacific and the Atlantic, into the understanding and affection of the rest of the world has always been a tremendous challenge for both the gringos and those who – happily or unhappily – belong to other nations, cultures, traditions.

What Fleur Cowles brings to her warm and wide-armed book is precisely that generosity, that embraceable quality that is uniquely hers, but that, in writing, she communicates to the immense variety of her subject-matter: the people, the places, the times . . . The friends are there, the memory is there, but what Fleur contributes is, indeed, a very American, North American, Unitedstater, Gringo, Yankee quality, which Longfellow perfectly distinguished in one of his poems: 'The song, from beginning to end, I found again in the heart of a friend'. This is what makes the greatness of US literature, from Twain, to Whitman, to Carson McCullers. Fleur Cowles has it and renders it in the form of literary medallions.

Tough but never malicious, warm but never mawkish, self-respecting but never self-serving, Fleur Cowles recalls to life, keeps in daily repair, and finds in the hearts of those she knows, the dual beauty of friendship and memory: bound to her soul with hoops of steel, they manage to take flight and remain, for ever, green.

'You have many friends, dear lady.' Perhaps this phrase from Henry James's portrait of the beautiful and tragic heroine, Isabel Archer, fits Fleur Cowles well, retaining the beauty, avoiding the tragedy, and simply, as James puts it, always finding something to write about in the vast universe of friendship.

CARLOS FUENTES

PREFACE

FEW WOMEN HAVE lived more multiple lives than I have: as editor; as that anomaly, an American President's personal representative, decorated by six governments; as a writer of thirteen books and contributor to six others; as a painter, with fifty-one one-man exhibitions throughout the world; patron of the arts and sciences, irrepressible traveller and, most importantly, a friend-gatherer. Having been editor of two of America's top magazines, *Look* and *Flair*, doors were regularly opened to me by Heads of State, royalty, Hollywood news-makers and others (no 'name-dropping' involved). Today the pattern continues. I have gleaned new friends in the arts, in journalism, diplomacy and politics. These I have nurtured and kept, and I am proud to have made lifelong connections of most. Tapping one to help another has helped make me a useful catalyst.

My world has always revolved around a pivotal threesome: expectation, achievement and friendship; they make up this book of memories. Since it is friends who lard this book, there will be no keyholing, no confidences broken – in fact very little malice, not even for the few who richly deserve it. Some things are better left *unsaid*, hence this anecdotal carousel is written without rancour. Could this be a welcome experience?

With luck the printed word can put a proper cloak on life, especially if it has been spent in part in the unrelenting glare of a goldfish bowl. Glass walls tend to get foggy from the hot breath of unsolicited scrutiny in the naked publicity spotlight. I once had my share.

I take my work seriously; myself, never. I was born with such a good memory that I have never needed to keep a diary or notes. I had the unsolicited help, while still in my early teens, of an elderly educator after he watched my memory being tested in a gimmicky way, involving rows of multiple numbers which I was asked to study, then to repeat without error.

'Stop it!' he cried out. 'Of what value is this nonsense? What possible use are all those numbers?'

I never again did such tricks. I might otherwise have gone on trying to accumulate and assemble a massive collection of useless data.

His zeal was God-given and my self-appointed mentor found me a willing collaborator even though I was often flustered by the old man's eccentricity. He felt challenged and decided to persuade this impressionable student to program her mind, to ignore what didn't really matter. Despite the occasional expensive mistake, I went ahead.

'You'll be a better judge when you're older, but get the habit *now* ... don't cram your brain ... stop building up useless storage,' he commanded.

He gave me one word which he insisted would help organize my life: the magic word was *select*. 'Select! Select!' he repeated and repeated. André Maurois reminded me of this wisdom when he once announced that a mountain of eggs was no omelette.

The assumption that one so young could deal with his order to 'select' might seem misjudged, but he paid me the compliment of assuming I could decide what to ask my untrained brain to remember. The system, which eventually bore fruit, was training my brain to behave like a computer.

'You'll be storing information for future calculation; it will become a pathway that re-excites itself,' he explained.

Early in our lessons, he asked me to describe my brain. 'How does it look?' he insisted. I refused to discuss it because, to me, that flabby object called the human brain was frightening. As the source of intellectual capacity and memory, how could this strange soft mass rule anyone's life? The mystery was compounded by its size, shape and texture.

He surprised me by agreeing: 'I understand. Why not design a new brain? What image would you prefer? Where would you like to store whatever you'll be selecting to store in it? And don't forget the Mad Hatter's warning to Alice: if she knew time as well as he did, she wouldn't waste it. Nor should *you* waste thought by cluttering up your brain.'

It took time but I finally could and did decide on an image to replace my real brain; it had to be beautiful, not 'flabby'. I chose to have an exquisite little chest, my storage 'bin', as an idea-warehouse and put into it only what I wanted to retain. Hundreds of tiny drawers would open and shut at will. Diary-like details and visual pictures would be sent into it for safekeeping and future use. That 'memory-bank' is now the whole of my experience. By selecting, I shaped my taste, my career, my choice of friends, how I wished to live.

I can still recall what I youthfully stored away; how a butterfly looked as I gently held it for a brief moment, how it folded up its tiny feet, how, inside, the wings were coloured differently from the outside . . . how looking long at a rose evokes all I still remember about its smell, its form, its shape, its leaves, how frost turned certain parts of it brown.

When an adult, I began to reconstruct any important experience by storing away how I was dressed, when and where it occurred, the first sentence spoken and the substance of the experience. Like pushing a button, all flooded back, like conversations with President Nasser in Cairo, which were then reported back to President Eisenhower. How Nasser grabbed my wrist to make a political point and explaining what the point was . . . or the memory of an experience with that 'royal' of Hollywood, Louis B. Mayer, in the library of his new home with wall-to-wall and floor-to-ceiling whiteness; white, white everywhere. How the mogul responded to my questions. How elderly Mme Banac, practically an uncrowned royal in Monaco, dressed and looked in her Balenciaga-designed outfits, beautiful 'uniforms'. They helped me decide to keep to my own style, to ignore fashion foibles.

Unforgettable was the sight of a young princess being crowned as Queen of Great Britain and the Commonwealth amid the sights and sounds inside Westminster Abbey, when I attended Queen Elizabeth's Coronation as American Ambassador. So were conversations while motoring with the Shah of Persia or with Queen Frederika at the wheel of her red sports car – or the prospect of finding a boa constrictor, supposed to be lurking in Madame Chiang Kai-Shek's summer residence in Taipei where I stayed for four *very* long nights.

I can retaste the 'real soup', as Jean Monnet called it, on the stove in the kitchen of the home outside Paris of this 'Father of Europe'. I recall the guns roaring over my head in Korea as I jeeped to and from Seoul to the Panmunjon Peace Conference which had been meeting for years right inside Korea's battle area.

On one of my visits to Athens, when I described my 'selection process' to Queen Frederika, she replied, in her fascinatingly impulsive way: 'Yes. If you have trained your brain this way, you can afford to jump first, think later – and expect to be right.'

Total recall helps me as a painter. I need not (do not) copy or look at models. I paint what I have loved enough to store as a memory. When painting flowers, the herbaceous border in my brain is my guide, with flowers which have been stored away in that mental diary. After fifty-one one-man shows, my passion for painting jungle cats and over-sized flowers remains constant; they both appear on landscapes which I have also carefully stored away in my imagination.

Many of my best memories have probably been kept current by telling the stories to the captive audiences I entertain at home. People and places thus stay alive, reappearing vividly. Some have already been given a life in print and more are added in an anecdotal form in this volume – deliberately not the cradle-to-grave style of memoir.

I have been buoyed up by Boris Pasternak's disclosure in his *Essay on Autobiography*. He wrote: 'It is more important to lose than to acquire. Unless the seed dies, it bears no fruit. One must live tirelessly, looking into the future and drawing on those reserves which are created not only by remembrance, but also by forgetting.' What I have chosen to forget is absolutely forgotten and will not appear in this or any other form in my personal life.

I was interviewed in America not long ago by a woman reporter who tried to provoke me to spice up her column. Fully aware of the danger, I remained polite and very cool, until she suddenly gripped my wrist.

'Okay. So you've done just about everything. So what? You are now dead. You won't be cremated, you'll be buried. What do *you* want inscribed on your tombstone?' she asked.

Who could be ready for such a question? Though stunned for a moment, an answer came off my tongue and I then grabbed *her* wrist to say: 'Thank you. You've just revealed *me* to *me*.'

My reply had been brief: 'I'd like just a few words to be inscribed on my tombstone:

SHE MADE FRIENDS
AND KEPT THEM.'

Fleur Cowles
1995

I

WOMEN ACHIEVERS

CONTEMPORARY EXAMPLES OF women high-achievers began to emerge in the early 1950s, overcoming the hurdles that had confronted them for so long. Some of these hurdles were long-held social beliefs, others stemmed from women's perception of themselves. Others were outrageous prejudice. One publication that caused a sensation at the time encapsulated it all: *A Generation of Vipers*, in which Philip Wylie dissected women's attempts to get ahead. He called it 'momism', a term so vicious that the word slipped into common vernacular as an expression of derision. Men applauded, angry women debunked it. The book was written to recognize 'the woman in the grey flannel suit' who began to challenge men in the workplace in the early 1950s.

Did Philip Wylie really hate women? I wrote to him to ask. He replied in no uncertain terms. I include some remarks from his long letter, which will amuse women who are still battling for equal places in the sun. His hates weren't 'hates', he explained, but intellectual criticisms deliberately expressed in emotional terms – 'because intellectual terms reach very few people'. He went on to explain that his celebrated attack arose from an immense *liking* for women: he takes a poor view of so fine a sex when, 'in many cases, it turns its back on the noble, fascinating and fabulous nature of itself as woman, and becomes something less, something vain and arrogant, cheap and vulgar, unlovely, unloving and unloved. A woman shouldn't try not to be a woman,' he advised. 'She shouldn't imitate what she imagines a man to be,' and he ended with a confession: 'I do not hate her but, as a champion of womanhood, I deplore her.'

Women like Evita Peron and Mme Chiang Kai-Shek (both of whom appear in a later chapter on 'Power-hungry Women') would have deserved Wylie's vitriol, but would not Marilyn Monroe's 'helplessness' have aroused his tenderness? Isak Dinesen would surely have evoked the same admiration she won from most men in her extraordinary life. Rebecca West once reminded me: 'People call me a feminist whenever I express sentiment that differentiates me from a doormat – and it was always meant as abuse.'

The pages that follow include such women. All of them have been friends and all of them are more or less safe from a Philip Wylie.

Until 1802, women had no official recognition; then Napoleon I instituted a new award, the now familiar Cross of the Legion of Honour, to replace the Order of the Saints Esprit, instituted by Henry III, last of France's Valois dynasty. Napoleon dismissed as sheer nonsense the claim that genius could possibly have any sex other than male or that a woman had any other claim for anything other than her fertility.

Later, in Napoleon III's empire, Rosa Bonheur, famous painter, was to be the first woman to be given the honour. By receiving it, she became a household name, but she didn't get it from the Emperor. It was a gift from the admiring Empress Eugénie, who was able to bestow it while temporary Regent of France during Napoleon's absence in Algeria. Pinning the medal on her, the Empress announced: 'I want to devote the last act of my Regency to showing that, as far as I am concerned, genius has no sex. You deserve it. You, a woman, have become a Knight.'

Bonheur's award opened doors, but among the female recipients there are only three Officers and nineteen Chevaliers; there are no Commanders. I was honoured by becoming a Chevalier in 1953. I have also been decorated twice by the Brazilian Government (raised by them from Chevalier to the rank of Commander of the Cruzero de Sud); by Great Britain with the Queen's Coronation Medal; by Greece with the Order of Bienfaisance; by Spain as a Dama de Isabel la Catolica.

There is a game I like to play: I ask women to name the ten women whose achievements make them most important in the world today. Few can find ten; *are* there that many, they ask? They are trapped trying to divide good women from bad. Queen Elizabeth II, Margaret Thatcher, Indira Gandhi, Queen Elizabeth the Queen Mother, Golda Meir, Evita Peron, Eleanor Roosevelt and Lady Bird Johnson regularly come up, although not all justifiably. Rarely does anyone who plays the game produce *ten*.

*   *   *

One woman, Lady Bird Johnson, makes every list, year in and year out; she is a role model to so many women. I know her well and I marvel over her strength of character, her spirit, her mind, her curiosity, her capacity for friendship and of course the way she handled herself as First Lady.

Within the Presidential circle, one woman must know a great deal about Lady Bird, Elizabeth (Liz) Carpenter, who was her right arm in the White House and today remains Lady Bird's close friend.

Lady Bird has no façade, no artificiality. She is no publicity-seeker, yet she was a memorable First Lady to Lyndon B. Johnson, the tough, remarkable President who needed a special sort of helpmate after coming to the White House. She never competed for the limelight. 'I will try to be balm, sustainer and sometimes critic for my husband' was all she admitted in 1963. After he died, we all felt sad for her loss of that relationship.

Like Winston Churchill and his wife Clementine, the President and Lady Bird Johnson wrote to each other constantly. Their letters exist from the time Lyndon B. Johnson dated Claudia Taylor in 1934. They continued to exchange letters all through their marriage, even during their White House days. Several of their letters were movingly read aloud a few years ago by the actress Helen Hayes in the role of Lady Bird, and by Kirk Douglas as Lyndon Johnson, at an evening in Lady Bird's honour in the vast theatre of the LBJ Library in Austin, Texas. Kirk Douglas seemed to grow in stature and voice to resemble LBJ as he read his early letters to his fiancée, whose real name is Claudia, and then to her as his wife. Helen Hayes was superb reading Lady Bird's. The performance ended with a letter revealing LBJ's surprise decision not to run again for office. We learned that his public announcement, made on television, had been suggested by Lady Bird, who really wanted him to retire. 'Lyndon, it's time to go home,' she added in one letter, and he announced it this way: 'I shall not seek and I will not accept the nomination of my party for another term as your President.' I chose several to read at the Valentine Evening at Christie's in London to benefit the American Museum in Bath, on whose Board I serve. They deserve publication in a book. They are history. Mrs Johnson has the collection, starting from those courting days. Friendly persuasion may help change her resolve not to publish them.

That Library celebration in her honour began humorously; Cactus Pryor, famous Texas broadcaster, was the Master of Ceremonies. He opened with: 'Ladies and gentlemen, Fleur Cowles is here tonight. She may have come all the way from London but lest she thinks she's come the farthest, may I point out that we have a man here from Amarillo.' That town is right there in Texas, but since most Texans consider their state to be larger than anywhere else on earth, the appreciative audience dissolved into laughter at the notion that I might think London was farther away from Austin than Amarillo.

Clementine Churchill similarly wrote letters to her husband, whether they were together or far apart. Hers were often sharp with advice, a typical one being: 'Please write quickly in your own paw before memory fades' (a reminder to thank Queen Wilhelmina of the Netherlands after being entertained by her). Others were in similarly instructive vein. Churchill signed his letters to her with his famous signature, his drawing of a pig!

To fully describe the Lady Bird I know as a friend would require the memory-bank of a computer, something I don't own and couldn't operate anyway, but locked in my mind are many personal remembrances that I can relate about the great lady. I'd say she was the perfect partner for an eminent and shrewd politician but, unlike others in the same role, she never lost her natural modesty, nor did she neglect her family in order to conduct her life as First Lady. When she moved into the White House, she said: 'I'm suddenly on stage for a role I never rehearsed.' What a performance followed.

Later, she enriched the already beautiful Washington DC by making it a garden city. She had also urged the United States to plant wildflowers on the roadsides, to the great pleasure of highway travellers across much of America. She would hold her hands up in dismay if she knew I consider her a botanist. 'I merely *love* flowers,' she would insist. She once wrote about the Maximilian sunflowers along Texas highways: 'Isn't it rather sad that one of the few things an *emperor* has named after him is a rough but colourful flower?' Yet no tiny white object in a field escapes her eye. No amateur, she knows their common names and their Latin binomials, the sort of scientific knowledge lost on most of us. Even in Spain, travelling about the countryside with her when she visits, in a cavalcade of cars driven by Secret Service men, followed by our other guests, we came to a halt whenever she felt the need to walk into a field to examine a small flower that others would not even have noticed. If she didn't know its name, it would be pressed into a book and brought back to Texas to her Wildflower Foundation to be named and reported. A new and beautiful building has just been officially opened there in her honour.

Her astute business sense and the purchase of Austin's radio and television stations from a relative (they are now sold) made the family wealthy. When her husband first took office as President a journalist criticized him 'for being rich', claiming that his wealth had given him political influence. I like the President's answer: he roared with laughter. 'If I ditched it (the station), it would break her heart.'

Her curiosity is endless. She *must* know. She *must* see. And she asks questions. 'She should be named the Prime Listener of our time,' her friend Elspeth Rostow says. She is probably the United States' most travelled former First Lady.

Every year, I visit her in Texas. Although she now also has a lovely home in Austin, it was usually at the original home, the LBJ Ranch*. Anxious that I know 'the other Texas', the artistic and creative side, not just the business world and its cities, Lady Bird takes me to areas that are part of her own life, the regions of Texas that are an amazing ethnic mix, produced by the men and women of every nation on earth who came to Texas in America's turbulent early days. The restless, oppressed and adventurous pioneer times, when settlers arrived and managed to survive the Indians, the snakes, wild animals and the seemingly arid land. She wanted me to see what was left behind, the important specimens of their nationalities and culture; original homesteads still exist and are cared for, as are simple village museums where the memorabilia of their lives have been tenderly gathered – the tools, the built-on-the-spot furniture, the artefacts, even the clothes they wove, made and wore.

We have listened to Mexican and German music, seen the dancing on the banks of the Pedernales River and have been stunned by beautiful young voices singing opera in the University of Texas – with which I am now involved. I learned to love Texas through her eyes and she has repaid me by her visits to London, Sussex and Spain, where I have shown her the sights I love and introduced her to my closest friends.

---

* Which she is leaving to the State on her death.

Lady Bird walked me through the Library built in LBJ's honour in Austin. Described as the Pyramid of Texas, it rises high above the landscape, six floors of cream-coloured travertine boldly set on a knoll of terraced grass and trees. It cost nineteen million dollars to build, the most expensive and impressive yet of the Presidential libraries, though I have not seen the Nixon, Reagan and Bush libraries so I am unable to make comparisons.

Until his death, Lyndon B. Johnson himself was probably the Library's chief magnet for visitors. Everyone who went there had the chance of meeting him, shaking his hand and 'chatting things up' because he liked to come unannounced to his office on the top floor. Because of his unexpected appearances, people tended to look over their shoulders when inside to see if by chance he was walking by.

A volume especially published for Lady Bird's eightieth birthday entitled *A Life Well Lived* now honours her. It was produced in 1992 by the LBJ Library Director, Harry Middleton, for publication by the LBJ Library. The idea was Tom Johnson's of CNN, and it contains personal comments by Lady Bird's friends.

Jacqueline Kennedy's contribution opens the book, followed by comments from Presidents who have followed Lyndon Johnson in the White House: Nixon, Carter, Ford, Reagan and Bush. All wrote with admiration and affection.

Tom and Edwina Johnson (he had begun in the LBJ White House as a member of the President's think-tank, and now runs CNN's vast communications centre in Atlanta) wrote: 'In countless ways, we have known her love, her goodness, her remarkable desire to leave the world a better place.' Her brilliant nephew, Professor Philip Chase Bobbitt, said with equal eloquence: 'In my universe, she is my steadily brightened comet.' I wrote as follows:

> 'She is one of the world's most admired ladies. A few other women have achieved similar greatness, but few kept the legend. If a stamp were made of her qualities, it would have to say: femininity, strength, efficiency, and a warm heart. We all admire her directness and well-informed views but for me, privileged by frequent get-togethers, her tireless mind uplifts me, her curiosity refreshes my own.
>
> 'To be a guest in the cosy LBJ ranch is to be surrounded by souvenirs of her days in the public eye, gifts from doting friends and a comfort equal to her concern and care for her guests. I especially

love the white-washed house on the LBJ Ranch on the Pedernales River – whose banks she has so beautified with carpets of the wild-flowers she has prescribed so successfully for roadsides all over the land. Indoors, there is not a Renoir in sight. Americana reigns instead, and smiles at you.'

'She is my strength,' LBJ once said publicly. Her friends understand.

Reflecting on other First Ladies: many have been political amateurs. Not Rosalyn Carter, who thought herself a professional, or Mamie Eisenhower who had no real taste for it. But Hillary Clinton orchestrated an unelected role for herself. She gave a hint of the kind of part she would play as the future First Lady when she reached into her pocket and handed her husband the cards on which were written his acceptance speech. A subtle gesture? Was she signalling her intention to participate in the President's affairs? After the election, she quickly took on a top unelected position in the Administration, her objective to improve the health care of America. History will have the final say on her efforts. We all want her to succeed; a health programme, accessible to all, is surely desperately necessary to the United States, but her plan has been almost totally rejected.

James Rosebush, who was Nancy Reagan's Chief of Staff in the White House from 1981 to 1986, gave me his views on the role of a First Lady, and suggested five courses of behaviour for any woman in this position. I summarize them briefly as follows:

> First, to take care of the President's health, recreation, intellectual and spiritual well-being – to help him unwind, to act as his and each other's sounding boards ... to be his most trusted adviser, but in confidence ... to remember you are the official representative of the American people so be careful what you say and wear and how you affect people. He used the example of Raisa Gorbachev and Barbara Bush holding hands, which sent waves of symbolism around the world. Do not forget you signed up to work for the American people (something Eleanor Roosevelt and Lady Bird Johnson recognized so very quickly). Last of all, to be yourself, to put your own stamp on the job and not to be phoney.

When the self-effacing and uncomplaining Pat Nixon died, it reminded me that when Richard Nixon was inaugurated as President in 1969, she admitted that politics was not what she'd have chosen for him: 'You don't see much of your husband and it's a hard life.'

The *New York Times* magazine published at that time a feature on her high school graduate class, a spread of tiny photographs of all the students, each declaring what their hopes were for the future. Pat Nixon's reply perhaps reflected her humble origins. She wanted to have a boarding-house. Presumably this was a huge step from her home as the daughter of an Irish-American itinerant miner in the small mining town of Ely, Nevada.

The controversy Nixon generated with his anti-Communist speeches led to his wife being portrayed in the press as projecting what would later be called 'twentieth-century-born-in-a-log-cabin image'. But the remarkably stalwart lady, when she reached the White House, opted for the traditional, likeable, limited role of a Bess Truman or a Mamie Eisenhower. I used to go and have breakfast with her while she was still in her bed after an early-morning meeting with the President. All three women apparently accepted their loss of privacy and family time, and the need to act in ways that would not get themselves or the President in any trouble.

Wives of British Prime Ministers also have a public role to play. In Margaret Thatcher's case it was her husband who had to accept a woman's usual place. It must be said he never put a foot wrong and supported her both during her premiership and after.

I am grateful for a special friendship with another remarkable woman, the late Rebecca West. We were close for thirty-two years, during which time I was fascinated by her intellect and the ardour of her life. There were many rich moments in our friendship, although on occasion her brilliance and intense passion could bruise my ego.

The ego can be fragile: even Ernest Hemingway's could falter! A book I constantly re-read is *West of the Wind* by Beryl Markham. When Hemingway first read it, he wrote to Malcolm Cowley, Editor of the *Saturday Review of Literature*: 'She has written it so well that I was completely ashamed of myself as a writer. I felt that I was simply a carpenter with words.' Not long after, however, her authorship of the book was questioned. Some said it had been written by Saint-Exupéry, others by her journalist husband.

I often wondered if Rebecca West wasn't in fact a philosopher masquerading as a firebrand? There were so many sides to her that I recall; for instance, her love of gossip which she laced with acerbic wit; usually sardonic and sometimes brutal, it could be as quick and deadly as a bullet and was often riddled with prejudices. An example comes to mind: we were talking about Margaret Thatcher, then Prime Minister. Rebecca West exploded: 'I cannot think of a Prime Minister in my lifetime one would want for a *father* unless it was Mrs Thatcher!' And on another occasion, over a crowded luncheon table during a weekend in Sussex at the time of the Profumo scandal: 'Christine Keeler and Mandy Rice-Davies are the two stars of the biggest sex scandal of the sixties, yet they are the only Ward girls too intelligent to marry peers!' When John Erskine met her in Manhattan, he said, 'I've been reading your clever articles and I wonder if they're sincere.' She snapped back: 'I've been reading yours and I never wonder whether they're clever *or* sincere!'

One of the truly great reporters of our time, Rebecca West was actually a one-woman investigating team: her study of treason was published in *The Meaning of Treason*, the collection of her reports on British traitors during the Second World War. 'In the twentieth century treason is a vocation,' she told me bitterly one day.

Her own political views were mercurial; she began as a Liberal and ended as a Conservative, although perhaps more *against* the Left than *for* the Right. *Time* magazine called her 'a Socialist by habit and a Conservative by cell structure!'

She had great taste and loved valuable possessions, although they were rarely kept in the best order. Some fine paintings would be hung, but others would be stacked like intruders around walls in rooms which were already cluttered with objects. Elegant curtains and chairs were often tatty and dusty but nevertheless grandly presided over by this very large, very old lady with intense brown eyes.

'Would she like to go up in space?' I once asked her in a letter during the period when spacecraft were headline news. She would, she agreed, but only if there was nothing else more amusing to do down on earth. If she was allowed to take a guest, who would she choose? She wrote back: 'None. One companion cannot be the perfect companion. I would find this true on a journey to the moon even if I was young. The lunar landscape looks unfavourable to love, though I was once offered a picture by a great artist representing two people finding happiness on a bomb site. But his was surely a special taste . . .'

Occasionally, she quixotically asked my advice about her home and its decor, but of course never took it, since she was either too irritated by the cost or too philosophical about the situation to bother. Before she died she did make one attempt to repair the tatters, but soon gave up. As for clothes, she had no interest in them and usually looked like it. Few who knew her cared. When young, she had decided to live a long time; in the end, she did endure for over ninety years, worrying less about those numerical figures than about the physical restraints age placed on her life.

Her ability to recall was total. The mention of a person, a place, a book, an object would evoke magnificent anecdotes, each a platform for her strong views. The stories could be as old as she was, but listening to her they always seemed of the present. To me, her writing was like a burst of brilliant conversation. Whenever I *read* her, I *hear* her.

Before we changed our route to Sussex at weekends when she drove with us, we used to go through an often riot-torn London suburb called Brixton. The troubled area became beautiful as we drove through it, because in her mind she immediately travelled back into her own past, having lived in that part of London at the turn of the century. The trip became a description of her family's lives, their garden and how she loved the stands of enormous ox-eye daisies as well as the neighbouring lavender farms. She described in great detail the now run-down mansions when they were the homes of the former big city margarine barons; she could name them all. I go through the district now with double vision.

Upset by the riots and problems of living in the area, she would point out, 'There was never a rift south of the river in those days. For hundreds of years foreigners of every colour and kind passed through South London on the way to the centre, making the inhabitants more tolerant. Even Mosley problems were north of it!'

For me, none of her impressive list of books has more significance than *Black Lamb and Grey Falcon*, which had been commissioned by the British Council. Few Yugoslavs believe she wasn't herself a Yugoslav. How else could she perceive people so accurately in pre-Second World War Yugoslavia? How could she write of their terrible struggles with such Dali-esque imagery and deep compassion?

As a writer and former editor, I have always been dazzled by the speed at which she was able to write. There is a claim which I heard some years ago of her 6500-word account of the trial of William Joyce (Lord Haw-Haw) for treason in 1945, written for the *New Yorker* magazine. *It had arrived by wire at the magazine twenty-four hours after the trial ended!* This remarkable ability was matched by the speed with which she could devour the printed word. This explains how she used to take five or six books to bed at night in Sussex and discuss them all with us over breakfast. She rarely had to give more than an hour to a book she was reviewing.

One wonders what the moral climate of 1914 was like when she had her illegitimate son, Anthony, by H. G. Wells. Forty years later, Anthony West produced a biographical novel, *Heritage*, an instantly recognizable, highly unforgiving account of his mother's ten-year liaison with H. G. Wells and of his own birth out of wedlock. In it he very thinly disguises her as an actress. She had been one for a very short time, when she changed her own name from Cicily Fairfield to Rebecca West, the name of the woman she played in Ibsen's *Rosmersholm*. When Anthony West's book was about to be published in Britain, its publication was prevented by his mother's doting husband, the banker Henry Andrews, who injunctioned the British publisher.

I hid the American edition I owned whenever she came to stay. She always looked high and low for it and once she found it, tucked right behind another book. I wouldn't allow her to take it away, as she demanded – not wanting to see either her or myself drawn into any legal action.

Her son remained bitterly antagonistic. His absence at her funeral, though half-expected, was nevertheless distressing to our small group of mourners. In fact, I felt we were acting out a Visconti film: the day was grey and very cold, with rain and sleet. Bernard Levin, in his address at the memorial service which he and I attended later, called her 'one of a basic handful of undoubted ageless masterpieces of our century'.

Once I had earned her friendship, she gave me her affection as well; one way this was demonstrated was through her nonstop letters. I've chosen a few paragraphs from countless written to me over the years in her not very legible writing. Words rushed along, the trivial mixing with the serious. Her handwriting was tiny and closely knit. It must have been a feat to decipher when it came to typing her reviews, essays and manuscripts.

One of her letters to me was: 'Attached you will find a letter I wrote you ages ago. It was never sent because I have a secretary who is incomprehensible and unless she is considered a Zen secretary, she transcends reality. Nothing happens, *very noisily.*'

In 1975, after a particularly malicious attack by her son (who was then aged about sixty-one), she wrote me: 'Anthony is going on and on writing these new attacks on me. I've been sent a proof of a review to be published in a coming *Harper's Magazine*. He invents an entirely new environment for my childhood and gives the most impudent and wholly false account of what Jane Wells' relations were with me. It is so nasty, so crazy. What I can't understand is why anybody publishes it.'

She described Eleanor Roosevelt to me in a letter as 'a victorious Cassius Clay'. She was then reviewing a book about her for the *Sunday Telegraph*. She wrote 'The book, *Joe Lash on Eleanor Roosevelt*, filled me with wonder. I had accepted it as gospel that Eleanor had had a hell of a time at the hands of Sara, her mother-in-law, but if I had been a St Bernard in the snow-covered mountains and the matter had come up, I would have gone right to Sara with my cask of brandy. She needed it more.' She continued: 'Imagine Eleanor weeping bitterly because her mother-in-law gave her some chintz covers. People would tell us that she had great sorrows in life – but I ask you. What sort of chintzes would Eleanor have chosen with *her* taste?'*

She complained in a letter: 'Next time I write a book I am simply going away for a month previous to a month after publication. My life has been complete hell due to a riot of enquiries arising out of my book *1990*. Also Warren Beatty's film *Reds* (in which I briefly appear). The BBC have been particularly maddening in this connection – utterly unbusinesslike and maddeningly tough to no purpose. This letter is a vale of tears.'

Her eye problem gave her considerable distress as she grew older; it dogged her later years and finally required surgery. In a sad mood, she wrote to me: 'I think the stress of modern surgery and medicine

---

* See Eleanor Roosevelt, page 19.

14

is hard on the timorous ego – which remains primitive and wants to hide at the back of the cave when the medicine man comes along.'

It would be worth hearing her acerbic comments today about the current mélange of dishonesty and greed. She pronounced that it was the public's responsibility to present themselves behaving well.

I once read a line in a play, 'The Major wanted to be an *active* verb.' Rebecca West was just that, an active verb. She will always be remembered for her report on the Nuremberg trials, the American lynchings, her views on treason and her reports on major murder trials at London's Old Bailey; and as a good friend to a chosen few.

Isak Dinesen, whose real name was Karen Blixen, was one of this century's most distinguished writers. She wrote under a collection of names, Pierre Andrew Zel for one. Her friends called her Tania (why not Titanic?). She wrote her first book when she was forty-nine and after that one on average every ten years. They included the brilliantly atmospheric *Seven Gothic Tales*, and must all be included among the finest books of our time.

Out of Africa is by far her most famous book, read by millions. It became an award-winning film starring Robert Redford and Meryl Streep. Her vision of Africa, rarely matched, was written with the passion of a poet. That she once painted so well helps explain why her words are so painterly, visual and hauntingly imaginative. When Ernest Hemingway accepted the Nobel Prize for Literature in 1954, in his speech he declared *she* should have won it for *Out of Africa*. It is in this book that we can absorb what her life on a 10,000-acre coffee plantation in the blue Ngong Hills of Kenya must have been like, and experience her struggle to maintain it after being deserted by her husband. Her life, in fact, was a series of tragedies following the suicide of her father. Her love-life was eternally sad. Married to Baron Bror von Blixen, she reluctantly went to live with him in East Africa where, fortunately, she learned to love the country about which she said, 'I am in a place where I ought to be'.

She liked to paint and that's why her words are often like the strokes of a brush. Because she found them so beautiful, she often asked the local women to pose in their native dress, highly disapproving of the efforts by missionaries to make them wear European clothes. To her it was 'like a harness on a lion or giraffe!' I love her neat little painting of her pet owl and those of scenes on her farm.

Six hundred acres were planted in coffee and two hundred in corn, but in the end they didn't provide a living and she had to leave the wild animals, pet dogs, flowers and the warm native friends she loved so deeply – to return to Denmark.

Her book *Winter's Tales*, written during the Second World War, had to be smuggled out of Denmark into the United States to avoid the prying eyes of the occupying Germans. She had written to a friend that 'Jews were in the kitchen and Nazis in the garden, the hair-raising problem was to keep them from meeting.' Her home is now a shrine.

Her marriage to von Blixen was a tragic disaster and he deserted her after reportedly giving her syphilis. Finally, there was her ill-fated love for Denys Finch-Hatton, the English game hunter who was killed in a plane crash in 1931, just as she was about to leave Africa for good. He had influenced the development of her writing, taught her Latin, read the Bible to her and encouraged her to love the Greek poets.

I had the good fortune to get to know her. Having admired her for so long, I was delighted to meet her in the late sixties, when my husband and I were in Copenhagen, the meeting arranged by a friend. The mental picture I had of this intrepid woman hardly prepared me for the apparition I saw crossing the room towards us. It was a wraith-like figure covered by a huge grey coat which hung down to the floor over her wasted body. Her head was lost in a tight-fitting cap-like hat which accentuated every bone in her face, which resembled a shell-like skull.

We talked for hours. Overlaying the conversation were passages from her book which I couldn't forget: descriptions in *Out of Africa* of the wild animals she loved, which I also love. (I paint all of them.) Such phrases as 'giraffes looking like long-stemmed gigantic flowers' and 'the elephant lumbering along as if it had an appointment at the end of the world' came to mind while we talked.

A few years after that Copenhagen meeting, Isak Dinesen came to visit us in London. Two of our mutual friends, Ruth and Zachary Scott, were appearing in a play which I knew she'd like to see. I arranged a dinner in her honour, asking guests I hoped would interest her as much as she would intrigue them: Clemence Dane, Rebecca West, G. B. Stern and actress Margaret Leighton, as well as equally distinguished men. At the last moment another unexpected guest was added, with the arrival in London that morning of Helena Rubinstein.

The cosmetic queen came to dinner dressed like a Mayan princess, wearing a heavily beaded mid-calf Balenciaga gown richly embellished with jewelled stones. A lavish selection of her famous collection of gems overlaid it all: baroque pearls twisted with emeralds hung on her throat and more were clipped to her ears and encircled her wrists. A tiny fedora hat, à la Peruvian native women and favoured by her at that time, was perched stiffly above her bun. Her face? A cosmetic showpiece.

Extraordinary as it was, her appearance couldn't compete with Karen Blixen's as she very slowly stepped into our drawing room on my husband Tom's arm. Conversation stopped. We saw a face with eye-lashes laden with black mascara, dark glaring eyes sunk in deep caves, outlined in mascara, every wrinkle in her heavily lined face set with layers of white powder and accented by a beauty mark worn like a beacon. Every curl of hair framing her face was positioned as if set in concrete. She wore a long coffee-coloured chiffon shirtwaister dress, gathered by black velvet ribbon tied tightly around her tiny body. Wrists and neck were ruffled, a black silk rose was pinned at her throat. She was a creation worthy of a Camille stretched out on a couch before death, incredibly romantic, an aristocratic wraith.

At dinner, she ate almost nothing and spoke little. She was genuinely frail. The illness that plagued her meant that she could eat very little of the food but knowing her needs I provided the two things I knew she loved, asparagus and grapes, which although out of season I was able to serve up especially for her. Even these luxuries were only nibbled; her bony body was evidence of such near-starvation. I knew that on her recent three and a half months in the United States she had nearly died of exhaustion, eating almost nothing, worn out by fame and attention. It was a diet of fruit and vegetable juices that probably saved her life. Her meeting in New York with Marilyn Monroe, whom she loved, was described by one who saw them together as 'the gaunt with the fleshpot'.

At eleven-thirty, having cast a spell over our guests, she floated out of my husband's arm to be taken back to her hotel. Others left slowly. Only the over-ninety-year-old Helena Rubinstein remained. She had said hardly a word at dinner or after although I knew her well enough to realize she had been observing closely. She sat quietly on the couch she'd chosen, her short legs dangling above the floor.

'Come here,' she beckoned to me.

'You didn't say a word to Isak Dinesen,' I remonstrated. 'Didn't you want to speak to that fascinating woman?'

Mme Rubinstein's immediate response in her heavy Polish accent was: 'Fleur darlink, all my life I've been trying to get *you* to use eye make-up!' With that reprimand, she struggled to her feet and left.

Isak Dinesen died soon after in 1962. For me, her epitaph is something she wrote to explain her philosophy: 'We must leave our mark on life while we have it in our power, lest it should close up when we leave it, without a trace.'

She wrote so often about myths; she is now one herself, a modern mythological lady who had claimed she had sat down with Socrates to talk of eternity.

The Roosevelts came to America centuries ago from the province of Zeeland in Holland. Several great ladies have borne the name; perhaps most famous is Eleanor Roosevelt, who created a large place for herself in history.

Everyone who hated the name 'Roosevelt' in Franklin D. Roosevelt's time, hated her, too. All of America's diehard right-wingers loathed the rich man who deserted their ranks to become a liberal President. Often the blame fell on his wife, for some knew how she had helped him formulate the master plan for the New Deal, but she was also thanked by millions of others. Fortunately, she made her reputation before violence became endemic in political disaster.

She was one of a unique band of American women. As his wife, she kept Franklin Delano Roosevelt up to the mark, not allowing his natural love of the good things in life to dilute his promise to change the face of America. She was a great political asset. Born in 1884, she died in 1962. She had grown up in a family noted for philanthropy. Her obsession with FDR's success as President is well known; it came from her early upbringing. The public knew it, probably because their relationship was so often written about and discussed – she the much-described ugly duckling who married the most handsome man in her family (they were distantly related).

Eleanor Roosevelt marvelled at her mother's looks, 'the most beautiful woman I've ever seen', but her own appearance didn't matter. Occasionally she did look lovely, especially as a bride in 1905, when she was perfectly coiffed and wore a very beautiful gown. When I met her, in the late forties, she already showed little sign of being seriously interested in what she wore.

Unlike the US Ambassador, Pearl Mesta, Eleanor Roosevelt cared little about decor. As First Lady, she spent none of the $50,000 allocated by Congress for White House repairs and upkeep. She furnished it with odds and ends, although rooms there sadly needed repainting and repairing. It is even said that it looked as though a ghost lived in it. Yet I read somewhere that when she left the White House as a widow, it took fifty army lorries to remove the contents. Harry Truman arrived with two lorries!

Somehow, she survived the domination of her mother-in-law, Sara Roosevelt. From the time of her son's marriage, the older woman had done everything possible to remain in control of his life. She actually rented their future house for them while they were on honeymoon – even furnishing it before their return, and hiring servants! Later, she moved her son and daughter-in-law into their second home on East 65th Street, New York, this time making a more ominous choice: the house was next to her own, and for good measure she put a door between the two to enable her to come and go at will. Antipathy between them must have increased when Eleanor Roosevelt began to exercise her own political influence over FDR. Her mother-in-law was perhaps responsible for the dreadful bouts of migraine which Eleanor suffered all her life.

Years before the days in the White House, Eleanor Roosevelt made a revealing statement to a woman journalist at the celebrations for her husband's election as Governor of New York State. 'What,' the reporter sarcastically asked her, 'are you *now* planning for your husband?' 'To make him President of the United States,' she responded with her toothy smile. The man she married and for whom the word charisma was probably invented, made good that prediction a few years later.

After FDR's death, the First Lady took on a new title as the Chairman of the Human Rights Commission of the UN, a post later taken over by two successful actresses, Irene Dunne and Shirley Temple Black. Eleanor Roosevelt soon began regular television broadcasts, as well as a daily column, 'My Day', which was syndicated throughout America, earning herself a formidable reputation as a broadcaster and columnist.

She and FDR seemed to thrive on the crises which abounded during his four terms; first the great depression of the 1930s, then the war. They agreed on most things and were seldom in conflict. This doesn't mean she was ever a 'second President' as Hillary Clinton* or even Rosalyn Carter have been accused of being. Eleanor was simply *influential*; her ideas counted to FDR.

Though she never openly indicated she knew it, she was painfully aware that her secretary, Lucy Mercer, was her husband's great love during White House days. It must have been a terrible shock to unpack FDR's bag and finding a bundle of Lucy's love letters.

Nevertheless, neither she nor Lucy's husband, Winthrop Rutherford, ever showed they even sensed there was a liaison. Secretly, however, Eleanor did offer FDR his freedom, but knowing the political consequences, he declined. The decision must have been the catalyst that brought about her own independence.

It was after the President's death and after her period with the UN that I got to know her. At an impressionable age, I was fascinated; never once did I find her the egghead she had been dubbed. To her, the search for knowledge was not a game. She once gave me a charming insight into one of her methods.

'Do as I do,' she urged, when she realized how serious I was about writing. 'Open your dictionary blindly every night before you go to bed. Let your finger rest on a word. When you open your eyes and see the word and *know* it, start again. If the word is new to you, study it, try to arrange it in a sentence, go to sleep, and your brain will work on it during the night. The secret is simple; you *must* somehow use that word in a sentence the very next day and it will then become a part of your vocabulary.'

I took her advice and often still use my dictionary as she dictated. Not a bad way to remember a President's widow.

---

* In 1993, Hillary Clinton surprisingly announced that she was having conversations 'in her head' with her predecessor, Eleanor Roosevelt (who died in 1962) which sent, according to writer Ben MacIntyre, 'a fresh chill of horror through part of the American establishment'.

Two other recent Roosevelts, man and wife, have given a modern lustre to the legendary name. We became friends when Archibald Bullock Roosevelt and his wife Selwa moved to London. He was posted there by the CIA to oversee Arab affairs. He was a successful Arabist, spoke many of the dialects perfectly and knew the people and the Middle East states well. He actually spoke twenty languages, including Russian which he learned from a family gardener, and Middle High German and Old Norse. He died in 1990 of a heart attack, after he had published his memoirs *For Lust of Knowing, Memoirs of an Intelligence Officer*.

Archie Roosevelt certainly lived up to his heritage as the grandson of 'Teddy'. He spoke like him and shared his looks. Like his grandfather, he sought out the exotic and got it in good measure when he married his wife, the dark-eyed southern graduate of Vassar, Selwa Showker, whose parents were Lebanese. Known as 'Lucky' Roosevelt, she was the black-eyed heroine he might have dreamt about. In his autobiography, he describes her as a woman with 'Arabian eyes and a smile that lights up the world'.

As a successful writer Selwa 'Lucky' Roosevelt made local Washington news when she wrote her defence of Nancy Reagan. 'When is the press going to give the First Lady a break?' The plea was published on the Op-Ed page of the *Washington Post* and became a much-talked-about defence of the woman being widely criticized for her extravagance and overdressing. 'Fun's fun, but the pummelling of Nancy Reagan has gone far enough,' she had written. 'How short are your memories? Only yesterday you were making fun of Mamie Eisenhower's bangs . . . her dowdy clothes and pedestrian friends . . . you maligned Pat Nixon for being so determinedly middle class . . . along came Jackie Kennedy and you extolled her for the very thing you now deplore in Nancy Reagan,' and so on. The column appeared everywhere in the United States and was reprinted in the Congressional Record. Not until the occasion when Nancy consulted an astrologer for advice to give the President was the vulnerable First Lady so strongly criticized again.

Later, Lucky was delighted by the suggestion of Mike Deever, the White House's Deputy Chief of Staff, that she replace Mrs Walter Annenberg, who had resigned after a year in office as Chief of Protocol in the State Department. Lucky Roosevelt filled the job superbly.

Her activities were diverse, coordinating visits by foreign dignitaries, arranging the purchase and presentation of gifts to them, as well as overseeing the maintenance and function of Blair House. This, the guest residence for official overseas visitors, is situated across the street from the White House and is many times its original size and considerably more beautiful, spacious and elegant, and thanks to Lucky's efforts, much more suitable for its purpose than previously. The Fleur Cowles Sculpture Garden is a gift I financed, a garden symbolized by a substantial bronze wall-sculpture, a replica of one of my paintings with the trees, birds, flowers and jungle cats that regularly feature in my work. The sculpture is by Walter Maia, one of America's fine artists.

No other Protocol Chief in American history served so long a term or worked harder than Lucky Roosevelt. We were very close over the years, and she wrote extravagantly of our friendship in her book *The Keeper of the Gate.*

The beautiful Margot Fonteyn and her dashing husband Tito Arias once held court in a lovely house in London when he was Panama's Ambassador.

One night in particular stands out among many spent there, the supper party she gave for the visiting Bolshoi Ballet on the first night of their engagement at Covent Garden. So many were invited that the stairs had to be used as seats for at least twenty of the guests. Margot and my husband and I sat at the top. The music was from the ballet and suddenly a shout went up for Margot to dance. 'No,' she replied, 'not in the presence of the Bolshoi's famous Galina Ulanova.' An incredibly modest gesture from Margot Fonteyn, who as *prima ballerina absoluta* and the greatest dancer of her time had the world at her feet.

It was Margot who arranged for her leading partner, Rudolf Nureyev, to be brought to London after he fled from the Kirov Ballet in Paris. When he first danced at Covent Garden, no one will ever forget the great leap to the stage which heralded his entrance. He left the audience gasping.

Margot and I became even closer after her paralysed husband was brought back to London with her by ambulance plane after the attempt on his life in Panama. He had gone to help re-elect his brother as

President. He had been at the wheel of his own car, stopped by a traffic light, when a close friend drew alongside, pulled out a gun and shot him twice in the back of his neck. His would-be assassin had been campaigning for the man running opposite Tito Arias' brother and he wanted to silence the popular campaigner.

Tito lay unconscious for days, bullets lodged in his spinal area. The assassin threatened to 'finish him off' in the hospital so Margot panicked, over-ruled the local doctor and insisted on flying Tito to England and safety. The full story of his suffering as a paraplegic is little known, but Margot confided it to me one day when I drove her out from London to Stoke Mandeville in Buckinghamshire, the famous hospital that specializes in the care of paraplegics.

She used to return there every evening after her exhausting ballet practice (nothing less than five hours a days would keep her muscles supple enough to dance, she confided). Each night she stayed in a nearby pub, took breakfast with him, then caught the train to London to continue the demanding practice schedule. Her iron will helped her survive that dreadful period. She was just happy that he was alive, even though paralysed. Her lover had become her child.

The awful truth was that the Panamanian doctor's fears had been justified. Tito's temperature on the plane soared to 108 degrees. This burnt out the mobility elements of his brain, leaving him unable to move anything other than one finger on his left hand, and quite unable to speak. He lay immobile, shrinking and ageing. I used to bring food from London with which to feed him, usually smoked salmon and brown bread cut into tiny morsels which I gently put into his mouth. He spent his life in a wheelchair until he died.

Once the four of us sat together in a box at Covent Garden; the Shah of Persia was in the next Royal Box. Margot stupidly wasn't allowed to dance before him because of Tito's political history in Panama, so Beriosova took her place, dancing beautifully while Margot watched, close to tears.

On several occasions Margot and Tito spent Christmas with us in Sussex, aided by the male nurse-valet who had to carry him about and strap him into a chair to dine. I often fed him, to relieve Margot. I learned to understand his guttural attempts at speech and was once able to reduce his despondency by inviting him and the actor, Jack Hawkins, to the same dinner party. Cancer of the throat had caused

23

Hawkins to lose his voice. It eventually killed him, but he helped Tito immeasurably by his courageous acceptance of his fate, persuading Tito to try to do the same.

Margot's love for him was pure and total. Nothing mattered more, not even giving up her career and success for life on the modest farm in Panama, which Tito preferred. But illness caught up with her; she had to make several visits to the States to resume treatment for cancer.

The last time we saw this lovely human being in London was when she came to the ninetieth birthday party I gave for Queen Elizabeth the Queen Mother. She was almost unrecognizable, her bony face half-hidden in a large hat. It made us all very sad.

Her love story is a tragic one worthy of the ballet. If ever there was a role model for femininity, devotion and talent, it was Dame Margot Fonteyn.

There was another wonderful heroine of mine, a woman considered by her contemporaries in the eighties 'the Incomparable, the Grande Dame of the Piano', Gina Bachauer. She was a great pianist who died all too soon; adored by music lovers, she ranked among the finest performers. Critics praised her in print. 'If Gina Bachauer didn't exist, she'd have to be created,' wrote Alan Hughes of the *New York Times* after a Philharmonic concert in New York. Physically, she resembled one of Manzu's great sculptured cardinals; small head, large, soft body; a majestic figure.

I invited Queen Elizabeth the Queen Mother to dinner on an evening when Gina would be playing. The Queen Mother wrote back delightedly to tell me that she was actually listening to one of Gina's records when my letter was given to her. I sent the royal reply to Gina to cherish.

She lived her life as a mother-figure to her own elderly relatives, as well as to strangers and friends, and was a generous patron to young talent. Her cool manner and substantial appearance hid volcanic emotions, unleashed at the piano but often, as well, in support of a friend. She was also one of the world's funniest ladies.

She had a close relationship to the Greek royal family. It was through them that I met her when she had been playing for them at a dinner party when King Paul and Queen Frederika were still the Crown Prince and Princess. After I first met the family as King and Queen in Greece, the King often told me that if he were not King he would like to be a concert pianist. He was, in fact, Bachauer's first royal pupil; later she taught his daughter, Princess Irene, whom Gina considered had great talent. They often played together and the Princess achieved a considerable reputation playing with symphony orchestras in Cincinnati, Dallas, Philadelphia, Seattle, Utah, and in Spain. 'Dat was ah miracle!' Gina reported with pride.

As a woman of the world, Gina Bachauer claimed an assortment of nationalities. When I pushed her to answer 'What is your *real* nationality?' she replied, 'How can I really know? I was born in Greece, my father was Austrian, my mother Italian, her mother was Russian and her father Czech. I consider myself Greek, but with these parents, I ask you, what do you call this person?' Her home was the 'commune' she had built above Athens for countless relatives, all living in separate houses but supported by her.

In 1947, she came to Britain to make her third attempt at a permanent career but found all doors were closed. The number of musicians waiting to be heard meant that few were interested in an unknown Greek pianist. She decided to return to Greece to accept a safe, if obscure life as a teacher in the Greek Conservatory. Her luck changed when she was given a chance to play in London for that great music-lover, Clarissa Davidson. 'This is really great music,' Mrs Davidson exclaimed after hearing her play. She rang a friend, the conductor of the London Symphony Orchestra, asking if he'd give her a concert.

'Who is this pianist you want me to engage over the telephone?' he demanded. 'I must hear her first.' After hearing her he, too, agreed with Mrs Davidson and offered Gina a concert in the Albert Hall. Her appearance was received with such excellent notices that it opened the doors to countless concert managers.

The orchestra's conductor was Alec Sherman, whom she married. He then gave up his own career to become her personal manager and to help develop her amazing gifts. Apart from his management role he also gave her the musical help and inspiration which all artists need. Yet he was her sternest critic. In post-mortems after every concert he told her what he liked and what he didn't, pointed out what was good and what had been wrong. Very few musicians can take their own personal critics around with them to criticize and direct with understanding and affection. Placido Domingo's wife, Maria, fulfils a similar role.

Gina and her husband never stopped travelling. She once calculated the distance they had covered – more than 2.5 million air miles. She never travelled anywhere without extraordinary misadventures. Retold later, they became an essential ingredient of our friendship, outrageously funny when reported by her. Though fluent in German, French and her native Greek, she destroyed the English language, fracturing it hilariously word by word.

Jack Benny, the famous funny man with the poker-face and throwaway jokes (all provided by a team of very highly-paid gag writers) said to me after a night in our home listening to Gina tell stories, 'She proves that the only really funny story is a true story, providing it has happened to *her*, and *she* tells it.'

No tour was ever free from the kind of comic near-disaster which seemed to lie in wait for her everywhere. A father was pestering her in America: 'You must hear my son, he is an eleven-year-old genius – one of the greatest pianists that ever existed in life.' Gina finally decided it was wrong not to listen to the child. On the day arranged the father arrived, alone.

'Where is your child?'

'I am terribly sorry,' he replied, 'but he is sick and couldn't come today. But I've brought a record.'

'All right,' said Gina, 'I will hear it.'

The record was played; she couldn't believe her ears. 'This is the greatest talent I have ever heard in all my life! I have never heard something so beautiful! What a technique – what musicality – what phrasing! When has he done this record? It's *unbelievable!*'

'This record?' said the father. 'This record is not the record of my child. This is a record by Horowitz. But believe me, my child plays exactly the same way!'

Another example occurred during a summer holiday aboard the splendid three-masted schooner, *Argonautis*, owned by a mutual Greek friend, the late John Carras. We often sailed on it through very rough Greek and Turkish waters during the August *meltemi*, winds howling dramatically through the rigging.

I don't get seasick so I could enjoy these trips. Gina Bachauer, though, took to her cabin, as did most others on board – my husband,

26

Tom, retired to the captain's deck. I sat alone in the saloon during one terrible storm, content to read my book. Suddenly I saw the top of Gina's head appear up the companionway, struggling against the ship's movement as she climbed from the sleeping quarters below. White-faced but elegant, I first noticed the pearls at her throat, then her black printed silk dress and her white gloves. She lurched forward to a firmly-fixed armchair. Nothing was said for the next grim moments until, suddenly, she broke the silence by pressing the bell as she sat upright, clenched fists holding onto the chair. When the ship's steward appeared, she said to the astonished man, 'Please order me ah tahxi.'

Another professional heroine of mine is greyhaired but young in heart, tiny in stature but large in reputation. I treasure this woman of spectacular achievement; she is photographer Eve Arnold. If a Nobel Prize were to be given for photography, she'd get it for the humanity revealed through her stunning work. She lives in London, which has given me the opportunity to know her well, a bonus after reading such wonderful books as *The Unretouched Woman**, *Flashback! The 50s***, *In China****. Through her many other books, I've learned more about Marilyn Monroe, about the British, and about the ballet.

Her latest book, *In Retrospect*, was published in 1995 in New York and in Britain. A major travelling exhibition was also launched at the same time, sponsored by the Harry Ransom Humanities Research Centre of the University of Texas (where I have been honoured). In early 1995 she was named 'Master' by the International Centre for Photography, a distinction rarely given (but last to Cartier-Bresson).

Clare Boothe Luce built a monument of her life. Before she died, she explained over dinner in Washington that she had decided against leaving her life-story to the vagaries of fate and considered that destiny would be better served if she chose and collaborated with a biographer.

---

* Published by Alfred Knopf, USA; Jonathan Cape, UK.
** Published by Alfred Knopf, USA.
*** Published by Alfred Knopf, USA; Hutchinson, London; and as *En Chine* by Nathan, Paris.

It was no surprise to me that she chose my brilliant friend, Sylvia Jukes Morris, an obvious choice: she had read Sylvia Morris's biography of Edith Kermit Roosevelt. Sylvia certainly has the talent to handle the recording of Luce's extravagant and controversial life since she knew the subject well. I await the book with impatience.

I vividly recall Clare's porcelain beauty as well as her sometimes acerbic wit. An example: when she was in Hawaii, where she lived much of her retired life, she heard an Air Force Catholic bishop expounding pompously on nuclear weapons. She considered herself a nuclear arms expert and decided he was talking drivel. She told him: 'I respect Roman Catholic bishops too much to take them seriously when they talk nonsense!'

Our lives as wives of two powerful publishers (my then husband, Mike Cowles, was the publishing tycoon, and Henry Luce, hers, was the founder of *Time*) coincided in some ways but never clashed. We remained close friends up to her death; by then she had become frail and almost blind. She wrote sometimes about my paintings, which she loved.

A brilliant blonde with a formidable talent, she was a journalist, author and playwright. She wrote an 'anonymous' review of her first book *Stuffed Shirts*, to appear in *Vanity Fair* magazine, of which she was then the editor. The book was not a success, but her play *The Women* was a considerable one.

She was also a war correspondent and politician, helped in that role by Bernard Baruch who was genuinely in love with her. So, it was rumoured, was Winston Churchill's son Randolph, the first husband of Pamela Harriman, United States Ambassador to France and the subject of a recent sensational biography by Christopher Ogden. Clare also served as a diplomat in Rome. Her eventual departure from that post was brought about by an occurrence in which arsenic fell from the ceiling of her Embassy bedroom on to her bed: the incident prompted someone to coin the now-famous phrase 'Arsenic and Old Luce'! Another cruel epithet which I read in a fashion sheet in the United States described her as 'a beautiful palace without central heating'.

Her notorious verbosity and tendency to know everything about any subject were demonstrated on a long weekend at my Sussex home. Because of her prominence I made sure her fellow-guests were from a range of occupations and professions, including politicians from all the main British political parties, in order to guarantee interesting conversation.

My guests did not let me down and many challenging and stimulating questions were brought up for discussion. Clare's response, on each occasion when her opinion was sought, and even when it wasn't, was to make a speech or deliver a seminar on her strongly-held views whether on Socialism, Republicanism, espionage, abortion or the economy.

It was all brilliant stuff but enough was enough, and by the time the final meal on Sunday was being served the other guests seemed exhausted and tired of being lectured. I tapped a glass for silence and said firmly, '*Shut up, Clare!* In my home, I also like to get a word in edgewise! And so would my other guests!'

To her credit, she produced an enormous grin, followed by loud laughter. 'Forgive me, Fleur, and everyone else. I didn't mean to monopolize,' she replied.

Everyone roared. When the noise died down, *general* conversation at the round table finally began – an unforgettable luxury!

On another occasion when she, my husband and I were together, she wanted to talk about birth control and to report on the Birth Control Conference in Paris from which she'd just come. My husband interrupted to say, 'There are two things wrong about that topic, Clare: one is that you're too old for a Birth Control Conference; and two, it should have taken place in India, not Paris.'

When I was visiting her in Rome, where she was Ambassador, she tried to convince me that it was silly to divorce Mike Cowles. The second wife of Henry Luce advised: 'Don't give up anyone so rich. It's not necessary. I would never give a divorce to Henry or give up his wealth or *Life* magazine .' I ignored her advice.

The Luces' own magazine, *Time*, reporting on her death in 1987, long after this conversation, was very frank about their marriage – mentioning Henry Luce's long-term relationship with Lady Jean Campbell, granddaughter of the British press tycoon Lord Beaverbrook; it lasted up until his death in 1967. Clare had said she might have to use the threat of suicide or editorial control of Time Inc. as the price of his freedom, but what would have been a headline-making divorce never took place.

Her flamboyant, late-in-life conversion to Catholicism was solid and deeply comforting to her, but it surprised many. Had her brother's suicide in a plane at sea disillusioned her, or her daughter Anne's death in a car crash, also rumoured to be suicide, or the suicide of four close friends? Whatever the reason, she was confirmed into the Roman Catholic faith in Fifth Avenue's St Patrick's Cathedral and wore her Catholicism as a mantle ever after.

She died at eighty-four, still with a gaunt beauty and a heroic reputation. At her burial, the Abbot described her death as an extinguished clear light.

Peggy Guggenheim, a contemporary woman of achievement, used art to make her name a byword in the history of Surrealism. There have been many great art collectors but this legendary American stands out not only as one of the most prominent, but also as one of the most eccentric.

Once she moved to Venice, visits to her amazing home became events for me. Her world and her talk revolved around art. She supported Surrealism as much or more than any other collector – she was something of a surreal person herself. So great was her reputation when she came to live in Venice that though she was far from grand in her manner, she was quickly dubbed 'the Duchess of Venice'. She lived in the Palazzo Venice dei Leoni on the Grand Canal, with a luxurious gondola parked alongside. On land, she had her Rolls-Royce. To enter her museum-home, you would have to pass the huge, beautiful, bronze Marino Marini horse, famous for its oversize penis, so out of scale it had to be made removable (a feature often made use of to avoid embarrassment on official occasions). Her home is now open to the public three afternoons a week.

Venice was her ivory tower. She loved it for its quiet and lack of traffic – there were no motor-driven launches then – and for its many great features. Fifteen years later, when the city became noisy and busy, she felt it had lost its attraction and charm, which distressed her – but she stayed.

Her closest admirers had originally conspired to bring her to the world of art. In the end she proved to have a staggering perspicacity for it, using a seemingly bottomless fortune, shocking her more conservative relatives, to help the surrealist movement. Her genius was in discovering talent and making close friendships with the artists. In the end she built the world's finest private surrealist collection. She fostered the most prominent among the 'lunatic fringe' of the time, regularly financing and feeding them. Among her several husbands was Max Ernst. She married him despite him being at that time a German enemy-alien, confessing that she suddenly preferred marriage to living in sin with him.

Samuel Beckett had also been a great lover of hers who tried his best to make her appreciate other kinds of contemporary art. Marcel Duchamp was another who also attempted to excite her into collecting abstract paintings. He failed. By consultation, and getting many of her favourite surrealists to come to America and exhibit in her own commercial art gallery, Art of the Century, in New York, she helped alter the course of Surrealism in the United States and in the rest of the world. Later, she was the first dealer to focus seriously on the work of Mark Rothko, Robert Motherwell and Clyfford Still.

Peggy Guggenheim belonged to the same family who built New York City's Guggenheim Museum of Modern Art, designed by Frank Lloyd Wright and financed by her uncle, Solomon Guggenheim, although she had no connection with it. Her father had died a dramatic death in the world's most famous sea tragedy, the sinking of the *Titanic*. Safely on board a lifeboat, he suddenly changed his mind and went back to his stateroom to change clothes. Dressed in black tie, he stayed on board and went down to his death, leaving his large fortune to all the Guggenheims. She could be no less dramatic than he, especially concerning marriage. She once said she had four husbands; 'none of these marriages by benefit of the church and only two by benefit of the state,' taking after her own father who was renowned for enjoying numerous mistresses.

At one stage in her life she lived in Sussex, but she soon described it as 'rural boredom'. It drove her back to Paris to which she had fled once before, in the twenties, to escape what she referred to as her own stultifying bourgeois background.

She knew her collection in Venice had to be found a permanent home when she died, and she worried about it. Museums on both sides of the Atlantic hoped she would bequeath it to them. I once thought I had persuaded her to leave it to the Tate Gallery in London, until she made all too clear her unacceptable conditions. The entire collection, she insisted, had to be displayed exactly as it was in her Venetian home (and not at her expense). Who could accept such conditions? In the end, there was no choice but for it to stay in her home, so it remains in the palazzo in Venice; she left both house and collection to the city, to be administered by the Solomon R. Guggenheim Foundation.

Visitors will find paintings, sculptures and her remarkable collection of bric-à-brac by famous artists which provide the main exhibits. There is no furniture. I have always been fascinated by her highly personal private possessions, the little artefacts made or given her by lovers, admirers and aficionados in the art world. The bottles, vases, urns and ceramics clustered on the walls were designed and painted by Picasso, Braque, Degas, Ernst, Dali, de Chirico, Magritte, Arp, Piet Mondrian, Cocteau, Léger, Delvaux and Klee. I hope I have remembered them all. Her 'jewellery gallery', an idea I loved, was the collection of her jewels, mostly spectacular earrings, which once hung on the walls on both sides of her bed. Even more fascinating, the silver headboard itself, a Calder mobile!

Her six Lhasa terriers were an integral ingredient in the decor, scampering after her wherever she moved. They were another reason she never moved her life or her collection permanently to England; the strict quarantine regulations determined that.

In 1960, she wrote an acid-dipped book, *Confessions of an Art Addict*, in which she voiced her opinion on non-objective art: 'I said art has gone to hell, now it's worse than going to hell.' She said she hated the Rauschenbergs and Johns (then housed right next door to her own palazzo in the American exhibit in Venice's *Biennale*).

Yet her name will always be associated with that of Jackson Pollock. She found him working as a carpenter on the site of her uncle's Guggenheim Museum. She took him off the job and gave him an annual contract with a monthly allowance that liberated him to paint. Eventually, she gave him an exhibition in her New York City gallery which brought him fame. It was a considerable act of faith in a contemporary art which she claimed she hated.

Lydia Dunn, one of Hong Kong's most remarkable (and beautiful) ladies, has achieved international fame both for her political skills and her big heart. When I had my fifty-first one-man exhibition of paintings in Hong Kong in 1995, as Governor Patten's guest, her generous efforts were responsible for a good slice of the success I achieved in its China Club launch* before the paintings went to Alice King's art gallery.

Her record is an amazing one. At the age of fifty, she was made a Dame of the British Empire and a member of the House of Lords in London. As The Rt Hon. The Baroness Dunn, DBE, JP, she is also a Director of John Swire & Sons (Hong Kong), a senior member of the Steering Committee on the British Nationality Scheme (a difficult political job) and convenor of the OMELCO Steering Group, whose job it is to promote Hong Kong as an international city. As she now lives in England, it will be exciting to hear her on the floor of the House of Lords espousing her causes for her first home, soon to be a part of China.

In 1988 she married Michael Thomas, CMG, QC, whose own impressive background as a Queen's Counsel includes his stint as Hong Kong's former Attorney General.

When I asked Lydia Dunn to tell me what she hopes to accomplish in her new life in London, her answer was to the point; brief and intense: 'Though my heart will beat for Hong Kong, there will be new challenges in London. Establishing a home there, taking on new responsibilities for the Swire Group, building a new platform for Hong Kong's concerns in the House of Lords, new friends, new interests and opportunities. I have never felt more motivated in my life.'

An even braver lady is Helen Suzman. Her reputation was made as a liberal white member of the opposition Progressive Party in South Africa. She never stopped battling against apartheid, not just in the recent somewhat safer climate of her country, but for as many years as I can think back in time. She was just plain brave: brave to visit jails on behalf of prisoners, brave to seek an end to brutality, brave to campaign openly for humanity towards non-whites.

As we slowly walked together around the lake in our garden

* See David Tang, page 306.

in Sussex, she exuded naturalness, not aggression; she was utterly feminine and, remarkably, she neither needed nor sought credit. I was proud of her then and will always be, even though she has withdrawn from the political arena in South Africa. Her hopes and ideals are a part of South Africa's past of turmoil and misery. After thirty-five years she simply ceded her seat, feeling exhausted.

When *all* the people of South Africa voted for the first time in its history in 1994, Helen Suzman was the voice sought by every network to speak for the liberal whites. Her greatest hope was that a democratic path would follow, with a respect for human rights and freedom of the press. Her fear is that the skills of government have to be learned literally overnight by the new black leaders and that the black population will grow impatient with the pace of progress.

Janet Suzman, her talented niece who chose the stage, not politics, has become a great star of television, films and the London theatre. Sharing the family blood, she has the same formidable intellect and passion. In the theatre, she has starred in all major Shakespearean and Greek tragedies. Recently she decided that directing plays and films would provide her with a new and exciting creative role. A number of such projects were in the wings. Late in 1994, relenting on her 'no more acting' decision, she joined the cast of *The Sisters Rosensweig* to play one of the strongest and funniest roles of her career, to rave notices.

A great heartbreak in her life was losing her husband, theatre's leading producer Trevor Nunn, who left her for another woman. Her son, Joshua, became her vocation for at least a dozen years; she took the view that he was her real 'career', and had the strength to put her ambitions aside in order to bring up her son. The decision has produced an unspoiled, intelligent, likeable boy.

Brave is a word I would like to use again in describing the woman who has been Director of the Victoria and Albert Museum in London for six years. She left the post to become Vice-Chancellor of the University of East Anglia in Norwich, to deserved applause for her achievements at the V & A. Her new role might also prove as challenging for her. Before he left in 1987 after many years as Director of the V & A, the elegant Sir Roy Strong described his function in an article in the *International Herald Tribune*: 'Part actor manqué, bash-throwing bon vivant, man about culture, amateur mathematician and ultimate survivor – just what it takes to run a modern museum'. He is now a trustee of the Museum tackling the problems he loves. Elizabeth Esteve-Coll succeeded him. I dare say her own description of the position would differ. She was brutally maligned in print by a different former Director from the United States, who described her as being more or less unfit for the appointment.

There was understandable public concern over the way she dismissed certain staff for what she considered their inefficiency. She was publicly criticized for her ideas on fundraising; they may have been essential, but were possibly badly presented and thus misunderstood. She calmly survived it all.

The Museum has become a very lively, family-oriented place. The façade of the Victorian Gothic building has been cleaned to emerge lily-white. It is *alive*. The staff are busy, alert and friendly. The seven miles of galleries are filled with visitors from all over the world, and many treasures once banished to the basement and infrequently seen are now on show. Major exhibitions from the Far East and other places fill the Museum, not all of equal popularity but giving proof that there is always something happening. They bring in the crowds, which is every museum's fond wish. Her changes have been painful, but she and the V & A Board wisely carried on and the museum is a must for anyone interested in the history of the world's art. Alan Borg, its new Director, is the new, imaginative boss.

I gave Elizabeth Esteve-Coll my personal sympathy (she never asked for it) when the campaign of abuse began. I admired her stoicism and bravery despite it all and I have since come to appreciate her unpretentious and firm manner.

I must admit that I like the way she instantly agreed to be a judge on my jury to pick the winners of the Fleur Cowles Award for Excellence at the Royal College of Art. She, like all the others on the panel, could scarcely spare the time for constant viewing and discussion, but gave it, nevertheless.

She is the widow of a Spanish sea-captain who, while he sailed Spanish waters for many years, could never go ashore because he was a refugee from Franco. She knows Spain now, our Spain, after regular visits to our historic home in the town of Trujillo.

Writing of Spain reminds me of one of the favourite Spanish pastimes, bullfighting. I often ask the questions: should anyone fight bulls – and who would want to? I put those questions to the world's greatest matadora, Conchita Cintron, and she gave an emphatic yes, they should, and that there were many in southern Europe who wanted to. But it is a question all animal-lovers must ask, and perhaps also the families of the participants.

However, the sport continues. The enthusiasm and the audiences may have diminished somewhat, but millions in Latin countries still want to watch this ancient exercise in bravery, the drama of humans standing arrogantly, temptingly, in the sand against the charge of an angry, pain-maddened bull. Each is in the ring to kill the other. What is the lure? Does it heighten the adrenalin because even those who abhor the spectacle join the crowds to watch?

I was fascinated by the very young Conchita Cintron when I saw her perform in Mexico City at my first, terrifying bullfight. To my astonishment, this teenage Peruvian girl was the star. She was the world's undisputed leading female bullfighter when we became friends after meeting in Portugal years later.

Though I had been sickened by that first sight, I was eventually able to control my revulsion sufficiently to write about the bullfight and the matadors, and to understand the ritual. A slow contest on horseback, not on foot as Conchita and the Portuguese do (they only dismount for the kill), they are called *rejoneadors*.

The teenager I saw in Mexico grew up to world acclaim. In Portugal, she rode elegantly, wearing a stark black and brown costume, eschewing the brilliantly coloured 'suit of lights' decorated and emblazoned with gold embroidery that is worn by all men. A 'suit of lights' costs over $5000 and a top matador has at least eight in his wardrobe. Sitting on a handsome horse, *she* preferred her own version: a truly great matador and very beautiful, still alive and unhurt today, she had killed over six hundred bulls when she retired at the age of thirty-one, already old by matador standards.

Her ancient female predecessors in Crete used a technique that is no longer legal, facing the bulls on foot, jumping up to grab their horns, then leaping like gazelles on to the animal's body. Conchita, just as brave, used to gallop around the ring on her fearless horse, teasing and enraging the bulls. I can still see her, dismounted, standing unafraid in the sand on her toes, in the classic pose, ready for the kill.

I asked Conchita for her opinion of one of the legendary idols, Spanish matador, El Cordobes: 'He is a phenomenon and kills badly. But the one truth about Cordobes is that he truly risked his life every time he fought. Approve or not of the bullfight, it should never be considered a painless way of life.'

And did she ever see the sport as cruel? 'Nonsense!' she replied. 'Every bull is born to be killed by man. The difference between a domestic bull from England and one from a fighting-bull farm is that one is only born to be meat and the other goes into the ring first to show how well he can die. In England the bull is killed at the age of two but the fighting bull is reared under the most idyllic conditions in the open fields. He has a wonderful life for four or five years!'

Her incomparable riding skill as a tiny eleven-year-old had caught the eye of a retired Portuguese bullfighter, Guy de Camara, who lived in Peru near Conchita's birthplace. Camara saw her astride her horse and was fascinated by her style and professionalism. He was persuaded that she was bullfighting material and taught her the craft. It gave her courage, which she never lost.

Conchita's heritage is an interesting mixture. She is half Spanish, one quarter Irish, one quarter American. Her appalled father, an American Army colonel, absolutely refused to condone her choice of occupation, but her Spanish mother, on the other hand, was more philosophical. 'After all,' she reasoned, 'she could have wanted to be a test pilot.' Eventually her father assented, extracting the concession that Camara's wife must accompany Conchita and Camara on every circuit.

Eventually she fell in love with and married the nephew of Camara and went to live in Lisbon. They had four sons and a daughter. Did any of them become bullfighters too? No, Conchita never wanted them to follow in her footsteps. 'Why, with the burden of my name?' she asked me.

*   *   *

37

The first woman ever to be President of the Royal College of Physicians in Britain, after 473 years' history of 'Men Only', was Professor Dame Margaret Turner-Warwick, DBE, MA, DM, PhD, FRCP, FRACP, FRCP (Ed.), FFOM.

This distinguished, well-qualified lady did not reach her lofty position by flaunting her talents and ambitions. One would have to go a long way to find a woman more modest, more solicitous or more friendly. She was elected as President after becoming an international authority on chest and lung ailments. She learnt about suffering as a young medical student at Oxford in the late 1940s, when she was suddenly stricken with tuberculosis, at that time a common and often fatal illness. In the year or more she spent on her back in sanatoriums, she learned more about the disease than in years of study, by identifying with the sick. She married another Oxford medical student, Richard Turner-Warwick, eminent in the field of urology.

Dame Margaret was my husband Tom's remarkable partner when she was Dean of the Royal Brompton Institute. For many years they worked very closely together, in particular when they were designing and building the Cardiothoracic Institute's new hospital during his chairmanship of all the London Heart and Chest Hospitals.

At one point, while I was writing these memories, the softly spoken Jung Chang was already *en route* to Tokyo to celebrate the sale of the millionth* copy of her remarkable book, *Wild Swans*. My husband and I have given countless copies away and persuaded most of our friends to read it.

It is not purely a work of history as such, although history could not be better served. It is the author's personal account of the lives of three generations of Chinese women, Jung Chang's grandmother and her own mother's and her life during her country's long years of violence, starvation and humiliation. Through the lives of these three women we are shown China's twentieth-century nightmare: years of civil war, foreign invasion, the disasters of imposed social experiments, the brutal madness of Mao and of the so-called Cultural Revolution.

She now lives in London, married to the delightful historian Jon

---

* In January 1996, the sales had risen to 6,500,000 throughout the world.

Halliday; they have been collaborating on a much-awaited biography of Mao Tse Tung. In the quiet of our homes, I have had ample opportunity to get to know and admire her simplicity and charm and her incredible sense of fun. With *Wild Swans* Jung Chang has given the world a truly remarkable book that has received many awards and prizes and has captured the hearts of millions around the world.

Few foreigners I've met are more articulate in English, a miracle which gives reading her books a remarkable extra tier of excellence.

Another woman of unusual character (and physical strength) who achieved a high position in palaeoanthropology is Mary Leakey, who is devoting herself to the search for man's origins. Her study of animal fossils at Olduvai Gorge in Africa has given proof of the exact timescale between ape and man. Her husband, Louis S. B. Leakey, continually tried to get me (as President of the Leakey Trust in Europe) to go out to Olduvai. I regularly refused because of my dread of snakes, and said so. In a moment of impatience over this obsession, he angrily blurted out: 'I'm sick of hearing that excuse. After all, my wife has only been bitten once!'

'Thanks. You've just lost me,' I announced.

Jane Goodall is also renowned in the same field. She has lived for years in Africa's jungle close to man's counterpart, the gorilla. She has written brilliantly about them, of the days in the wilderness, her infant son by her side. This beautiful woman was a great help to me in the early years after I formed the Trust – so was her mother, Vanne. Jane's 'Roots and Shoots' organization was created to take positive action to encourage young people with the same ideals. She has been a serious contributor to the growth of interest in anthropology, searching for knowledge of our human past.

II

MEMORABLE GENTLEMEN

INTERESTING AND MEMORABLE gentlemen are not a scarce commodity. I have had a fair share of such friendships in industry, in
government, in the arts and among royalty, but my husband must
be at the top. We have shared a good life for over forty years after
meeting in Persia in 1953. Two years later, in November 1955, we
married and I left the United States for a new life, new friends and
new activities.

Everyone who knows my husband, Tom Montague Meyer, thinks
him remarkable. He winces at attention, being almost paranoid about
personal publicity,* yet his life has been fascinating enough to warrant
his writing the autobiography two publishers regularly try to persuade
him to produce. 'One writer in the family is enough,' he announces,
but I shall persist in trying to get him to write it.

A potted biography appeared in 1990 in London's Royal Brompton
Hospital's house organ; he was the hospital's highly effective Chairman
for over ten years. It was written by the staff when he announced he
was retiring. I quote it in its entirety.

'Tom has had a most interesting and varied life, which started when
he left an English public school at seventeen, and thus began to
show his own spirit of enterprise.

'He went by train and boat to British Columbia in Western
Canada, where he worked in saw mills and became a lumberjack,
making enough money to buy a car and motor to Los Angeles. In
the Port of San Pedro (Los Angeles), he signed on as a deck hand
on a small cargo boat, working his way round the Pacific for the
next six months. Signing off in Shanghai, he sailed down the China
coast on a Japanese cargo liner, eventually returning to England,

* His father taught him never to invest in any company if the Chairman appeared in
the press more than twice a year.

where he became Assistant Manager in one of the docks owned by his father's company in the East End of London – until the outbreak of war.

'He was then commissioned in one of the crack British Regiments, the Rifle Brigade, seeing service in the Western Desert in 1940 and 1941, including the first siege of Tobruk. He had been captured at the end of 1941, twenty-five miles behind the enemy lines, mapping minefields at night. Because of this, he was considered a dangerous prisoner-of-war and so was moved all over Europe – from Alsace to Czechoslovakia – until the end of the war, nearly four years later.

'He regained his health in Canada and helped the British Government produce the timber they required for essential post-war re-housing. During the next ten years, he led surveying expeditions in East Africa, Borneo, Sarawak, Malaya, North Persia and the Amazon. Later he became a Chief Executive in Europe's biggest timber organization.

'Always interested in the less fortunate, Tom Meyer was asked by the Government to serve on many Health Boards and in 1974 was given the job of looking after the 750,000 people living between London Airport and Central London in all matters concerning National Health, while continuing to take on other Government responsibilities. He has just retired as Chairman of all the Post-Graduate Heart and Chest Hospitals, working directly for the Minister of Health, and has also worked as Chairman of all the Post-Graduate Hospitals when they meet as a body.

'He has had many hobbies, having played cricket and rugby football at a high standard as well as becoming an internationally known racing driver, taking in most of the leading events in Europe. For over thirty years, he has been a successful and innovative farmer – concentrating on the cross-breeding of continental and British animals, both cattle and sheep.

'In 1955 he married Fleur Cowles and together they have lived one of the broadest international lives, interested in everything from politics to people.'

I now take up the tale: the son of two wealthy parents, he inherited the pioneer character of his father, who established the family's international timber company. After his death, it was built into the biggest timber business in the United Kingdom, a 'statistic' which is usually followed by another – it became 'Russia's single largest customer' by purchasing such vast quantities of their timber products.

Before we met, he had enjoyed a hobby that must have been the perfect antidote to the time spent as a prisoner-of-war, cooped up for nearly four years in ever-changing cells in ever-changing camps all over occupied Europe, the treatment meted out by the Germans to any prisoner who tried to escape. He became a racing driver competing in the major European events, somehow fitting this added career into his business life.

This love of fast cars also appealed to me at a different time in my own life when 'the dangerous' was a wishful experience. After we met, he obligingly designed a fast Jaguar car which could fly me over the European roads, then less crowded. They were first marked off for me on a map by King Paul of Greece. He wished, with a sigh, he could fly over them himself.

My husband and I used to do the racing circuits together on non-racing days and it soon became obvious to me how dangerous professional racing was as a vocation. I knew enough not to say *stop*. Instead, I announced one day that I wanted to sit beside him in his next race. It was going to be the Mille Miglia (1000-mile) race in Italy, reputed to be one of the most dangerous in the world. Result? He never raced again. Later, we watched sadly as one by one some of his companions were involved in terrible crashes, often to die.

Public service replaced racing for him. At sixty-five he retired from the timber business to continue, full-time, the work he had begun years before on a part-time basis, always wanting to contribute to public health. He did this for seventeen years without pay, and did it with honour. All he has ever really cared about has been the respect of his colleagues.

After those seventeen years of service, his retirement did evoke at least the following letter from Virginia Bottomley, then number two in the Department of Health (later its Minister):

'I am writing to thank you most warmly for the contribution you have made to the National Health Service over a great many years.

'Your record of service has been outstanding. I know that your work for the NHS goes back to 1974 when you were appointed as Chairman of the Ealing, Hammersmith and Hounslow Area Health Authority. We are all aware of the enormous debt of gratitude which many people owe to you over all these years.

'I would particularly like to pay tribute to your leadership of the

Special Health Authority of the Royal Brompton National Heart and Lung Hospitals for the past eleven years. Under your chairmanship the SHA has progressed impressively and has carried forward major developments to its estate, culminating in last month's opening of the new Hospital.

'The Secretary of State and I want you to know of our deep appreciation for all your hard work during what have been years of great change for the Health Service. I should like to add my personal best wishes for the future.

'From all accounts the opening was clearly a marvellous occasion; many congratulations on all you have achieved.'

London's new Royal Brompton Heart and Chest Hospital is his pride, which after ten years as Chairman he saw erected. His portrait, by Bryan Organ, hangs inside its entrance with a simple statement: 'Tom M. Meyer, who made this hospital possible'. He considers this his real reward.

What was once housed in the original huge, musty Dickensian Brompton Road giant had become a beautiful modern (and welcoming) building a block away. It ranks as the finest heart and chest hospital in Europe (some say anywhere), as much for its superb atmosphere, equipment and research capabilities as for its renowned medical teams, many of whom he had personally drawn to its doors from far places. Minister Bottomley actually tried to close this remarkable place a year later, for ridiculously unfathomable reasons, but failed.

After being granted the now rare use of 'Royal' in its name, the official opening was honoured by the Queen. The occasion ended (one could hear a pin drop) as someone very slowly came forward to present flowers to the Queen, after my husband announced that it would not be the usual tiny child but a woman who had just recovered from one of the first heart and lung transplants successfully done in the hospital. A quiet drama.

Another tribute came to him from the London Chest Hospital, one of his many other responsibilities. When he opened the new Operating and Recovery Units, named the Tom Meyer Wing, the Princess of Wales officiated. I tried to be unobtrusive, looking out for my modest husband, but he was standing quietly behind *me*. Yes, hiding. The Princess finally located him and beckoned him forward. 'Come here,' she demanded quietly, 'after all, this is *your* day!' 'I hope I didn't embarrass you!' she said to him later. 'Now you know how I feel!'

It was thanks to the Shah of Persia that he and I actually first met. He had been out in the untravelled, dangerous north, prospecting timber at the request of the British Foreign Office. They were anxious about the low standard of living in north Persia and the increasing influence of the Russians along the Caspian coast.

I was in Teheran on my second visit as guest of the Shah but also on a confidential mission for President Eisenhower. I later succeeded in persuading and bringing the Shah and Queen Soraya to the United States on a private visit because, for political reasons, he couldn't be invited officially for a state visit. The trip had its hoped-for success with the signing of the Turkey-Pakistan Pact.

Tom Meyer, whom I hadn't yet met, had finished work on his timber project and was on the airplane on which I was to leave Teheran. It had been irritatingly delayed by the Shah, who kept me too late to join it at the scheduled take-off time. A sea of angry faces greeted me when I finally arrived.

One seat was available; it happened to be on the aisle, directly across from the timber executive. Worn out after having made the journey from New York to Teheran three days before and having endured a perilous near-arrest in Beirut while *en route*, sleep was on my mind, but I was too revolted by the contents of the pocket facing me, bulging with sticky Cola bottles. I took one out gingerly, and as I did, the man I ultimately married leaned over. 'Give them to me, I'll deal with them.' After thanking him, I pulled out a black chiffon scarf, tied it around my eyes, dropped the seat lower and went to sleep.

Nonstop journeys were then unknown; the first landing was Athens. The seat next to Tom Meyer became vacant (after the occupant had been persuaded by him to get off by urging him with the advice, 'World travellers shouldn't miss the beautiful, ancient sights of Greece.') As the man left, he asked if I would like to have that seat. 'Yes, *indeed I would*.' I jumped at the chance to sit by the window.

From then on it was incessant conversation: 'Did I know anything about Walter Reuther in the US?' he asked. He didn't know that I was an editor of a mass-circulation magazine, that I did know about Reuther. Little did I know that labour conditions was one of his prime concerns in life. Walter Reuther was making headlines as the American labour leader who insisted a worker had a right to job-security.

Like his father, Tom Meyer had always been troubled about workers' conditions, particularly that dockers in Europe were never paid for the time when they weren't working. His family company, with sixteen docks around Britain, was the first to change the system in 1937, when they arranged that men be paid for Christmas Day and the day after – *the first time dockers received pay for any time they were not labouring*. Christmas had been their nightmare. Slowly, through the years that followed, Tom Meyer kept improving the system, leading to labour relations he could approve of.

If ever there was a seemingly unromantic chatter on a plane, it was about labour relations. He and I later breakfasted in Rome's airport while waiting for the connecting plane to London for my three-day stop-off at Claridge's. The amiable bachelor was returning to his own London pad.

What started as an interesting meeting between two people sharing the same views, gradually became a serious relationship. Problems had arisen with husband Mike Cowles. I often had to be away and I suddenly learned of his relationship with another woman, which I refused to countenance. Two years after the meeting on the plane, I divorced him and married the dashing Tom Meyer. My American life had ended; a European life began.

In 1992, after my husband retired from the Royal Brompton chairmanship, a noted American cardiologist, Dr Bernard Lown, who received the Nobel Peace Prize for his disclosure and warnings on the medical effects of an A-bomb, invited Tom and myself to join him and several other dedicated men on the Board of a trail-blazing medical scheme called *SatelLife*.

SatelLife is now in full-stream operation – a satellite service supplying isolated doctors in nineteen Third-World countries with the free medical information they need. *SatelLife* focuses on the whole world four times every twenty-four hours for fifteen minutes and gives doctors in the Third-World countries the free research they knew was available as required reading while they trained in the United States and Europe – but which they lose completely when they return home, often to remote jungle localities. The easy way to think of *SatelLife* is as a 'library of the air' – the Flying Doctor of tomorrow. Doctors ask for (and receive free) whatever information and research and news they need – even books by satellite.

We are now both proudly involved as two of ten founders of the Institute for American Studies, which will be built on Oxford University land. The campaign, going well, was the idea of Lord Rothermere. He and his sister, Lady Cromer, are co-Chairmen. We played a major part in influencing the building committee at Oxford to employ a New York firm of architects, probably the first from the United States to work in that ancient university.

The aim of the Institute is to encourage Anglo-American cultural and political ties at a time when Britain's close cooperation with the rest of Europe could in the future make this more difficult.

Passing from my husband to friends I also treasure, I begin with the most unforgettable friend in my life, the tall, tall aristocrat, Bernard Baruch, the elderly 'Elder Statesman' who, for fifty years or more, figured so importantly in the political life of the United States. Our friendship was practically father-and-daughter and though I was not officially adopted, I was taken by him into his 'family', chosen to be treated as a daughter. This privilege taught me, enlightened me, and contributed immeasurably to the fullness of my life. Bernard Baruch was my 'thought processor' and a lovable, courtly friend.

I recall nothing about Baruch that wasn't praiseworthy, unless it was his love of publicity, a criticism sometimes made by enemies. Yes, he did love the press's attention, yet he refused every offer of public appointment, any one of which would have automatically ensured attention. His 'Park Bench' press conferences suited him to a tee. Immaculately dressed, he simply walked across New York City's Fifth Avenue from his home to sit and bask in the sun, giving his views informally. I first met him at a luncheon on Long Island in the home of Alicia Guggenheim. He was already seventy-six years old. We had driven down a long, long drive from the road to her house. The sight of the deep carpet of crocuses in the grass contributes to my memory of that meeting. Soon after, he decided 'Fleur has a brain' and began his 'thought processing' training which certainly made me focus on current events, and to treat facts like a religion.

Bernard Baruch was as well known as any President of the United States, yet he never had or wanted that kind of power. He refused office, wishing only to have the ear of whoever *was* President. He got it. He gave freely of his time, no financial considerations were involved, and he was an adviser to six Presidents.

He did hold important administrative posts; heading the American Delegation to the Atomic Energy Commission was his last. He gave advice, wrote reports, influenced Congress, generals, diplomats and party leaders as well as the public. When I asked why he refused official power, he answered: 'Why should I kiss off my potential influence?'

During the First World War, he was Chairman of the War Industries Board. Put in charge of all industrial mobilization by President Woodrow Wilson, he actually controlled America's entire industrial capacity. Among countless other unpaid jobs, he assisted with the Treaty of Versailles and his Baruch Plan for Atomic Energy remained the policy of the US Government for years.

This elegant gentleman was first of all a financial wizard. He made his first dollar million (worth at least ten million today) when twenty-one years old, but he made his fortune honestly, by intuitive skills; no inside trading, no gambling – these were not his ethics. As a great industrialist he helped mobilize for World War II. He underwrote the entire cotton crop of his native state, South Carolina, to ensure that it would command a fair price.

Although President Roosevelt described him as 'that old Pooh-Bah', he respected his sagacity, regularly sought his advice and always took it seriously. Once, however, on an unexpected occasion, another President, Truman, challenged him, arguing harshly over their difference of opinion. Baruch never spoke to President Truman again. Nor did he speak well of him again. Despite this, in his wisdom Baruch was about the only political figure to place a bet that Truman would win against Thomas Dewey in the race for the Presidency. He sent me a handwritten note predicting Dewey's defeat six months *before* the election – while every other pundit, Congressman, Senator or diplomat, either in the press or in private, wrote Truman off completely. 'No chance at all,' they agreed. In fact, *Life* magazine made the mistake of its *Life*-time when it published a portrait of Dewey on its magazine cover, headlined as the 'New President of the US'. This issue was actually on the news-stands nearly a week before the election took place. Truman, not Dewey, won it.

Age never concerned Baruch. When a reporter asked him, at ninety, when he intended to write his autobiography, he smiled; 'I'm putting it off for my old age.'

He brought great warmth to my life after 'adopting' me. He always stressed the importance of news and the need to be perceptive. Although I refused his suggestion that I enter the political arena, he never let up on his wish to see me a full-time diplomat. I preferred my role as an editor and to undertake special diplomatic assignments, in the manner of the American system. He was pleased whenever it happened. However, when once I sent a written statement to the State Department about the condition of the US Information Department, he wrote back: 'I could spank you for not presenting your report personally to establish your own authority and open doors for yourself.'

The privilege and pleasure of his friendship continued even after I moved to England. He 'vetted' Tom Montague Meyer in person in New York City before we were married, pronouncing him 'exceptional' and wishing us well. Despite the oceanic distances involved, we managed to see each other and correspond regularly until his death just after his best friend, Winston Churchill, died. He had already given me the opportunity to know Churchill.

I was one of the few women in his circle. Others were Elizabeth Navarro, his highly capable nurse, and that glamorous favourite, Clare Boothe Luce, with whom he was genuinely in love. He had met her in 1923 at a Democratic National Convention. Her beauty and mind captivated him for the rest of his life. Hedda Hopper, Hollywood's tart-tongued reporter, fascinated him with her sharp language and even her right-wing politics, normally an anathema to him, but intriguing to him as a Democrat.

How devoted we were is exemplified in the following quotation from his authorized biography by Pulitzer prize winner, Margaret Coit, whose biography of Vice-President John C. Calhoun so impressed Baruch that he offered her free access to the vast collection of papers covering his own life. He talked endlessly to her and was delighted by her resulting impressive book, titled *Baruch, the Man, the Myth, the Eighty Years*.

The book's cover photograph shows him simply dressed, sitting on that famous park bench, the view of himself he loved the best, though he was also known for his elegant appearance at formal events, dressed in his tailcoat, wearing cufflinks of emeralds surrounded by a blaze of diamonds.

Miss Coit wrote:

'Another of his children was the effervescent Fleur Cowles. In every crisis of her life he would give her advice and then thank her for seeking his help. Once, near Christmas, she was startled to hear his voice on the phone late at night. He had not been well, but had sent his hard-working nurse, Elizabeth Navarro, away for a change of scene. He was alone. Would she come over? Mrs Cowles slipped on a coat and went at once. The butler showed her into Baruch's room, where the old man was lying on his bed, stretched out, his eyes closed. He began to talk and he talked for hours. He spoke of Truman and why he did not like him, and on across the whole range and roster of his life. He had received letters and cables and telegrams from all parts of the earth this Christmas season, yet had sought out this one warm, personal friend.'

This telephone call came at midnight on a cold winter's night. I put a fur coat over my pyjamas and rushed four blocks away to his side. Looking at him, I thought he was dead, so pale and still. I held his cold hand in mine for hours as he talked, watching his tired old face, worried desperately about his condition.

Miraculously, he was almost himself again two days later. I had hardly said a word as he lay there not moving, soliloquizing about the many men who were so deeply etched on his mind: President Truman, President Wilson, whom considered a very great man, George Marshall, the general whom he deeply admired for authorizing the Marshall Plan, and countless others. When I saw Marshall later, after the Coronation of Queen Elizabeth II which we both attended in an official capacity, I recalled Baruch's four-word description of him when he was Secretary of State; 'America's first global strategist'. Marshall smiled with pleasure.

Margaret Coit also wrote amusingly of the social side of our friendship:

'Nothing annoyed Baruch more than to be used as bait to lure others to a party. One evening he dined with a person who had told him that his good friend, Fleur Cowles, was to be among the guests. In the drawing room Mrs Cowles and Baruch compared notes. Mrs Cowles accepted the invitation only because Mr Baruch was to be the guest of honour – he had been told that *she* would be. They stuck it out during dinner, but as soon as coffee had been served, Baruch rose and announced: "Fleur is going to take me home." In the elevator, Mrs Cowles teased Baruch about getting old, to which he replied: "I want to go to the Stork Club." '

The Stork Club was New York's 'in' place to eat (it has long since gone) but this was to be his first and only visit to it. Mr Billingsley, the owner, was clearly shaken when I walked in with this very famous companion. I used to dine at the Stork Club regularly so Billingsley and I were friends. Everyone in the special room on the left of the club, the dining room set aside for chosen guests, was delighted to see him arrive.

The social climber's trick of using a name to lure someone to a party is an old one. Another time in Washington my former husband and I went to an infamous social climber's dinner for the distinguished essayist and editor, Walter Lippmann. He and his wife met us just inside the front door. 'If this wasn't in your honour, Walter, we'd never be here,' I whispered. To which Walter replied in astonishment, 'What! We were told the dinner was for *you*!' All four of us turned on our heels and went elsewhere for dinner.

To explain why I call Bernard Baruch my 'thought processor' I must describe his affectionate, continuous and mind-boggling method which never varied. He would telephone me at eight-thirty every morning to bark out what he considered was the question of the day. Being quite deaf, he never knew how loud he was. The question would be impossible to guess in advance; it could be the day's headlines, financial news, something scientific, or it might be political, even social. I simply had to be respectably prepared.

If occasionally I disappointed him, it was not for lack of trying. I needed very little sleep so the three papers delivered every morning at six o'clock were always devoured. Reading them became a 'mania' and remains so to this day. I did my best to absorb at random whatever I guessed he might choose. Sometimes, when the question stopped me in my tracks, I made a stab at answering it and the gods were sometimes kind enough to help me get it right.

Just where his mind would light was always a chance. Such questions as, 'Fleur, what are the goddamn Russians up to today? . . . What the hell is the stock market doing? . . . What's your view on old age pensions? . . . What on earth is going on today in Cairo? . . . Who *is* ready to take unilateral action against China? . . . What do you think of the Kefauver inquiry?' And so on and so on.

He also often talked out his speeches or articles with me: 'to hear him think' was how he put it. Or there would be general discussions in which he more or less ordered me to make sense. When it worked, I was very happy. The results of his method have been permanent. To this day, I 'keep track'. Baruch had made facts a religion and this has become my old friend's legacy to me.

When I hear certain words, Baruch always comes to mind. Whenever anyone uses the word *appraisal*, I think of him and his definition of it: once a man asked him, as a woman walked by, if he'd ever seen a better complexion or better figure. Baruch silenced him by saying that a beautiful woman only asks for attention, not appraisal.

But judging famous politicians was and still is fair game. I was able to gather two very different appraisals of the gallant Adlai Stevenson in the early fifties. The first came after an invitation from Gladwyn Jebb (later Lord Jebb), who was then UK Ambassador to the UN, to attend the farewell dinner he regularly gave to the Security Council at its end-of-session.

I found myself seated at table next to Russia's Ambassador Malik, a particularly interesting experience since neither interpreter nor informer was at Malik's back or elbow, a rare situation. I made the most of the fast and often amusing volley of friendly insults which flew between us without censorship.

I lived then on East 69th Street in the townhouse next door to the side entrance of Malik's Park Avenue Russian Embassy. Evidence of mysterious goings-on there rarely escaped me, particularly the scandalous time Mme Tolstoy, the famous Russian author's descendant, was either dropped or jumped to the sidewalk from the fifth-storey window of the room in which she was incarcerated. She survived, although terribly injured. No details were ever given, and it was reported as an accident by the press.

At dinner, Malik and I discussed this tragedy; he gave no explanation, so we moved on to another custom which interested me. It involved the arrival of bus-loads of men, women, and their children, baby carriages and all, which disgorged at the side door next to our main entrance every morning at seven-thirty. At seven each evening they were paraded back to the bus to be taken to an unknown address, presumably a hostel somewhere on Long Island. I watched them as they climbed into the bus, no one looking to the right or left, no one putting a foot out of line – a grim Moscow scene enacted daily on our elegant street a few steps off Park Avenue in New York City.

I chided the Ambassador: 'Why are you afraid to let these nice people see anything of New York?'

'I certainly deny that. They simply dislike New York!' he retorted.

'That's nonsense. They're obviously not given a chance. You realize that I keep an eye on what goes on there, Mr Ambassador?'

'I expect that!' he replied. 'And *we* have *you* bugged!' he responded, grinning broadly.

My experience with Soviet tactics had already been frustrating. Despite five years of trying to get to Russia, I never could get a visa, probably because *Look* magazine was then so anti-Soviet. After Ed Murrow mentioned my difficulty on CBS television both Ed and I were flooded with outraged denials.

'Fleur Cowles is always welcome. All she need do is to ask for a visa!' I continued to request one, but a visa never came, despite countless embarrassed assurances from the Russian Embassies in New York and Washington. My name was obviously blackballed in Moscow.

After dinner at the Jebb residence, Mr Malik and I walked together to the ballroom to watch the arrival of guests invited later for supper and dancing. All were talking about Adlai Stevenson's expected nomination that same evening as the Democratic Presidential candidate to run against Eisenhower. No one was surprised when Stevenson's acceptance speech was broadcast. Most guests discussed the 'spontaneous' speech which all smilingly knew had arrived at the Convention in his pocket.

Beatrice Eden, the estranged wife of Anthony Eden (who was then the British Foreign Secretary before becoming Prime Minister) arrived after dinner on the arm of her son. Spotting me, she crossed to us in the ballroom. 'We're talking about Adlai Stevenson,' I said after introducing Ambassador Malik.

'Mrs Eden, you must know the candidate. What do *you* think of Adlai Stevenson?' Malik asked her.

Then came her astonishing appraisal: 'Yes, I *do* know him,' she replied. 'Mr Stevenson is exactly like Anthony Eden. *Both are excellent Number Two men!*' After that outburst she moved on, leaving us with frozen faces.

The election campaign that followed Stevenson's nomination was notable but for me it became a disquieting experience when I agreed to take part in the *Herald Tribune*'s Forum debate in New York City over the merits of Stevenson versus Eisenhower (I was for Eisenhower). During the campaign, America had listened with delight to the two performers: Stevenson's superb prose was weighed against Ike's homely, even clumsy campaigning, but the odds were against Stevenson because of Eisenhower's engaging smile, his worldwide reputation, firsthand knowledge of postwar Europe and Soviet Russia and his personal popularity. Whenever he sent his upstretched hands in the air to make his characteristic V-sign, votes flew his way – a national love affair with the public in which he carried forty-one of forty-eight states, including Stevenson's own state of Illinois. Stevenson not only didn't beat Eisenhower in 1956; in 1960 he lost the Democratic nomination to John F. Kennedy.

The Forum debate in which I participated took place on Election Eve in 1952. I was then (and still am) that oddity, an independent voter, occasionally choosing the man and not the party. I knew and greatly admired Eisenhower; I first met him when he was Director of SHAPE headquarters outside Paris after the Allies, under his command, won the war in Europe.

I knew and also greatly admired and respected Stevenson, but I simply could not vote for him as President. He'd given his *voice* to the hopes and ideals of liberal Americans of both parties but I thought many of his strongest virtues would be fatal drawbacks in the White House. Despite his undisputed idealism, tenderness and honesty, there were personal weaknesses – most of all his anxiety when faced with any decision. 'He even struggles with his bid at bridge,' Mike Cowles often reminded me.

In the debate, I drew attention to a sad litany of personal facts: Stevenson had little faith in himself; he had self-doubts which he admitted to close friends he couldn't really manage. His marriage to a beautiful woman went haywire, largely due to her serious medical problems, but their break-up didn't build his confidence. He often used a sad phrase: 'gain brings pain'. The Forum occasions can be nerve-racking at any time, but particularly so for me on that night as the debate was the last on the crowded agenda.

The Forum was a yearly event in which world figures appeared, and it ran for a week. To be asked to speak was flattering; few from the political, philosophical and scientific arenas ever declined. The paper no longer exists in America today. Renamed *The International Herald Tribune*, it is now published in Paris, with printing presses on three continents, even in Asia, a bible for Americans abroad and all serious newsgatherers. It is now owned by Katherine Graham and Arthur Ochs Sulzberger.

Mrs Ogden Reid, then owner of the newspaper, personally persuaded me to take part in the debate. Dorothy Schiff, publisher and editor of New York City's *Evening Post*, which was conducting a blazing campaign to elect Stevenson, was my adversary. On this night, many notables were seated on the dais directly behind Mrs Schiff and myself, including candidate Dwight D. Eisenhower. For me, the debate was a tricky one for many reasons, especially the fact that Adlai Stevenson was a lifelong friend of Mike Cowles. Would my husband be agreeable to my debating against him? Yes, he was; as an undeviating Republican, General Eisenhower was his obvious candidate and when I explained the line I had decided to take, which was Stevenson's record as Governor of Illinois, he unequivocally agreed.

Stevenson was aware of his personal difficulties. After having been elected Governor of Illinois, he wrote that he needed help, understanding and encouragement. 'I have none,' he concluded. Again, in the acceptance speech as the Democratic Presidential nominee which we heard him make on radio while at the Jebb party, he said, 'I have asked the merciful Father to let this cup pass from me.' Since he wrote his own speeches one assumes he spoke honestly, and he was shrewd enough to warn the Republican opposition with a brilliantly clever threat: 'If you stop telling lies about us, we'll stop telling the truth about you.' Even such a comment didn't help him.

I began my contribution to the debate with statistics and facts: after praising his good qualities, I asked if one could expect so sensitive a man to tackle politics at the low level to which it normally sinks. Could he be more successful in the White House than he was as Governor in the state capital of Illinois? What of his promises of racial equality . . . a superior school system . . . the ending of vice and corruption in the political system itself? Such concerns had motivated every speech and every effort Stevenson made during that term of office in Illinois. The results, which I listed, gave a picture of a man whose hopes had become unreachable dreams. Racial bigotry? It reached its worst when he was Governor. Education? Attempts to raise the educational level in the state had failed. Corruption? Racecourse scandals surrounding government officials were rampant. And there was more.

I won the debate, although the report in the press the next morning was probably too late to have been of harm to his candidacy.

After John F. Kennedy was elected President, it is said that he promised Adlai Stevenson the only post the internationalist really hankered after; Secretary of State. But Kennedy reneged, giving him the post of Ambassador to the United Nations instead, appeasing the shocked man by the novel promise that he would, nevertheless, be a member of his cabinet.

Stevenson's passionate disapproval of a limited blockade of Cuba was made clear. He won his point (according to a report given to me) by confronting Ambassador Zovin of Russia at the United Nations with photographs taken of the USSR's build-up of missile sites in Cuba.

There is an aside to this story which my British husband revealed to me at the time. Directing Europe's largest timber-importing business and buying heavily from the Russians at the time of the Cuban crisis, his contracts with them, current and outstanding, were suddenly abruptly delayed or postponed. When pictures in the press revealed a Russian armada on its way to Cuba, my husband recognized many of the ships as familiar timber carriers (all of which had been designed to be able, at times of war, to carry missiles). They were headed for Cuba with their deadly cargo instead of being on their usual timber run from northern Russian ports to the United Kingdom.

After the crisis was over, my husband's British dock workers, who over the years had become friendly with the Russians, were told by them that delivery delays were caused by Russia's mobilization which involved every port worker under fifty years of age. Traders like my husband had realized that something strange and unusual was afoot because normally the Russian deliveries were punctilious. *How near we had come to war.*

Stevenson, who loved London, actually died of a heart attack on a

Mayfair pavement. Millions had lost their favourite loser, and they wept.

Far less popular was another loser in a bid to become President: General Douglas MacArthur, the man of the clenched jaw, corncob pipe and over-decorated cap, a lover of publicity who arrogantly decided he was the more likely candidate to succeed Truman. After dismissal by Truman as Commander of the armed forces in 1951 he actually intended to wipe him off the slate. His support was short-lived, over almost before it began. The audiences and the street crowds he enjoyed on his return from Korea simply disappeared. The parade on that occasion was the most dramatic welcome ever accorded anyone by New York City before the astronauts; the people turned out in force for a ticker-tape celebration. Right-wing Republicans cheered his return and cursed that Democrat in the White House, Harry Truman, for his dismissal after MacArthur after he had disobeyed the President's command. His Presidential campaign consisted of dramatic speeches to partisan voters but ended with his famous tear-jerker, 'Old soldiers never die. They merely fade away,' which he also repeated regularly on TV.

I spent the evening of his ticker-tape welcome in New York City in the Fifth Avenue apartment of Charles Cushing. Other guests were the Duke and Duchess of Windsor and Mrs George T. Baker, Long Island socialite, all of us watching the television, following his open-car motorcade as it crawled up from the caverns of the downtown city and on to Fifth Avenue. There wasn't a dry eye in the room – *except mine.*

MacArthur had mistaken his welcome as a measure of his popularity, and permitted himself to be drafted as the Republican candidate to replace his enemy. He had a triumphant start, with masses of hastily-formed support. The *Chicago Tribune* gathered a group; they clamoured for Truman's impeachment. Nixon even demanded MacArthur's re-instatement. Marches were held on his behalf, flags flown at half-mast. Despite the frenzied plan, MacArthur never won the nomination. In fact, he suffered so severe a trouncing that he probably never got over his belittlement, the most painful failure of his life.

Not long before, I had seen his vain posturing and formed a highly personal impression of the man's ego from an innocent habit of his remarkable wife – something I had seen when in his Tokyo residence (he liked to be called the 'Proconsul' of Japan). As occupation chief of the vanquished Japanese he had good cause to be proud because they actually loved his monarchist ways.

I've never been able to forget Mrs MacArthur hovering about in seeming awe, not daring to call him anything as simple (or as endearing) as 'dear' or 'darling', or plain 'Douglas' or 'Doug'. When the military butler announced a meal, she would turn to her husband very hesitatingly to enquire: 'General MacArthur, the food is ready. Would you like us to go in?' Had he no name but *General*?

MacArthur's demise followed his undisciplined revolt against Truman's Presidency. The general (considered the hero of the Philippines) had been stubborn enough to want the armies in Korea to cross the 38th Parallel, the Yalu River and to bomb China – all this against Truman's orders. For this arrogance, he was abruptly dismissed on 11 April 1951 on the last day of Truman's sixth year in the White House.

Truman and the general had met for the first time the year before on Wake Island on 15 October 1950. Truman had been holidaying in Hawaii; MacArthur was summoned from Tokyo for a 4000-mile round trip to meet him there. Outwardly, the meeting was cordial. The two men conferred alone for at least an hour in a Quonset hut, later meeting a brilliant galaxy of Army and State Department officials and ambassadors. After five hours, Truman had high praise for MacArthur, rewarding him with the Medal of Merit. But five months and some days later, the President, sitting this time in a dilapidated old car, ousted him from all his commands; it was the second dismissal of a military chief in American history. The first occurred when President Lincoln ousted his Civil War commander, General George B. McClellan in 1862. If Truman hadn't stopped MacArthur and he had bombed above the Yalu it is universally agreed that Russia, allied to China, would have retaliated. The result? A third World War. MacArthur did have Senator McCarthy on his side, but that helped not at all.

The straw that broke the camel's back was serious; despite orders to the contrary, MacArthur refused to curtail his demands for a further offensive against Red China, contrary to the policy agreed by the United States and the United Nations. The situation was grave: on 20 March 1951, MacArthur was advised that a new offer to discuss peace was to be made. South Korea had been virtually cleared of the enemy; a feeling persisted among all Allies that every diplomatic effort should now be made towards a settlement before any dangerous advances to the north.

MacArthur had simply been asked for his recommendation. Instead, he defied the President and United Nation Allies four days later by issuing his own public statement; the UN should crush Red China by attacking North Korea directly, a plan which would take the 8th Army across the 38th Parallel to continue the fight into China. To worsen matters, MacArthur offered to hold his own personal peace parley to negotiate a surrender with the Communist commander. Truman promptly asked the Joint Chiefs of Staff to remind the general of his directive of 8 December requesting that all statements had to be cleared first.

MacArthur had indulged in extreme action for any field commander: he had been warned, a word intolerable to him, not to carry the war to China or to make more than routine statements in the field. By communicating directly with the enemy he had, in fact, cut the ground from under his Commander-in-Chief as well as the Allies, gravely exceeding his authority.

The White House charged (and General MacArthur denied) that he had repeatedly ignored their orders to avoid making personal statements. President Truman went on radio and television to explain that the action MacArthur advocated would touch off World War III. He was forced to dismiss the general to prove that civilian law had control over the military. To quote the President: 'I fired him because he wouldn't respect the authority of the President. I didn't fire him because he was a dumb son-of-a-bitch, although he was . . .'

MacArthur learned of his dismissal just after lunch in Tokyo, on 11 April. His military secretary, Major General Courtney-Whitney, described to newsmen how his commander had taken the news of the dismissal: 'Magnificently. This was his finest hour.'

One day later, the ex-overlord of Japan, the former 'Proconsul', accepted a position as a director executive, at $100,000 a year, from the Remington-Rand Company. Lt General Matthew B. Ridgway, who was later to be so helpful when I went to the Korean War front, replaced MacArthur in all his posts, thus becoming Supreme Commander of Allied Powers, Occupation Chief in Japan, Commander-in-Chief, UN Command (for Korean War), Commander-in-Chief Far

East (US), Commanding General, US Army, Far East. A brilliant man, without pretensions.

In October 1995, I returned from my second visit to the Pattens in Hong Kong. We had spent time with them in January, when my husband and I went out there to celebrate my birthday at the invitation of Governor Christopher Patten, and later (again as his and his wife Lavender's guests) to have the fifty-first one-man exhibition of my paintings in Hong Kong.

Each time was an electrifying reunion with a changed world from the mythical place I last saw on visits in the late fifties when it was a colourful small port for shipping to the western world; it has now become the fantastic centre of rich sophisticated international banking and trading activities, a city through which passes an enormous amount (at least 40%) of mainland China's gross national product. In 1997, it will be returned to China after more than one hundred and fifty years of British rule.

In the intervening years since I was last there, this beauty spot has lost much and gained much: lost its sandy shores through reclamation of land from the sea and gained a world of dizzying activity. Gone were the colourful slums of the boat people I once saw living on junks and sampans, mingling with the clutter of ocean-going vessels dipping in the waters of the harbour. Airplanes now fill the sky, dangerously skimming rooftops to land at the airport. Hong Kong is now crouched like a mouse; China, close by, is the cat with outstretched paws.

Hong Kong is a marvel of man's success in reaching the heavens, an empire of tightly knit skyscrapers. The tallest one is a hundred storeys high. It is an Oriental world, but a modern one, tumultuous with the activity of the city's six million people, mainly Chinese but crowded with many other groups. I found the city's colours to be quite grey, the buildings a riot of imagination. The perfume in the air? Gasoline. Roads climb up, up, in a city with little level space. Rolls-Royces are far from a rare sight on their way to the high hills which have become Hong Kong's elegant mountainous Mayfair. The views of the skyscraper landscape below are so spectacular they are completely unreal.

Former penniless squatters (now more fortunately apt to be employed) live in these same but segregated 'needle cities' inside small cell-like flats, most of them air-conditioned, which they reach by modern lifts. All is neat and clean, all cheap, all crowded and all laid out as new high-rise suburbias.

The British have been trading here for one hundred and fifty years, and Hong Kong is still governed by an English gentleman, this time the politician, Christopher Patten*, was chosen instead of the usual foreign office diplomat. He arrived in July 1992 and will stay, he confirms, until the city is handed back to China. He is our warm friend. To us he is the bravest of men, in the thankless job of overseeing a huge population in an uncertain world at the final act of giving up Britain's most fabulous possession. He is a part of important history.

Both he and his brilliant (former barrister) wife, Lavender, have redone the Governor's mansion with great skill. It is now a pale beauty, marrying Chinese antiques with contemporary British, pleasing both worlds. The calmness that now exists is a compliment to them and to Britain.

As he has never been a headline-hunter, I asked Christopher Patten what he hopes for after he leaves this difficult post: 'That Hong Kongers would say that I've done my honest best to preserve the decency and the freedom of Hong Kong's way of life . . . to feel that the way I've done the job has helped to ensure that Britain was seen to be closing the last chapter of British Empire in a decent and honourable way, leaving behind a reservoir of affection and moral respect'.

His hopes for a future Hong Kong are already clear to many of the ordinary Chinese men and women, a fact easy to judge on the many walk-abouts we did with him, mobbed by these people. The extraordinary warmth from this public towards their Governor (who is also their Mayor) was moving and reassuring – unburdened as it was by politics. They are grateful for his commitment to a democratic future, no matter how unpopular in Peking. They showed this in spontaneous

---

* The Rt Hon. Christopher F. Patten, born in 1944, was forty-eight when appointed Governor by the Prime Minister. He will be a mere fifty-three at the end of his stint in Hong Kong. He began in the Conservative Research Department after Balliol College at Oxford, aged twenty-two. He then had four important appointments before being elected to Parliament, aged thirty-five – since when he rapidly advanced to ten important parliamentary positions, including appointment as Chairman of the Conservative Party. He lost his parliamentary seat in the 1992 general election having given his time, energy and ideas instead to the successful re-election of the Tory party.

and grateful ways that cannot be otherwise registered as it would make them vulnerable after 1997. Few in any walk of life want to be recorded as anti-Peking (understandably). This attitude is an irony yet Patten bears it gamely.

David Tang of Hong Kong recently reminded us that Dr Sun Yat-Sen, the founder of modern China, had already tried hard to democratize China back in the early 1900s. Wouldn't he applaud Chris Patten's efforts if he was alive today?

As I write, he is being skilfully touted by some of his British Tory party friends as a logical candidate for election as leader of the party – an acceptable notion for the more liberal members of the Party who are less enthusiastic about the swing to the right of certain other members (some of them preening themselves for that same role).*

On days when Patten and I meet we like to talk politics – candidly. Asked what he sees as his role in future, he replied: 'perhaps more public service after this stint is over, perhaps one more job in public life, perhaps on the European or international scene'. But he didn't rule out something at home: 'if I'm not asking too much, I'd like to have an academic berth which would enable me to write and read and think. I am extremely fortunate in not really wanting much more in the way of epaulettes and gold credit cards'.

He would do well in academia because he cares for and understands students (having three lovely young daughters). When speaking to foreign Atlantic College students while on a visit to London he was asked how they could change the world. (Whenever they got home they faced the grim reality that people there didn't want change.)

He replied: 'You must recognize that you can actually make a difference. If you didn't try, the world would be an incomparably drearier place ... *have a go*. It will give you a more interesting life. There is not much point being here at all unless you make a contribution to what the world is like'. This is his role, thankless or otherwise.

A statesman of the press who took seriously his obligation when writing for the public, a man who set so many standards, whose friendship

---

* On 4 March 1996, it was reported that the Prime Minister, John Major, named Chris Patten as a possible leadership candidate in a future election.

meant so much to me, was Walter Lippmann, whom I still see with Baruch in double vision. Presidents also consulted Lippmann, the essayist and editor, as did Cabinet officers and foreign Heads of State. He wrote whatever he chose in his column, expressing his views in a forthright style. When a crisis occurred, a huge readership looked for his opinion. He was interested in facts, ignored rumours, and learned early in his career to rinse the acid from his pen. His articles could read like a fireside chat, although occasionally he seemed over-intellectual.

As a young man he was buoyant, confident, and a gifted spokesman for liberalism. He believed capitalism was freedom's best guarantee and he was inspired to use the press to express his opinions. His first columns appeared in the *New York Herald Tribune*, and later they were widely syndicated in one hundred and eighty newspapers all over the United States until his death. They soon made him an institution, not as a news analyst or news commentator or for 'inside dope', but as a man who used his considerable intelligence and an agile mind to comment on and assess the problems of the day. He became America's most influential columnist; his writings were read seriously, trusted and admired. His opinions were often addressed to those in high places, reminding them of their responsibilities and he liked to think he was a moral mouthpiece for the population. I am biased in his favour, but so were millions of others.

As one of the world's best political writers, he was an influence for more than fifty years. Nearly thirty million Americans turned to his column three times a week as he helped form policy and opinion, right up to Presidential level. President Roosevelt called him 'the most brilliant man of his age in all America'. He was also a source of ideas for Woodrow Wilson, whose policies he characterized in the tragic phrase, 'peace without victory'.

He was founding editor of *The New Republic*. He also conducted hour-long television interviews for CBS and wrote twenty-four lucid books. He undoubtedly helped increase the vision and quality of other political reporting, despite a tendency to preach. Some of his columns could be re-run today, such as those reflecting his opposition to a united Europe – not because he didn't believe in it, but because he feared German domination. Sadly, he didn't live to see the collapse of Soviet power, nations being freed, European unity debated. The painful progress towards a united Europe is still hampered by the fierce nationalism he recognized and hated in his time.

His private lifestyle was fascinating: he lived in a beautiful townhouse in Washington, with no nonsense about hiding his success or embarrassment at living elegantly. He scheduled his life as if by computer, setting time aside for each of his interests and for travel. New York was a city he loved, often finding it as important to observe on his regular travel-beat, as Europe was, where he was warmly greeted.

We knew him as a good friend. He rarely came abroad without a scheduled weekend visit to our house in Sussex, where we always tried to surround him with interesting people to sit in a circle and listen as he talked to us from his favourite armchair. The visits became regular occasions to be savoured and prepared for, and we traditionally gave a dinner for him midweek in London following the weekends. Invitations to both were coveted.

Once, in Sussex, after a trip to Russia to visit Nikita Khrushchev, he recounted a strange experience. Expecting to go to the Kremlin, he and his wife were quickly ushered off their transatlantic flight in Moscow to be put immediately on to a small government plane, without a word of explanation. Much irritated, they eventually discovered they were being flown, without their consent, to the Russian leader's dacha, an implied compliment which totally missed its mark through its clumsiness.

Startled and annoyed but impatient for explanations, they were driven to a huge estate whose gate opened on a long tree-lined drive with a mansion positioned in the distance. They soon spotted a man ponderously walking toward them, lost in a greatcoat which hung down to his ankles, so big his hands disappeared inside the sleeves. It was their host, the smiling Khrushchev, who had assumed this unexpected detour would give the Lippmanns pleasure.

What Khrushchev didn't know was that Helen Lippmann understood Russian (in fact, she was fluent in four or five languages). At Walter's insistence, she attended all meetings, taking notes of what was actually said. Later she would give him the accurate version, which was not necessarily the same as that offered by the Russian interpreters. The verbal pictures of those encounters given to us in Sussex by Walter made fascinating listening and made me feel as if we had been there with the Lippmanns.

A few days later in London at the dinner for Walter, a certain Ambassador sat directly across from him at table. With cool rudeness, he disagreed with Lippmann's column in that morning's *International Herald Tribune* about the visit he had made to General de Gaulle. He rudely questioned Lippmann's flattering view of the French leader. The unfailingly graceful (but livid) Lippmann refused to reply; instead, he reached for his cane, got up from the table and silently limped to the front door, his wife following, hushing my apologies with 'I could not and would not stay in the same room with that man'. Henry Brandon, then Washington Bureau Chief of the London *Times*, was one of the other astonished guests. He promised not to print the unpleasant encounter.

If he were alive today, Lippmann, a German Jew, would be distraught at the constant acts of war between Arabs and Jews. Although never a Zionist, he was ever scornful of Judaism as a weapon. Both my husband and I wish he were still writing; we should like to know how he would deal with the outrage over the BCCI, the Savings and Loan corruption and the Barings scandal and the technique by computer which plays with our currencies (not one penny of which is invested in goods or production).

Lippmann's death was sad. I didn't know he was seriously ill until our mutual friend, Drew Dudley, telephoned me from Washington to say how unhappy and lonely he was and how much it would mean to him if I could fly over to see him. I flew to New York at once. I didn't find him at home; he'd been banished to an expensive Park Avenue private nursing home. Neither a person nor an object was familiar; the atmosphere entirely lacked any suggestion of home, and I found him terribly upset.

Why? Was it too unpleasant for his wife to keep him at home? The former Helen Armstrong, married previously to Foreign Affairs editor Hamilton Armstrong until she ran off to marry Lippmann, was a woman everyone thought would have been glued to his side. He never travelled without her, he listened intently to her views; she never forgave his critics and she was obviously deeply devoted to him.

Even so, she frankly admitted that she couldn't survive continual bedside care. She had already gone back to Washington before I arrived, leaving him alone in the nursing home. Ironically, they never saw each other again.

I wasn't prepared for his death. We had been friends for over thirty years, marked by long, sometimes bantering discussions about people and events, rarely in disagreement. It was so sad that we would no longer be able to appreciate his extraordinary intelligence and wisdom.

Few had more success in Britain during the Second World War than American journalist Ed Murrow, who arrived in London on the very day that Hitler's armies marched into Poland. The famous Edward R. Murrow was volatile. If he felt strongly, he shouted. If he was concerned, he needed to find a solution. We met in the basement of Claridge's in 1945 when I was in London during the closing weeks of the war. He had become a legend. To the British, he was the American hero who broadcast daily from London to America. His vivid accounts of the misery endured by the brave population were also heard all over the British Isles. Like CNN reporters in the Gulf War, Bosnia, and the Somalian battles, he lived under constant fire – although in a little more comfort in the basement of Claridge's Hotel. Americans across the Atlantic listened and agonized with him over the plight of bombarded British citizens.

Back home in the United States he achieved further greatness when he fought and won his own war against Senator McCarthy. It took courage; the Senator had massive support, and those opposing him were labelled 'Communist-lovers'. Undaunted, on his top-ranking CBS television programme watched by millions, Murrow's attacks were the opening shots against McCarthy's witch-hunt and he hammered and hammered away at the Senator's character.

He dealt McCarthy a fatal blow by bringing on air a very old, scared, black lady cleaner in the Senate offices. She'd been seen in tears during the Senate hearings, cruelly interrogated by McCarthy who accused her of stealing papers for the Communists! This shrunken little woman in tears, a secret agent? Murrow asked his audience. The public reacted with outrage after seeing and hearing her deny the nonsense on his programme. McCarthy was finally censored *and ousted* by the Senate – crawling away to his home state of Wisconsin, he drank himself to death, giving many American enemies the occasion to use a favourite phrase which suited the circumstances so well: 'Good riddance to bad rubbish.'

I will never forget Murrow's TV attacks because above all else they significantly led to McCarthy's demise. Few others dared do the same, whatever their beliefs. While head of the US Information Agency, he simply ignored any Senator who tried to spread McCarthy's doctrine in overseas broadcasts.

When Murrow died of cancer, aged fifty-seven, his death was mourned by all Americans as well as by many in the British Isles; that crisp Murrow voice had been a brave symbol.

In 1954, I appeared on his celebrated *Person to Person*, which lasted an hour, watched by one of television's largest audiences. The show took place in homes, not in the CBS building, where Murrow remained, interviewing guests from his studio there, heard but not seen. A camera and his voice simply followed as you walked about from room to room – following a route he was able to direct after having gone through it in a rehearsal for equipment and discussion.

I confessed that I was 'better if spontaneous', and jumped at his suggestion that he'd let me have his questions the afternoon before the evening programme was aired, giving me time for thought. Once we were actually on the air, and by now relaxed, Murrow sprang his trap. He launched into completely new questions, not one of them having been rehearsed or discussed. I responded as I had wanted to, spontaneously, and it was with gratitude I watched the rerun in private the next day. Here in Britain on television, we have the unrivelled political watchdog, David Frost, now internationally celebrated.

To my American list I must add the late Eric Sevareid, the CBS correspondent in France in the first year of the Second World War. After he broadcast the surrender of the Vichy French to Hitler's armies, he was recruited by Murrow to London and later, from 1946 to 1959, to the USA where he symbolized liberal political thinking in Washington.

Like Murrow, Sevareid was a most attractive celebrity. I knew him and his wife all the years he was living and working in London. Once, he brought to dine in London an astronaut who had just been to the moon and the four of us relived that piece of history.

R. W. (Johnny) Apple, now Bureau Chief and Director of the *New York Times* in Washington, has always been a favourite read in the

International Herald Tribune or in the *New York Times*. He often donned his gourmet hat – he is a man who loves and understands food.

When Iran and Iraq were at war he left for Iran and went straight into the front line, after a struggle for permission from the Iranians for that dangerous privilege. Scotty Reston was right when he said: 'Johnny Apple taught a whole generation how to cover war.'

Everyone who knew the late Czech-born Henry Brandon admired the man who was on such friendly terms with Heads of States and other important world figures. I knew him for forty-odd years, and he never betrayed a confidence.

He died of a heart attack in 1993. After retiring as head of the London *Times* Washington Bureau, he continued to write books and syndicated columns. He understood money as well as he did politics and wrote with great clarity about the seemingly chaotic world of finance and its institutions. His daughter is my god-daughter.

In London's press media I particularly admired William Rees-Mogg (now Lord), Simon Jenkins and Bernard Levin, who are quite a trio. In their newspaper columns they all express perceptive and sound opinions, amusing readers as well as giving occasional raps on the knuckles.

I was very apprehensive about my first meeting with Bernard Levin, just after I arrived from the United States. I was invited by the BBC to join him on a 'Brains Trust' to be broadcast to America, and he had a ferocious reputation. These days my heart beats normally, as we've become close friends. Two of his books were written in our garden in Spain. I can see him in the sun at the Roman wheel he uses as a table, protected by one of my largest hats, parasol perched over his head.

The easiest way to describe his rapier mind is by quoting his admission that 'Schubert may be better than Wagner but if it is made public, I shall deny it and sue you.' I am grateful that at his insistence we travelled to Colmar in Alsace to see one of the world's greatest paintings, Grünewald's *The Life of Christ*.

*   *   *

When editor of *The Times*, William Rees-Mogg was Levin's boss. Now, having retired, he has become a columnist on the paper he once ran. His articles appear on the leader page two or three times a week. His ability to turn out lucid prose on matters of real concern can be devastating. He has also sat in high places, as Vice-Chairman of the BBC and Chairman of both the Arts Council and the Broadcasting Standards Council; and of course in the House of Lords, where he sits on the crossbenches. When visiting us in Spain in 1995, Colin Powell was frequently discussed. As I was Chairman of the Committee in England to elect him as President, I was grateful for Rees-Mogg's enthusiasm.

Simon Jenkins, a neighbour of ours, followed him as editor of *The Times* having previously edited the London *Evening Standard* and an important area of *The Economist*. He was Journalist of the Year in 1988 and Columnist of the Year in 1993 for his pieces in *The Times*. He pleased me by agreeing to appear at the Flair Symposium, on 'The Future of the Printed Word' which honoured me at Texas University in November 1994. After I opened the debate, he was the first speaker, assuring the audience that in his judgement the printed word would outlast computer innovations, just as it has survived radio and TV.

Looming large in the communications world is a friend with whom I go back to the White House years in President Lyndon B. Johnson's days. Tom Johnson was a member of the President's 'Think-Tank'. Later he went to direct the radio and TV stations owned by President Johnson in Austin, Texas, and next became Chief Executive of the *Los Angeles Times*. While there, he was head-hunted to become Chief Executive of this generation's trail-blazing TV company, CNN, in Atlanta, Georgia.

He took up this post in 1991 at the very beginning of the Gulf War. Few across the world are unaware of CNN's part in revealing the details of that war to millions all over the globe. Johnson, its remarkable leader, became, overnight, respected and loved by his very large and diverse staff. CNN is a signal appreciated by millions.

His character was obvious when he was still a young man, at a time when unwanted black students, the first ever, were being taken by bus into his university in Athens, Georgia. One of those brave forerunners was a black girl who was being disgracefully hounded and brutally insulted by the white girls. She was rescued by Johnson, then a senior student. It took great courage; he needed plenty of it at a time when cruel racial hatreds erupted in riots and reprisals.

We often visit the Johnsons in their beautiful Atlanta home when *en route* to Texas; we appreciate their straightforward friendship. While with him, one feels totally in touch with what's going on – aided and agreeably abetted by his remarkable wife, Edwina. When there, we are privileged to enter the magical new world he has inaugurated for TV transmission and to meet many of CNN's talented cast.

Another great friend I have known since I came to live in London. He is also at times a word-creator, so we have much in common. He recently retired as Chairman of the Radio Authority. Alun Chalfont (now Lord) was the most powerful man in the country's commercial radio, fearlessly safeguarding the standards and integrity of the air waves.

His talents are not only considerable but varied, and he has combined government, diplomacy and industry with his career as a professional army officer. He has held posts as varied as Minister of State at the Foreign Office and Chairman of the House of Lords All Party Defence Group; in business, he has been on the Boards of IBM UK, Lazard Brothers Bank and many others. He has published five books including a biography of Lord Montgomery of Alamein, and for years was defence correspondent for the London *Times*.

His wife, Mona a distinguished physician, is known for her work in combating alcohol and drug addiction. We enjoy the Chalfonts' luncheon parties on the terrace of the House of Lords amid illustrious company. The weather is usually kind and the view of the Thames is a treasured experience. They are 'regulars' who visit us in Spain, two valued voices in the save the world breakfast decisions we tend to debate.

From the media to medicine takes me to a remarkable trio. Geniuses are few and far between but my husband and I have come to know three well enough to say they enhance our lives as we are both trustees of the same charitable organization, *SatelLife*, which meets regularly in Boston to bring free medical advice by satellite to nineteen Third-World countries.

One of the three has played a vital role in this organization; Bernard Lown, *SatelLife*'s chairman and Nobel Prize winner – the world's gratest expert on sudden death. He was responsible years ago for keeping my own heart beating.*

Two others on the Board are Jerome S. Rubin and Dr Kenneth Warren. Jerome Rubin is chairman of MIT, Media Lab's newest research initiative, the *News in the Future* consortium. He joined the Massachusetts Institute of Technology in Boston in 1992 after retiring as Chairman of the Times-Mirror Company's Professional Information and book Publishing Group, whose publications cover legal, scientific, technical, medical and university textbooks, together with professional training companies.

He had the skills to develop the LEXIS computer-assisted legal research service in 1973, followed by NEXUS, an on-line news research service which he launched in 1978. These revolutionary products now constitute the world's largest textual information services. Such pioneer achievements may be well beyond the comprehension of non-technical readers like me, but the information industry itself inducted him into its Hall of Fame.

His CV in publishing covers pages, as does the international acclaim for his writings. He and his art-expert wife, Ida, presented us with the gift of a magnificent book of flowers, *The Arboretum*. When they arrived to visit us in Spain the pair revealed themselves as friends and great lovers of nature. The book was so heavy it required both of them to carry it all the way from America.

Kenneth Warren's story is also one of trail-blazing as one of the world's leading public health doctors, a most eloquent and moving speaker on his subject; he has played a major role in the Rockefeller Foundation and is admired by everyone in the international medical fraternity. Although at the very forefront of medicine, he's no grey-beard. His sense of humour matches his intellectual prowess.

Recently he even advised me financially by bringing me into the

---

* See also Dr Jorge Rius, page 325.

mysterious world of communication. Time will tell, but our very great friendship with him and his wife will outlive any stock market vagaries.

Greatness comes in diverse ways: in a later chapter on Heads of State, I describe my experience with Mohammed Mossadeq of Iran while this eccentric maverick was in power, having forced the Shah to flee, for the first time, temporarily from his country. A tall, handsome man from the Netherlands was then making his own considerable reputation in Iran. Jonkheer John Loudon was a leading figure in the then-current oil negotiations as senior managing director of Royal Dutch Shell, later becoming its chairman. His father, Hugo Loudon, had been one of Shell's founders.

Mossadeq nationalized the oil holdings in 1951, provoking the international oil industry to declare 'no more foreign interests in Iran'. He was ousted in 1953 (with the help of the CIA), and the Shah returned. General Zahedi became the Prime Minister and an inter-national consortium was formed by major oil companies to negotiate a settlement so that oil would flow again (it had completely stopped in 1951). In these negotiations John Loudon participated with his usual great skill.

The tall aristocrat, whom my husband and I consider the best-mannered man in Europe, was quickly recognized as one of the ablest minds in Teheran during the warlike posturing of Mossadeq toward the western oil entities. Loudon's kid-glove approach did a great deal to lift the iron curtain Mossadeq drew between the oil companies and Iran.

I, too, had much to thank him for: we had met in America in 1947. After that he provided me with an invaluable asset for any editor. He approved my being met wherever I travelled in the world by the resident Shell Executive, no matter how distant the country, to be given a confidential report on all local matters. Meeting whoever and seeing whatever made the news in each locality: this was my private intelligence service and a gift beyond repayment.

We remained warm friends. When he celebrated his eightieth birthday, my husband and I arranged a surprise birthday party. He came over from The Hague, expecting to dine just with us and his niece, Lady Lydia Stewart-Clarke. Instead, I had asked twenty-five guests whom I knew were his close friends. He was stunned to find them behind the closed doors at our London home and was almost moved to tears when Queen Beatrix and her husband, Prince Claus, arrived. 'My Queen!' he murmured in delighted surprise.

I was already on the International Board of the World Wildlife Fund when John Loudon became its President, succeeding Prince Bernhard of the Netherlands who, with Sir Peter Scott, had actually created the organization many decades ago, after publicly expressing concern about the decline in animal life. This was long before calls for animal preservation and welfare were heard. 'PB', as Prince Bernhard is known to his friends, and I consider myself one of them, elected me to the Board more than twenty years ago. After him, when John Loudon's official time as President came to an end, he was succeeded by Prince Philip, Duke of Edinburgh.

Until he died, early in 1996, regular meals with Jonkheer Loudon at Mark's Club in London were tradition, keeping us close to this remarkably ageless man. He was a regular visitor to Sussex and Spain, always making it an exhilarating experience.

I have known many leaders in very different fields, including the armed forces. Some of them, Dwight D. Eisenhower, for instance, became 'special gentlemen' after they gave up warfare.

Another historic (and particular) one was General George Catlett Marshall. Choosing him as Secretary of State was one of the greatest appointments President Truman ever made. A speech made in June 1947 at Harvard University brought the unpretentious blue-eyed man with sandy hair international prestige and gratitude. He spoke to seven thousand guests, bringing to life the now historic Marshall Plan when he told the United States it must save western Europe from the ravages of war, the threat of Soviet Communism or sliding into dictatorship.

This architect of an historic rescue operation urged Europe to create a working economy to replace the poverty and hunger and chaos he'd seen at the war's end. To unite, not to separate, to work together, not against each other. He even left the door ajar for the Soviets to join, but Stalin refused. Marshall had presided over a turning point in our history: NATO followed. The Western Alliance, led by Reagan, then won the Cold War some four decades later.

The European Recovery Plan, renamed the Marshall Plan, received the support of President Truman and Dean Acheson in raising the eighteen billion dollars needed. Congress introduced the idea and a year later, in April 1948, both Houses approved it with an overwhelming majority. President Truman pointed out: 'We are the first great nation to feed and support the conquered'. He was reminding us of Germany, the aggressors who had waged all-out war from 1939 to 1945.

In his speech when he was awarded the Nobel Peace Prize in 1953, Marshall admitted there had been considerable comment over its award to a soldier: 'this does not seem as remarkable to me ... I know a great deal of the horrors and tragedies of war'. His job had been to supervise the construction of many of western Europe's military cemeteries, the cost of war in human lives was written on those gravestones.

It was my good fortune to join General Marshall at the Coronation of Queen Elizabeth II in June 1953, as part of the panoply and drama that proclaimed the young woman a Queen. I had been appointed Ambassador to represent the people of America ('a woman for a woman's great moment in history' is how Clare Luce described it). General Marshall went as President Eisenhower's personal representative.

A week or more after that beautifully organized pageant, doing our rounds together, General Marshall suggested I must get to know a certain great lady, Queen Frederika of Greece, whom he had met during his overseas trips in connection with the Marshall Plan. He described her to me as a defiant woman who had shown incredible bravery during her country's civil war in 1944 when the National Liberation Front had tried to seize power.

One day he took a handwritten letter from his pocket for me to read. 'This is from the remarkable woman I want you to know. It is confidential, but I trust you.' I longed to meet her after reading her account of conditions in Greece. Anxious that this happened, Marshall quickly wrote to the Queen and I was soon invited to Greece for the beginning of nearly forty years of friendship with the entire royal family, which still continues.

During the Coronation, I had constant reason to be proud of General Marshall. Whenever he was spotted by the crowd he was cheered. Court circles held him in awesome regard. The venerable Winston Churchill made a splendid gesture in the flawless ceremony in Westminster Abbey when he spied Marshall sitting there. He stepped out of the slow moving procession along the Abbey's blue carpet to clasp Marshall's hand – an impulsive and revealing gesture. Bent over in his ermine-trimmed, huge red velvet robe of the Knights of the Garter he looked like a regal cabbage. He had ignored rule and circumstance to greet the man he once called the 'noblest Roman'.

Those were the days when Joe McCarthy was at the peak of his trouble-making career and all talked of him constantly. I kept thinking how the dreadful man wounded Marshall by vilifying him. I was embarrassed, even disgraced by McCarthy's behaviour which was headlined in the British press. English friends clamoured for explanations which I could not possibly give.

Now, in the nineties, I have been brought back in touch with Marshall's world as a member of the Board of Marshall's former home, Dodona Manor in Leesburg, Virginia (under the auspices of other distinguished Americans: Ambassador Vernon C. Walters, Powell Harrison*, its Chairman, and Diana Keesee, its dynamo).

Marshall may have preferred anonymity, but we are determined to honour him and preserve his home as a museum open to the public, like Washington's 'Mount Vernon' and Jefferson's 'Monticello'. We shall turn the property into a place to perpetuate Marshall's name and promote the principles of a great American of our century. It will help me feel I've helped to repay my debt for George Marshall's friendship. He ended his life almost a forgotten man. *Not* true now.

D-Day has been remembered in Europe in 1994, with ceremonies and celebrations and tears. It was appropriate that on that day I received a copy of a letter from General Marshall to the Burpee Seed Company in the USA, written in 1942 at a grim, low point in the war. He ended his letter: 'The business of seeds and flowers tantalizes me because I have been an amateur gardener, both flowers and vegetables, since a boy of ten. There is nothing I would so much prefer to do this spring as to turn my mind to the wholesome business of gardening rather than the terrible problems and tragedies of War.'

Another truly unforgettable person, Jean Monnet, the patron saint of the European Community, whose hope was to bring about the

---

* He has since retired, and has been replaced by Nestor Sanchez.

restoration of Europe. His hopes for the unification of Europe, so fiercely debated in Britain's Parliament today, began almost fifty years ago. He first fought for the League of Nations between the World Wars, then he began to care more than anyone else about actually bringing Europe together. He originated the Coal and Steel Community.

He spoke four languages, and advised China, Poland and Austria on financial matters. Apple-cheeked and bald, trustworthy and dedicated, he was born a member of a cognac vintners' family. He died in 1979, aged ninety-two. Like Bernard Baruch, although French, he had also been an inside adviser to four American Presidents and, again like Baruch, he never wanted to occupy high places, preferring to influence people and events unobtrusively. He could speak with de Gaulle, although he once compared him to Hitler. He spent most of his life patiently fighting for European cooperation. He had no vanity, and never asked for credit despite seventy years of effort. Although without real power, he had great influence.

We met in 1950 in Paris. I was drawn to his idealistic views. He lived in Paris but also had a lovely old farmhouse outside the city, to which we once drove for dinner. 'Let me show you a real farm meal,' he had suggested. We drove out to Hourjarray to enjoy it, eating in the kitchen where we scooped ladles of soup from the pot that always sat on the stove there. Leftovers always ended inside it, enhancing the flavour.

I learned a lot about how the French cook during that plain meal in that simple farmhouse. Driving back to Paris, we stopped talking about Europe to discuss French food instead, a unique departure from his usual stubborn concentration on the political future for Europe.

Whenever he came to London after I moved there, however brief his visit he always at least left his card at my door. Whenever I went to Paris, I looked him up – if only for just a few moments – if he wasn't flying from capital to capital. I always remember him whenever I think about China today. Years and years ago he suggested: 'Wait until China grows up. Russia will suddenly decide she's got to be part of Europe.'

He was a great help in spreading the Marshall gospel. Even then, he always worried about the nationalism of the individual European states. When he became the father of the European Coal and Steel Community he asked, 'What would Europe do in future without unity?' He would still ask it, even of those who are personally against it. In his book of memoirs, Monnet asked why national barriers must remain so permanent. The debate for an answer rages on, particularly in the United Kingdom.

According to a servant of his who was with him for more than thirty years, he loved walking. The loyal man explained it this way: 'It is simple. Monsieur puts his ideas in front of him as he walks, talks to them – and then decides.'* He was one of the most memorable men I ever knew.

If anyone questions the qualification of business men in government I like to point to John Alex McCone, who first had impressive experience in defence matters before he was selected by three Presidents for delicate, important posts.

He started in business by forming the Consolidated Steel Corporation, and then the Bechtel-McCone company which built oil refineries and power stations in the United States, South America and the Middle East during the Second World War. Then he became President of the California Ship Building Corporation, which produced, with Kaiser as partner, 467 Liberty ships for the war effort. After war ended, he took over Joshua Hendy Ironworks to operate tankers and cargo ships in the Pacific.

The first President to seek out his service was Harry Truman, who appointed him to the Air Policy Commission. A year later, he became Special Deputy to James Forrestal, the Secretary of Defence. McCone was the man who helped create the OSS, the forerunner to the CIA. Later, in 1950, he was named Under-Secretary to the US Air Force.

Eight years later, President Eisenhower chose him, because of his defence experience, to be Chairman of the US Atomic Energy Commission. There he made a reputation by advocating cooperation in international research – which has since proved so hard to come by in North Korea, for instance.

* From an essay (January 1992) on Jean Monnet by Walt W. Rostow, who teaches at the LBJ School of Public Affairs, University of Texas.

The CIA came next when in 1963 John F. Kennedy named him to succeed Allen Dulles, which markedly improved the quality of the relationship between the CIA and other agencies. He also set about rebuilding CIA morale.

He and Kennedy disagreed on how to handle the Cuban crisis but once Kennedy opted on a blockade, McCone loyally helped him carry out this decision. His involvement in government ended in 1965 when he resigned from the CIA after President Johnson declined to back his attempts to bring all United States intelligence activities under the CIA's wing. One of his great friends was Harold Macmillan; between them they worked for or with five American Presidents.

The McCones and I were first introduced by the Norman Chandlers, owners of the *Los Angeles Times*. After dinner at their home, I was unexpectedly asked to recount my experiences and my impressions of the Korean War front from which I had returned that very day. The guest list was a distinguished one and I was far from wanting to take centre-stage with what would be the first off-the-cuff exposure of my opinions of the war, but vanity came to my rescue. I 'went on' and fortunately did it well enough to impress my audience, including Walter Lippmann and John McCone.

When John McCone died in 1985 aged eighty-five, I lost a most extraordinary friend, and also a treasured source: gone were the confidential letters in which for years he had kept me informed on American and foreign events.

A typical example, now safe from security considerations, follows: 'I hope that you will not be carried away with the "no nuclear" concept, for NATO cannot sustain conventional forces in significant numbers and fire-power to meet the capabilities of the Soviet Union and the Warsaw Pact countries. To attempt to do so would seriously impact the economies of all NATO countries and the United States as well as the Soviet Union and the Warsaw Pact countries. I also feel the no-nuclear concept is not in our interest – and this I have felt for many years. In fact, I debated this with Oppenheimer before the Soviets had developed a bomb. He was going around the country advocating that we throw all our bombs into the San Francisco bay. Fortunately, we did not do so, but my views on this issue have been constant and not changed in the past over forty-six years.'

Gone are our trips together, the two McCones and my English

husband and I, when we had the luxury of sharing his special know-ledge of the government's thinking. Gone are the answers to delicate political questions, provided on the basis of absolute confidentiality, which I solemnly upheld.

Gone is their active acquisition of my paintings; the McCones had chosen eleven from gallery-exhibits all over the world. Once I was commissioned to produce a painting, the subject to be of my choice, to hang above the mantel of the fireplace in the home they were building on the coast at Cotton Bay in Jamaica. I'd never been there, nor did I know the house, only that the painting, when hung, would face the beach and the sea.

Magic was involved. My painting reflected identically the scene through the window facing the location where the painting was to hang: deep white sand on a horseshoe curve. I added three cheetahs basking in the sun. A photograph couldn't have given a more exact view than the one I had created. How did it happen? I still wonder.

As Chairman of the Atomic Energy Commission, he became known for his steely mind and brilliant analysis. Both stood him in good stead as the head of CIA, from which he resigned when he realized he couldn't get LBJ's ear.

My husband and I and Lord and Lady Carrington probably got to know each other best in Spain, rather than in the political arena in London, as they are regular guests in our peaceful home hidden inside high castle walls. There we talk freely about all manner of topics and events. We discuss the state of the world at breakfast, where we always enjoy the Carringtons' wisdom and humour. We share hopes and confidences. These tête-à-têtes are repeated when we happen to visit them in Buckinghamshire, where, like many with his family back-ground, he farms on a large scale. He acts and looks like the 6th Baron, but instead he has devoted the best of his talents to serving in government.

In 1995, we celebrated New Year's Eve in this Spanish home, with a fine cast of guests, amongst them Lord and Lady Carrington and Jung Chang (author of *Wild Swans*) and her husband Jon Halliday. For days we heard our anecdotes float about, like darts, to laughter (once or twice in tears of pleasure).

The best of Peter Carrington's dry wit intermingled with his inimitable mimicry of a favoured friend, former Prime Minister Harold Macmillan. The Hallidays 'took us through China' on their recent long journey to research their coming joint book on the biography of Mao Tse Tung – fascinating, informative and occasionally funny. My husband and I recalled our own experiences (his often dangerous in a life worth the book I am trying to persuade him to write). Mine were often 'historic', otherwise detailed in this book.

Lord Carrington and his wife give parties in the garden of their home in London, where Lady Carrington's green thumb has turned a small area into an enchanting place. You see the hands of both of them in the selection of sculpture as well as the skilful choice of plants wherever they have a garden.

Behind his sometimes formidable manner lies a man of fun. His anecdotal repertoire is vast. He began his career as a regular soldier in the Grenadier Guards. During World War II, he took part in the action to capture the Nijmegen Bridge, one of the bloodiest episodes in the months that followed D-Day. After the war he entered the House of Lords. At the age of thirty-six he became High Commissioner to Australia, probably the youngest ever to reach such a position. Following this, he went on to several Cabinet posts: Agriculture under Winston Churchill, Defence under Edward Heath, and eventually, in Margaret Thatcher's first Cabinet, Foreign Secretary.

I can only speak of his resignation from that post with bitterness. He had found himself in Israel, the wrong place at the wrong time, two or three days before the Argentinians invaded the Falklands. He was there for two reasons: he had already cancelled three visits to Israel, creating the unintended suggestion of pro-Arab bias. And his staff, who should have known better, had falsely assured him there was not a chance that the Argentinians would make a move. His intention was to negotiate a land-lease settlement with Argentine's military government.

Typical of the man, he resigned honourably. Margaret Thatcher accepted it, to the astonishment of many who saw her simultaneously refuse the resignation of the Minister of Defence, John Nott. It delighted the Conservative right wing in Parliament who had never forgiven Carrington for solving the maddening Rhodesia problem by what they saw as 'giving the nation to the blacks'.

He took the blame like the gentleman he is and left politics. He was Chairman of General Electric for a spell before leaving to accept the post of Secretary General of NATO. We like to remember him on a Spanish visit to us just before he left for Brussels, occupied for a good deal of the time reading Agatha Christie *in French* to ready himself for a new French-speaking life.

When he left NATO, he became Chairman of Christie's, the auction house, challenging their powerful rival Sotheby's in the highly competitive international art and antiques market. I have often dined with him at Christie's and have seen how much he loved his position and the pictures, old masters and contemporary masterpieces, the antique furniture and porcelains, which he used to call 'the tea cups' he never found 'in the Foreign Office'.

Diplomacy intervened once again while he was still at Christie's: he was asked to spearhead the peace negotiations in the developing crisis in the former Yugoslavia. As impossible as it looked then (and was) he felt that having been Foreign Secretary and Secretary General of NATO he was qualified to bring peace as the Serbs, Croats and Bosnian Muslims fought for control of land.

His international contributions to a better world are well known but I, for one, believe we should know the truth about his Yugoslavia experience. He is never one to explain – even when to do so is in his interest. But I was able to get him to explain it this way; the facts were as follows: the invitation to intervene in the bloody affair came from the European Community with whom he was on friendly terms after his successful stint at NATO. Carrington said he would agree on two conditions: that there should first be a cease-fire, and that everyone must be prepared to accept him as a negotiator.

All was agreed, but the war went on without a sign of a cease-fire. He was then urged to start negotiations anyway, without a cessation of fighting. He agreed, leaving promptly for Yugoslavia's war zone. He proceeded cautiously, getting certain agreements to his own personal plan, which was to put Yugoslavia together again as a flexible federal system in which each faction associated itself to the centre as loosely or as closely as they then felt inclined. He got some way down that difficult road. The big issue was Krajina, the part of Croatia which the Serbs occupied.

He got both the Serbs and Croats to agree there should be a system of near autonomy in Krajina, although it should remain a part of Croatia. Then an unexpected blow came from Germany, who proposed that Croatia and Slovenia should be recognized as independent states. This sparked an even fiercer and wider conflict, when Cyrus Vance was at that very moment bent on reaching a negotiated cease-fire. Despite knowing this, the Germans apparently felt that recognition of Croatia would stop the war.

The consequences of the recognition of Croatia and Slovenia were twofold: it totally torpedoed the peace conference by giving two of the six republics their independence, and it removed any reason to continue the conference. Independence would have to be offered to the Bosnians and other three republics.

The Bosnian Serbs then claimed that they were not prepared to accept an independent Bosnia under the constitution which *existed* (because of the Muslim majority), and they were prepared to fight to prevent it. Civil war would therefore be inevitable. Lord Carrington immediately warned the Foreign Ministers of the European Community that this would happen if they, as well as Germany, recognized Croatia and Slovenia. Nevertheless, they followed Germany, particularly the British government under Margaret Thatcher. Civil war did follow, as he had warned.

Carrington and his aide, José Cuttiliero, continued in hope. They devised a plan for a federal Bosnia, divided broadly but not wholly into three geographic ethnic groups, Muslims, Croats and Serbs. This scheme was thwarted by the American recognition of territorial claims. The use of force and ethnic cleansing then accelerated, finally putting paid to Carrington's efforts. Ironically, two years later, almost the exact same scheme was put forward and supported by all concerned in the UN and the USA. Disillusioned, Carrington returned to Christie's to stay until retirement age arrived.

In the United Kingdom, immediately after World War II was over, I earned the friendship of the man once called the architect of Britain's post-war industrial recovery, Sir Stafford Cripps, Chancellor of the Exchequer 1947–50 in Clement Attlee's government. A mutual friend suggested we should meet and Sir Stafford graciously invited me to luncheon at 11 Downing Street, his official residence. Little was he aware how young I was, and little did I think our first encounter would be in his home. I simply hoped for an informal meeting with Britain's Chancellor, and got it. A strong friendship developed. I wanted to suggest what products I believed American women would first look for as imports from Britain, the kind of British goods they would snatch up and buy as soon as they re-appeared. Shouldn't these be put into immediate production by women who had, up to then, been turning out the products of war? I asked.

Cripps, who had mapped India's independence and planned Britain's policy for postwar economic recovery, had little time for such a young girl's passing advice. His original reaction was cool: 'No,' he replied simply. But later his attitude changed when he realized that I was genuinely serious and in a position to be helpful.

The currency crisis of the 1990s is still in full swing as I write this so I cannot help remembering our last conversation in London. 'Fleur,' he said, 'no problem can be met today, on either a monetary or military level, unless we get at the basic long-range issue ahead: nothing is ahead of Common Currency.' Few terms produce more heated arguments today than 'Common Currency'. Tempers flare. Election campaigns are riddled with the phrase – some in favour of and most, it would appear, against the radical idea. We talked about a devalued pound, to which he insisted he would never submit. To his dismay, he finally had to devalue in September 1949, despite the anguished promise.

He seemed roguish and bouncy during dinner at 11 Downing Street, a miracle of energy after having attended tense conferences in Paris and London in expectation of the US Treasury Secretary's arrival in London. We dined on his normal vegetarian menu, and then went down into the garden to sit amid the geraniums, hollyhocks and lilacs. We raided the drawing room furniture for cushions to make the wooden benches more comfortable and we sat there talking for a long time in the slowly darkening evening.

In the twilight, I was suddenly aware how old and ashen he looked. His health was admittedly bad; he had already given up smoking. Churchill, though an admirer of Cripps, had recently made a priceless remark about 'the smokeless chimney'. Soon after that evening, he had to go into hospital. A vision of that sudden change in his appearance came back to me later at the news of his sudden death. When he resigned the Chancellorship in 1950 he announced: 'My trouble is a tired heart.'

By then, we had accepted our political differences, becoming so friendly he came twice to stay in my New York home. On the second occasion, in September 1949, he had first to fly to Washington for the very unpleasant business of discussing sterling's devaluation, but before flying back to London, he detoured from Washington to visit us again in New York. The decision to devalue was unbearable for him, although it actually took a heavy load off his mind, and in New York he was ready to relax. I went with the small group that gathered on the station platform very early one morning to welcome his arrival on the overnight train from Washington. It crawled in very slowly, in the usual fits and starts, on the way to its final stopping point. Cripps couldn't wait. He jumped off as soon as he thought it safe, actually skipping towards our little gathering.

I rushed to join him. Linking arms with me, to the astonishment of the British Consul-General and the rest of the watchers, he whispered: 'Fleur, guess what I was doing yesterday morning at dawn in our Washington Embassy? I was up long before the house had arisen. It was very hot so I jumped into the pool in the garden – naked!'

When both Sir Stafford and Lady Cripps first came to stay, I had set aside the fifth floor in my townhouse for them and had a tiny kitchenette unit built in so he could make his own four-thirty a.m. tea-breakfast at this almost uncivilized wake-up time.

The not-so-austere political side to this solemn man was slowly being revealed. The night he arrived we gave a large dinner party in his honour, with an impressive group of guests. We sat together and the lucid, entertaining man whispered confidential anti-Socialist ideas to me. One I'll never forget: 'Remember, Fleur. Communism is on the wane, so is Socialism.' This confession from Socialism's standard-bearer was almost unbelievable in 1949. By then, I had come to know them both well enough to conclude that the kind, very likeable Isabel Cripps was the one who worked hard at controlling her husband's political line. From the time when he was a wealthy corporation lawyer and an ardent Socialist idealist, Isabel, heiress to the Coleman's Mustard fortune, was the strong force in keeping him on Socialist rails. His father, Lord Parmoor, had switched from Conservatism to vague

Christian Socialism, giving inspiration to Stafford Cripps's political ideals.

After the first visit with us in New York, Isabel Cripps stayed behind when he returned to London. It was autumn, so I took her on a long motor trip through Maine, New Hampshire and Vermont to show her the incredible palette of red, yellow, brown and green of the trees on the vast mountains above the roads en route to Canada. It is one of America's most unforgettable sights. However, what she talked most about after that trip was not the extraordinary scenery but a restaurant that no longer exists, New York City's self-service establishment, the Automat. Food was displayed inside glass drawers; when the correct money was placed in the slot, a door opened, food slipped out and was instantly replaced from behind.

My own favourite purchase was the oversized honey-dipped cinnamon bun. A year later, when I nearly died after surgery, I could not and would not eat. 'What, *please*, will tempt you?' I was constantly asked. 'The Automat's honey buns,' I finally admitted. They were brought to me. They broke the fast. They saved my life.

I never thought I would fully earn Stafford Cripps's friendship but the measure of it was the telepathy that existed between us when he became ill. Very early one morning, about six o'clock, I woke with a start, feeling that he was in trouble. He had been encased in a plaster cast from neck to knee, hospitalized at the Bircher-Benner Clinic in Switzerland for many months, suffering from rare spinal tuberculosis. Three hours later, at nine o'clock, a cable arrived from Isabel Cripps, sent from his bedside to say he had just died, aged sixty-three. A treasured friendship had come to an end.

Praise mounted up after his death. Churchill and Cripps, as different as possible but both of similar extraordinary intelligence, often stood together. The learned, audacious mind of Cripps appealed to Churchill, who led the nation's praise after his death, calling him 'a statesman of national pre-eminence who was the soul of honour throughout his complicated political career'.

Born wealthy, Cripps freely gave away his large fortune. The dedicated idealist renounced his immensely remunerative legal practice to enter public service. Churchill sent him as a diplomat to Russia and India. At the war's end, and in a new Labour government, he was obviously a future candidate for 10 Downing Street, but his illness put paid to such hopes. He had imposed rationing, heavy taxes and wage freezes on his people, but all mourned his passing.

Another distinguished politician, Selwyn Lloyd, was a very different friend. He became Secretary of State for Foreign Affairs in 1951 in the Conservative government under Winston Churchill, and came from time to time to the United States to appear at the United Nations, when I saw a lot of him. It was on such a trip that I brought the term 'bebop' significantly into his vocabulary.

At the United Nations at that time, Sir Pierson Dixon was the British delegate following in the footsteps of Gladwyn Jebb, whose reputation for crackling ripostes to the Russians had made him a star performer in the tedious verbal duels between East and West. Jebb's shoes were not an easy pair to fill but Sir Pierson wore his own very well.

Selwyn Lloyd, on a visit to New York to deliver a speech to the Security Council, spent some days beforehand in our weekend Connecticut home. He looked perturbed on arrival, in fact he and his assistant both seemed terribly preoccupied. 'What's up?' I asked. 'Bad news?'

'No. It's not the news, it is next Wednesday which worries me. I shall have to reply to Vyshinsky at the closing session of the Security Council,' he said. 'We'll have the usual tirade against Wall Street bankers and Western imperialists, the lot! I've run out of original retorts. My reply has to be written this weekend.' Because he had always derided the UN to me as a place of endless postponement of decisions, I appreciated the problem. 'Fine! We have a house full of guests but I'll see that your rooms are kept quiet and undisturbed. Work away,' I told him as I walked the two men to their rooms.

When dinner was announced, I teased the still-concerned Foreign Secretary seated on my right. 'Stop being so serious. Why don't you ridicule Vyshinsky's boring repetitiveness? You did it successfully once before, in Paris!'

This was true: a year before, he had headed the UK delegation to a General Assembly of the UN, meeting then in Paris. Vyshinsky made the usual speech, high on attack and low on constructive suggestions. Selwyn Lloyd had the responsibility of replying, and on that occasion he had no difficulty. 'Your speech reminds me of the old Russian proverb,' he announced. 'The cow which moos the loudest yields the least milk.'

Mr Vyshinsky indignantly reminded Selwyn Lloyd during a debate the next day that this was not a Russian proverb. A day later Selwyn Lloyd continued the game by charmingly apologizing, admitting the proverb was Polish in origin.

'Why not do it again?' I asked him. 'Why give his tirade the dignity of a serious reply? Make a joke of it!'

'That's not easy. Have you ever tried being humorous under such circumstances? If you think it is that simple, make a suggestion,' he challenged.

'I accept,' I replied. 'Why not give him a dose of *bebop*!'

Anita Loos, the tiny author of *Gentlemen Prefer Blondes*, was sitting next to him at dinner and beamed instant agreement.

'What on earth are you talking about? What is *bebop*?' he asked in amazement.

Anita Loos, and I, between us, then explained; *bebop* was the teenage language of the moment, a lingo which started *every* sentence with the word 'Dig'. We gave him examples to explain how the language worked: 'Dig that crazy bathroom', for instance, would describe the white-tiled tunnel to New Jersey under the East River. Others at the table lent a hand with their examples to make the ridiculous slang-language clear to two incredulous British gentlemen.

'You really have no choice. Nothing could possibly be more effective than replying to Vyshinsky in *bebop*!' I concluded. 'I shall write your speech for you. I promise to make it short and *you* must promise to deliver it.'

He gave this promise, never expecting me to take it or the speech seriously, but he reckoned without my determination. I did write the speech, and delivered it to him on Monday morning. For the next two days, I plagued his staff by continually telephoning them to 'remind the Foreign Secretary of his promise to use *my* speech'. At three o'clock on the famous Wednesday in 1952, his secretary telephoned me to announce that Mr Lloyd had, in fact, just done so. I simply could not believe he'd done it.

Vyshinsky had, indeed, pulled out all the stops in denouncing the West. When Selwyn Lloyd stood up, delegates dug in for the usual style of reply. To say that the Assembly was speechless when they heard what the British Foreign Secretary delivered would be a crazy understatement. The chaos that resulted has never again been repeated.

Gales of laughter were followed by sheer bedlam. The *bebop* language had totally disrupted the translation facilities of the UN! One can imagine the consternation of the Chinese and the Russians and most other foreigners in *trying* to translate the dialogue, which went as follows:

'Mme President (Mrs Pandit of India), may I have your permission to reply to the learned Russian gentleman in the language of the young generation of the country in which we are all guests?'

'Of course,' replied the puzzled President.

Then, with studied care and proper enunciation of the words, which I had carefully taught him how to underscore because of their importance, Selwyn Lloyd replied: '*Dig* that *CRAZY* broken record!'

And he sat down.

Selwyn Lloyd's wit delighted America. I'm not sure how well the speech went down in Whitehall, but I did try to find out from Anthony Eden later when having tea with him and Lady Eden in London. He was non-committal but definitely not smiling, so I didn't admit I'd written it, although I was secretly proud at having contributed humour to the deadly decorum of the UN.

I never mentioned to anyone that I had written that '*bebop* speech', but years later I was seated next to Selwyn Lloyd at a dinner given by Lady Cooper-Key at Warwick House in London. He suddenly repeated the *bebop* story to all the others at table. I was shocked but absolutely delighted! Now that he had thanked me openly and so effusively the truth was no longer sacrosanct. I could tell it at last, and do.

On that same evening, he also whispered to me a shattering piece of news (in confidence). The Prime Minister, Harold Macmillan, would be making the next day's headlines with what was immediately dubbed 'The Night of the Long Knives'. Not only Selwyn Lloyd but one-third of Macmillan's entire Cabinet had been abruptly and unexpectedly dismissed that afternoon, just before we dined. Being a gentleman, Selwyn Lloyd simply left 10 Downing Street after his shocking dismissal, went home, dressed and came on to dinner, keeping the disastrous news to himself. The headline news wasn't mentioned to anyone else at dinner except to me.

He liked to reminisce about another dinner party which I had given for him at home while still in New York. 'Why did this evening mean so much to you? How come you never forget it?' I eventually asked him.

'Oh!' he said. 'How can I ever forget? You gave me *Garbo*!'

I often went to play Scrabble with him in the late afternoon before he left London. His death in the country from cancer was grim – and too soon.

Bernard Baruch was the first to treat me like a daughter but another great man, Osvaldo Aranha, not long after, also 'adopted' me into his family of two daughters and two sons (his 'American daughter', he used to say). He and his children became a second family: two daughters have married diplomats and been posted near us. One son-in-law, Sergio Correa da Costa, came to London as Ambassador to the Court of St James's – then went to Washington (where his wife's father had preceded him as Ambassador). The other daughter, Dede, married Antonio del Lago, and he went to Paris as Brazil's Ambassador. The two sisters have between them produced countless nieces and nephews who are now in my life.

I became fascinated by Brazil's potential after I began to fly there frequently. I met Osvaldo Aranha, an extraordinary national hero, in 1949 on a journalistic tour; he was introduced to me as the man who helped boot the sleeping, awkward, backward giant Brazil, into the twentieth century. This elegant internationalist (who had a spider as a symbol of his family name embroidered on his shirts and used it as his coat of arms) was also a scholar, parliamentarian and diplomat who began life as a gaucho. In 1930, he ousted Brazil's hated dictator; he was the first great man to see Brazil in relation to the rest of the world. He is called 'Brazil's Churchill'.

If instant friendship is possible, we found it. I was struck by his personality, his political views, his patriotism. In me, he discovered something he thought very rare – an editor of a large American magazine who was actually keenly interested in Brazil's politics.

In the 1940s and 50s, Latin America held little interest for the war-torn world, not even to Americans, although Nelson Rockefeller did make a serious attempt to sell South America to the Americans. In the Argentine, the glittering Perons shone as if part of the movie world. Evita's clothes and jewels were highlighted by American tabloids before they knew anything more about the wicked woman. I take credit for my role in unmasking her character, having written a bestselling book to draw attention to her activities.

My ties to Aranha were twofold: I persuaded important Americans to take an interest in Brazil, and eventually I was asked to undertake errands there for President Eisenhower. Dr Aranha afforded me the necessary direct and friendly contact with President Getulio Vargas, and persuaded the benevolent dictator he could trust me. I was able to convey messages to him in a very personal way, one not so easily available to the Ambassador posted to Brazil.

Vargas had been elected President after Aranha refused the role. Undoubtedly inspired by Dr Aranha, he honoured me by making me a Chevalier of the Order of Cruzierio du Sud in 1950. In 1973 I was upgraded to become a Commander of the same Order, this ceremony taking place at the Brazilian Embassy in London, presided over by Ambassador da Costa. The medal of the Commander is usually given only to Heads of State and foreign ministers, according to the rules of the Order. I received it for my continuing interest in and knowledge of Brazil's affairs.

Once, in a frivolous mood, when I had called on President Vargas with Osvaldo Aranha, at that time Minister of Finance, I was told that Brazil's longstanding and popular Ambassador to the United States, the doyen of the diplomatic corps there, was retiring. I impulsively suggested the name of the man I felt might be a logical successor. To my surprise and delight, the Brazilian banker was quickly appointed to the post.

On his arrival in the United States, Ambassador de Salles called on me. 'President Vargas said I must first present my credentials to you,' he admitted with a broad grin and a low bow. We have remained close friends.

Every visit to Dr Aranha's home gave evidence of his humanity in action; he was dedicated to the poor, the troubled and those unfairly treated. Doors were never locked, his hall constantly full of people seeking help and advice. An overflow of politicians, wanting his support, also waited apart in the library. Food was always available, gifts of advice or money or books were given. In that vast house overlooking the city of Rio de Janeiro, legal problems were sorted out, jobs found, homes saved and political strategies arranged. For me, still young, it was a privilege to enter and feel that I belonged, if only for short periods, in that Aranha world.

Though refusing to be 'top dog', Aranha nevertheless sat in many seats of power: Minister of Justice, twice Minister of Finance, Foreign Minister, and Ambassador to the United States, where he had a special relationship with President Roosevelt who also fell for his charm and erudition and made him a close, trusted personal friend.

He was elected as President of the United Nations, after just having been a delegate, a rare honour. Important people who knew him found him a unique person. Henry Luce, in his book *Ideas of Henry Luce*, called him 'one of the greatest, most irresistible personalities I've ever encountered ... with the forthright, belligerent honesty of Wendell Willkie and the easy charm of Roosevelt, and an inexhaustible energy which neither of those Americans possesses.'

Aranha once remarked that some diplomats are given a tongue in order to conceal their thoughts. Not Aranha. He always came to the point and said exactly what he meant. His easy charm, backed by his insistence on knowing all the essentials, whatever was involved, led to the dispatch of some amusing cables to Ambassadors when he was Foreign Minister.

He liked to tell me of them. Humour as much as annoyance was involved in an exchange with two diplomats in the Middle East. One had cabled he'd been insulted by his Japanese opposite number who 'threatened to use karate on me, whatever that meant'. Aranha cabled back: 'You are being posted to Japan to find out.' Another diplomat who took three and a half pages to report a conversation was told in reply: 'The essence of your conversation should have been confined to a long first paragraph and you are being charged for the rest.' Any good professional journalist knows that however long a report, the summary of its entire contents should be in the first paragraph.

Aranha was also a hypnotic orator and actually played a crucial role in bringing Brazil to the Allied side during World War II. In 1942, at Rio's Conference of Inter-American Ministers of the twenty-one South American republics, he threatened to resign 'if Brazil doesn't get away from the Nazi gangs'. His threat worked. A few dangerous hours before the conference ended, Vargas, up to then in favour of the Nazis, had to give in: Brazil declared war on the Axis. History's course was changed.

Aranha's ability was so great that during those sensitive, tricky war years, he, almost singlehandedly, changed Vargas's policy of *pretended* neutrality. As Foreign Secretary, he had constantly and skilfully rebuffed every Nazi sypathizer and councillor in government. Though the public may have been passionately pro-Allies, President Vargas was adamantly in favour of the Nazis.

By changing that policy, Aranha denied the Nazis the use of Brazil's vital bases, ruining Nazi plans to bombard the United States, and preventing U-boats from sheltering in Brazil whence they could make dashes to North Africa. This action actively helped end the war, which Aranha never doubted the Allies *would* win. In a book by Goebbels* the former Nazi official confirms this in his report on Brazil:

> 'A bitter fight is going on between President Vargas, who is pretty much on our side, and Aranha, the Foreign Minister, who has evidently been bought by Roosevelt and seems to be doing everything he can to provoke a conflict with the Reich and the Axis Powers. We have, alas, no facilities for reprisal. We have about 600,000 Brazilians in our land, whereas in Brazil alone there are 150,000 Germans. The possibilities of economic retaliation are also extraordinarily limited, as we don't own one-tenth as much Brazilian capital as they possess of ours. So we have to be fairly careful.'

The great grazing land in southern Brazil played a part in the country's history by raising such men as Aranha who rode those plains and changed governments. He was the most distinguished Brazilian gaucho. Along with Getulio Vargas, he led a small band who marched towards Rio in an amazing revolt on 30 October 1930, finally freeing the country from its dictator, Washington Luiz, and his despotic rule. They fought on the streets as the civilian leader of the revolution acted to unseat the dictator. With a handful of men, in a brave action, they took over the headquarters of the Federal Army in Porto Alegre and joined it with Rio's garrison. While on this march to the city, Aranha took a leg-full of machine-gun fire – part of his heel was blown away. He refers to the event as 'a bloodless coup'.

He was not only a superb orator but a talented linguist. As President of the United Nations, he spoke French, immaculate English, Spanish and Portuguese. He officially declared Israel a state. President Truman

* *The Goebbels Diaries, 1939–41*, Hamish Hamilton, 1992.

had wanted this but defence chiefs feared it would close the boundaries to Arabian oil. Aranha went ahead and did it regardless. The State of Israel was proclaimed on 14 May 1948. President Truman could then officially recognize Israel, which he did eleven minutes after Independence was declared. Arab troops immediately prepared to invade the new State.

I was deeply saddened by his death. He was buried with the full honours of a President. To this day I vividly recall one moving comment he made to me. He said: 'Fleur, when I dream, I am sure I will live for ever. When I am trying to achieve that dream, I act as if I am going to die in a minute.' He told me to live that way. I try.

He will be remembered for his unique urbanity, intelligence and diplomatic skills. Few have ever left more friends and admirers.

Another of Brazil's history-makers was a quixotic man with the improbable name of Assis Chateaubriand, a Robin Hood, South American style. In very different ways he, too, helped mould his country.

The enormous difference between Aranha and 'Chateau', as he was known, was in their techniques. 'Chateau' was a Hearstian publishing mogul, who used to watch with glee as internecine warfare sprang up between his countless employees in his dozens of publications and TV and radio stations.

He looked and acted like a sultan; short, squat, big-nosed, dark-skinned, with black shining eyes below a mop of black hair. His inexplicable success with women often evoked surprise but somehow he did seem to hold great allure for certain beautiful European ladies. He roamed the world as if he owned it, in his own airplane, scooping up the people he considered were attractive enough to travel from Rio to Paris or New York and back. In a smaller plane, he'd fly foreigners up the Amazon to show them his plantations. This may not seem so unusual today, but in the early fifties it made an impressive invitation.

He maintained that his French name came from a family background in northern France. If this was true, and no one minded whether it was or not, he nevertheless gave his devotion and enormous largesse to Brazil, not France. He created Brazil's first nursery system to look after impoverished children who today roam the streets, some to be murdered, it is said, by paid killers to stop them from looting food.

He organized Brazil's civil aeronautics system, one of the biggest communication networks in the world.

Lunch in my honour was routine whenever I arrived in Rio. Once, to my horror, he insisted I go with him to a luncheon that I didn't know he was hosting for hundreds of men. He introduced me as his guest of honour – *the only woman there!* He started with a paean of praise for me (I was quite unknown to the astonished dignitaries). Further embarrassment came when the companion sitting on the dais on my right was ordered to translate his speech into English for me as Chateaubriand sped on at his usual 100-mile-an-hour conversational pace. The shocked interpreter was the governor of Natal, Sylvio Pedroza, a Tyrone Power look-alike.

A few years later, I was happy to visit and write about newly-built Brasilia with Sylvio Pedroza's help, after he had been appointed President Kubitschek's official construction coordinator and brought his family to live in the area across the lake overlooking the new city. While visiting them there, I spent much of the time secretly praying not to meet the poisonous snakes, coral snakes in particular, which abounded.

Chateaubriand and I were later appointed by our governments as Ambassadors to Queen Elizabeth II's Coronation. I could write a skit about his hilarious attempts to persuade me to present the Queen with the handsome necklace and earrings of diamonds and aquamarines which he brought as his personal gift. 'You're a lady, you should make my presentation,' he insisted, regularly trying to force the box into my hands.

'Official guests are *not* expected to bring personal gifts. They will not be accepted,' I explained over and over again as I refused. Yet they *are* worn by the Queen, because when later he became the Ambassador to the Court of St James's they were accepted by her as an official gift from Brazil. Visiting him when he presided over the London Embassy often meant being present at some bizarre events. He was Brazil's most colourful export. Once, all chairs were removed and dinner was served as forty of us sat on huge pillows on the drawing-room floor. The difficult Brazilian meal ended with rice strewn all over it.

A massive stroke left him speechless and almost totally paralysed after his return to Brazil. I went to see him when he arrived at

England's Stoke Mandeville Hospital. After weeks there, finally having regained the use of one finger on each hand, he arranged for them to be placed into stirrups hung from the ceiling above his bed. Slowly, he punched out a daily column for his newspaper on the typewriter which was also hung on a slant from the ceiling.

A few years later, my husband Tom and I went to visit Chateaubriand, paralysed, at Claridge's Hotel in London. He had just returned from a trip to Moscow to study their cattle! Totally *motionless* in bed, eyes glazed with excitement, he faced the wall which was plastered with photographs of the Russian cattle he'd seen and wanted to introduce to Brazil. He communicated, incredibly, by moving the muscles of his stomach. Two nurses, one a tough gentleman, the other a red-haired woman, 'read' his words by putting fingers on those muscles. Listening to what they said, he grunted disapproval if it wasn't accurate. If correct, they were rewarded with a grotesque grin.

He is no longer alive but his Robin Hood activities gained him a unique place in Brazil's social history. Using his vast communications system as a threat, a weapon mightier than any sword, he forced men of means, whether or not Brazilian nationals, to purchase art for Brazil. Most businesses seemed to have skeletons in their closets and somehow he always got to know them and used the threat of disclosure. I was an unsuspecting witness to one of his successes when I joined him for lunch at the home of one of his friends. This, I later learned, was without the prior knowledge of his host, the chairman of a highly profitable foreign company in Rio. Pandemonium arose as we arrived late, as was his habit, because I was an unexpected guest. The table had to be reset and the seating rearranged.

A degree of tranquillity was eventually achieved, but after dessert Chateau sprang to his feet, eyes gleaming, to describe a beautiful El Greco painting he'd recently discovered in Europe. 'This,' he stated, 'belongs to Brazil. It is so wonderful of you' (pointing to the host), 'to buy this for the museum!'

The host blanched; it was the first he had heard of it as Chateau raised his glass to toast this latest victim. The El Greco soon hung in the museum as a superb reminder of a modern 'Robin Hood' at work. The technique ultimately brought a considerable reputation to Sao Paulo's Museum of Modern Art. Chateau built a museum in which to house masterworks from Goya to Picasso.

He made a mad decision before he died when he decided that his new Rio de Janeiro publishing headquarters must be more than merely architecturally interesting. The building must be 'unique', he insisted. While still on post in England he brought a botanical expert to lunch with us in Sussex to explain what he meant by this. The building's top floor, high on Rio's skyline, was to become a vast botanical garden – with a difference: *no electricity*! This expert had been hired to gather together millions of fireflies to fly about the huge roof area, twinkling in the darkness of the night sky.

It never happened. Chateaubriand's serious strokes put paid to the idea, but it made great conversation as he explained his plan at the lunch table to his shocked listeners in his broken English.

The Chateaubriand network of communications was vast: his press empire consisted of thirty-three newspapers, five magazines, five TV and twenty-seven radio stations. He used them to achieve all sorts of results, on one occasion to revenge himself on one of my American friends in Sao Paulo who was married to a Brazilian millionaire.

The United States Secretary of State, Dean Acheson, when on a State visit to Brazil, stayed at their home in Sao Paolo; it had been selected because the wife was American, and sufficiently rich to have a ballroom substantial enough for a glamorous dinner-dance in Acheson's honour. The couple were also well connected politically. The hostess chose not to invite Chateau to the ball, although he always took his attendance absolutely for granted. Sick of his ego, she simply ruled it out, pretending that it was a Foreign Office decision. He knew this was nonsense; she soon rued her decision. He plotted an extraordinary revenge; it was devastating. For two days before the event, he published an advertisement he had personally designed. It went into each one of his thirty-three newspapers, positioned prominently at the top right-hand corner of the important page three. To ensure its conspicuousness, a thick black border surrounded it.

The headline was 'LOST, TWO CATS', and a huge reward was offered. Each cat was described; a white Angora cat identified by its collar of large emeralds and a Blue Persian by its necklace of square-cut diamonds. The name and address of the Secretary of State's hostess was boldly printed. She had no cats, but the result was havoc. For the length of Dean Acheson's stay, the Communist party organized a crowd of banner-carrying, angry, chanting members to stand at the gates of the house protesting at such extravagance in the face of Brazil's poverty. As one group was dispersed by the police, another crowd fell into place, all dressed in rags. Robin Hood had turned *mafioso*.

A very different man, but one of the world's most fascinating, influential and admired intellectuals, Carlos Fuentes, unexpectedly entered our lives with a bang some years ago.

After completing his tour of duty as Mexico's Ambassador to France, he was the guest of honour at a dinner at the Mexican Embassy in London. After dinner, all fell into separate groups in the drawing room, but my husband and I, disliking crowded rooms, were slow to leave the dining room. Suddenly we were beckoned by Ambassador Sepulveda: 'Come with me,' he commanded, 'you are the person Carlos Fuentes wants to meet!'

With that flattering invitation, a treasured friendship began. I was greeted not by a handshake, but by two hugs – one from him, the other from his beautiful wife, Sylvia. I knew Fuentes by reputation but we'd never met. The title of one work of this admired historian, writer and teacher was particularly famous; *Old Gringo*, the book which later became such a successful film, jumped into my mind as we talked. One of the latest of his many other books, which I have just finished, is *The Buried Mirror*, reflections on early Spain and the New World. It taught me considerably more than I already knew about the land of the Conquistadors in which we now live for months each year.

I knew less about his amazing blonde wife but I soon learned of her reputation as a television star in Mexico. Her interviews with major world figures make her programme one of the longest-running and most significant in the country. What kind of friends have they become? Pure gold, is the easiest way I can describe them.

Worldwide honours acclaim the worth of this brilliant Mexican. Prizes for intellectual and literary achievement could paper one large wall and honorary degrees another. Everywhere students know him: he has held special Chairs as Simon Bolivar Professor at Cambridge in England and was the Robert F. Kennedy Professor at Harvard. Literary prizes have been many: three from Mexico, one from Venezuela, the Picasso Medal from UNESCO, one from Italy, another from New York and three from Spain, one from the hand of King Juan Carlos himself, Spain's equivalent to the Nobel Prize. Many of us wait impatiently for him to receive that ultimate honour.

Any blank wall space could be filled by honorary degrees from Cambridge, Warwick and Essex Universities in the UK, and ten others in the United States, from Harvard, Weslyan, UCLA, Miami, Georgetown Washington and Oregon Universities, Bard College, New School for Social Research and CUNY in New York. As a distinguished citizen, he has been awarded honours in Mexico and Buenos Aires, Santiago, Chile and Denver in Colorado. He wears the Legion of Honour from France and Order of Merit from Chile.

He is a disciple in disguise – having lived his life in ways to better the world through his words, plays, serious books, essays and poems which are normally published in twenty-four languages.

He honoured the first *Flair* Symposium on *The Future of the Printed Word* at Texas University by agreeing to attend. He listened for two days and then brilliantly summarized what had been said, adding his own views on the subject, and received a standing ovation from the audience of 690. The entire contents of the Symposium is being printed in a book by Texas University.* His name added lustre to the list of prominent speakers; it was a sold-out event a month in advance, with many disappointed ticket-seekers from far places.

Forget the weight of his worldwide reputation. Carlos Fuentes and his wife are fun to be with, especially as they both share our love of opera. When we are together in Spain we sit after dinner on the stone patio outside our castle. There, music on discs floats through the Roman arches in the cloister and under an almost black sky we watch the stars light up. We count the satellites as they race above our heads on their trajectories. We listen to half an opera one night, the other half the next – in tune with the music and with each other.

Kisho Kurokawa is the man who occasioned my return to his country, Japan, in 1990 for the three exhibitions of my paintings he had personally arranged in Tokyo, Kyoto and Kanazawa.

My husband and I flew eastward from London to Tokyo in a 747 jet, taking eight long hours simply to cross Siberia. We saw the earth

---

* *The State and Fate of Publishing*, published by the University Press.

change from icy, uninhabited tundra to a crowded land before we arrived in the neon-lit labyrinth of Tokyo's airport. A two-hour motor trip had still to be endured before we reached the city itself.

It was my first sight of Japan for over thirty years since the annual round-the-world hops I used to make as an editor, and nothing prepared me for the Japan I found: bumper-to-bumper spotless cars, clogged streets, dense but well-behaved traffic, streets clean enough to eat on, shoulder-to-shoulder pedestrians, all in a hurry. Order was personified, despite what appears to be chaos.

Kisho Kurokawa, a renowned architect whose philosophy and creative achievements are admired all over the world, not least in Japan itself, had made this visit and the three exhibitions possible. It had been immaculately planned and organized by Kurokawa after he visited us in London. There he saw my paintings and decided they should be known in Japan, and the exhibitions were the result; there could be no better introduction to the Japanese world. He opened all doors. His interest in and support for my work brought the added bonus of the help and friendship of his beautiful wife, Aiko. These days we see them both in London, she dressed in Chanel clothes enhanced by beautiful jewels designed by her husband. She is Japan's leading actress, and while we were there she appeared in a TV soap-opera about the Samurais, who once ruled Japan. European stars would gasp and envy the audience of fifty million viewers.

Collaborating with Kisho Kurokawa was one of Tokyo's most respected art critics, Shin-Ichi Segi; together they provided me with three superbly appointed galleries: the Wako in Tokyo, the Gion Sango in Kyoto and the Art Centre in Kanazawa, and they handled all the difficult intricacies of such a complicated project: the dates, importation papers, shipping arrangements, and a catalogue in Japanese which illustrates how decorative my name is in that language.

The two men even created a reception committee: Princess Shimazu, daughter of the Emperor; Mme Aso, the British-educated daughter of former Prime Minister Yoshida (she and I have been friends for years), and ten influential businessmen whose companies, such as Sony, are known worldwide in communications, motor cars and other high-tech manufacturing. They gave heartwarming personal evidence of Japanese interest in Western art and as most of them collected my work, I can now think of my paintings hanging in impressive company.

They were our hosts for nearly three weeks. In Kyoto's superb gallery, I was pleased to see that such important Western painters as André Miraux, Serge Poliakoff, Antonio Clavé and Ben Nicholson had preceded me from Europe.

The Crown Prince Hiro has one of my paintings, probably the first Western art to hang in the Imperial Palace. When we were invited to visit him there later, he shyly observed to me: 'You are not American. You must be Japanese to have painted this picture.'

'What can you mean?' I asked politely. 'I *am* American, as American as apple pie.'

'No. You must be Japanese to paint as you do; only Japanese painters hang in the Imperial Palace.'

The Japanese critics wrote that my work must have been influenced by Japanese art. Not true: I am not influenced by anything.

Kisho Kurokawa and I got to know each other when we both served on the Rolex Jury in Geneva which, like a mini Nobel Foundation, presents financial awards to deserving men and women with aspirations to improve the world. It was hard and confining work but gave great joy nevertheless. It required hours and hours, sometimes days and days, of personal time as well as meeting and debating regularly in Geneva with the jury (composed of judges from Tokyo, Brazil, Germany, France, Belgium, Italy, USA and the United Kingdom). Fourteen thousand entrants competed but government and other agencies sifted out all but the thousand it was to be our task to judge. I considered it a privilege to assist Rolex in their generosity.*

Our diverse group included an explorer, an architect, a doctor, a businessman and the physicist who had put up the first spaceship. We were all differently talented; in fact, in our incessant debates to arrive at unanimous decisions required to select the ten winners, we learned from each other. I was genuinely sad when our work was done after three years. The elegant Kisho Kurokawa was a calming influence at meetings. We saw no sign of his 1960s' reputation as an 'enfant terrible'.

The three weeks spent in Japan were made even more eventful by

* The other jurors were: Andrew Heiniger (Chairman), George Cochran, Xavier Fructus, Yoshimine Ikeda, Kisho Kurokawa, Hans Joachim Panitz, Carlo Rubia and Robert Stenuit.

another of Kurokawa's gifts: he lent his English-speaking personal secretary to us for our stay as a guide and translator. She was Americanized enough after a university degree in the United States to understand our Western needs as together we saw beautiful temples, shrines and palaces. I can't help wondering if they had all been built according to a decree which required visitors to climb at least one hundred steps to reach their doors. Worthwhile when accomplished, but often an ordeal.

We shall long remember sitting crosslegged in Kisho Kurokawa's tea house in his penthouse garden, one of the few areas in crowded Tokyo big enough for a tea garden today. Prime Ministers have come to contemplate there. The penthouse stretches over two tall apartment houses which he designed to face each other across a Tokyo street, spanned by a bridge which continues as part of his apartment.

We learned to sit correctly on the tatami (the tea house matting), drinking formally, noticing the elegance of each cup before returning it. Kurokawa had constructed the tea house and it is like a rare gem. Nothing, not an inch, that is not ancient and memorable.

Kurokawa's ideas on how best to show his work brought an amazing freshness to his London exhibitions in the mid-'90s at the Sainsbury gallery in the Royal Academy of Arts, where he displayed his most recent projects for museums in Japan and Europe, presented in rooms decorated in pristine and peaceful white. Reproductions of his black and white architectural drawings were on the floors of the exhibitions underneath transparent Perspex which we walked over! The framed originals hung on the walls. In each room, a huge model of a museum project was lit from inside. It was a marriage of drama, serenity and elegance.

There are Kurokawa cultural centres in museums all over the world, including China, where this Japanese friend even teaches at the University of Tsinghua! At twenty-six he helped found the Metabolism Movement and since then has been an astonishing leader in the architectural world. Best of all, for me, is his ability to explore the interaction between Oriental forms and the modernism of the West. I await with special interest the new wing he has designed for the Van Gogh Museum in Amsterdam, a favourite port of call of ours.

*   *   *

I met the oldest gentleman I have ever known through a friend who also lived in our historic building, Albany, in London's Piccadilly. In 1895, 'Mr Stone', a gentleman only referred to as 'Mr', presided over it as the Trustees' Chairman, and in the course of his life he acquired a large slice of the vast estate which was originally built by Lord Melbourne, Queen Victoria's Prime Minister. Mr Stone lived over one hundred years.

The amazing old gentleman remained Albany's 'curiosity', gossiped about for his eccentricities, his miserliness, his collection of Georgian jewellery (including the tiara he was reputed to wear at night at home), but also for his incredible vitality. He would shuffle off with his nurse for his daily walk to Regent's Park, a vast distance for a man of his age. He did this until he reached the age of ninety-nine. When he died, he left his thirty sets of Albany chambers, called flats or apartments elsewhere, to Cambridge University's Peterhouse College, creating a most unusual landlord for some of the residents.

His one-hundredth birthday sparked off a tribal ritual, an Albany birthday party given by his own tenants. Committees were formed for libations, for cake decorations and birthday greetings, one to be received from the Queen who always sends a telegram to centenarians. Another committee dealt with speeches; *who* should be asked from the distinguished list of Albany's Oxford dons, publishers and intellectuals? Yet another tackled invitations. Welsh Guards bandsmen were to be engaged to play directly outside in the garden, the music to drift through windows (their repertoire to include Mr Stone's favourites: Mozart's *Eine Kleine Nachtmusik* and Ketelbey's *In a Monastery Garden*). Could the old boy survive all this excitement? Decisions were taken with tender care.

I was the only American present, thanks to a friend, Mrs Frederick Roe, in whose large chambers the party was held. Such an occasion would interest me – she reasoned, and arranged for a vote. I, although not one of *his* tenants, was allowed to attend. At the end, guests formed a queue to shake his hand and wish him well. He knew I was not one of his tenants and that I was an American living there.

When I reached him in the queue he moved away from the high-backed chair selected for him near the windows. I couldn't help noticing how loosely his morning suit hung on his bony shoulders, and how obtrusive was his Adam's apple and, finally, his wandering,

LEFT: After our first meeting in his Cairo office, future talks with President Nasser took place in his army camp home, inevitably surrounded by buzzing little children and his very shy wife. The house was tiny but the parlour furniture gilded. It lacked any evidence of Nasser's position as the Head of State of Egypt.

RIGHT: Lady Bird Johnson came to Beverley Hills to attend the dinner given by the Louis S.B. Leakey Foundation to raise a fund in my name for AIDS research. The study examines why, other than man, the monkey can also carry the virus. My interest in anthropology was inspired by Louis Leakey himself and I am President of the Louis S.B. Leakey Trust in Europe.

BELOW: A visit to the Argentine during the Peron era. Evita somehow chose to consider me her friend. She took me everywhere to 'see the wonders I have arranged for my poor'. This visit was to a children's home; temporarily borrowed tiny expensive dresses hung in closets to be displayed on our walkabout – but where were the children? 'They are on holiday,' she explained.

LEFT: Dwight D. Eisenhower generously honoured me in his time, including appointing me as Ambassador to the Coronation and to other diplomatic duties. Here I am describing to him how I intended to create my magazine, *Flair* – a bewildering proposition. Otherwise talk was of politics, on which we rarely disagreed: an exception to this was the momentary friendliness he showed Senator Joseph McCarthy whilst campaigning in 1953.

RIGHT: Isak Dinesen, that noble Danish writer, gave me this photo taken of her in New York City with Marilyn Monroe. She found the 'Sex Symbol' so cuddly and funny she spoke constantly of Marilyn Monroe when we entertained her in London after that American visit.

BELOW: One of the first one-man exhibitions of my paintings (I have now had fifty-one worldwide) was in Athens, opened by Queen Frederika. Here Crown Prince Constantine (now King of Greece), his wife Queen Anne-Marie and sister Princess Irene show their interest in a cheetah painting.

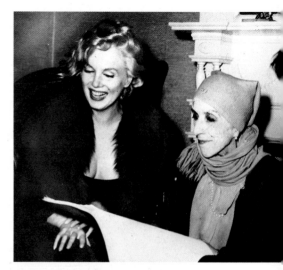

ABOVE: The rains suddenly came pelting down just as Cary Grant, my husband and I sat down to the picnic he'd arranged on the hills overlooking Toledo on a day off from shooting *The Gun*. Instead, we returned to the Palace Hotel in Madrid to this picnic, laid out on a tablecloth on the floor of his sumptuous suite.

RIGHT: Ayesha Jaipur (now Raj Mata of Jaipur) discussing her decision to run for Congress in India. The beautiful Maharanee who symbolized Indian wealth campaigned with jewels and superb saris amid the poor of her country, and won on a platform against her friend, Nehru.

LEFT: President Reagan at a White House evening – in a merry mood, listening to a spontaneous poem by the inimitable Archibald Roosevelt (grandson of former President Theodore Roosevelt) formerly an Arabist specialist for the CIA. His wife, Selwa, was the State Department's Head of Protocol.

RIGHT: General Zahedi, Iran's Prime Minister, giving me personal notes about the former Prime Minister, Mohammed Mossadeq. He then arranged for me to visit this madman – whom I found cross-legged on his cot in his prison cell. After his trial he was imprisoned for expropriation of the oil industry.

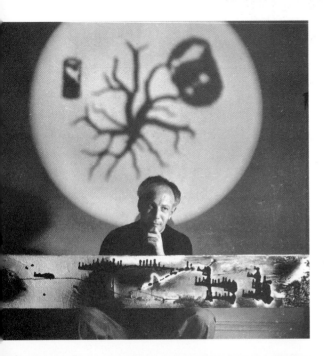

LEFT: My devoted friend, Enrico Donati, successful painter (member of the New York School), art collector and the tycoon Chairman of Houbigant perfume, always found time to help less fortunate painters. And he recently even gave his perfume company to his employees. This is gallantry personified.

RIGHT: Bernard, Prince of the Netherlands ('P.B' to his friends) and I are deep in discussion about a World Wildlife project when he was its International President. Such smooth sailing on this work continued when he was followed by the late Jonkheer John Loudon as President. We all remained warm friends.

ABOVE: The untimely death of King Paul left a deeply saddened population. Here I am, dressed in mourning, close to tears as his body was carried to the church for the funeral. He had always been a wonderful friend, and decorated me with the Order of Bienfaisence for my efforts on the Cyprus issue.

INSET: A few days after the tragic death and funeral of King Paul of Greece, Queen Frederika invited me to visit his grave with her. Our tears were followed by a moving gesture: the Queen handed me this affectionate photograph of her and her husband together, her favourite photograph. It sits now where I see it when I wake up in the morning, which had also been her habit.

LEFT: Dame Margot Fonteyn and Rudolf Nureyev brought an extraordinary genius and romantic quality to ballet: it was Margot who brought Nureyev to London from Paris after defecting from the Russian Ballet. On Margot's last visit to London before she died, she was at home with us for the celebration of HM Queen Elizabeth The Queen Mother's ninetieth birthday. All were saddened by how ill Margot had become.

RIGHT: Olivia de Havilland, flanked by her newly-married husband, Pierre Galante, then editor of *Paris Match*, with Jean Prouvost, its publisher, and me, before cutting the wedding cake. I gave her away as her 'temoin' as she and her mother and sister, Joan Fontaine, were not on speaking terms at that time.

ABOVE LEFT: I never look at the gentle green hills clinging to our Sussex weekend home without recalling waking up to hear Yehudi Menuhin playing his violin as he took his morning walk. In this photograph, we are discussing the piano concert we'd just heard by the amazingly gifted Gina Bachauer.

ABOVE RIGHT: I had difficulty in persuading the already very busy Lord Clark (Kenneth Clark of TV's *Civilisation* fame) to write a book to coordinate with my worldwide museum project for the World Wildlife Fund, called 'The Animal in Art'. In his book which followed, *Animals and Men*, Clark records me as 'the begetter'.

RIGHT: Greeting Prince Philip, Guest of Honour at the Tate Gallery's impressive Picasso retrospective exhibition in the mid-fifties. Alongside him is his famous former equerry, Michael Parker, now living in Australia.

BELOW: James Stewart and his wife Gloria with a friendly lion cub in the California zoo where Mrs Stewart was a docent. The Stewart's regularly went on safari to Africa (to film, not kill, wild animals) always stopping off in our Sussex home, whether coming or going. Amusingly, two lions in San Francisco were given the names of Fleur and TomTom by their zoo!

BELOW: The Duchess of Windsor visiting me at my *Look* office after she and the Duke came to live in New York City. Later, I gave a mock 'Book and Author Luncheon' in my home to launch the Duke's book, *A King's Story*, lampooning the vicissitudes which he should expect ahead.

ABOVE: After a nasty arrest in the Lebanon by the Beirut police when the unacceptable Israeli stamp was found in my passport, US Ambassador Hare came to my rescue (President Chamoun and his wife then invited me to breakfast to apologise). Meanwhile, I'd missed the plane to Teheran to visit the Shah, arriving a day late.

INSET: I made my good-byes to the Shah's brother, Prince Abdorreza Pahlavi, and his wife and son after my visit to their home to meet the man often referred to as the handsome Tyrone Power of Iran.

LEFT: Just-married, Tom Montague Meyer and I were met at Heathrow by an avalanche of press as we arrived in London. Despite all the attempts to minimize publicity, it had become known we'd just been married. We had just flown from Los Angeles as guest of Howard Hughes, who reserved the rear of the plane entirely for us, putting on an extra chef to look after our needs.

watery eye. *'You're an American!'* he croaked. Without another word, he took me by the hand and slowly proceeded to the couch across the room which he had obviously longingly eyed all afternoon. Clumsily sinking into it, he took me down with him, dropping me without a murmur *on the floor*, his hand still gripping mine.

After pushing back his Adam's apple, arranging his butterfly collar and cravat, he started his interrogation. 'Do you remember Beauregard?' he asked. And answered himself: 'You Americans were so unkind to him after your Civil War. General Grant sent him back to his farm, but –' he continued angrily, 'Beauregard *had* no farm – so he joined the mercenaries and fought on Britain's side in the Sudan!'

That point settled, I looked for the exit but he was not yet finished. Settling back, he asked searchingly: 'Did you know the great friend of mine who invented the combustion engine?'

'No,' I muttered. 'I wasn't alive.'

Next question: 'Were *you* on the Pony Express?'

'Good Lord, no! It was somewhat before my time . . .'

He interrupted; 'Of course you weren't on it! But I *do* know exactly who *was* on its first journey.'

Before he could finish listing the names of everyone who rode on that early postal transport, I jumped to my feet, wished him well and fled to the comparatively modern confines of my own eighteenth-century set of chambers on the floor above.

Albany is one of the most coveted addresses in London, some are pretentious enough to say in the world. It is where I came to live when I arrived in London. Although the historic mansion is on noisy Piccadilly, it sits back in its own courtyard, oblivious to buses, traffic, or any street babble. Once inside, all you hear is the sound of birds. Our windows face towards the back, a sight unique in England, perhaps anywhere, a covered 'rope-walk' between two rows of small houses which stretch from the mansion where I live for the length of a city block to the next street; there are flower beds, and tame blackbirds whose song is the only sound we ever hear. It not only reminds me of the countryside, but of another century.

It was intended to be a man's world: married men were admitted in 1878, but not their wives (other women?). Ladies were only officially accepted in 1919 after so many men were lost in the First World War that the rules became impossible to enforce. Lady Lee, the first woman to live there, was the American married to an English peer who gave Chequers to the British nation for its prime ministers. She was still alive when I arrived in 1955 so I had the pleasure of knowing this lovely old lady.

Albany was built in 1770 by Sir William Chambers for the first Lord Melbourne as a gift to his bride. It acquired its current name later in the 1770s after the Melbournes exchanged houses with the King's brother, the Duke of York and Albany. The Duke was soon on the verge of bankruptcy and about to have to give it up to his creditors when seven trustees paid the bills and turned the house into sets of chambers. It remains the same to this day, an enclave of peace and distinction, favoured by Byron, Gladstone, Disraeli and Macaulay. Today such names as Lord Clarke (of *Civilization* fame), Edward Heath and other politicians and artists continue to give it a significance. For me, since London has become the crossroads of the world, international visitors and locals can meet in my drawing room where the talk is such that I often think of that room as a Roman forum.

When we are not in Spain, weekends are spent in Sussex. There I have the contrast I love; instead of the high Georgian elegance of Albany, I turn to the flower-laden charm of a small Elizabethan manor house. Adjoining are a huge ancient barn and gardens, including a farm and a kitchen garden which provide everything we eat. I describe the house as a debutante at the time of the Armada. It was built in 1572.

Wherever I live, London or Sussex or Spain, my passion for flowers has to find expression, something my English friends understand. Fortune brought me to Britain where growing them is part of the national character. Claude Monet's phrase clings to me: 'More than anything, I must have flowers always, always.'

A remarkable man who lived to improve the lives of his fellows, a gifted surgeon, a medical genius distressed by the misery of the mutilated, John Marquis Converse is my next memorable gentleman.

He came into my world when facial mutilations were a fact of life after the horrors of two wars and acts of terrorism. The study of reconstructive surgery was almost unknown until this brave doctor's plan for its future. To him, terribly mutilated children were the most heartrending; some born without mouths, ears or noses, with cleft palates. So were the Nazi mutilations of women.

I was given the chance to help him and his patients in 1946 – the idea of a remarkable elderly lady, Ouida da Costa Breckenridge, whose own great personal vision created the world's first Eye Bank: eyes from the dead to give sight to the living. She and I were strangers but she called on me at *Look* Magazine to ask if I, younger and well-placed, could do what was needed for the vast army of mutilated. Of course, I agreed.

She arranged for me to meet Dr Converse. His dream was to build a hospital for reconstructive plastic surgery and to introduce the magical skills to postgraduate students, in order to save as many patients as possible from a life of isolation and hell. I was able to help him. Today there exists a great Institution and teaching centre in whose birth I participated: The National Foundation for Facial Reconstruction.

Dr Converse's own dedication stemmed from a touching incident. After studying medicine in Paris, where he was brought up, his San Francisco-born father had become head of the US Public Health Service in Europe, and later, director of the American Hospital in Paris. He felt he had to follow in his father's footsteps, and was ready to do so when a dramatic event decided both his life and aspirations.

It happened in the south of France, when an attractive girl was his passenger in a fearful motor accident. Her face was so badly smashed he despaired for her unless he could find the one man capable of repairing the terrible damage. The man was to be the gifted Dr Thierry de Martel, one of three men who introduced neuro-surgery to medical science. Dr de Martel had undertaken plastic surgery during the First War, but this medical discipline had fallen into disrepute between the wars. The Second World War brought it back into prominence.

Dr Converse watched de Martel at work on the woman's battered face; the effect of seeing her disfigurement repaired was so inspirational he immediately went to work with Dr de Martel to learn the elements of a surgery that was not being taught anywhere else. Secretly he had longed to be a sculptor, and soon realized that this type of surgery was in itself a form of sculpture.

He later went to work in Boston at the Massachusetts General

Hospital with the famed Dr V. H. Karanjian, but with war still on he returned to Europe to help the French, joining the Red Cross volunteer ambulance service. When warned that the Germans were on their heels, his unit crossed the river at Bordeaux and he fled by Embassy car to the Spanish frontier, then on to Lisbon and finally aboard the SS *Manhattan*, back to New York. But he couldn't find peace of mind there, so he sailed back to England, being thwarted at his first attempt when the ship he had chosen was sunk on its way to America.

In London he joined Sir Archibald McIndoe and Sir Harold Gillies, who became the 'fathers' of wartime reconstructive surgery. This team worked on airmen whose faces and hands had been burned and destroyed, often beyond recognition, in the Battle of Britain, men who became McIndoe's 'Guinea Pigs'. I met many of them with the McIndoes and marvelled at their courage, especially when they eventually returned to normal life.

The 'Guinea Pigs' had an earlier counterpart in France, called 'Les Gueules Cassées', mutilated men who were shut away from the public gaze in a large château donated for the purpose by the American wife of a Kodak Company executive. No mirrors allowed.

At the war's end, Dr Converse came back to America to dedicate his life to the facially mutilated; gaping holes left by cancer, hideously disfigured Nazi victims, burns that left children without neck or head movement, others born with unspeakable malformations. Most of them led a life hidden away, not daring to be seen. No hospital existed for their treatment and the public was generally completely unaware of their plight.

Some patients had cleft palates that were so extensive they almost split their faces. Some looked 'elephantine'. Some were noseless and one, whom I helped personally, had no mouth, no chin, only a hole. The news of our activities had reached Lyon in France and Dr Converse was asked if he would treat the daughter of a level-crossing gatekeeper. He never refused a patient. When the girl arrived in New York she looked about five years old, stunted and gaunt, but she was actually fifteen! I decided her future was my personal obligation.

I paid for her mother to come from France to stay near her in New York for the first four months of her hospitalization so that she could be with her daily, to lessen her fears and to prepare her for nearly four years of treatment including thirty future very painful operations. The 'child' finally left New York four years later, aged nineteen, now grown to a size normal for her age. She had been taught to read, write, to speak English and to type. Returning to Lyon, she opened a secretarial bureau specializing in the English language, a heartwarming success indeed.

Converse had begun simply by taking unofficial walks through the wards of the original decrepit Bellevue Hospital in New York, now rebuilt (a magnificent place), to search its crowded corridors and wards for patients who needed his reconstructive surgery. These missions were conducted by him and his team consisting of a dental surgeon, a sculptress for new ears from cartilage, and a photographer, all volunteers.

Having met Dr Converse at Mrs Breckenridge's insistence, I came to their assistance, beginning at first by supplying the necessary photographic equipment to begin a medical record. The next *official* centre was at the Manhattan Eye and Ear Hospital. At this point the fund-raising began to gather momentum; one cheque for a million dollars came from the Avalon Foundation, generously given by Ailsa Mellon, and it was the single biggest boost to our efforts.

From it and other contributions, our own new Institute was born and with it Dr Converse established the first endowed chair of reconstructive plastic surgery in the United States. Three million dollars followed in 1970: one million from the De Witt Wallaces, proprietors of *Reader's Digest*, and two million from the Billy Rose Foundation, earmarked for the establishment of a Centre for Cranial Anomalies. Billy Rose originally wanted the money to be used for face-lifting unemployed actors! Dr Converse refused to accept it for that purpose: 'My activities are for badly disfigured people,' he said. To Billy Rose's credit, the money was used for this serious medical purpose.

Reconstructive surgery is not to be confused with nose-changing and chin-lifting. It is a surgical technique that demands the ability to visualize and create forms and shapes for both aesthetic and functional reasons.

I have remained a member of the Board of the newly situated Institute of New York City's rebuilt Bellevue Hospital, where not only surgery but inspired teaching is carried on, including, now, treatment for victims of accidents to limbs.

For the record, one of Dr Converse's most famous 'faces' was that of a French woman. He was invited to Paris in 1950 to the Elysée Palace to examine the face of the President of France's daughter-in-law, Jacqueline Auriol. Even after extensive facial surgery she was still so severely disfigured she felt quite unable to allow her two sons to see her. A miracle was needed to make her face acceptable. She had been one of the two leading female flyers in the world. While she was test-piloting a new jetplane, it suddenly nose-dived into the Seine. She was thrust against the instrument panel and was barely alive when pulled from the wreckage, the bone structure of her face having received more than two hundred fractures. Her mouth and nose were severely distorted. Her eyes miraculously escaped injury, but the rest of her face was virtually destroyed. Could Dr Converse build her a new one so she could live a normal life again? He agreed to try.

She was brought to the United States under a false name; only Mme Bonnet, wife of the French Ambassador in Washington, and I knew her true identity. Though we had never met, she accepted my help. Dr Converse's incredible skills produced a completely new face which he took several years to design and create. A bone graft from her hip, for instance, replaced the non-existent nose; and there were many more painful acts of surgery. Her new face dramatically altered her appearance; whether or not it resembled her old one was immaterial.

Yes, Mme Auriol had a new face; but a new personality also emerged to go with it. She made a remarkable post-surgery recovery and then insisted she must fly again. When she was considered physically and psychologically fit for the experience, we arranged with Larry Bell, Chairman of Bell Helicopters and on our Board, to let her come with a false identity to try to fly one of their machines. After that, I arranged for her, still incognito, to meet General Vandenberg of the US Air Force to ask him to let her fly a plane again in order to try out her nerves and her skill. Courage won.

When she felt ready to meet people again and before she returned to France, I took her on her first public outing. I chose New York's Pavilion Restaurant where I had a regular table and it would be possible to come and go without much attention. The experience nearly destroyed her willingness to face strangers again.

We were just about to slide into our seats when the French general, Pierre de Benonville, who was on a visit, recognized me. He came over and bowed low over my hand, smiling at the same time at my guest. She knew this distinguished war hero far better than I did, but he didn't recognize her and I did not reveal the identity of my guest. As soon as General de Benonville finished his meal, he came back to the table to say goodbye. Turning from me, he looked at Mme Auriol intently and apologized. 'Do forgive me for smiling at you before. For just a fleeting moment, I had the mistaken idea you were Jacqueline Auriol,' he explained as he turned on his heel and left the restaurant.

She dissolved in tears and I had trouble hiding *mine*. 'I've lost my identity. My own friends don't know me. *Who am I?* she sobbed.

She got over it in a year or so and now leads a new life, still flying.

1992 was a great year in my life; I entered quite a new world, seriously involved in academics in the University of Texas, irrevocably committed to the Harry Ransom Humanities Research Center, after being honoured by them in unique ways. I had gone on to a new pursuit, education.

I am now a rare kind of academic. My private study in London has been exactly reproduced in that building (when I walk in I am still stunned) and teaching and lectures go on inside it. There are now also Fleur Cowles Fellowships (global and in perpetuity) available to postgraduates in the three disciplines I love: art, literature and publishing. Also, every two years, a university conference for 'big brains'. The first of these was in 1994 on *The Future of the Printed Word*. It was and will always be held to honour Fleur Cowles and *Flair* magazine.

This magical place is directed by Thomas F. Staley, who became its current Director in 1988. Harry S. Ransom had given the institute its name and began its continuing growth in the world of education and research. If alive today, Mr Ransom would see how much the literary giant, Tom Staley, has added to its prestige and to the archival collections Ransom started.

The Center has a remarkable record: currently there are nine million manuscripts by such writers as Isaac Singer, John Fowles, Tom Stoppard, W. B. Yeats, Evelyn Waugh, Graham Greene, C. P. Snow, Tennessee Williams, Henry Miller and Jean Rhys, to name a few.

Of research material, there are twenty-four miles of shelf-space, one million books, five million photographs (including the oldest in the world, dated 1826), also David O. Selznick's film library (the largest anywhere, given by Jeffrey Selznick) and an extensive art library whose life and breath is fed into it by a brilliant assistant of Staley's, Sue Murphy.

Dr Staley is the acknowledged expert on James Joyce; his phenomenal forty-two articles on this author have made him required reading. He has also written fourteen books, major essays on literature and five encyclopedias on individual British writers. Since at least nineteen professional and civic activities on several continents are attributed to him, he must live much of the time in the air, where he could be finding the added peace he needs to deal with the work he turns out. Meanwhile, new friendships are made and never overlooked by him.

In that wonderful year of 1992, I had the unforgettable experience of leaving London, to step for the first time thirteen hours later inside the facsimile of my London study-office, after it was finished in the Harry Ransom Center – it was incredible to see my room exactly duplicated (including furniture, fabrics, carpet, books, paintings and photographs, even bric-à-brac). It is now in daily use for teaching and conferences. I lecture there yearly to students in my world of art, literature and publishing, mainly to those who are recipients of Fleur Cowles Fellowships. The University teaches 250,000 students in its many institutions which cover southern Texas.

In Austin, they have a remarkably young-in-heart, attractive Chancellor, William Cunningham. His Argentinian wife Isabella is a fully-fledged lawyer who also teaches advertising (she is nationally turned to in regard to advertising law). Both husband and wife are now treasured friends and their beautiful home becomes our home when my husband and I come on regular visits to the University. The privilege is a luxury.

Talking to students there is one of life's good moments. Most teaching heads of the countless colleges, as well as other executives, come from far places. I have yet to meet more than a few locals. Consequently, there is much outside influence, creating a remarkable sophistication. Robert M. Berdahl, an imaginative new President of the Universities, arrived from the West in 1993.

*   *   *

Anthropology is one of my interests, one which keeps me in the different world of education. About twenty years ago, I formed the European-based Louis S. B. Leakey Trust and became its President. It was a somewhat unplanned act of my own devising, odd for someone neither a scientist nor even a budding prototype to be so seriously involved with anthropology. But it was a natural sequence after getting to know Louis S. B. Leakey. He was an old, terribly tired man when we became friends. He would drop in for a cup of tea in London after a money-raising tour of America. He was lame (leaning on a cane after recently having been very ill) yet his champagne-like energy and youthful zest for the future were contagious.

I had first dipped my toe into Leakey waters the year before we met when I was appointed to the Board of the successful Leakey Foundation in California. After that, whenever he came to London, he would repeat his hopes for a European-based Foundation. Before he died, he had the pleasure of seeing it finally formed. After it became obvious that Leakey should be honoured in England where he had been a remarkable undergraduate and a Research Fellow at Cambridge. He had discovered young students and helped them make their contributions to the field (Jane Goodall is the most famous). Our new European Board unanimously agreed on an uncomplicated *raison d'être*: to focus on students, to give them simple means to go off as researchers to foreign locations. This made Louis Leakey, the man who dominated the science of anthropology and paleontology, very happy.

III

SAINTS AND SINNERS

FRIENDS GAVE ME THE CHANCE to know five historic figures – three 'saints': Mother Teresa, the Dalai Lama and Pope John – and to sit in on trials involving two sinners. One was *of* the merciless Nazi, Otto Abetz, the other the hearings conducted *by* the notorious Senator Joseph McCarthy.

It was the wish of two close friends, Naresh and Sunita Kumar of Calcutta, that my husband Tom and I should meet Mother Teresa, and they ultimately provided the opportunity for us to do so – in the winter of 1990, we flew to India for four days to accept their invitation.

Mr and Mrs Kumar are both very important to Mother Teresa; the beautiful Sunita has been the link between her and her co-workers for more than twenty-five years. Naresh, a top Indian industrialist, gives his support in other ways. He has an international reputation as a tennis player, after playing at Wimbledon and elsewhere, and has captained India's Davis Cup team. He still maintains his tennis contacts, commentating for Indian television every year from Wimbledon.

Mother Teresa (Agnes Gonxha Bojaxhiu) was born in 1910 in Skopje, which was then in Albania. She was the daughter of a professional businessman, who died when she was eight. The good-looking, rather plump girl decided at eighteen that her future was in India. She first had to join an order and chose an Irish one, The Sisters of Loretto. After a brief period of service in Dublin, learning English meanwhile, she made her way to Calcutta. Nineteen years later, she decided to leave the convent to work in the terrible slums on her own. She was so poor she often went hungry, but she went on to achieve miracles and her momentous work was recognized by the Vatican in 1965.

Sunita Kumar took us to meet her at the Missionaries of Charity House, a nondescript building in an alley off a typical crowded Calcutta street, like all those that are home to so many thousands of pavement-dwellers. When we arrived, the tiny, wraithlike nun emerged from a dark doorway and sat beside me. For over an hour we talked, sitting together on a rough wooden bench. I found the bench hard on *my* bones but it didn't seem so to *her* fleshless body.

My husband and I were prepared for a frail old lady but reality brought a considerable shock; the eighty-one-year-old woman looked so feeble. She had been very ill, and her stooped figure and deeply-creased face were mere skin and bones. Her customary garment, the blue-trimmed white sari, hid everything but her cheekbones and searching eyes. Yet there was a warmth and, oh! what a smile. It melted our hearts, an effect she has on everyone.

The frail woman might not have been alive to greet us if she had not been helped by Sunita Kumar. Mother Teresa had collapsed while Sunita was flying from London on her way to New York for a visit. Everyone in India had already learned about it and had heard that her illness was serious. She was in intensive care.

Sunita arrived at her New York apartment later in the day. She found a hysterical Indian staff awaiting her: 'Mother Teresa is dying! Everyone is trying to reach you from India!' they cried.

After calling India to learn exactly what the diagnosis had been and what particular specialist was needed to give emergency treatment, she set to work telephoning one recommended New York heart doctor after another, seeking advice on who would be the best virologist, the specialist needed. At nearly midnight, she tracked down the distinguished doctor.

'Would you be willing to fly to India early tomorrow morning to save the life of Mother Teresa?' she asked him.

'Of course!' he replied. 'But there are serious problems. I have no visa and my passport is out of date.'

'I will call you back,' she answered.

First she telephoned the Prime Minister of India's office, 'Couldn't it be arranged that the doctor be met and *not need a visa*?' This was readily agreed.

Next, she began to try to find a Washington friend who knew someone in the State Department who had the authority to get the passport seal to Kennedy airport early the very next morning to meet the doctor, to validate his passport before the next plane to India. Helped by an American contact in New York, the documents arrived at four o'clock in the morning. The power of Mother Teresa's name broke down bureaucratic barriers. An official seal arrived, the doctor's passport was validated and he flew out to India, where he saved Mother Teresa's life.

Sitting beside her a few months later, I held Mother Teresa's hand in mine, never forgetting for a moment that I held the hand of a saint. Tom, my husband, sitting close, asked, 'Mother, why don't they make you a saint while you are alive? Why wait until you're dead?'

Her face lifted and lit up in laughter. 'Oh, they're waiting for me to go up there first,' she replied, the first finger of her right hand motioning in a twirling climb upwards above her head.

We discussed her work, her travels, her homes for the sick and dying all over the world, two hundred and twenty of them in ninety countries! As we talked, there was the continual silent parade of nuns of all ages and sizes passing by, nodding to her as they left the building to minister to the poor in the slums of Calcutta, just as she has always done. All were in voluminous white saris, those of the Sisters edged with blue; the novitiates have to work seven years to graduate to the blue trimming, and wear all-white meanwhile. They always walked in pairs.

Before they started the day's work, they prayed. My husband watched in a doorway as they fell to their knees on the rough floors of an empty hall to celebrate an anniversary of their building. The cross was so primitive a child could have nailed the two pieces of wood over each other. It was placed on a simple chair, to be returned to a space by a wall when mass was over.

Daily, they feed crowds of starving people, and thousands of abandoned and homeless children are picked up from the streets to be fed and educated by the Sisters in the various homes Mother Teresa has built. The many who die do so in those homes with laughter and hugs, dying in dignity, unlike death on the streets. Countless dedicated Indian women enlist to help her in this work, which can be draining and cruel and certainly heartbreaking, but they get on with the job. Five million poor die each year of malnutrition and disease. To Mother Teresa and her staff there is no distinction of caste and creed.

It couldn't have been easy in India when she needed support from the Church. Many men and women in the Calcutta community whispered to us that the official Church had a hands-off attitude to her.

Some dared to suggest it was jealousy; who is *she*, they ask, to meet the Pope and Heads of State and find enough money to build and build in ninety countries? *And to receive the Nobel Prize*, as she did in 1979?

There are other problems; she finances her own global network of charities entirely through private donations, but rogues use her name to collect money which they simply pocket. These unauthorized collections, she explained, go on in Europe and the United States, even India, using her photographs and signature, so easy to copy.

An instant friendship resulted from our visit. We write to one another but with a proviso: I was never to write directly to the Mission but through the Kumars. Two men are now in gaol in Calcutta for stealing her mail and the donations enclosed. The proceeds must have been large; both men were found to have fat Swiss bank accounts. This incident reinforces my image of her. In spite of such scoundrels, she is a figure with a saintliness very few can achieve. I feel her hand softly enfolding mine as I write. Her popularity remains undimmed outside her own territorial arena. It pleased me to read in mid-1995, the national survey of candidates for the American Presidency: 'the warmth toward the still-undeclared Colin Powell was exceeded only by that for Mother Teresa'.

I felt much the same on the day in Washington when I lunched with the Dalai Lama. The way he takes one's hand in his on meeting is a good omen. He took mine gently to welcome me and then covered his and mine with his other hand, lightly pressing them down; 'enfolding' is a better word. If you believe in his aims, as I do, you feel enfolded in goodness. or should one say godliness? He is, after all, the sixty-year-old spiritual leader of every Tibetan Buddhist. Known as the Dalai Lama since he was discovered as a child, the once-named Tenzin Gyatso lives a holy life, while trying to enlist government leaders of the Western world in his struggle to free Tibet from the Chinese. Few governments seem prepared to talk to him and take up the Tibetan cause. With the market in China opening up and offering trade opportunities worth billions, the West is not inclined to offend the Chinese and put such a lucrative opportunity in jeopardy. The world outcry when Kuwait was invaded by Hussein was far greater than when China took Tibet. But the Dalai Lama goes on in his patient way, hoping that he can help free his people from serfdom, religious torment and murder by using only passive means.

The present Dalai Lama is the fourteenth to represent the earthly incarnation of the Tibetan God of Mercy. Born on 6 July 1935, the tiny boy was discovered by a travelling group of monks and proclaimed as the Dalai Lama after they found the necessary tiger stripes on his legs and his extra large ears, both valid signs of his deity. Shown a tray of objects, the two-year-old boy was also able to pick out those that had actually belonged to his predecessors.

The smile he wore when we met was wide and genuine. I was in London when the phone rang and I was asked was I free the next day, and would I like to lunch with him – in *Washington*!

The ocean between us did not prevent my accepting. I left at ten-thirty the next morning by Concorde and arrived in Washington in time for lunch at the appointed hour, having changed to a shuttle flight in New York at nine-thirty local time. I flew home to London after lunch, deciding that just having met the Dalai Lama was excitement enough for one day.

I had received a letter from him many, many months before this occasion to thank me for helping to get Nancy Nash, an American journalist who lived in Hong Kong, the recognition and money she needed to continue her work with the Buddhists living anywhere in or near to China. She is brave and a giver and deserved the Rolex honour I helped to bestow upon her when I was a member of the Rolex Jury in Geneva.

She has worked in Hong Kong long enough to speak many of the Chinese dialects, developing a personal influence sufficient for her to be able to open China's door in order to introduce Prince Philip and the World Wildlife Fund to Chinese officialdom to discuss saving the panda! What matters most to her is to persuade Buddhists to include in their pacifist religious training the need to save animals and flowers as well as human beings. The Rolex Award money has helped in her work; with millions of dollars involved, this Nobel-style prize is given not for achievement but for aspiration. Nancy Nash used the money she won to produce affordable printed literature for Buddhists. The Dalai Lama wrote to thank me after he discovered from Nancy Nash how hard I worked in getting her the prize. Hence the sudden invitation to meet him in Washington while he was there on a short visit. Nancy Nash remains close.

On an earlier occasion, I had a meeting with the saintly Pope John XXIII in the Vatican after a private audience had been arranged at short notice. The unexpected invitation had come through the auspices of a friend high in Catholic circles. Perhaps one could hardly call it private as there was also a handsome Roman prince in attendance, a snob whose style hardly befitted the friendly Pope.

I was in Rome in order to have an exhibition at Rome's Obelisk Galleries when the invitation to the Vatican arrived. I borrowed the required lace mantilla, put on the regulation black dress and soon found myself escorted through one room after another along the maze of Vatican corridors. When I reached a vast hall where hundreds of others waited, I realized that the card I held in my hand was hardly conventional. As soon as it was spotted, I received special attention, and was sped on my way from one room to the next, each with fewer and fewer people waiting, until I found myself in the elegantly panelled chamber where Ambassadors present their guests. The Pope's personal attendant came forward to whisper that I was to have a private audience – and would I follow him?

I was concerned – a private audience for which I was unprepared. What to say? In what language does one address His Holiness? I asked the Prince in attendance. '*I* speak every language,' he coolly replied.

Before I could collect my wits, Pope John and I were together in his library, he beaming with friendliness. I needn't have worried. While I remained too tongue-tied to think of an opening remark, he asked: 'And how is your exhibition going?' We soon chattered away informally, he in as much English as he could manage, before the infuriated Prince parted us, having other rooms and their audiences on his mind.

The Pope told me that he had been stopped that very day from going again to visit prisons as it was considered too dangerous for the Holy Father to go to any public places. The edict also excluded restaurants; they, too, were now 'off-bounds'. 'Tell me your favourites,' I suggested. 'We will eat in each – and drink to your great good health, one by one.'

He gave the names, then blessed whatever coins I had brought along to give as gifts to Catholic friends in Rome before he was swept out of the room, but not before the indiscreet, hopelessly impulsive hug I gave that wonderful man. It was too much for the royal aide to bear!

That evening, my husband and I and friends ate at the Pope's favourite bistro, from which he was now being kept; we went on to visit his other favourites each night in Rome. *We ate well.*

In contrast to such saintliness is a monstrous sinner, a Nazi war criminal, Otto Abetz. I sat just opposite him during his secret trial in Paris which he had ruled and abused as German Ambassador to France during World War II. I do not include Otto Abetz as any sort of friend, but the hideous scar he made on my memory was with the help of a friend, his lawyer, who knew how much it would mean to me to attend the trial in a nondescript Paris building.

It was held in camera, after Abetz had already spent eight years in a French jail. The public was not admitted, and neither was anyone connected with the press – I was only able to get in by the pretence that I was his lawyer's secretary. However, even the notebook I carried to support the deception was immediately confiscated. No notes, no record, I was warned.

A chill of evil hung over the small room where Abetz was tried, and I sat there in rigid, frozen silence throughout. A few feet directly opposite me sat the war criminal himself. Listening to his defence – the claim that he saved more lives than he condemned – Abetz suddenly sprang to his feet shouting: 'Stop this trial! Stop! Stop!' His final outburst was: 'Stop this nonsense. If I had the chance I'd do it all over again, I would do exactly the same!' He wasn't ashamed of his past, nor interested in avoiding the truth. He was proud.

In the moments that followed, my mind went back to a slim little book I had just finished reading the week before (and can never forget) by a Jewish lady doctor who described how thousands had been shunted into cattle-cars from Paris depots – shoved in tightly to force them to stand upright, cheek to cheek for the long journey. The only air they could breathe came through cracks in the wooden sides. If they needed to urinate or defecate they had to do it as they stood. *The sole purpose of the Nazis, her book was intended to point out, was to change each man, woman and child from a human being to an animal as fast as methodically possible!*

When Abetz shouted out his infamous statement, a hush fell on the courtroom. Every face looked shattered. His defenders were shocked into silence.

His story is typical of a dedicated Nazi. He was born on 26 May 1903 in Karlsruhe, near Mannheim, the port and city at the confluence of the Rhine and the Neckar rivers, a well-known centre of Nazi activities. He became involved in the Hitler Youth Movement and eventually joined the German Foreign Office, where he earned the admiration and respect of those in high places. He was sent to Paris as a so-called 'expert on France' in the late 1930s, but was expelled in the summer of 1939 for Fifth Column activities. He returned to France in 1940 with ambassadorial status, a position awarded him personally by Hitler's Foreign Minister Ribbentrop. The two men had much in common: Abetz, like Ribbentrop, was a man with exquisite manners and an exquisitely cruel heart.

He was 'expelled' for a second time in 1944 by the advancing Allied armies. His final arrest came in 1945, in Germany; he was brought back to be imprisoned in a French jail to await the trial which I was now witnessing. During the eight-year delay his hair had turned white.

Multiple charges against him included looting and incitement to kidnap, the deporting of Jewish people, being accessory to their murder, the taking and shooting of hostages and involvement in the assassination of the French resistance hero, Georges Mandel. He had ruled Paris with great cruelty. His trial lasted nearly two weeks, and the last day was one which I cannot erase from memory.

I finally found out by secret means that Abetz was sentenced to twenty years of hard labour, yet he was released in eight years when his health failed. Unlike his victims, he was allowed to go home to die, instead of in a gas chamber. Whatever happened to his wife is an unanswered question.

A recent study of Vichy art-confiscation* alleges that Abetz was implicated in the looting of French art and literature, abetted by his assistant, his French wife.

I found a fitting epitaph for this sinner in Edward Lucie-Smith's

* *The Rape of Europe* by Lynn A. Nicholas, published by Macmillan, 1994.

book, *Art Anecdotes*. He was writing of Picasso, who was being visited during the German occupation by the cool German Ambassador. When Otto Abetz saw a photograph on Picasso's studio wall of the huge, gruesome painted outcry against war, *Guernica*, he exclaimed: 'Oh, so it was *you*, Monsieur Picasso, who did that!'

'No,' came Picasso's swift response, '*it was you.*'

Le Comte de Chambrun, his defence lawyer, is a direct descendant of Lafayette; he prides himself on his family's ownership of the Baccarat crystal company for nearly three centuries (it was sold in 1993). He has a large legal practice.

His decision to defend Abetz was obviously linked to his long attempt to vindicate the name of Pierre Laval, the father of his wife, José Laval. Le Comte de Chambrun claims Laval was a patriot and that he became a collaborator only in order to save lives, even of Jews. He has authored book after book, and is now working on an encyclopedia of the history of the German occupation. His huge office on the Champs Elysées has the atmosphere of a library, filled to over-flowing with references, books and letters, Laval-data and documentation. He insists he will never stop trying to clear Laval's name.

America's own terrible sinner was Senator Joseph McCarthy. If self-induced martyrdom can be considered peril, I *was* in hallucinatory peril when I decided in 1953 that I must be the one to assassinate the Senator. My arrest would follow, so would headlines. Although some would call my action commendable, I would be tried for premeditated murder.

I had just returned from Egypt, where I had met Gamal Abdel Nasser.* My former husband, Mike Cowles, met me at the airport and insisted: 'No matter what has happened in Cairo, as an editor you must just go home and watch television, to see what the despicable McCarthy is doing to America while insisting he is saving it from Communism. Washington can wait.'

So instead of flying to make my report to President Eisenhower I remained in New York, glued to my TV set, a new daytime experience, for two full, harrowing days. I choked with rage every time I heard

---

* See Gamel Abdel Nasser, page 156.

McCarthy's tirades and his bullying of helpless witnesses. I vowed vengeance. I simply had to attend the Senate Committee hearings. 'Not even a fly could get wedged in,' I was told. But I was not put off, and the influence we had in Washington was quickly mustered. The next day a chair was hastily placed directly behind the Chairman of the Senate Committee, Senator Stuart Symington. A few short feet away, directly facing me across the narrow table, was the despicable Joseph McCarthy, the man Harry Truman called a moral pygmy.

On each side of him sat two smirking henchmen, Messrs Cohn and Schine. And next but one, a future Attorney General and Presidential candidate, Senator Robert Kennedy, later to be assassinated. It may seem hard to realize today that a Kennedy brother was a part of Senator McCarthy's infamous 'prosecuting team', but Harry Truman never forgot Bobby's role. In Merle Miller's *Plain Thinking* Truman commented: 'I never liked that boy and I never will . . . He worked for old Joe McCarthy, you know, and when old Joe was tearing up the Constitution of the country, that boy couldn't say enough for him.'

A single day at the McCarthy hearing was all I could take. Seemingly strong men were reduced to mumbling incoherence by brutal bullying and fear. The gentlemanly defence lawyer, Joseph Nye Welch, was hardly a match for the hostile and menacing McCarthy and his men: lies after lies fired like missiles, with little effective response to shoot them down. I kept thinking of *Darkness at Noon*, Arthur Koestler's book on the Moscow trials. I left the hearing in a melancholy mood. That McCarthy's lip curled so quickly, that he could remain unchecked, battering victim after victim, I felt was too much to bear. His character assassination of men and women was often merely a device to grab the headlines. I was also upset by the applause he received from many sources. Isolationists and extreme right-wingers, John Birch Society members for instance, even launched a brief campaign to back him as a candidate for the Presidency. The hero of the Pacific war against Japan, General Douglas McArthur, was a supporter.

Why doesn't someone assassinate McCarthy, I wondered. Obsessed, I decided that I was the best possible person to do it. I could afford the best legal counsel, I wasn't one of his vengeful victims, it would be a trial of good against evil. It never occurred to me that I had never held a gun in my hand. Only once had I ever been in a U.S. court, and then only as a witness in a traffic case. Even being a witness for the defence had been a frightening experience. Killing, for any reason, had always been repugnant to me, even killing spiders, but when I explained my decision to Mike Cowles, he didn't bat an eyelid or try to dissuade me because, unknown to me, he had a plan in mind. We were ready to fly to Des Moines the next morning for our regular four-day monthly visit to meet the staff of two of the Cowles papers, *The Des Moines Register* and *Des Moines Tribune*. They had all been briefed before I appeared. 'Don't cross words with Fleur, just agree politely. Be understanding. Don't force her to take a stand.'

So, when I calmly announced my decision to kill McCarthy, no one demurred, except one of the editors, who put paid to the crazy notion simply by insisting on knowing exactly how I intended to do it. 'With a gun? With a knife? How? How?'

I finally realized I couldn't use any weapon. In a few days sanity returned. They had done the job well by withholding derision or guffaws. I never mentioned the idea again and to everyone's credit, neither did anyone else.

A year later McCarthy lost his chairmanship of the Senate Committee, having been condemned in a Senate resolution. President Eisenhower confirmed the man's demise from any public role by announcing: 'The year began with McCarthy riding high and ended with his being practically a political cipher,' and that was putting it kindly.

Three years later, in May 1957, McCarthy died, some said of cancer, but it was officially declared of natural causes. He did love his alcohol. He did at least die discredited after a sad, sad moment in the United States' political history. America's reputation could now slowly recover.

For me, the Senate's action after his death was inexplicable, unacceptable and unforgivable: they gave his body a place of honour in the Senate, followed by a memorial service for a hero. He had started his political life far, far on the left, but changed his party of liberation to the more popular extreme right. Chasing Communists became the better vote-getter.

These honours came to him despite the fact that for nearly a dozen years he threatened the Senate, ridiculed the President's foreign policies, captured sensational headlines and, worst of all, for a long time used merciless techniques to claim he was single-handedly 'destroying' Communism. Such malevolence is trying to resurface today in

Nationalist and pseudo-Nazi campaigns, in terrorism and such night-marish bombings as in Oklahoma.

At a dinner given for me years later by CIA Director John Alex McCone, I was seated next to Stuart Symington who had chaired the Senate's McCarthy hearings. I raffishly described my 'near-murder' of McCarthy to him, at which he joked: 'Gosh, Fleur, aren't you glad you didn't? You'd have been the Jack Ruby of the McCarthy era!'

IV

HEADS OF STATE

W HEN I THINK OF presidential men, I sometimes think of
Plato, that maestro of political philosophers. In writing this
chapter, 'Heads of State', I asked myself an interesting question: what would Plato have made of our declining democracies, the
calibre of the new emerging Heads of State, the resulting cynicism
about politics today and the democratic problems caused by America's
immensity, where citizens think as *states* not as a *nation*, and of the
aims and values of the new Europe where the vision is the end of the
nation states, to be replaced by a federal European state. It would be
fascinating to sit at Plato's feet to hear him pronounce on such a world
and *our* forms of democracy. *Democracy is, after all, just an invention.
If we lose it, will it ever again be re-invented?*

In his time, Plato thought the best form of government would be
an Aristocracy not elected by citizens, the best and wisest of a *ruling*
class who would be *chosen* to be the government. Today, if we were
to look for aristocrats to govern us, few would accept.

Plato thought every Greek had the right, or should at least have
been given the democratic right, to become a member of the ruling
class. In his system, gifted young people would be chosen for special
education by the state, a policy adopted by Soviet Russia after the last
war in establishing the University of Siberia. There, youngsters with
mathematical flair or excellence in science were taken with their parents
to live in a newly-built Siberian town where they were groomed as
future students in the new University. After graduation, many had to
work *locally*, in different ways, often by exploring for and extracting
uranium. Meanwhile, they had to learn perfect English.

Through the years, I have met and judged many Heads of State,
some of them women. All offered different versions of the democracy
they espoused. In Brazil I watched candidate Kubitschek on his presidential campaign. The one speech he made constantly was brief, and

effective. He lit a candle, held it high in his hand; 'I shall light the way!' Then in the other hand, he raised a broom aloft; 'I shall sweep Brazil clean!' He not only won but built Brasilia as the country's capital, a deed considered as eccentric as the man himself. But he was right to choose the location he did, in the heart of his vast country.

I never knew Franklin D. Roosevelt, but I have never overlooked the chance to learn more about him; for example, that his campaign slogan of '3 R's' – Relief, Recovery and Reform – came from the 'R' in his first name. He became our first 'fireside' orator and others have copied him, not all of them successfully. To him, words meant ideas. The Rooseveltian style of speech was essential at a time when industry, agriculture and the banking system were all in chaos. The Great Depression was ended with his New Deal for America heralded by the unforgettable words: 'The only thing we have to fear is fear itself.' A new agenda was created and the country put on its feet before the United States entered the war in 1941. Since then, I have got to know most American Presidents. The following are those whom I would call my friends. Some live on in slogans, some in deeds.

Harry S. Truman, the Missouri farm boy, could well have fulfilled Plato's criterion as 'the wisest man in the state' but the little man only became President of the United States by a trick of fate, Franklin D. Roosevelt's sudden death. His wisdom proved to be such that he came down on the right side of all but one of the moral issues of his day (the order for the second bomb at Nagasaki). Though tough, he was highly emotional, a home-loving, decent man, who against his wishes had to bear seeing his family lose its privacy. What's more, could he have enjoyed slipping unexpectedly into Roosevelt's famous shoes?

Dwight D. Eisenhower might also have met Plato's description in his first term of office, after being Europe's most admired man as Commander-in-Chief of the Allied Armed Forces. Both American political parties tried to persuade him to become their candidate. Republicans won.

I met General Eisenhower for the first time when visiting him at SHAPE Headquarters outside Paris, one of many who went hoping to persuade the unwilling soldier to bring his qualities to politics by running for the Presidency. It led me to a series of fascinating experiences. As a journalist, calling on him there would have been normal practice, but there was a political purpose as well. The Republican Party urged many personalities from the US to visit and try to persuade Eisenhower to become their next Presidential candidate. The General was not keen to take on the role and, in any case, wasn't committed to *either* party. He wanted nothing more than to leave war-ravaged Europe and return to his Gettysburg farm – and the golf he loved.

The Republicans netted him in the end because the good man felt he must help to defeat a potential rival, Senator Taft, whom he considered a dangerous right-winger. Eisenhower was the tenth general to become an American president; he never aspired to the post, but a massive display of adulation from the Americans who called on him had its effect. He finally came home to pursue the unfamiliar round of whistle-stops and endless speeches as a Presidential hopeful, and in the end, America elected the perfect President. Eisenhower was needed at that historic moment; he was the one man whose popularity abroad could help heal the wounds of war.

His campaign was coloured by charming amateurism, which proved a great asset at the starting gate. Once, on a short journey with him on the campaign trail in Denver, I had a glimpse of the aspiring Vice-President, Richard Nixon, and saw how his machine-tooled brain worked as he went before widely differing groups. He altered his speech on an identical subject from *pro* to *con*, often within the same hotel on different floors, getting votes from *both* sides.

On one of Eisenhower's campaign whistle-stops in Wisconsin, his exhibition of camaraderie for the vile Senator McCarthy caused me distress. He actually put his arm around the man who had just finished a speech in which he insulted the great General George Marshall, the man responsible for bringing Eisenhower's army career to its peak. Calling Marshall a Communist was, for me and countless others, quite unforgivable, although some did find it understandable for an inexperienced politician to do what he was told to do by political bosses – McCarthy was to be 'treated nicely' so as to retain his wide support. Unfortunately, Eisenhower agreed to this expedient.

After he became President, I saw Eisenhower frequently, normally at early morning meetings in the Oval Room, usually followed by chats on the floor above with the somewhat miscast Mamie Eisenhower, still in bed. He soon realized how many friendly contacts I had in important places and this led to 'errands for the President', in Iran, Cyprus, Greece and Brazil. John Foster Dulles, Secretary of State, was likely to be asked to sit in when I made my Oval Room reports. On such occasions, Eisenhower's frank support for me irked Dulles, who although he was completely friendly and even cordial, took every opportunity to use his veto, even if what I had done accorded with his advice and had his blessing. Being a member of the President's 'club' was exciting, but it did not ensure automatic entry into the Dulles camp.

The leader and peacemaker role fitted Eisenhower well, but this splendid hero of World War II lost his prized reputation by being railroaded into accepting a second term. He had been coerced by the argument that the Republican Party *needed him*, although he thought he had fulfilled his mission and promise in the one term. He did not enjoy the role. His second term seriously reduced his standing; if he had retired, as he actually longed to do, his record would be untarnished. It was sacrificed to win the second election for the Republicans.

Of all the Presidents, I knew him best, and I owe much to him. He appointed me Ambassador to the Coronation of Queen Elizabeth II, and later sent me as his personal emissary on countless missions, a very American practice: for instance, to Greece on the Cyprus issue, which proved fascinating and cemented my friendships with the Greek Royal family and two of Greece's Prime Ministers. I got close enough to Gamal Abdel Nasser and his family of five children and his shy wife to know them well, and became acquainted with Brazil's President Vargas. Doors to him were opened so splendidly for me by Osvaldo Aranha. Through Eisenhower, I went to the Korean War front as an observer, a period covered in the chapter I have called 'Perils of Friendship'.

Bernard Baruch was always so pleased when I did anything for Eisenhower, because he never gave up wanting to see me become a fulltime diplomat. One piece of advice, written by hand from Little Hobcaw, his shooting lodge in South Carolina, read: 'Lay low and keep quiet; your number will come up. Best to you. You rate OK in my book and my book is a good book.' Baruch also warned me: 'Never forget it, Fleur, behind Ike's grin is a man of iron.' However, the truth is that I never really wanted to give up being an editor and gratefully took on Presidential 'errands' instead, which allowed me to remain in publishing.

I actually received my first White House assignment long before – from Harry Truman immediately after he became President. Like most good things in my life, a friend was responsible for this plum. It fell into my lap while I was in Washington, writing speeches for the War Production Board, having added years to my age to get the job.

The establishment of the Famine Emergency Committee, one of Truman's first acts in office, was on the advice given by Washington's Wartime Advertising Council. Anthony Hyde, now in London, was a principal. Eugene Meyer, who then published the *Washington Post*, father of its present publisher, Katherine Graham, took the suggestion of the Wartime Council to the President, persuading him to create such a unit. 'To feed starving Europe is your first job,' he counselled. He also advised Truman to invite ex-President Herbert Hoover to be its Chairman and recommended I be taken on for the White House role. Hoover hadn't set foot in the White House for sixteen years since leaving as a very unpopular President, but Meyer persuaded him to change his mind.

Luckily, President Truman accepted me on Eugene Meyer's recommendation: my White House job required a good deal of lobbying, to persuade wheat growers to promise wheat at the *source* to send to Europe. I spoke countrywide on radio and on one occasion to all schoolchildren in the United States. On another special broadcast I asked them to persuade their parents to set an extra place at table to feed a hungry child and to donate what they didn't actually eat to hungry Europe. This was purely propaganda; its real purpose was to embarrass wheat growers into cooperating with the Famine group.

On one weary day when I was having difficulties with the Secretary of Agriculture, Clinton Anderson, I cornered him in the White House lift as we were *en route* to our next Committee meeting. I insisted that he stop holding out, that he must give his promise (despite his fears for his mid-Western votes) to be in favour of a quota system to get the wheat. *He said yes and we got the wheat.*

I had been sharp-witted enough to have wangled a permit to fly to

Europe just before VE Day, the first civilian American woman to get there before the fighting had stopped. The shock of the experience was helpful in those White House days. My work for the Famine Emergency involved public relations, marshalling top journalists and broadcasters to awaken a nation which didn't know war firsthand and had never experienced starvation to release aid for Europe. After I had been to Britain, France, Holland and Belgium I returned so distressed by the spectacle of destruction and haunted faces that I longed to do something really useful.

Being thin for *fashionable* reasons was wrong after seeing people who hadn't eaten properly for years. I was thrilled to see millions of tons of wheat finally shipped to Europe. I used to go exhausted to my hotel after each fourteen-hour day, but the results were worth it. It was impossible to erase the memory of the exhausted, grey people and blue-faced children I'd seen on my visit to Europe. I had been the lucky foreigner, warmly dressed. I wore *stockings*, few women had any. I could get *away* but they were prisoners of geography – as they continue to be in so many war-torn areas today.

I recently re-read an ageing newspaper clipping dated 7 August 1946, in which I was asked by Martha Ellyn of the *Washington Post* why I worked so hard. 'To get back my peace of mind,' I replied.

I greatly enjoyed every contact with Truman but I really got to know him best after he left the Presidency. I had spent nearly a year in the White House, seeing evidence of Harry Truman's humanity and noting how quickly he became accustomed to the Presidency, but our later meetings after he left Washington to return happily to Independence, Missouri, remain more vivid.

One took place in New York City's Pavilion restaurant when Tom, my husband, and I were in America. We lunched with the President and Mrs Truman and Mr and Mrs Victor Weybright. Truman and I reminisced about his visit to England in 1956 when he went to receive an honorary degree from Oxford University. I was by then living in London and remembered the press coverage of the modest man I could still recall peering over his silver-rimmed, old-fashioned glasses under floppy velvet headgear, accepting the honour on this, his only visit to Britain. Americans were proud of him and of the press's friendly, even affectionate, reaction to him and his speech.

Sitting next to him years later in the restaurant, I remembered that occasion and asked, 'Why haven't you ever returned to England?'

'Why should I do that?'

'Because people love you there,' I said. 'Have you any idea what an impact you made on the Oxford visit?'

'No, of course not. You don't mean to say I'm popular in England?'

'Just come back and find out. Your heart would feel good!'

'Are you *sure*?' he demanded.

'Of course I am, or I wouldn't say so,' I insisted.

'Then do me a favour, will you?' he asked, pressing his hand firmly on mine. 'Do me a great favour.'

'Of course, anything you ask. What would you like me to do?'

'Go and tell Bess,' he quietly suggested.

I changed places with my husband for a few minutes, and left Bess beaming.

Another question I asked him at this same luncheon was about his controversial decision to order dropping the second A-bomb on Nagasaki.

'Did it ever bother you, knowing the devastation of the first one?' I asked him.

'No,' he snapped back, 'I never lost any sleep over that one. I saved the lives of at least 100,000 American soldiers. That was reason enough.'

This decision, supposedly taken by this man all alone in a vast War Room was probably as momentous as any President ever faced, but Truman simply 'wrote off' Hiroshima and Nagasaki. To him, it was an essential military strategy to save the lives of so many men who would otherwise have been mown down as they waded through the lapping waters on Japanese beachheads.

He had an iron backbone. 'Once I made a decision, I sent it on a one-way journey in my mind,' was his explanation.

Another conversation with him took place in Athens after the funeral of King Paul of Greece. President Lyndon Johnson had sent Lady Bird as his *personal* representative and Harry Truman went to represent the American people. I was there as a close friend of the Greek royal family, deeply distressed by the King's death.

The funeral was haunting for everyone who loved the King, and the ceremony was exhaustingly long. We had to be seated very early in the morning at the Greek Orthodox Church, which is tucked down at the lowest point of the city of Athens. After the service we were required to walk behind the coffin which was carried aloft in a procession led by the obviously frail seventy-year-old Archbishop of Greece. The heroic old man held high a heavy sacred icon as he walked up, up, up the hill to the centre of Athens and then again uphill to the top of the city to the Hilton Hotel, crowds on all sides. The coffin was then placed on an army catafalque and guests were seated in black limousines for the slow procession to Tatoi, the country home of the royal family, where lunch was served hours later.

When I went to pay my personal respects to Harry Truman the next morning at the Hilton Hotel, I found him looking old and tired, but he was his usual bluff self when I showed how concerned I was that he'd had the long hard walk from church to hotel.

'How did you survive?' I asked.

'Why should I be tired? Not me. Who walked? I didn't. I just sat in a comfortable car, following all of you.'

'What about food? You must have starved waiting until nearly four o'clock to eat after such an early breakfast.'

'Who starved? Not me! I had my own chicken sandwiches.'

The image of a former President of the United States sitting in the back of a big black limousine munching away on sandwiches out of a brown paper bag seems a wonderful way to remember the great man.

Henry Labouisse was the American Ambassador on post at the time of the funeral. He and his wife, Eva Curie, who was the famous author, daughter of Marie Curie the discoverer of radium, had gone to the airport prepared to greet a seriously exhausted former President after the long air journey of those days. They reminded him that the hotel was very comfortable and not far away, reassuring him that he would soon be able to rest.

'Hell, no! I don't want to go to the hotel. Take me to the Acropolis first!' he demanded.

Nothing that Eva Labouisse could say about the steep climb up the hills to these ruins daunted him: they had to go to this Greek monument first. He set off like a mountain goat, knowing the dates and all pertinent details of the site. I was reminded of former Secretary of State Dean Acheson's opinion that 'Harry Truman knows more about history than Roosevelt and Churchill combined'. Truman loved to read, especially American history, but he had managed Greek history too.

On yet another occasion, I asked Truman what *he* considered his most important single act as President. Without hesitation he replied, 'My decision to go into Korea.' It had been his angry retort to the first major thrust of the Soviets. 'We hadn't written South Korea into our announced list of areas of the world to defend, so the North Koreans moved in. We had to get them out!' he explained. He showed courage in declaring war but he chose to do it through the United Nations so they too would always be identified with that event.

He died in 1972, aged eighty-eight, a President of big decisions. His death brought to light the charming letter he wrote his mother, Martha, on 12 April 1945, when Roosevelt died, having that *same day* been declared by doctors to be 'in good health'. 'Dear Mama, it was the only time in my life I think that I ever felt as if I'd had a real shock. I hurried to the White House to see the President and when I arrived I found *I* was President. No one in the history of our country ever had it happen in just that way. All the stars and the planets fell upon me.' (He had added, 'and a load of Hay'.)

Against all the political pollsters' opinions and the gamblers' odds, he experienced the pleasure of winning the Presidency on his own merits when he ran for re-election in 1948.

He was a very different man during his first days in the White House, insecure and uncertain. I was there and saw his insecurity quickly evaporate; nervousness turned to firm control, sometimes, even, larded with arrogance. At his very first visit to Congress as President, jittery and unsure, he began to speak immediately. 'Wait!' admonished Sam Rayburn, the Speaker of the House. 'Wait, Harry, I have to introduce you first.' He was so troubled by the global problems he told one of his visitors, 'The world has fallen on me.'

The former haberdasher was surely one of America's greatest Presidents – for many reasons: he had recognized the value of the UN and used it to protect South Korea, preventing the action from becoming merely a US intervention. He dismissed General MacArthur. He stopped Tito from moving into Trieste. He saved Europe after the fighting ended when he backed the Marshall Plan. He sent the Mediterranean fleet into the Persian Gulf, heading off a Soviet thrust into Iran, a favour that Iran soon forgot.

He concluded the NATO Treaty; what better has superseded it? He gave the go-ahead to the Berlin Airlift, proving to Russia that the US wasn't fooling when it came to American rights in Europe.

His continued collaboration with British intelligence is still intact despite the fading relationship with America, and despite the fact that he was totally ignorant of intelligence when fate sent him to the White House.

He was an old-fashioned family man, and the Presidency didn't go to his head. An insane man made an attempt to kill him but that did not deter him. He could, and did, take his 'constitutional' on the streets of Washington every day and even, at a fast clip, on Park Avenue in New York City when there on UN visits, one lone detective trailing behind him. He was the last President to know such freedom.

He may be as well remembered for his foibles, especially his rage when an unfavourable review of his daughter Margaret's voice appeared. What he thought of the critics became headline news when he virtually slammed them for doing so.

Bernard Baruch's best friend was Winston Churchill, so I often heard him being discussed. Although Churchill was some four years younger than the venerable Baruch, they were near enough in age and experience to be genuinely close partners. Baruch died after Churchill but he felt younger and, regardless of the difference of those few years, the two touchingly chose to act like nannies towards each other. Baruch's home in New York was Churchill's home on American visits and on these occasions I had the good fortune to see him. Baruch also took me on a visit to Churchill at Chartwell after I moved to London.

Churchill's last visit to America had been Baruch's idea; he arranged for him to make a major speech at Boston's Massachusetts Institute of Technology, to be sure Britain's great man left a memorable statement for Americans in case he was unable to come again. Churchill arrived a week before the date of the speech with a tightly packed schedule for the time preceding the trip to Boston. The days before and after his arrival were always worrying for Baruch. Everyone wanted, or thought they needed, to see Winston Churchill.

Because I had already met Churchill, Baruch telephoned to shout

out to me, a week before his arrival: 'You stay away this time!' and he kept calling me daily to repeat the command. It was clear I was always on Baruch's mind but that he was frustrated by the avalanche of appointments stacking up for his visitor.

I had never ever raised the matter. 'Don't worry,' I continually placated him. 'Get me off your mind, I *understand*,' feeling a bit like Pagliacci, but proud of my good grace.

The day before their departure for Boston, he called again. 'Are you busy at tea-time?'

'I'll be there!' I responded. At the stroke of four-thirty I made my way through the barrage of police, secret service and other guards and found myself in the long hall of his elegant apartment. There I found him dressed at that early hour in white tie and tails for the stag dinner to be held three hours later in honour of his guest. He barely nodded, pacing back and forth nonstop, deadly pale. 'What has happened?' I demanded. 'You look ill – or is Mr Churchill ill?'

'No. He's fine, but *I* am not. Three days from tonight he has to deliver his speech. He hasn't even put pen to paper or even dictated a word. It is all my fault for arranging a trip which will now be a failure,' he snapped back at me.

'*Please*. Sit down. Let's discuss it,' I begged. 'Stop worrying. This man's capacity to write a speech is legendary and he tosses one off *brilliantly. Stop worrying.*'

That Churchill came though with his speech two days later at MIT is a matter of history, but the worried Baruch simply couldn't risk it. I pushed him into his favourite chair in his drawing room, pulled another one up so close our knees touched, urging him to shut his eyes and rest.

Suddenly, a look of surprise crossed his pale face. I felt a presence beside me. I looked down and saw two pink waxy bare feet. Above them was Churchill, dressed in a dangerously small towel. There wasn't even a greeting from him, just a grunt as he started to navigate the room, stomping about between and around furniture like a large cat, noisily muttering his irritation about having to write a speech. 'I'd rather play gin-rummy,' he complained.

He finally returned to the door, as we watched, speechless. One hand held the towel firmly in place, the other gripped a huge cigar. He waved, said farewell to me by my name and trotted out to disappear down the hall. Baruch was ready to collapse. His only reaction, though, was to insist that I swear I would never tell anyone about this incident. 'This never happened,' he repeated and repeated. Reluctantly, I agreed, but thought what a delightful anecdote I was being asked to bottle up for ever. However, I was unexpectedly released from this promise a few months later. Baruch and I were both in Paris and I went to have a cup of tea with him at the Ritz. Churchill's son, Randolph, also arrived. Staring at me, he began, without hesitation: 'What a hilarious greeting you got from my father when he was in New York.' Baruch turned pale again.

'How do you know?' I demanded. 'Let me establish one thing right here and now – that is that you never heard about it from me!'

Randolph refused to say how he knew the story, and I never discovered the source of his information. He even boasted that he had written about it! This revelation freed me from my promise.

On a later occasion, I went to Chequers with Baruch. At luncheon I was seated at Churchill's right, a doubtful honour because he hated small talk. This time proved no exception so I finally decided to 'jump in' and discuss that New York incident after other chatter failed to interest him.

'You *do* know, Mr Churchill, that I never told your son that story about the last time I saw you in New York?'

'*What* story?' he demanded.

'Oh, you know, the time you were wearing only a towel in Mr Baruch's drawing room,' I began.

A red-faced, very angry man looked straight at me and erupted: 'That's a g.d. lie! It *never* happened,' he thundered as he turned to concentrate on his roast beef and brandy. The coolness disappeared in a very few moments, but my equilibrium was temporarily shattered.

After lunch that same day we had a personally conducted tour of the beautiful house and grounds. It was fascinating to see that only a bust of Napoleon Bonaparte faced him on his desk as he sat in his chair.

In the garden later, Churchill pronounced on every detail as we walked about. 'This is the wall I built myself, brick by brick . . . those are my goldfish and I know each one by name. Come and see them answer my call . . . here's where I like to sit and make decisions . . . this is a very steep step, dear, don't fall!' he warned Baruch, in unabashed sweetness, man to man.

All the time he was wearing his famous sky-blue siren suit, padding about in gold-initialled black velvet slippers. His complexion was white, his eyes blue. We finally reached his studio, a long, narrow basement room lit by windows at the far end. A huge globe, the gift of an American, was the room's only adornment unless one counted as decor the meticulous arrangement of paints on a table. It was a luxury to see where and how he worked. I had already admired his skill from the painting he gave to Baruch, one of the few ever given.

Two easels stood side by side in the basement studio: on one, he had placed a photograph, blown up to the exact size of the canvas he was working on. On the second easel, his painting of the same scene. Churchill's daughter, the delightful Mary, Lady Soames, DBE, wrote of this in her remarkable book about her father, discussing this twin-easel method and pointing out that it was a technique following the advice and practice of his favourite painter, Walter Sickert.

Years after the Churchill towel story, I invited two widows to lunch at my home in London, Lady Spencer Churchill and Mrs Edward R. Murrow. It was an occasion to remember because, like all great ladies, Lady Churchill's mind had great clarity, not always an attribute of the ageing. Anecdotes were a favoured topic, so we three did a lot of reminiscing. Lady Churchill greatly enjoyed the Baruch story, 'the story that wasn't', but when I told her about her husband's reaction, she replied: 'Oh, that's explainable. My husband always called something he didn't like a *lie*!'

I have carefully banked the copy (given me in confidence) of the Official Top Secret minutes which were written after my visit in the early fifties to the Colonial Office in London, a three-page report of a meeting which was held there 'at the direct request of President Eisenhower, whose confidence she enjoyed'.

It spells out in detail what my mission involved after the President asked me to do anything possible to see that the Enosis issue be withdrawn from the United Nations. I was warmly thanked for 'probably having influenced British policy'.

I also filed with it a letter from Lord Colyton, former Colonial Secretary, and another written by Stephan Stephanopoulos, then President of Greece; thanking me – for 'efforts on the Cyprus question, which always moves my countrymen deeply'. Not long after, I was decorated at dinner with the Order of Bienfaisance by King Paul of Greece.

Churchill thought I was too young to be 'official', I was later told.

Could great men be socially cruel? I have a personal recollection: a face-to-face encounter with General de Gaulle after his return as Head of State in Paris.

A close friend of his, editor of a Paris newspaper, invited him to meet the Associate Editor (me) of *Look* magazine, in the USA. Luncheon was secretly arranged in a small bistro alongside the Seine, just opposite beautiful Ile St Louis, in a private room on the floor above the public restaurant, entered by a side door. The two of us sat there awaiting his arrival.

I'll never forget his face as he entered the room and saw a female editor too young, even too glamorous, not his expectation! His manner changed, talk was difficult. A political discussion was met in monosyllables, often curt.

I suddenly exploded and blurted out: 'Obviously you don't like Americans!'

'No, I don't,' he replied as he rose, opened the door and slowly trod heavily down the stairs. The sounds grew dim as he arrived at the busy Paris street, having left a half-eaten meal on the table.

A very different man rose to pre-eminence in Iran in the 1950s – an elderly, frail, long-nosed man with a haunted look, his eyes like laser-lit buttons, who had recently been the Prime Minister. On one of my trips to Teheran, he provided me with a memory which, after all these years, is still fresh. Mohammed Mossadeq was a man who loved his bed, and I don't mean of roses.

I met this Head of State in his Teheran prison in the early fifties; he was in his tiny cell, waiting to be carried (he refused to walk) to face trial for treason. I had been given permission to see him by General Zahedi, the Prime Minister, the father of my great friend, Ardeshir Zahedi, who was then the equerry who accompanied the Shah on the visit to the United States that I had arranged.* I hadn't had time to absorb all the facts about Mossadeq's case before being ushered into his tiny cell. There I found an obviously insane man sitting crosslegged on top of his unmade prison cot, unshaven, wearing crumpled pyjamas. The pyjamas and cot would have been familiar to his countrymen. Though shocked, I stepped slowly towards the extraordinary figure; I offered my hand, gave my name and expressed my thanks for his willingness to see me. He hadn't, of course, even been asked for consent. He refused my hand, just turned his head high and screeched a loud cackling laugh at me. For ten or fifteen minutes (they felt like years) I tried to pretend I didn't mind his loud laughter whenever I spoke. He knew English, but preferred French. It made no difference what I said. If I stopped to control my thoughts, the silence was broken by even louder cackles.

Eventually, feeling close to madness myself, I slowly backed out of the cell and went directly to the courtroom where a seat for me had been arranged. Mossadeq was soon carried in by two men, just as I had left him, in the same crosslegged seated position, and was placed in the defendant's chair.

This time he did speak, making the occasional impassioned plea in his own defence (as well as giving vent to sporadic cackles). At other times he simply sat there, leaning his head on his right hand, radiating boredom. All this was good for the press. The leading newspaper's circulation went up eighty per cent. Two peacocks strutted and shouted in the garden outside the court, acting as if they, too, were Mossadeqs.

He was found guilty in August 1953 and spent three years in prison. He then lived out the rest of his life under house arrest, where he returned to his experiments in homeopathic medicine, which he had begun thirty years earlier when Reza Shah's father had put him under house arrest the first time.

His immense personal popularity had forced the Shah to make him Prime Minister in 1951 but a CIA-supported military group ousted him in 1953 after he began to favour Russia. The once pin-striped aristocrat slowly became the man I saw, the man who had humiliatingly brought about the temporary demise of the Shah and tried hard to wreck the oil industry, preferring Russia to the West. He used to

* He later became Ambassador to the UK and USA. See Zahedi, page 000 and the Shah of Iran, page 211.

boast that he was, after all, the one true royal, claiming that his own great-grandfather had been a Shah of a former dynasty. With a gleam in his eye he used to refer to the Shah as a tyrannical impostor.

When alarm bells rang in Washington over the oil crisis he precipitated, Averell Harriman went to Iran as the President's personal representative to discuss the disastrous situation with Mossadeq. He had the embarrassment of meeting him in his bedroom, not his office. He was lying on the bed, hands fluttering beneath his neck, presumably as a greeting.

This was how he conducted all the urgent meetings that followed. Though partially deaf, he would often pull the pillow over his head, laughing uproariously, slyly changing his mind. For a time, he outwitted the oil companies who were concerned to avoid irritating Iran's right-wing Mullahs. They rule Iran today; Mossadeq's political actions brought the country close to ruin.

He had become prominent in politics in 1944, and in 1951 created an international crisis by nationalizing the country's oil. He made life very difficult for the Western oil companies, using a rabble-rousing technique which echoed Hitler's. Not even the Shah could break his power or suppress his hatred of the West, especially the British.

President Truman was very concerned about Iran and its oil. In 1951, in a tense discussion on the Korean War, he warned those with him that the Soviets would move into Iran and take control of Middle East oil production. I just happened to be in Iran at that fascinating time.

The Shah dismissed Mossadeq in 1953 as Prime Minister and appointed General Zahedi in his place, but was forced to flee the country in panic when Tudeh supporters of the former Prime Minister began to riot, tearing down all royal statues and fighting against the Shah's own supporters – to whom they lost the battle. The Shah returned six days later in triumph. The victory had in great measure been due to the work of Kermit Roosevelt, grandson of President Theodore Roosevelt, acting for CIA.

The mad Mossadeq never appeared except in pyjamas, weeping copiously; the rich Persian who hated the British, who dreamed of destroying and expelling them and did – by nationalizing the entire oil industry.

*　　*　　*

Few Prime Ministers have acquired more personal supporters from all walks of life than James Callaghan, who left 10 Downing Street in 1979. He is a personal magnet wherever he goes, constantly invited to address serious gatherings.

At the moving and inspiring ceremony when Nelson Mandela was sworn in as the first black President of South Africa, Jim Callaghan was placed close to him as he accepted his new role. Some years before at a different event, when Katherine Graham, owner of the *Washington Post* and *Newsweek* magazine, celebrated her seventieth birthday, he was one of two people from Britain to fly to Washington to attend. I was the other.

Whenever he comes to stay with us in Spain, invitations are eagerly sought by Spaniards wishing to become an audience for the lucid conversations that are a feature of his visits.

But Jim Callaghan, remembered for many political acts, has but one thing in particular recorded by history: his authorization to send troops into Northern Ireland in 1969 – not to make war, but to protect Catholics in answer to anguished pleas. Bullet-and-bomb responses from the IRA resulted until late in 1994, when the IRA called a cease-fire. An eighteen-month peace was consigned to history when, on 9 February 1996 a huge bomb exploded in London, followed by others. The agony was reborn.

During his time in Parliament Callaghan was certainly never the darling of the Left. It is the breadth and soundness of his opinions together with his humanity which make him such a magnet to our guests.

He loves the soil; he and my husband debate the land, since they farm in the same Sussex countryside. Years of friendship bind him and his wife Audrey to us and Christmas would not be the same if they did not share part of it with us.

He said to me once: 'Fleur, you should sail like a swan, calmly above the waters but paddling hard beneath.' This is a good description of the man himself.

The colourful Lyndon B. Johnson became President in the saddest possible manner, after President John F. Kennedy's murder in Johnson's own state of Texas. He and Lady Bird had waited in Dallas to greet him but fate intervened. Johnson was suddenly the new President of the United States, catapulted into office as Harry Truman had been.

I met him long, long before that, in 1947, already making a name as a politician from Texas, far from a modest or shy man even then. The meeting took place after the stag dinner given in honour of President Truman by the Washington Press Corps' Gridiron Club, a yearly event where the President was always mercilessly ragged. Truman took it gamely, let it be said. So did most Presidents.

Mike Cowles and I always gave a supper reception later for the same Gridiron guests, this time including their wives, and in this way I met Lyndon B. and Lady Bird Johnson.

Our friendship grew, even after I left America to live in England. The relationship encompasses their two daughters, Lynda Bird and the far-from-shy beauty, Luci, whose personal independence was such that she became a Roman Catholic while living in the White House. Her conversion was to provide her father a place of secret refuge late at night at the St Dominic Roman Catholic Church, when he felt despair over Vietnam. Lynda Bird developed her father's political acumen and independent and passionate views, and an astute, knowledge-seeking mind. This striking brunette married Charles Robb, who was Governor of Virginia, then its Senator, and fought and fortunately won in the 1994 mid-term elections against Oliver North of Irangate 'fame', who was described in one national magazine as 'the most frightening man in America'.

A great friend of mine from Seattle wrote a terse epitaph for Oliver North: 'Ollie North is 4F: 1) failure, 2) fraud, 3) fool and 4) fascist.'

Visiting the LBJ ranch in Texas, which I often do, is a heartwarming experience. It is a simple, whitewashed clapboard house sheltering under a giant oak tree facing the Pedernales River, fifty miles from the state capital, Austin. There isn't a Renoir in sight but plenty of colourful American art is on view. There is beauty and peace here, as there was even when it was the country's second White House.

The ranch was like an armed camp then, but there were few outward signs of the security. It was a home, not a public place, looking and feeling like any thriving farmhouse in the centre of a spacious countryside. Chintzes were symbols that epitomized the comfort of a home redolent with family life.

Visitors such as South Vietnam's Nguyen Cao Ky, a Columbia Broadcasting television anchorman and crew, and Henry Kissinger who, interestingly, used to fly regularly between the White House and the ranch to bring LBJ briefings, a practice which had been originated by John Kennedy when away from the White House. 'I insist that these brief reports come directly from Kissinger. I don't want to wade through too many words,' Lyndon Johnson explained to me.

The stream of important visitors didn't affect the relaxed atmosphere. On one of my visits towards the end of his life, the President seemed to be living out the final chapter in a merry way, behaving as if he were able to turn off the past. He was restless, but untroubled and very entertaining. I always had a stroll around the ranch with him. He did this with all his visitors but it pleased me to experience it alone with the President, just the two of us. I heard his pithy, often earthy, views on livestock and the land which I used to report back to my husband in Sussex, who loves our farm as much as LBJ loved thisone.

The family table was one of his great pleasures, not only for him to preside over but also because he could grow the food presented there, which he would gulp down: black-eyed peas, potatoes, onions, squash, corn and beans, the fillings for ranch pies, what he called his 'cow butter', the 'cow beef' and his beloved Tex-Mex casseroles. Meal times were great occasions. LBJ, a commanding presence, always took in the scene, surveying his table, his food and his guests. At dinners given by the Johnsons, the landing field was always full of private planes; Texas distances being so vast, air travel is commonplace.

At times when the Johnsons and I remained together after the guests had departed, there were opportunities to be quite frank, imprudent even, in our conversations. He was never in a mood to turn off the talk. 'Go to sleep? That's out of the question!' he would announce. 'The evening's just begun. If you insist on leaving in the morning, Fleur, don't think of rushing off too soon *tonight*!'

He arranged for me to spend a day at the NASA centre in Houston, where I received the kind of welcome given to Heads of State. The second man to step on the moon, Buzz Aldrin, was my host. I had the excitement of being photographed inside the space capsules; claustrophobic hardly describes how I felt enclosed in those cramped quarters.

That night, Lady Bird and I curled up in a huge couch, facing the restless talker. Confidences flowed. I felt relaxed enough to ask questions and I knew that LBJ liked that game. One concerned the journey he had been scheduled to make to Moscow as President just before the elections in 1968.

'Is it true that the men in the Kremlin didn't know that their army planned to invade Czechoslovakia? Wouldn't they have let you plan your trip at that precise moment if they had. Didn't the totally unexpected invasion put an end to your journey? And had the purpose of that same trip involved an effort to settle the Vietnam issue before the elections? If that trip had been successful, unlikely as that may have been, would it not have elected the man you scarcely lifted a finger to help, Hubert Humphrey? Peace in Vietnam would have scotched all complaints about this unpopular war and kept the Democrats in office! Wouldn't it have been Humphrey's chance?'

'Yes, yes! *Absolutely!*' LBJ admitted, with a very wry smile.

In 1967 I attended the wedding at the White House of Lynda Bird; she was in flowing white, followed by a corps of maidens in medieval red velvet, as she became the bride of Charles 'Chuck' Robb, a young lawyer soon to go to Vietnam as a Marine. This was the first White House wedding since that of Theodore Roosevelt's daughter, Alice.

In the receiving line after the ceremony I took President Johnson's extended hand briefly to ask a question as we moved slowly, very slowly forward. I had flown the Atlantic to attend the wedding – one of three British guests (Lord and Lady Bessborough were the others). As I stood before the President I whispered: 'May I have five minutes with you tomorrow before I fly back to London?'

The weary man, perspiring through his make-up under a mass of TV lights and cameras, replied with a broad grin, 'Hell, no! Tomorrow's Sunday. I'm going to Texas for a rest. Ask me what you want *now*, right *now*.'

'*Now?*' I blurted out. 'Okay! Can't you stop spending so much on bombing Vietnam and put the money into housing instead?'

'Congress won't vote for it,' he whispered as I moved on my way. I am an independent voter so I had the luxury of his friendship without political overtones. I have always tried to judge LBJ in a completely personal way. I never witnessed the tantrums or outbursts and politicking which the press was given to reporting. He could be wickedly sarcastic, but I never experienced it personally, although his conversation could have a sharp edge to it. I shall always remember his humour, his friendliness and acts of kindness. He had a talent for exacting social legislation, in contrast to the failed attempts of his predecessor, who promised so much but never delivered. Using eloquence and cunning, his legislative skills were highly effective. The Democrats had a majority in both houses so he was able to go forward on civil rights; he launched his War on Poverty with his 'Great Society' programme although anti-Vietnam sentiment eventually destroyed it. He demanded justice for blacks, honoured Martin Luther King and hated bigotry.

On a walk round the ranch, the President once gave me an insight into his insecurity when he looked straight at me and confessed sadly, 'I know I don't look like a President.' It was hard to comment after that – 'But which President did?' I countered. 'Did Coolidge, Hoover, or Truman look like Presidents?'

LBJ's insecurity also stemmed from his Southern background. He expressed it frankly in his memoirs, *The Vantage Point*, in which he admitted he knew a Southern President could never rally the Northern press around him. Secretly he must have ended his life a tormented man, realizing that he was less glorified for his remarkable achievements than maligned for Vietnam, which, after all, he inherited from Kennedy. But if, as it has been reported, he retired to his ranch so unhappy and troubled that he drank too much, let it be said that I never saw any sign of this when I was there not long before he died. Behind him were forty years in Washington in different seats of power, ultimately at the centre of it. Yet, as one of the most active of ex-Presidents, he seemed to find a way to fill every moment of every hour in his modest white house in Texas.

LBJ did run victoriously for election in 1964 – to finish his 'Great Society' plans, he spoke of war on poverty, better education for children, medical care for the elderly, building plans to ease the shortage of houses, and how to protect the environment.

Johnson won with an amazing plurality, having secured his following by reminding the public of his programmes and his record in the Senate on civil rights (over the years, he built into the law changes promised but never delivered by Kennedy). In the end, Vietnam was his Waterloo. His tough leadership style had lost him vast popularity.

He was 'a complex and wonderful man full of temperament and

even bitterness'. Those are the words of a man who scrutinized him mercilessly for years, both as a journalist and as a friend; Hugh Sidey, Washington Bureau Chief of *Time* magazine. Just after *The Vantage Point* was published, Sidey characterized LBJ this way: 'Lyndon Johnson has seen and heard more of the important affairs of this nation's world than any other living American. He is like Mount Rushmore, a sort of elemental part of the land, shaped by man and events, but enduring.'

His marriage to Lady Bird had been a romance. He proposed to her twenty-four hours after they met and they married two months later. Her father, meeting LBJ for the first time, announced, 'Daughter, you have brought home a lot of boys but this time you brought home a man.'

A tiny ring from a Sears Roebuck catalogue, a ceremony at St Mark's in San Antonio, a honeymoon in Mexico – and a historic pair started their life together. His first act as a young Congressman in Texas was to bring electrification to their raw and sun-beaten land. It changed thousands of lives. They loved him for it and he must have drawn future strength from that deed. He was a born protester and brought that troublesome characteristic to the White House. Lady Bird shared all his thoughts – they wrote to each almost daily while he held high office, just as Winston Churchill and Clementine did.

Despite lifelong protestations against war, he ended his life identified with Vietnam's worst horrors and national humiliation. He had promised, 'I am not going to be the first President to lose a war.' It was an irony and a tragedy for a remarkable President whose first war had been on poverty, not Vietnam.

The best way I can describe the times I spent with another sort of world leader, Harold Macmillan, is to relate a few anecdotes which we heard regularly in our homes. After years of seeming coolness, we had become real friends.

A memorable evening occurred in London in 1984 when I gave one of my dinners for Queen Elizabeth, The Queen Mother. Because she comes alone, I decide carefully who to invite to 'pair up' the numbers. Someone she would enjoy during the evening, not just a 'token' gentleman. I thought of Harold Macmillan. Since his retirement to Sussex, one saw little of him in London, so I thought he might enjoy coming to town.

Yes, he was delighted to accept – but I had dreadful second thoughts when my husband and I stood in a queue in the hall of his home two weeks later, waiting to be greeted at his ninetieth birthday celebration luncheon with dozens of tables and a galaxy of names and personalities. I wasn't prepared to find him looking not only dreadfully old, but terribly frail.

When we said goodbye, I said impulsively, 'Harold, you don't need to come all the way to London; I'll understand, and the Queen Mother won't even know because I haven't yet sent her the guest list.'

'Oh no!' he replied, in his inimitable thin voice. 'I want to come, I *am* coming.'

I worried even more after that because I knew *how* he would come, not by car, in comfort, but by train in order to take advantage of the pensioner's concession which he loved to use! I began to call every few days to ask his secretary if he felt well enough to make the journey.

The day before the dinner party she responded sharply: 'Mr Macmillan *must* come to London; he's going to become a member of the Peerage and the ceremony takes place on the very same day, in the afternoon. He'll be with you!' When I heard that, I knew I would have to make the event into an extra-special occasion.

I had a sudden idea. I telephoned the American singer Robert White, who was by chance then in London. Considered a modern John McCormack because he has the same, pure golden voice and sings the same repertoire, I asked him if he was free the following night and, if so, could he come to see me immediately? He came. We rewrote the words to 'The End of a Perfect Day', working in the events of Harold Macmillan's life. I then called Clarence House to ask for a list of the Queen Mother's favourite Scottish songs, one of which Bob White could sing first before the song for the new Earl of Stockton.

In the event, he was very moved by the song. All think we saw a tear. My husband had risen before coffee to say a few words to explain how special the occasion was, celebrating the honour bestowed on the great man, and to wish him good health and happiness for the years ahead: 'It is rare when someone has such a new experience at the age of ninety. We congratulate you on becoming an Earl, we are all delighted.'

Lord Stockton struggled to his feet, and I *mean* struggled, but we knew from experience how he hated to be helped, so he was allowed to pull himself halfway up, when he announced: 'I'm not going to make a speech. I just want to thank our hostess and her husband for this memorable occasion.' Then, to everyone's surprise, he slowly raised himself to his full height, and embarked on a fifteen-minute history-making speech, first about the world *before* he was born, then about the years of his long life, and finally the world he envisioned *after* his death. There wasn't a dry eye in the room. Everyone chastised me later for not having a tape recorder, which, if I had owned one (all my friends know I don't) and had used it, would have lost me the trust which has enriched many, many conversations in all of our homes. They are not on tape and never will be.

For fleeting moments, I have to admit, I have wished I had possessed a tape recorder to capture some conversations. For instance, when Jack Benny or Victor Borge or Ronald Reagan took over and filled the rooms with humour and wit or meaningful conversations. All speech, it has been suggested, is floating about in space, waiting for a simple electronic device to make it audible.

Harold Macmillan's anecdotes are famous, and many have appeared in books about him. There is one particular story which he used to love to tell himself at lunches in Sussex, where he came often. He admired the changes on our 600-odd acres, mostly made by my husband who redesigned the landscape beyond the house. Macmillan reminded him that he was merely continuing the tradition of the eighteenth-century gentlemen who levelled and re-landscaped their acres. He called him 'Capability' Meyer. A little persuasion was all that was needed to draw out the story, an anecdote about Charles de Gaulle's visit to his home while he was Prime Minister. The two men had become friends in years of peace despite de Gaulle's reservations about Great Britain, especially in regard to Europe.

The French President wanted to talk privately with Mr Macmillan. He made it clear he wanted no pomp or ceremony so the visit was carefully arranged to take place when the British monarch was overseas. De Gaulle did not wish to go to Chequers but to the Prime Minister's private home, Birch Grove, in Sussex. This was inconvenient but was nevertheless agreed.

Weeks of preparation were involved, with security a prime concern because shortly before there had been a dramatic assassination attempt on de Gaulle. As a result, the official French aircraft, landing at Gatwick airport, had quite a human cargo: de Gaulle's private physician, dozens of French security men and detectives in mufti, met by the requisite complement of British security men. A supply of blood of de Gaulle's group was locked in a special refrigerator in case of need.

The conversation, according to Macmillan, started in earnest the first evening after dinner. 'Perhaps conversation is the wrong word,' he told us at luncheon when describing the occasion. 'De Gaulle occupied the stage and pontificated for at least forty minutes when we were interrupted by a junior male secretary who, with fear and trepidation, passed a small note over my shoulder. The note read: "Mac wants to see you". Mac was my Scottish gamekeeper.

'I ignored it, of course,' Macmillan told our enthralled luncheon guests. 'But an hour later, another note arrived in someone else's hand; I was needed at once. So I rose at this urgent summons, leaving de Gaulle scowling; he was still in full sail.'

Macmillan expected some crisis of State but was astonished to find only Mac, the gamekeeper, standing at the door. The fellow-Scot had served the Macmillans for years and years; he was a blunt man and he was plainly in a rage.

'Either he goes, or I go,' he threatened. 'All those French detectives in the bushes and fields are ruining the pheasant covers and we're meant to be shooting on Monday!'

Though highly amused, the Prime Minister, who had taken the threat in his stride, replied seriously, assuring his irate gamekeeper: 'The President and his retinue will leave in a day.'

He chuckled over the incident, and thinking it would also amuse Monsieur Le Président, he returned to the library and told de Gaulle what it was all about. 'It was greeted with icy silence and open disapproval, I'm afraid,' Macmillan enigmatically ended his tale.

At another occasion at luncheon in Sussex, he announced with a wry smile: 'The trouble with de Gaulle is that he never forgave the British for defeating the Germans.'

Once, when John Alex McCone, ex-Head of the CIA, Secretary of the Navy, America's largest shipbuilder and former Chairman of the United States Atomic Energy Commission, was staying the weekend with us, I also invited Harold Macmillan, being aware the two men had known and between them had worked for or with four American Presidents: Roosevelt, Truman, Eisenhower and Kennedy. Over lunch my husband and I were amazed and gripped by both men's razor-sharp memories as they reminisced over contemporary history; the *truth*, that is, not the generally-reported versions of the great events of the past fifty years! When we rose from the table I thanked them both for their trust in letting us hear history being retold from their firsthand experiences.

'If we weren't here in your house,' Macmillan said casually to me as he strolled from the table, 'we wouldn't have spoken as we did.'

No. No tape recorders will be found in my home.

I met the astonishing Gamal Abdel Nasser in 1952. My first introduction to the man who tried to save Egypt and turn it into a modern nation, but came close to ruining it, was on a visit to Egypt made as a travelling editor. Our meeting was actually arranged by the American Ambassador, Henry C. Byroade. I had been tipped off beforehand about Nasser by Britain's Ambassador, Sir Ralph Stevenson, who suggested: 'Keep an eye on the brilliant young Nasser; he is giving the real instructions.' By the time we met, he had become Egypt's President.

The ten-minute interview Nasser agreed to give me became more than an hour, during which time I had his full attention and a promise to see me again.

I reported this back to President Eisenhower. 'Keep going. Such a rapport is useful,' he announced. In fact, I saw Nasser whenever I asked for time, but the venue changed from his crowded, busy office to the army camp outside Cairo. I came back to see him many times with specific objectives after discussions with President Eisenhower. We certainly clashed, especially in conversations when he denounced the West, particularly the USA and England. Yet I was pleased to have the chance to argue. The give-and-take was stimulating and rewarding.

George Marshall, then Secretary of State, had named his favourite, Henry 'Hank' Byroade, then Assistant Secretary of State, as Ambassador to Egypt, thinking well of the idea since both Byroade and Nasser had the same heritage. Both were born poor, both achieved military success; Byroade before he was thirty rose to the rank of Brigadier General, the youngest in American history. They were the same age, thirty-nine. Presumably a likeable match for each other – but not to Nasser, who believed that a much more powerful or distinguished man should have followed the autocratic, aloof Jefferson Caffray in the Embassy.

Nasser it was who had masterminded the coup in July 1952 that led to King Farouk fleeing the country, a feat accomplished without bloodshed. He later admitted to me it was originally meant only as a feint to test Farouk's strength. However, the action of the Revolutionary Command Corps fooled Farouk, who instantly left the country and accepted exile on the Riviera instead of staying to fight. The monarchy was abolished and a Republic proclaimed. Farouk's five-million-dollar annual income, his four palaces, his two yachts, his fleet of planes, his carloads of erotica, were all commandeered by the state. In one palace all the rooms I visited were fitted out as shops with differing gifts for girls.

Twelve men had managed the coup, led by Nasser; not one ranked over a major. Another four hundred young men were in the Revolutionary Command Corps, calling themselves the Officers' Committee. Together these four hundred and twelve men automatically became Egypt's ruling class. Since all were so young and low in rank, General Mohammed Neguib, who was over fifty, and resembled a good, solid father-figure, was chosen as Head of State. He seemed kind, unassuming and unambitious when he found himself named as Egypt's first President.

Nasser went to great lengths later to explain to me why Neguib was ousted in November 1954, and why he assumed power in his place. 'Neguib was too simple-minded. He soon fell in love with attention from the public. It went to his head and he began to negotiate with our national enemies, the extreme right-wingers. Those crafty old men never did anything for Egypt but milk it – so for Egypt's good, we placed Neguib under house arrest.'

After that first meeting in his office, further discussions took place in Nasser's home. I always stayed at the Embassy Residence with Ambassador and Mrs Byroade. He arranged the appointments and sent me off in his Ambassadorial car.

I started each journey in that car but at a certain point, a crowded two-storey café, a man would wait for me. I would leave the big black Cadillac for a quick drink with Dr Mohammed Hatem, later adviser to President Sadat. After the Cadillac moved safely away, a small, rather dilapidated car drew up to take us to the heavy, high doors of the fortified army post in which Nasser lived until he died in 1970. It was probably only a mile from Cairo's centre, but it seemed far, far away.

The first time these gates opened, I had no idea what to expect. I had heard that Nasser and his wife and a fairly large brood of children lived in absolute simplicity; the house was in fact small and mediocre with five rooms the size of large boxes, sparsely furnished. The parlour was reserved for special callers and in it the ubiquitous suite of lavishly gilded furniture, upholstered in vivid brocade, of the type so favoured by Egyptians, as the sole decoration. It was touching if not ridiculous to find a Head of State jamming his large family into such small quarters, but he had moved into the army camp for security reasons.

On one occasion the Nassers and their three sons and two daughters and I spent hours being photographed together with very active little Nassers flitting around like mosquitoes.* The child who caught my fancy was his father's pet, a wild-eyed, frisky boy of six or seven whom Nasser had nicknamed Jimmy Cagney after his favourite movie star. The little boy really wanted to be like Davy Crockett. Remembering this, the next time I came, I brought him a raccoon tail to attach to his cap.

The timid Mrs Nasser was only persuaded to have conversation with me after several visits. She had not changed her life, continuing to live as she did before his coming to power; no parties, no receptions, no recreation. I once heard Nasser's aide say: 'Go to the movies, do something!' She never did. Nasser took his country from the heavy protocol under the monarchy to no protocol at all. He didn't even have a formal uniform to wear to his first important conference abroad.

What did we talk about? I tried once, crazily, to persuade Nasser to meet Prime Minister Ben-Gurion of Israel on a neutral ship at sea to discuss their problems. This appealed to him, but he did not dare to attempt it. I tried another time, nearly succeeding, to persuade him to lend the Tutankhamun and other treasures to the National Gallery in Washington, although I had not had time to consult anyone beforehand. Many years later, when these treasures did go to Paris and

---

* Not long ago I was reminded of those amazing circumstances when lunching at Cecconi's restaurant in London: an unknown woman introduced herself to me as Nasser's daughter. 'We still remember your visits,' she declared.

then to Washington, I was irritated by the irony. Nasser's refusal had been to the point: 'The Egyptian people would lynch a leader who would send away their national heritage,' he had announced to me. What a pity! If they had been lent to Washington, Nasser could have come to the United States on a 'cultural journey' – without the imposs-ible official invitation as a Head of State. An informal White House meeting could have been arranged, perhaps changing Middle East policy. Even if hate was then almost fever-hot, negotiations might have had a chance.

He spoke bitterly to me of American senators from the South who were afraid that if American aid was granted to the Aswan Dam project, it would lead to the sale in the United States of Egyptian cotton, and enable Egypt to compete against American exports in the world market. Instead, the United States had embargoed Egyptian cotton, leaving it to collect and rot on Egypt's docks.

I had begged him not to go to the Afro-Asian Bandung Conference in 1955, but he played a leading role, instantly allying him to the East. China bought the cotton. Russia did the same and then gave financing to the Aswan Dam. 'The Chinese treat me better,' Nasser had boasted, and Russian arms deals also followed.

One error of judgement was Nasser's, not mine, when he invited me to attend the Feast of Ramadan. I accepted, not knowing that six thousand men, Egypt's entire Officer Corps, would be present – and no other woman. I have a photograph of the massive array of men with me as the one and only woman which was published as a full-page picture in the press the next day. I also kept a copy of the top-table menu for the dinner to which I was ultimately invited by Nasser.* At the table guards stood close, guns on shoulders, grenades in hands.

Nasser seemed a very lonely figure sitting there, with little to say, even to the Prime Minister of the Sudan. It was a big mistake for me to be singled out in a historic night of pageantry which concluded with a spectacularly complicated fireworks display. Since early in Egypt's history the armed forces had given a male-only banquet for

* The menu, translated into English for me, reads: 'First, amerideer (a cake of happy regime), then birds from our own country with oriental rice, Egyptian vegetables, lamb, salad of spring, canafa, fruits of the season.'

their king at the feast of Ramadhan. For the first time in history it was for a commoner, not a king. I soon learned my female intrusion in that photograph did me no good when it was published.

I am constantly asked about Nasser's personal characteristics. What was he like as a Head of State, as a man? He was complicated, of great charm. His nose was large; his eyes were his best feature, but they were hard to fathom. Was he intrigued by my straight talking? Were our political conversations, in fact, his first with *any* lady? Was I not, in any case, the first Western lady he had ever come to know? Was he educated? Certainly more than most Egyptians, though far less than his successor, President Sadat. He spoke English and read voraciously; his mail even included a subscription to that favourite of America's political intellectuals, *Foreign Affairs* magazine.

He paid me the compliment of total concentration, doubling over in his chair as we talked, looking intently at me. From time to time a broad grin would punctuate the conversation and when it did, I knew I was losing the game. His goodwill wasn't my objective, but nudging him into action was difficult. When anxious to emphasize a point, he would grab my wrist to make sure of my attention, an idiosyncrasy of which I have a photograph.

Although my relationship with Nasser was presumably as an editor and he never allowed himself to think of me as anything else, I never left Cairo without a gift, which was often presented in a stiff ceremony by a minister seeing me off at the airport. The range of presents was intriguing; sometimes they were picked from the mountainous piles of Farouk treasures still kept locked away. One gift he insisted I accept, however, was a brooch, a jewelled scarab which I learned later used to highlight Farouk's royal turban at official events. I protested, to no avail.

Another, equally valuable, was a gift Nasser asked his wife to give to me while I was in his home. 'It's too personal for me,' he explained, but she was too shy. I left in a hurry to avoid further embarrassment. Ambassador Byroade saw me off at the airport that same evening and the usual little farewell ceremony took place. One of the three Egyptian officials deputized to attend plucked up courage to announce splendidly, 'President Nasser requested us to present you this gift as a token of his esteem, too personal to give you himself.' I looked beseechingly at Ambassador Byroade: 'Just thank them, Fleur, and take it,' he promptly announced. Once inside the plane I opened the huge, awkwardly wrapped brown package. 'This is Coptic embroidery,' the card said. 'The President wants you to make it into a dress.' There was enough for a ballgown, but the valuable yardage remains untouched, rolled up and covered in black paper in a closet.

Another scarab was delivered some years later at Christmas from the Egyptian Embassy in Washington. I had by then already dropped all communications with Nasser; we were miles apart politically, and I sought no further contact. During the Suez Crisis, the beautiful engraved silver salver he had given me on another occasion was never polished by our indignant former English char lady, but she regularly shone it to brilliance after his death.

After five visits, I decided not to go back to Egypt. The men around Nasser were irritated and there were immense obstacles to overcome before they would ever agree to any plan I offered. I was the wrong sex to be in the President's favour in an Arab country. Being American became more and more a handicap since the United States was looked on with such distrust. Finally, when it became known in Cairo that I had Nasser's attention and had gone frequently to his home, I began to feel hot breath on my neck. After the spring of 1955, by which time USA–Egypt relations had almost totally deteriorated, I left for ever.

Things had changed drastically since Nasser toppled General Neguib when he was only two years older than King Farouk. Though he looked inconspicuous, he was recognized as a young zealot in uniform and he soon became the most powerful personality in the Arab world, using authoritarian methods to carry out reforms. He controlled a subservient press, a disciplined army and a tyrannical police force.

Yet even disaster and defeat by the Israelis didn't harm his god-like appeal to the people. Travelling elsewhere later, I saw his photograph hung inside mud houses of the Hadhramaut in Arabia and in the caves and tiny huts outside Muscat. His face had become a symbol of brotherhood between Arabs. Yet in attempting to change their world, the government became the oppressor. Innocents were jailed and feudalism was installed in the name of freedom by a man driven on by the memory of his own childhood poverty. He constantly talked to me of his mother: 'She often went hungry to send me forward,' he said. His devotion to her is made clear in his autobiography.

Soon Cairo became a symbol of a frightening contrast between wealth and poverty. He had become a revolutionary in the best of all revolutionary breeding grounds, the student riots, when he was seventeen. He wanted to become a lawyer, to use that profession to bring about political reforms, but he changed his mind in 1938 at twenty, when he was commissioned in the army.

The turning point may have been in 1942, when the British actually sent their tanks against Farouk's palace. Though Nasser loathed the King, nationalism reared its head: Farouk was, after all, his monarch and Nasser was offended by this affront to Egypt's dignity. But exactly ten years later, he did the same thing, dethroning the profligate King with tanks.

Nasser had been born poor, the son of a postal clerk. He constantly reminded me that because of this poverty and his early struggles he was determined to raise the country's standard of life. Using radio, he beamed his ideas across the Middle East, damning the West. He planned a new Arab world, which he would lead; he wanted to eliminate Israel, to control the Suez Canal; the money from its tolls would be a new source of wealth.

His death came when he was just over fifty years old, a little more than five years after the Rabelaisian Farouk had a heart attack while dining in a restaurant in Rome. In that very same week Nasser had been re-elected President of Egypt by 99.999 per cent of all votes cast. A changed man had gone to his people; tired, cynical, pressurized and ill, allowing no other candidate to appear on the ballot or in the headlines of his controlled press. He had nationalized the Suez Canal, enacted land reform against the rich, seized foreign assets. Helped by Russia, he finished the Aswan Dam.

If he had the capacity to look back before he died, he would have seen his country as an example of a mismanaged state, his army humiliated, his national economy in tatters. He may have nudged his country slightly forward, but not very far. Idolatry and sycophancy ruined him. The idealistic figure I thought I knew had disappeared.

George Bush is the charming man whom I first met when he was the US Ambassador to the United Nations. He became President in 1988. He left office four years later as a warrior, not the man for the gentler American world he had promised, who went abroad and made life better for foreigners. He had to turn to military options, plunging into two conflicts; one against Iraq, the other against Noriega in Panama. Both had moral dimensions and both were of short duration. He knew the world well before he became President; as Congressman, UN Ambassador, envoy to China and as Head of the CIA. He knew his own nation less well.

Barbara Bush is remembered as his secret weapon, although she failed in one serious matter; she made no attempt to dissuade Bush from standing against abortion during his election campaign. The President was passionate in his opposition, but why did this popular mother-figure, who had been on the board of Planned Parenthood in Washington, remain *mute*? Precious female votes disappeared as many women wondered what had happened to the principle of free choice.

The war against Saddam Hussein (whom he called 'worse than Hitler' and vowed he would 'kick in the ass') resulted in a victory that made him the most popular President since poll-taking began. 'We are the only nation on earth who could assemble the forces for peace,' he declared, an embarrassing claim if one turns to later events in Bosnia and Rwanda.

Wars cost money. The nation became further impoverished while the needs of welfare and education went unheeded. It must be said, however, that in Bush's last year of office he instituted a fiscal pro-gramme which put the United States on course for recovery, ironically benefiting President Clinton in his first year of office.

Bush had angered the Republicans by raising taxes. His foreign policies went badly in Yugoslavia, echoed by similar dismal problems for dedicated meddlers since. He was rebuffed by the Democratic Congress, stung by scandals in the Post Office and the Savings and Loan Bank collapse. His approval-rating dropped with a thud. But he did achieve the long-sought arms agreement with Gorbachev and Yeltsin, and he also promoted the far-reaching Disabilities Act. Would these help him to win the re-election? He seemed to campaign as if he didn't expect to win, and he was proven right.

I felt very sad for George Bush and his wife after the votes were totted up in 1992. Even before the campaign, the rumour was that Barbara hoped he would not run again. Both had been ill; she had recovered from Graves' disease. Health considerations could have played a part in her thinking, so their departure from the White House could have been celebratory as well as melancholy.

Both President and Mrs Bush have been good to me during their public years. I shall never forget the handwritten birthday greeting handed to me on 20 January 1992, at home at my party which I disguised by pretending it was for a guest. My birthday is also the day when Presidents are inaugurated. The Bushes didn't forget. Their message was written and signed by them both on the day before the inauguration of his successor, Governor Bill Clinton. In fact the Bushes left the White House that very day for the Middle East. More important things must have been on their minds, yet they remembered me. The birthday message might have been among the last things the out-voted, tired man signed as he left the White House. I was thrilled to be remembered at such a difficult and moving time.

Harold Wilson was described by author John Gunther as a man who was too choosy to be a member of the multitude, 'a man with a cold mind and a dry posture'. Nevertheless he rose to the top of Labour's hierarchy. He had one thing that even bitter enemies envied: an incredible memory. I had known him for more than twenty years before he became Prime Minister, and had seen that memory leap to the aid of his tongue many times.

How good was this fabled ability? Was his brain really a computer? How did he program it? How did he recall at will any date, any fact, any quotation, any comment? How early in life did this Prime Minister who won three elections learn to create his remarkable memory-box? I have one amusing personal proof of it, to be told later.

Before becoming Prime Minister, he had been economic adviser to my husband's timber company, Montague L. Meyer Ltd, but he came into my life long before I met my husband. It was just after the war when at the age of thirty-one he accompanied Sir Stafford* and Lady Cripps to the USA; they stayed at my home during the New York stage of this visit, and again later.

Wilson had already moved up the ladder as President of the Board of Trade, England's youngest Cabinet minister since William Pitt. Stafford Cripps plainly thought the world of him. He had begun political life as a Liberal but won a Labour seat in Parliament in 1945.

* See Stafford Cripps, page 85.

Before that, aged twenty-one, he was the youngest-ever don at Oxford, teaching economics. Such brilliant young men may not be so much a novelty today, but a youngster among the senior fellows was remarkable at that time.

The memory he was training must have played its part in all his roles, academic, commercial and political. His reputation for producing facts and figures and seemingly forgotten incidents and using them in debate is well established; many political adversaries had been impaled on the lance of his data. Equally, he confounded friend, enemy and press by his memory-gymnastics, never giving the impression of being briefed. In fact, he could and did speak 'off the cuff'.

Another side to the man was his dry sense of humour. The most affectionate use I ever heard him make of it was at the party given by *The Times* to celebrate Harold Macmillan's eightieth birthday, when Labourite Wilson's wit made the Tory speakers seem dull. It was not a new experience but the largely Conservative audience was riveted by it and impressed by the friendliness between two former Prime Ministers who had opposed each other in Parliament for many years, cleverly and acerbically, with rapier precision (although they had been known to leave the floor of the Chamber arm-in-arm for a drink together).

Some of my own friends had an opportunity to see Harold Wilson's remarkable memory at work at close hand one evening in 1970 when as Prime Minister he came to dine with us. After dinner he and twenty or so other guests gathered in our drawing room for the usual tribal-groups of conversation. He and I and several hardier types chose to stand in a corner of the room. The group gradually widened around us in a semi-circle.

The conversation became personal when we both began to reminisce. I started by recalling his invitation to me in 1959 to appear on my first 'Brains Trust' in England, which he chaired. Finally, I blurted out: 'Do you remember how many years we've known each other?'

'Oh, come along!' he protested. 'That question is too simple! Of course I remember. But do *you* remember the date of the last time you gave me dinner in New York City?'

'Good heavens no,' I admitted frankly. 'How could I? It happened in 1951 in the USA and it is now 1970.'

'Well, I remember. It was on January the twentieth, 1951,' he announced.

I almost collapsed. 'How could you possibly recall the exact date after over nineteen years?'

'How could I possibly forget?' he demanded, with a sly smile. 'After all, it was your *birthday* . . .'

I glowed for a very long time while recovering my composure. The conversation had not only evidenced his machine-tooled memory, but was handsomely flattering.

Later, the Prime Minister moved to another part of the drawing room where he chose to sit next to Lady Diana Cooper, the same beautiful Tory guest who had rudely and openly snubbed him when he arrived. 'How could you have that *awful* man here?' she managed to hiss at me as she turned her back on him in an impeccable example of snobbery, which he had not failed to notice. After dinner, he decided to sit down on the couch beside her and started the conversation with a cool, 'No one will ever forget your husband's gallant war.' She melted in surprise. Twenty minutes later he got up to talk to someone else and left her in a softened mood, though I dare say far from converted.

Like Prime Ministers Thatcher, Callaghan and Wilson, Sir Edward Heath was also definitely not 'upper class', but he nevertheless triumphed as they did by reaching that high office. He eventually accepted a knighthood from John Major in 1992 although he had always seemed lukewarm about the subject of honours. In his time at 10 Downing Street, only nine men were named for knighthoods. Yet Socialist Harold Wilson had a middle-class love of the system. He received the Order of the Garter, Britain's highest honour and Heath has been equally honoured recently.

In Parliament, Edward Heath's speeches became 'box-office attractions' for those on the benches both during and after Margaret Thatcher's time. The House of Commons bar could empty if 'Ted' was about to speak, few wanting to miss his acerbic interventions, whether at the expense of Thatcher or Common Market antagonists. A few may have wished they had his courage.

As one of Britain's earlier enthusiasts for the Common Market at the European Union negotiations, he still bridles at remarks by the Eurosceptics in Parliament. I remember Heath's skill in the sixties when he debated the Common Market at the Oxford Union. Calmly, speaking without notes, he trounced two other noted spellbinders, Barbara Castle and Peter Shore, who had to shout their way through student jeers. They lost the debate to Heath, hands down.

Pleasure is there in his home in Salisbury where we often go, very willing to drive for three hours from our Sussex home on a Sunday, to attend his 'jury-lunch'. I am one who assists Heath in his role as judge of the *Praemium Imperiale* Prize given yearly to the world of art by a group in Tokyo. The official jury chosen by the Japanese for this 'Nobel Prize of the Arts' includes Jacques Chirac, President of France, ex-Chancellor Schmidt of Germany, Amintore Fanfani, former President of Italy, and David Rockefeller of the United States (now replaced by his son). It is a fascinating activity, but frustrating; I have never succeeded in getting a prize for anyone who was not already very successful. I would like to see the award got to someone who is less well established and who needs the accolade and perhaps the money. I continue to try to have photography included as an art, with Eve Arnold in mind.

A few years ago, I had a personal experience which gave me a chance to fully appreciate Heath's musicianship. He and I both journeyed to Barcelona to answer a cry for help from my friend Mme Monteserrat Trueta de Trias. She had written to ask if I could persuade Mr Heath to conduct a charity concert to benefit the Trust she created to help Spanish children who are born with Downs Syndrome, as was her first son. She dedicated her life to helping other victims as well as those sometimes forgotten sufferers, the families of the children.

Heath agreed he would go if I also went. The symphony orchestra probably hated him for making them rehearse twice daily for three days but the result warmed even their hearts; they had never played so superbly and the reviews made them proud. While in Barcelona, we were given very privileged treatment, including a comprehensive preview of the plans for the coming Olympics, which were fascinating.

It was interesting to hear it claimed that everything being done was necessary to improve the conditions in Barcelona in the long term, not just for the short-term drama of the Olympics. The World's Fair at Seville, on the other hand, proved a different story: overbuilt, over-spent, still in debt, including, it is said, for wages and salaries.

Today, Sir Edward might be the country's 'official' Elder Statesman, and deserves to be, if he were less outspoken on issues like the European Union and the American and British handling of Saddam Hussein, but I believe it means more to him to say what he believes than be restrained by such considerations. He overcame the drawback of his modest background to break through the Conservative Party's class structure to become its leader and Prime Minister. Margaret Thatcher, whose parents were grocers, followed him through the hallowed portals of 10 Downing Street, often, say his supporters, riding on ideas he had expressed but had not implemented when in office.

When he lost the February 1974 General Election, Margaret Thatcher ousted him from the Party leadership and went on to become Prime Minister in 1979, a post she retained for over eleven years. No other person, however, has been an international racer who won the Sydney-to-Hobart in half a gale, at the same time being a superb musician *and* Prime Minister of Britain!

Hollywood made its unbelievable entrance into the White House through Ronald Reagan. He brought with him a magnetism so irresistible he was elected twice, despite often facing disapproval. This did him little harm and he left office as one of the most popular Presidents in American history, having worked effectively and brought about the collapse of Communism through his policy of fully-realized military superiority. He also left office as the oldest retiring President, and is now, sadly, suffering from Alzheimer's disease.

Watching President Bill Clinton smiling, hugging and kissing during the inauguration ceremonies, one inevitably compared him with Ronald Reagan, who needed only a spontaneous smile to bring him very real political support. Much of Reagan's popularity arose from his hatred of Soviet Russia, which he called the 'evil empire'. He never stopped borrowing money to build a suitable defence, helping the United States become the world's biggest debtor, with a federal debt of $2 trillion.

Even the banking scandals which surfaced didn't *seem* to hurt him; nor did the bigger military appropriations, such was the strength of his personal popularity and his fund of 'street wisdom'.

The last time I was with him and Nancy Reagan in the White House was at the dinner they gave for King Hussein, when I enjoyed being seated between Vice-President Bush and the Queen of Jordan's father. We followed the Reagans to the East Room where concerts usually took place in a setting hung with portraits of every previous President. Waiting on the stage were Benny Goodman and his band and guest star, Buddy Rich, the great jazz drummer. These musicians were chosen as a special treat for the 'jazz-buff' King of Jordan. There were countless encores and rapturous applause. Reagan finally stood to address the performers.

'I needn't thank you,' he told them. 'You faced your audience and obviously know how much they enjoyed your music. But there's one thing you couldn't see and that is the portrait of George Washington behind you. Whenever I'm in this room listening to music, I watch our great former President. *Tonight was the first time I've ever seen him tap his toe!*' A roar of applause followed.

Ronald Reagan and I had met in Hollywood at the beginning of the 1950s when *Look* Magazine gave him a *Look* Award for his part as a cowboy in a film, an award which, like the Oscar, is given after being voted for by film distributors.

I introduced him to English political friends at dinner in London when he was Governor of California, but the last time I saw him and his wife was after his retirement when they were in the London home of 'Kip' Forbes, son of the colourful man who left a history of financial and other successes, including *Forbes Magazine*, when he died. At this Forbes dinner in honour of the pair, I spent a good deal of the evening with the Reagans, an old friend among less familiar English guests.

On other occasions, while Charles Price was America's Ambassador to Britain, we dined in the President's honour at Winfield House. On one such occasion, I whispered to Nancy: 'You should eat more. You're far too thin!'

'How can I eat?' the tiny lady replied. 'I've never stopped worrying about Ronnie after the terrible assassination attempt. I'm too nervous to eat,' she concluded. The President seemed to have got over it, but she simply couldn't; a sad price to pay.

When in the Philippines on a round-the-world tour, I called on President Ramon Magsaysay, and later had a chance to be helpful to him. I had talked so long with him that I decided this brave man should be better known by other Americans to help counter the tales of corruption and misuse of American aid which were commonly believed back home at that time.

He was an incorruptible national hero during his time in office between 1952 and 1957. If he had been allowed to finish his term, the Marcos regime which followed would have met stiffer resistance since people hallowed his name after he had routed the dangerous HUKs from the Philippine hills when World War II ended.

A man of his obvious honesty should be seen in America, I decided. When I asked *why* a trip to the United States would not be in order, he reminded me that an official invitation would be required. After I returned to New York, I thought of a subterfuge and wrote him to ask: 'Why not come to the USA by saying it would be for health reasons, whether true or not, to get opinions from American doctors? No official invitation would be involved.'

The ruse worked; President Magsaysay came to New York, and I have a superb photograph of the two of us lunching in my office to remind me of it. Once he was actually in America, *informal* talks at the White House were easily arranged: my mission was accomplished. Americans, hearing his name for the first time, realized that a decent man was at his country's helm. He was killed shortly after this when his plane crashed mysteriously when taking off for a regular local flight to the interior. Sabotage? Assassination?

A great drama many of us remember living through was John F. Kennedy's assassination. I was in my weekend home in Sussex on the fateful Friday in 1963 when the music on the radio to which I was painting was abruptly halted. 'President Kennedy has just been shot!' was announced, like a bolt of lightning. Hours later when he died, there was an inevitable blackout on everything but the memory of the tragedy. Although I never really got to know JFK, despite several meetings, after his death I did a great deal of soul-searching. One horrible fact kept repeating itself in my mind: *that I was not surprised.*

I had returned from Florida just before he was murdered, visiting friends for the first time for many years. I met dozens of conservative Democrats and Republicans, all of whom, regardless of party, became apoplectic at the mere mention of Kennedy's name. 'He'll get killed if he comes down here,' I heard again and again, said by men whose eyes burned with rage. I was so appalled by the atmosphere I left for England earlier than planned, getting back to London in good time before giving a dinner for Walter Lippmann.

It was exactly five days before the murder. The Florida experience weighed so heavily on my mind, I knocked on my glass during coffee to ask Lippmann a question, knowing his answer would be of interest to all guests.

'I may be mad, Walter, but I don't think Kennedy stands a chance of being re-elected. I've just left the vitriolic American South where he is violently hated, mainly for his civil rights program. After all, he only won the election by the narrowest possible margin, so can you tell me and our guests if *you* think Kennedy can be re-elected?'

Lippmann carefully weighed his reply: 'You may be right, Fleur,' he said. 'Kennedy's re-election is possible but certainly not *probable*.' No one at dinner forgot that comment when the assassination was announced a few days later.

I made a special trip to the United States to persuade Supreme Court Justice Earl Warren, whom I knew well, to answer these questions about the assassination which concerned people in Europe. 'Will they be dealt with in the coming Warren Report?' I asked.

'No, they won't. The report is already printed,' he replied reluctantly.

Like many other Americans, I had to deal with trying to answer worrying questions from my English friends; it was not the easiest time for any American abroad. The distress was in many ways touching and reassuring and I shall always remember my pride in knowing an American President was held in such esteem.

Misunderstandings about America's culture and its politics still exist. Americans tended to offend when abroad, especially the ingenious ones, because Europeans mistook American confidence for arrogance; they are disliked for the ostentation of their apparent wealth; it is forgotten, *of course*, that there is little difference between them and all the arrogant, rich, overbearing Europeans travelling outside their *own* countries.

Was it true that 15,000,000 Americans carried guns? Yes, the number regularly increases. Did a murder really occur every 48.5 seconds in Texas, as a BBC reporter claimed? Does the Second Amendment of the Constitution give every US individual the right to hold

171

firearms as part of the sacred right of the individual to defend himself? Yes, and still does as I write, in spite of President Clinton's recent legislation, a move that the horrifying bombing by militants in Oklahoma must highlight.

I reminded friends that every state in America interprets the Constitution in its own different way. In New York State at one time, for instance, you could hold a rifle to the back of a pal on Times Square and it would be legal; but if the weapon was *concealed, that* would make it an offence.

I tried to deal with widespread notions about John Kennedy's assassination was simply a grand plot by either right-wingers or Communists. The question brought out the paradox of our American history: *we were born in a revolution but large pockets of our people are entirely intolerant of revolutionary ideas.* John Birchers on the right and Black Power on the left were then equally fanatical; each wanted change, but only *their* kind.

I still have the list I made at this time to demonstrate the problems *shared*, even then, by the United States and Britain. Many still exist:

1. Falling standards of education: too many children, too few schools, too few teachers, too many of whom were politically biased. *Still true.*

2. Over-education (particularly in art colleges): too many gifted graduates for too few jobs. *Still true.*

3. Gravity of juvenile and young adults' delinquency. Educated students without jobs or hope, followed by crime on the streets. *Truer than ever now.*

4. Emphasis by university graduates on knowledge for *financial* gain rather than for its own sake. *Still true.*

5. The complexity of government, and with it, the steady growth of bureaucracy. *Too true today.*

Americans were being blamed for changes in European society in the sixties yet most of them were inevitable. Mass culture, automation, high-pressure selling and vulgarization of taste are absolutely and unfortunately concomitant with any industrial and economic revolution. Look at post-Communist Russia today and its mafia.

Americans were often scapegoats for behaviour the Europeans disliked in themselves. Europe was not compelled to drink soft drinks, copy American clothes, watch American motion pictures and placate their children with terrible comic books, or wear blue jeans. Things that Europeans thought were American *luxuries* were often simple *necessities* in the American way of life. People tended to forget that there was no real collective view in America. A *particular* American should never be asked to bear personal responsibility for Americans *in general.*

As for President Kennedy, in hindsight, whatever one's politics, not only must we thank him for the inspiration he gave to millions, but for the Apollo space program. He pushed it through against strong opposition, and opened the skies to science – a man actually stood on the moon. Centuries from now men could judge his term of office by this one historical act. It could even overlay other judgements of the man.

V

POWER-HUNGRY WOMEN

CERTAIN WOMEN DESERVE the description 'power-hungry'. Evita Peron, whose excesses I revealed in my book *Bloody Precedent*, deserves a place of honour on the list. Madame Chiang Kai-Shek's record as former First Lady of China gives her a place, too, especially for her vengeful wish expressed personally to me to see her own country destroyed. She has tried everything to return to power in the China which at one time she wished to crush.

Indira Gandhi, whom I never met, earned a place in this group every time she showed her contempt for democracy. By ordering the unwarranted house arrest of her distinguished aunt, my friend Madame Pandit, she provided me with final evidence.

Imelda Marcos, the lady of the two thousand shoes and billions of missing dollars, showed her true character when we were at the Philippine Embassy in London.

'Why not come and visit my country?' she kept insisting, 'I will send my plane for you.' I had to tell her: 'No, I *do* know your country, Madame Marcos. When I was last there I got to know well your former President Magsaysay.' At the mention of his name, her face dropped, and she promptly turned on her heel and walked away. Our friendship was over. Magsaysay, predecessor to Marcos, had been a Philippine hero.*

A total of five to six *billion* dollars was bled from the country in the twenty-one years of Marcos's Presidency. Imelda Marcos claims that this was all *private* money, that their wealth simply resulted from clever investments, and included a large quantity of gold they 'discovered' before he became President of his impoverished country.

* See Magsaysay, page 170.

In late 1993, Madame Marcos faced trial in the Philippines for corruption. She was convicted and sentenced to twenty-two years in prison, having somehow escaped the possibility of such a fate in her trial in the USA. She and her husband were alleged by their own government to have embezzled $6.5 *billion* during their rule. Hundreds of millions were still in Swiss bank accounts in 1994). She also claims that she will never go to jail, and the years continue to roll on without her imprisonment.

Alexander Walker, the London *Evening Standard*'s respected film critic and author, frequently visits us in Spain. In 1994, as I was writing this chapter, I remembered that he was a 'Philippine-regular'. He admitted he knew Imelda Marcos well enough to contribute to this book.

Judging those in the limelight is not an unusual role for him; he has written about such celebrities as Audrey Hepburn, Garbo, Vivien Leigh, Bette Davis, Joan Crawford and Marlene Dietrich, as well as the authorized biography of Peter Sellers, among some twenty books. He gave me a vivid explanation for Imelda's behaviour and motivation in the following fascinating account of her 'secret' health disability which affects the way she lives. It gives an interesting insight into her character.

'Imelda Marcos owed a great deal of her power and influence to a peculiarity of her metabolism. She was unwell – or unwilling to rest and thus determined to deny other people their rest, too. Early on in life, she had discovered that she had a medical problem to do with the retention of fluid in the body: if she lay down to sleep, she arose looking puffy and bloated.

'The solution was simple, if drastic – not to lie down at all, not to sleep, or to do so as little as possible. Thus she busied herself with the many projects in hand for far too long hours. Then, even the most dedicated bureaucrats, in turn, were kept busy, on the go, serving her commands, holding themselves in readiness for some new order, some fresh requirement – never daring to call it a day or slope off home, or take their pleasure, or indeed do any work of their own until "Ma'am" permitted them.

'People's work hours were a matter of her whim. If her husband, the President, set the agenda of government, Imelda Marcos set the clock.

'People dropped with fatigue in Imelda's service. Even when she took her pleasures, they were fatiguing ones for those in her retinue. They never knew when the dance would end, or indeed where – for sometimes Imelda, to keep herself upright and awake, would transfer the guests to three or four different locations in an evening. They went from the dining room at Malacunon Palace to the Japanese disco in its roof and then to the night club at the Manila Hotel and then to an early morning – *very* early, almost pre-dawn – buffet arranged around the helicopter pad on the palace roof. And, finally, stuffed, sated, enervated and tired out, the guests, who might number fifty or sixty, would be allowed to depart at sunrise to their homes or hotels, dying for a sleep, while Ma'am would allow herself to close her eyes for half an hour, usually sitting bolt upright and seldom, if she could help it, lying down, thus keeping the liquids from diffusing themselves through her face, cheeks and eyes. This ability to wear others down physically had its statecraft – usefulness in preventing opposition to form politically.

'Louis XVI used a similar technique to keep his courtiers in line through the enormously complicated protocol and etiquette prac- tised at Versailles, where those who served the King and, even more, those who merely rushed to approach him, had to observe a series of commandments and prohibitions that were rigidly enforced and formed a hugely complex kind of game whose serious purpose was to protect the person of the King.

'By contrast, protocol at Malacunon Palace was very relaxed, almost informal, and the President and Imelda frequently made themselves accessible to their subjects in ways that might have been deemed "inappropriate" or downright "imprudent" in the state regimes of other less easy-going countries. But the penalty one paid was to fall under Imelda's spell and be whirled along, reluctantly but impotently, in her jet trail.

She got through a lot of work as a result of never resting and the compensation was that she energized people who often did need someone on their tail, or their back, pressing them to get their work done in a country where it was more pleasant to put the work off until "tomorrow". In a phrase, she kept others at it. Though a lot of what they did was designed to enhance the prestige and public face of the Marcoses, the country did gain as well in the speed with which the commands of Ma'am to beautify a building or clean up a town, plant more flowers, stage a festival, put out more flags or simply throw another party were executed all down the line.

Much of Imelda's "work ethic" derived, of course, from Imelda's power complex. But there are worse forms of tyranny than keeping those who serve you in an almost permanent state of fatigue.'

After reading Alexander Walker's contribution, I smiled over her thousands of pairs of shoes, idiotic stacks now on view as a tourist display in her former palace.

This shoe fetish is one she presumably copied from Evita Peron, who like Imelda later, had secretly accumulated hundreds of pairs of Ferragamo shoes.

And that's not all. Evita was like a 'goddess' to Imelda, who admitted it to an Argentinian friend, Roberto Devorit while he was in Manila. He lives in London but his family in the Argentine survived Evita's revengeful campaign against the aristocracy in her time. Imelda's secret passion, he told me, was to become the Evita of the Philippines.

In fact, Evita's own book, *La Razon de Ma Vida*, is kept as if a bible in a place of honour on a desk in a room in the old Palace – opened and on a pedestal in Imelda's parlour. Imelda also proudly showed Devorit the major portion of Evita's famous collection of lavish jewels, sought and bought by her as the principal bidder at the auction of those gems.

Both Marcoses devoted their lives to money. Imelda may point out an art building, a theatre or a new park as public symbols of her largesse to the people, but they cost pennies compared to billions of dollars still unaccounted for in scattered places, safe from the needs of the desperately poor of their land.

The First Lady wasn't the only one who had a mania for adornment. Even the President's wardrobe reveals an obsession equal to his wife's; a collection of 365 suits – an equivalent of her shoe-mania. Shopping tales survive. Diamond purchases clung to sticky fingers, $300,000-worth in one disclosed quick foray to a Geneva jewel emporium, for instance. Property was bought all over the expensive areas of New York City. There was always enough cash in hand for any exigency, every time, everywhere. Their regime was a bad dream, even if a section of their population has been fooled into believing otherwise.

Despite all this, in the fall of 1995, she actually made her comeback into politics by taking her seat in the Philippine Congress. This enraged Aquino's family who blamed President Marcos for his assassination. At the ceremony when Imelda Marcos took her oath of office, Aquino's sister Teresa said: 'Mrs Marcos now stands among us in the institution that Mr Marcos padlocked and abolished in the martial law system he imposed'.

In September 1995, the Philippine State prosecutors filed draft charges against her deposits of a half-billion dollars, and charged her with having maintained false accounts and deposits in a number of Swiss banks. The Swiss government agreed to return $300 million to whomsoever the Philippine courts decided should get the money, meanwhile the money is kept in escrow.

One woman who openly and confidently used her position of power was Evita Peron, the blonde, rabble-rousing Argentinian. She exerted it for revenge, to get even with the rich, at the same time accumulating the vast secret fortune from the wealthy country she helped make poor.

The Peron partnership, Evita and Juan, gave Argentina a bitter dose of dictatorship, although for a time she managed by her activities to camouflage this. Getting to know her, as I did, was a chilling experience. I watched her deal out cruel 'justice' to her wealthy victims. Grim accounts of every form of practical revenge exist, springing from a hatred which stemmed from her early life as the daughter of a woman brothel-keeper. As soon as she became First Lady she openly set out to repay all the snubs she had received from Argentine society.

I became her companion in Buenos Aires, after she mistakenly decided I was a friend. I shivered when I saw the mob-hysteria created every time she spoke to the thousands who crowded the streets to listen. I yearned to expose her as a tyrant to the world outside, which was bedazzled by her clothes and her jewellery and treated her as a movie star. So I wrote a book.

In *Bloody Precedent*, I was able to couple her and Juan Peron with the husband-and-wife team who ruled and likewise bled the Argentine people one hundred years before the Perons came to power. They duplicated all the tactics and techniques used by Encarnación and Juan Manuel de Rosas in the nineteenth century.

Juan Manuel de Rosas, described by Carlos Fuentes in his book *The Buried Mirror* as a Machiavellian character, was both lion and fox. Juan Peron may have been the lion, but Evita thought of herself as the angel. She convinced the population of this while at the same time destroying the country's fabulous wealth in cattle and wheat by ordering them not to work in either industry, which helped ruin their economy and change their civilization.

My book is in two parts, starting with the dictatorship of the earlier pair, the de Rosas. Because their history had been rewritten in the Argentine by the Perons' dictate, I could find accurate records only in Britain. *Part I*, the de Rosas, and *Part II*, the Perons, have many duplications. Both men had to flee, Peron to Spain, de Rosas to England; both women died of cancer; both men used their women to attain power; both men needed their wives' ruthless talents to achieve their goals. I described the two women this way in my introduction to the book:

> 'I cannot see the blonde Evita without the distraction of a double-image. My mind's eye always produces the blonde and the brunette together: the blonde Evita, in a dramatic double-negative merging with her black-haired predecessor, Encarnación. It is Encarnación who was the more remarkable for she was the trail blazer; she lived in an era and among a Latin people who never permitted a woman to move outside the narrow affairs of the household and the bed.
>
> 'Encarnación, like Evita, used marriage to build her own prestige and power. Both Encarnación and Evita ranted about the man to whose personal welfare and political and social programs they claimed to have dedicated themselves (while each plotted, directed and policed the public's idolatry for themselves). Each walked eagerly and fearlessly where their men feared to tread. And each has been cruel, terribly cruel, far crueller than their men ever dared or needed to be when they had their women to dispatch the worse vengeance for them.
>
> 'I vividly remember the attentive, hand-rubbing, handsome, masculine Juan Peron, but it is Evita who continues to haunt me ever since I met her and sat and walked and rode at her side and talked to her, though the time was short. I cannot obliterate the image of this woman-politico with too much power, too much rage, too many flunkies in high government places, too little opposition, too much greed, too much money; a woman too fabled, too capable, too sexless, too driven, too overbearing, too slick, too neurotic, too sly, too tense, too sneering, too diamond-decked, too revengeful, too hateful of North Americans, too ambitious – and far, far too under-rated for far too long by the world.'

Indira Gandhi's story is less dramatic, indeed very different, but her obvious love of power could be seen in her often stony face. During two terms of office she succeeded in undermining many democratic institutions if and when they threatened her authoritarian rule.

Her reputation was shattered for me when she put Nan Vajaya Pandit, Nehru's younger sister, and Indira's own distinguished aunt, under house arrest. No one loved her country more or represented it better than Nan Pandit. Few women have achieved a greater political reputation. She was the only female President of the United Nations, became Ambassador to Russia and finally, High Commissioner to the Court of St James's (as well as to Ireland and Spain). One could only assume her arrest was a petulant attempt by her niece to isolate her from an admiring world, or to prevent her from becoming a political rival.

Indira Gandhi was assassinated by her own Sikh bodyguards; later her son, Rajiv, following her as Prime Minister, met a similar fate at the hands of Tamil Secessionists. The inherited danger even followed him outside his country to the United States. In Selwa Roosevelt's book *The Keeper of the Gate*, the former US Chief of Protocol describes how she needed to arrange tighter security for him than for any other Head of State. 'Tents were constructed to cover his comings and goings. We never entered a building by its proper entrance. I came to know cellars and secret doors in every stop on our itinerary,' she wrote.

The decision to 'closet' Madame Pandit in her house was an ugly one. It was followed by a similar act by Indira Gandhi when she arrested Nan Pandit's daughter. Author Nayantara Sahgal hadn't confronted her relative while she was the Prime Minister but once she was swept out of office, Mrs Sahgal felt safe and gave her personal view of Mrs Gandhi's regime in a national newspaper. Indira Gandhi was re-elected and prison was Sahgal's final reward.

I knew Nan Pandit for nearly forty years. We met when she presided over the UN while I still lived in the United States. I had constant opportunity to appreciate and enjoy not only her political skills but her capacity for friendship, both over there and in London where she later came as High Commissioner. One example of this occurred in our Sussex home. After she had threatened for years to cook us 'a real Indian meal', a Sunday luncheon-party was ultimately arranged. The *soignée* greyhaired High Commissioner, dressed in a gold-trimmed sari, wrapped herself in a huge apron and went to work in our kitchen, our interested staff watching while keeping out of her way. The delicious buffet of Indian food that followed was her gift.

While cooking, she was serenaded by two guests: Line Renaud, the French chanteuse, who sat on a kitchen bench accompanied by her music-publisher husband, Loulou Gaste, who played his guitar at her feet. 'Oh, mon God!' actress Anna Massey exclaimed when she caught sight of all of us. Food was served in the garden under one of Sussex's great summer skies, amid a multitude of flowers; the conversation was unforgettable and is still a special memory.

After retiring to India, Nan Pandit longed for trips to England. The last one she made was almost wrecked when Indira Gandhi limited her to the sum of only one hundred pounds for plane tickets and all other expenses. We and other friends in London helped her out. We found her much less voluble, very pale and genuinely sad. She must have known her life would finish badly and it did, after a long illness.

She was still alive when my husband and I were arranging to go to India in 1990 to meet Mother Teresa, so I wrote to her to say how much we hoped to see her. She wrote back, begging us not to try. 'I'm too ill, and embarrassed by my condition. I don't want to be seen.' Loving her, we agreed with heavy hearts to honour her wish.

India's leading female today is a woman I've never met, but her power-drive deserves at least a mention: Jaya Lalitha claims she is the Virgin Mary.

Madame Chiang Kai-Shek is one woman who wouldn't at all mind being called power-hungry, for power has been her life-sustainer. Aged ninety-nine in 1996, now living on Long Island in the United States, ailing and frail, she has lost every possibility of a power base. When I visited her during the Korean War, I found her blazing with contempt for the weak-willed allies, America in particular, with whom she no longer had any influence.*

My visit to her in Taiwan was unscheduled. It happened by chance when leap-frogging on army planes to get back to the United States

* See chapter 'Perils of Friendship', page 361.

after leaving the war front in Korea. I was excited by the idea of seeing this famous woman again when the pilot of the navy plane announced that he could only go as far as Taipei. I had met the wife of General-issimo Chiang Kai-Shek before, during her visits to the United States as First Lady of China. She had brought a queenly retinue to the White House, wearing lavish clothes and jewellery, and bringing the famous silk sheets she insisted be used on her bed, all of which brought her questionable publicity.

I knew it could be an interesting stop-off in Taipei; she would be the first person to call on before even checking in with the American Ambassador. She was at home, painting a Chinese scroll, the new hobby in her boring life of exile. She later gave it to me, and with it a beautiful little marble seal bearing the word 'Fleur' translated into Chinese, *May Hua*, meaning flower, which she told me to use on stationery. Her scroll, six feet long by two feet wide, was a fast-brush ink drawing of a branch of blossom, a traditional design. Sadly both the scroll and seal were lost in my move to England. Looking at her working in Taipei, I marvelled that frustration and contempt for her modest surroundings had not interfered with the delicate ink-wash Chinese technique she used in painting.

She was openly irritated, no, actually angry, to be found in such reduced circumstances, a small, nondescript house of the size and type usually found in poorer neighbourhoods bordering big cities any-where. She tried to hide her embarrassment at being discovered in such a setting by insisting on offering hospitality, an invitation which she issued like a command. More about this in the chapter 'Perils of Friendship'.

Before I departed four days later for the United States, we were together for a formal farewell in her small sitting room. She was not only in a bad mood, but infuriated by America's behaviour. The former First Lady of China (I can only think of her as their worst *man*) turned on me without a word of warning and hissed out: '*You Americans are fools. You have the Atom Bomb. Why don't you throw it on China?*'

Mme Chiang gave other evidence of her hunger for power, accord-ing to Mike Cowles, who told me the following story just after we were married. Later he wrote about how it happened on the 'One World' trip he made with Wendell Willkie in 1942.

That 31,000-mile trip was made in forty-nine days in the fastest

185

available bomber to ensure Willkie's safe return. Having defeated Willkie in the Presidential election campaign, President Roosevelt gave his permission for him to make the 'One World' trip but obviously had to see him safely back to avoid being accused of having rid himself of his political opponent. Mike Cowles was invited to go along.

In Chungking, China, the two men finally met the Generalissimo and his wife, Mme Chiang, and discovered that the Chinese couple were comparative strangers. It was said they had married strictly for convenience, so that he might become a part of the fabulously rich Soong family who had once shaped China's history. On this historic trip, Mme Chiang had her dangerous, short-lived affair with Wendell Willkie after a huge welcoming reception by the Generalissimo. This brief love affair had an amazing consequence. It had taken place in Mme Chiang's secret apartment on the top floor of the Women's and Children's Hospital. Mme Chiang was so besotted by Willkie she asked to see Mike Cowles privately before they left China, pleading with him to make sure that Willkie would beat Roosevelt in the next election for the Presidency. *She offered to pay any costs!*

The conversation concluded with her agitated promise: 'If Wendell could be elected, he and I would rule the world, I the Orient, Wendell the rest.'

VI

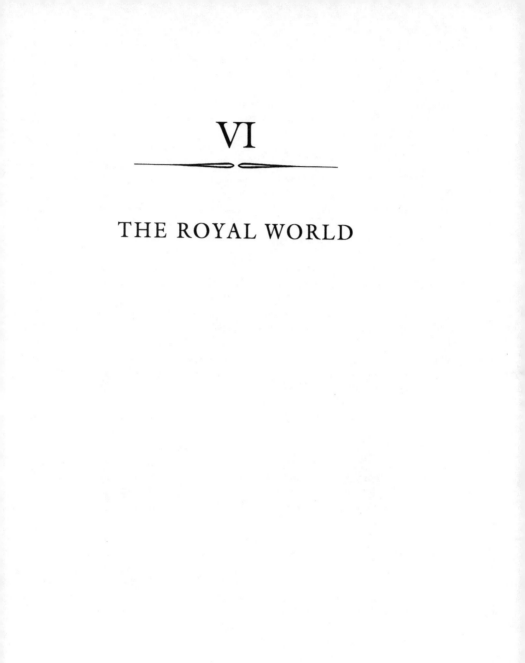

THE ROYAL WORLD

EVERYONE'S FAVOURITE ROYAL in Britain is Queen Elizabeth the Queen Mother, whose friendship has truly enriched my life.

I had been presented to her in New York City at a small dinner party in the fifties given by the American Ambassador to the United Kingdom, Lewis Douglas, who had accompanied her and King George VI to the United States on a State visit. The Queen charmed everyone with her lively mind and inviting personality. Talk was never difficult; a soft smile and a hand outstretched put one at ease instantly.

Soon after, I came to live in London and began to experience her celebrated warmth and curiosity. Her eagerness to *know* inspires those who meet her socially at dinner parties in our London home. My guests are always chosen by keeping a vow I made many years ago: never to invite the same cast. Potted biographies of all guests are sent in advance to Clarence House, a list often spiced by friends from around the world and always with a mixture of artists, writers, political figures and just plain, but interesting, friends.

At one such occasion, for the Queen Mother's eightieth birthday, I invited Luciano Pavarotti and sat him at her side at table. He gave her his favourite recipe for making pasta. He ended up singing 'Happy Birthday' in which we all joined.

On another occasion, international banker Edmund Safra and his wife Lily arrived in London and were delighted when I asked them to dine with the Queen Mother. Mrs Safra expressed her pleasure in a special way: attached to a tiny box which arrived an hour before dinner was a small bouquet of rare flowers. Their own personal florist always arrives a day in advance, wherever they go, to ensure that their homes all over the world are properly flower-filled on their arrival. I wore the gem, which attracted notice from our royal guest. Her letter the next day mentioned its beauty. I had pointed out to her the woman who gave it to me and 'that lady in pink' was mentioned in the letter. I was able one day to show it to the extravagant giver, to her delight.

After another dinner, we showed a film of anthropologist Jane Goodall's work. The brave woman was then living in an African rain forest, studying the behaviour of wild gorillas. Baron Hugo von Lawick, her husband, had made a superb film documentary of her life in Gombe, near where Mary and Louis Leakey made their famous anthropological discoveries. As luck would have it, Queen Elizabeth and King George VI had spent part of their honeymoon there, and had seen those same sights, and announced to us how much they enjoyed the experience.

My husband and I enjoy our visits to Clarence House. On one occasion I was telephoned by a lady-in-waiting to see if I would be free for tea a few days later; I didn't ask but I wondered if it was to be a big tea party. Would I need to wear my one and only hat (for weddings and funerals)? Carry gloves? My husband laughed. 'The Queen Mother knows you never wear hats!' I did carry gloves, just in case.

I found myself alone in a room which is normally full of guests. I sat there waiting, until I heard lively footsteps. I knew the Queen Mother was on her way. The door opened. She was alone.

We talked about mutual friends and current news and what I was up to. Suddenly she asked if I understood why I was invited.

'No, I haven't a clue, but you have made me very happy by having me on my own, a very special honour.'

'Then let me tell you. Although you've been in the country for many years, in these changing times have you ever been asked to a *genuine* English tea? The old traditional kind? I wanted to share that with you.'

The doors to the dining room opened to a splendid sight: the large round table was set out with a gold samovar, an array of at least four cakes, scones, bread and a variety of jams, and biscuits, all sitting on beautiful lace, and served on elegant porcelain and silver, enhanced by a glorious display of flowers.

'How would you like your tea?' I was asked. The Queen Mother was ready to serve it herself from the samovar.

'I'm afraid I can't take tea,' I replied. 'My heart specialist insists on *no caffeine*.'

'Then I won't take any either. But what cake would you like to *start* with? The chocolate or the lemon?'

Words fell out of my mouth: 'Good heavens, if I start with one cake, I'm afraid I'll go right through them all, as well as everything else on the table. That would be fatal!'

'Good! Neither shall I,' she announced, getting up.

We went back to the couch on which we had been sitting, taking up the conversation where we had stopped, until I felt it was time to depart. Before I rose to go, I was informed that I wouldn't need to leave by the door I regularly used; my chauffeur had been told to come to the family entrance instead. We both walked down the hall, past the equerry's room and pantry to the door where my car waited. I departed with an affectionate farewell.

The family entrance is in Ambassadors Court. Facing the wrong way, we had to circle around the courtyard and then to move slowly forward. As we reached the family door again, the Queen gestured us to stop. 'You've forgotten your gloves! They were left on the couch.'

The day before we went off on our summer stay in Spain last year, we went to lunch at Clarence House. This time our visit began in the beautiful sunlit flower garden, where under a large, bright umbrella the Queen Mother sat, upright, directing the occasion. We were served by familiar footmen in traditional scarlet livery. Most of the staff are known to us – one in particular, a genius at flower-arranging. We went inside for delicious food and highly entertaining conversation.

In Clarence House diverse pieces of art live in harmony with elegant furniture. The paintings that particularly attract are Augustus John's portrait of the red-bearded George Bernard Shaw (though a small painting, it makes a considerable impact), Walter Sickert's superb painting of the Queen Mother's father-in-law, George V, and the remarkable early Monet that hangs in one of the drawing rooms, previously in the Clemenceau collection. The Queen Mother has an eclectic eye for paintings, and collects the works of such a variety as Sidney Nolan, Alfred Sisley, Graham Sutherland, Paul Nash, Duncan Smith and L. S. Lowry, whose scenes of pre-war northern industrial landscapes peopled by matchstick figures are so widely popular. There are also works in bronze and fine porcelain. My heart always lifts when I go into the Garden Room and see one of my own paintings of a friendly cheetah sitting boldly on a Louis XV table.

This is the Queen who pioneered the walkabout on a visit to Canada in 1939, a practice all the royals have followed since. During the London blitz of 1940, her small figure picking a way through the rubble in the East End was an inspiring sight to the people, showing her courage during what was then a new kind of war on civilians. Buckingham Palace was hit but she and the King refused to move to safety; they were glad, she announced, to share such an experience with so many others. This was said with smiles, good humour and a dignity that she has never lost.

She is mentally indefatigable. Though patron of hundreds of organizations, her attendance at functions witnesses her genuine interest. I have been present at a few, and noted how everyone responds to her ability to turn to perfect strangers as if they are old friends.

How does one characterize this great lady, her irresistible grace, even a raffish sort of charm? I started by reminding myself that she *is* her century; she was born with it in 1900, to become a beloved symbol of the British royals, known within the family as 'The Firm'. Ninety-five in August 1995, her energy astounds, her stamina amazes, and her curiosity is still as lively as ever.

As much as I would like to be in tune with her favourite pastimes, I am quite out of hoof when it comes to her love of horses and passion for racing. She has had over four hundred winners to date and she can and does discuss their form. I fare better on fishing, as once upon a time in a former transatlantic life, I did love to cast a line in Canadian streams. These days I often see another image of the Queen Mother I carry in my mind's eye, the sight of her standing thigh-deep in the water, casting her fly in a Scottish stream.

Yes, I am totally devoted to the Queen Mother, and grateful for her friendship. I love my copy of Godfrey Talbot's book on her which she inscribed in her own distinguished hand: 'To Fleur Cowles, by her friend, Elizabeth R'.

It was Clare Boothe Luce's idea that I be named as the Ambassador to the Coronation of Queen Elizabeth II. She had said: 'A remarkable young woman is going to be made Queen . . . this is an assignment made to order for a woman – and you, Fleur, are that woman.' A whisper into President Eisenhower's ear was all that was needed.

When the President announced my appointment, Clare Luce may have beamed with satisfaction, but not everybody did. It caused a furore among certain of the older socialites waiting in line expecting to receive the honour themselves, in particular one sad, jealous female relative who conducted a silly vendetta against me. Also raised in protest was the voice of that died-in-the-wool Republican, cosmetic queen Elizabeth Arden, who, perhaps rightly, felt that the sums she contributed to the Presidential campaign entitled her to be named. Another objector was the grimly-determined female British politician, Lady Astor who had chosen a friend in Washington for the honour. All this cut no ice. I survived the turmoil, much too happy to be sidetracked by maliciousness.

I still have memorable recollections of the experience. My commendation from Foreign Secretary John Foster Dulles was a long warm letter thanking me for the prideful way I'd conducted the assignment. It pushed all the female nonsense into the waste-basket of time. The President had given me a rewarding experience – allowing me to become a tiny stitch in the historic tapestry of the event.

I go back to 1953 to recall the ceremony which crowned a young Princess. Times, ideas and even loyalties have changed since then. Today, the disturbing question of the future of the monarchy is discussed openly, and 1995 in particular was a year when public respect for the royals started to drain away significantly.

Morality and the monarchy's costs are worries. Monarchists, and I am one, prefer it to the Presidential system, which would be a disaster here, even though much has changed since the days when Britain wielded worldwide Imperial power, when fifty per cent of all manufactured goods were made in Britain, when the Royal Navy could dictate world politics. Today, we live in a hard-pressed, small island, one I love.

It is quite impossible for me to forget the atmosphere and the incredible joy around us when as American Ambassador I attended the Westminster Abbey Coronation. I found myself in a cocktail of glitter, a superbly organized fairyland, an unforgettable pageant. Among the many delights was the lasting friendship I formed there with the great George C. Marshall, who came as President Eisenhower's personal representative.

Art Buchwald wrote in the Paris *Herald-Tribune* that it was

'England's wettest hour'. The Coronation procession to and from Westminster Abbey took place in pouring rain while millions stood on wet streets in a cold wind with soaked clothes and blown hair – yet I saw only happy faces. Millions watched at home, most of them on their very first black and white television set.

Crowds slept on kerbstones for forty hours to reserve their places. I saw a tent pitched by an American man; fortitude knew no nationality. One very old lady parked her stool on the pavement for twenty-four hours. 'This will be my fourth Coronation,' she boasted to me that night. I found it very hard to slip inside my linen sheets and warm eiderdown in our luxury hotel when I knew she was out there below in the cold and damp. Children were everywhere, schools having been given places of honour on the route.

Inside the Abbey, despite the opulence of everyone's dress, I remember most of all the colourful spectacle made by Zulus, Arabs, Indians, Chinese, Nepalese tribesmen, Germans, Russians and coroneted British and European nobility, tiaras obligatory for all women whether royals or not. We were mixed up, like confetti, side by side. Turbans, plumage and 'emerald jewels' blended together with Western opulence. There were some with grim smiles but differences were ultimately resolved by a sense of sharing in the greatest show on earth. The Princess, a tiny, dignified figure, was a moving sight as she was given the new robes of Queen Elizabeth II to cover her simple dress. I kept thinking of her predecessor, Queen Elizabeth I, so passionate about her clothes that she left a thousand ball dresses at her death.

Psychological and political barriers were temporarily broken down; gathered together were the disparate elements of the widespread British colonies, many since gone. First they stood aloof, strangers in a crowd, not mingling, not speaking, but gradually they melted. Political frictions didn't cease automatically, but they were lessened.

The logistics involved in fitting the limousine for General Marshall and me into the procession were typical of the Foreign Office's incredible organizational skills. It might have been an army landing! We were given an enormous chart every morning, with every conceivable necessary data for the day in minute detail: what time to leave (never a moment later), when and where we would eat, the time to arrive and what time to leave a party, what to wear and when a change of clothes was required, including *exactly* what – down to jewellery (if any).

Because of General Marshall's age and prestige, it was arranged that our car would be the next to the last in the procession, to give him not only a longer night's rest but also the shortest wait in the Abbey. All had been rehearsed, down to the split seconds: exactly when breakfast would be at our doors, a lift set aside just for us, even the fact that General Marshall was to get right into the car *first*, not to lose needless seconds in unnecessary politesse towards me. We did our job, leaving as planned, driving at a pre-set speed to arrive at the correct moment when our car had to glide into the empty space maintained for it at the precise instant the procession appeared.

Guests at the Abbey were given lunch in Westminster Hall. The darkened mahogany-brown stone walls were hung with huge fuchsia and orange-coloured ropes of flowers which had been flown in from Africa during the night. I now never lose an opportunity to put fuchsia and orange flowers together, difficult as it is to find them both at the same time.

Trooping the Colour took place nine days later and once again, all the main streets of London were clogged by cars and crowds. Only a few people ever got anywhere near the ceremony but they stood on kerbs everywhere as if they could see. I watched from the Foreign Office in Anthony Eden's reception room, but thousands accepted just being in crowds *anywhere*. They didn't *need* to see. Incredible? That was Britain, 1953.

The British public's attitude today towards the monarchy is such that I thought it would be of interest to have a postscript to the Coronation, to remind us of what it was like over forty years ago.

The year of 1995 provided shattering disillusionment on all fronts, with a tired government, the inadequacies of the law, the police, the royal family, and even the Church of England divided within over the ordination of women and the acceptance of homosexuality in the clergy. Sleaze in government and greed in corporate business were bywords. Winston Churchill could never have realized how prescient were his words when on Coronation Day in 1953 he described the new young Queen this way: 'The gleaming figure whom Providence has brought us in times when the present is hard and the future veiled'. So I have listed the diverse elements which made up that unforgettable event, the things that I remember most about the Coronation.

Most moving: The Queen, divested of her ermine-trimmed crimson velvet robe and train while in the Abbey, in an austere white dress, seated in the huge King Edward chair made in 1297, as Handel's beautiful anthem 'Zadok the Priest' was sung. Elizabeth looked like a small, defenceless girl until anointed and invested with the royal garments as a symbol of her sovereignty.

A near accident: As Prince Philip stood up to kiss his wife's cheek he touched her heavy crown, moving it off balance. Almost imperceptibly, she nudged it back before it could fall. A human touch to the ritual.

Gayest moment: Dancing with Prince Bernhard of the Netherlands. He and I were without our spouses and were often paired.

Most unforgettable: An African wearing a lion's mane, his face pushed through the open jaws, directly opposite me across the Abbey aisle. African kings in conventional jackets, shirts and ties, over little more than loin cloths or short skirts or fur pelts – below them bare knees above short black street socks and black street shoes.

Most dazzling: Huge ropes of emerald 'eggs' worn by Maharajahs against the whiteness of their royal Indian costumes.

Most influential: The Duke of Norfolk, the Earl Marshal and Senior Catholic of England, who stage-managed it all. He decided who was invited, what guests must wear and who sat where. In fact, there was such a clamour for seats that for the first time in history, England's peers had to *ballot* for them.

Most engaging: Queen Salote of Tonga, six foot tall with a smiling face, in an open carriage in the pouring rain, moving all English hearts.

Most innocent: The teenage Crown Prince of Japan (now Emperor), probably the youngest person there, with his delightful court whom I always found standing close by me, no matter where we went. His English was non-existent, so we always exchanged the same few words of greeting. On the shy Prince's first visit to the West, he apparently chose me as a 'friendly' figure.

Statistical facts: More than forty years later, they still fascinate. The cost, even in our moon-journey age, was staggering. Millions worked for a year for a twelve-hour event which cost six million dollars at the 1953 rate.*

The Queen's 1761 coach: Weighing over a ton, it was at that time worth more than £150,000 ($225,000); though completely overhauled, it was still hardly comfortable. The Queen rehearsed in it and she also had to learn to walk in her robes, balancing the huge imitation crown made for rehearsals by a theatrical costumier.

Most of the 7500 Abbey guests sat in a new extension whose unsightly framework had to be covered in 1500 yards of blue and gold damask. 770 square yards of blue and gold carpets were laid on the floor. 6000 stools embroidered with the Queen's cipher were made for more important guests in the Abbey. Mine now sits in my drawing room in London. By the way, only half were able to *see* the ceremony.

The six and a half miles of the Coronation procession's route were lined with covered stands with seats for 100,000. Sloping uncovered platforms were placed beneath *them* (so that another 'favoured' 24,000 could *stand!*). All positions were for sale, more for the covered places and a little less for uncovered. The press, radio and TV had to pay about £5000 for their places.

The cost: The Queen spent about £250,000 ($375,000) on the official entertaining which began, for her, in May and lasted through July.

Security arrangements: These were complex to protect the Queen, other royals, and the street population, for whom 16,500 policemen had to be trained in crowd control methods, and finally, each of us as representatives at the Coronation. How much, I wonder, did I personally cost? Everyone entering the United Kingdom was screened. 800,000 overseas visitors had to be watched. 250,000 came from the Commonwealth, 350,000 from Europe and 200,000 from the USA.

Crime: A Black Book of criminals was issued and a search made to find and keep a check on each. The identity of every person who would sit or watch from a window, a shop or rooftop had to be given to the police and every workman in the Abbey.

---

* All sums quoted are based on 1953 currency rates worth probably ten times more today.

The horses had to be taught to be indifferent to screaming, waving, pushing, hysteria! What an enormous work-out for these animals. 15,500 policemen, 100 on horseback, were detailed to the route itself, 5000 brought in from other parts of the United Kingdom. All were quartered in tents in Kensington Palace Gardens. 150 ambulances and first-aid stations were on the route alone. 150 to 200 police cars patrolled in the back of the nine-foot crash-barriers erected behind the route to keep out crowds trying to penetrate the sealed-off area.

Flowers: for over a year, government greenhouses grew flowers in the 'reds, white, blues and yellows' needed; 300,000 extra rose plants, the future Queen's favourite flower, had to be set out a year before.

Accommodation: floating hotels, including large liners, were docked in the Thames; channel steamers were chartered and forty private yachts also anchored on the river, to be used as small hotels. The Goring Hotel became the Buckingham Palace Annexe to take the royal overflow.

Remembered conversations: Talking with Heads of State and royals from all over the world, occasionally politically, though always under direction, informally. There were always odd moments at which to drop the official status and to ask questions. It was later with the El Glaoui, then the Pasha of Marrakech; he had hardly spoken a word at the Coronation, but he was loquacious in Paris at a dinner we shared, when he invited me to his palace in North Africa. He was at that time one of the world's most powerful individuals who could, at any moment, summon over 500,000 mounted and armed tribesmen ready for battle. Not many years later, he was dead, having been deposed, stripped of his position and his fortune, together with his sons. Our conversation now seems medieval.

Causes célèbres: Everyone tried to pin me down to discuss McCarthy or the Rosenberg spy case. Communists had managed to promote the idea that even our Supreme Court was being intimidated, mainly by McCarthy. When he toppled, Americans could again hold their heads high in Europe.

Jealousy: The talkative Nancy, Lady Astor, visiting America, actually named in an interview the woman she had personally chosen for my job. An American, married to an English peer, Nancy Astor is often considered the first woman to be elected to the Commons.

Apparently not so (in fact Countess Markiewicz, a Sinn Fein candidate in a Dublin ward, was elected to Parliament in 1918, but never took her seat).

Recently written: In May 1994, Sir Roy Strong, former Director of the Victoria & Albert Museum, whom I believe to be very much a royalist, wrote an article for the London *Times* on the image of the Queen today entitled 'Fitting Image'. He reminded us that we live in the age of the long-range camera. Certain photographs of the Queen, often unkind and unflattering, which would once have been inconceivable and thus not available for publication, are now printed regularly.

He went on to refer to the Commonwealth, 'in terminal decline'. 'By the next century,' he continued, 'the monarchy will be virtually back to where it was in 1603, on a par with the Netherlands, Denmark and Spain.'

It has been estimated that the present cost of the House of Windsor is £300,000 a day – a price which would never have been questioned on those inspired occasions of pageantry – the loyalties, rejoicing and expectations of Coronation days. In 1994, *The Times* organized a monarchy debate: it broke the ancient taboo of silence and opened wide the door to further discussion. Later, the Queen herself spoke of her *annus horribilis* after a year of miserable royal happenings: broken marriage (Charles and Diana), toe-kissing (Fergie) and the fire at Windsor.

If the septuagenarian Andreas Papandreou, Prime Minister of Greece, thought he was consigning Greece's King Constantine to oblivion, when on a day early in April 1994 he decided to confiscate his property, deprive him and his entire family of Greek citizenship, and make them *persona non grata* in their own homeland, he was mistaken. He merely elevated the 53-year-old King to world prominence and damaged even further his own tattered reputation.

In an early-day motion, thirty-three members of the House of Commons in London condemned Papandreou's intention 'to destroy the former King Constantine of the Hellenes as a Greek citizen, removing his citizenship and his passport, by appropriating his property without compensation including his family graveyard, through use of edicts imposed by military dictators and by destroying his basic human right of recourse to the courts of his own country to challenge the validity of these edicts and law'.

The same outcry came from the US Senate's Committee on Foreign Relations, originated by Senator Claiborne Pell. A brave Greek newspaper, the *Apogevmatin*, took a poll of 2400 people to test their reaction to the shameful edict. Constantine received a higher proportion of support than he had in the 1974 referendum.

Trouble is no stranger to this Greek royal, whom I have known since he was very young. When he was an infant the family had to evacuate to Crete to escape the German Army's advances, launched to bolster the failing Italian invasion. They fled to Egypt, then to South Africa to the welcoming arms of Field Marshal Jan Smuts.

When at twenty-three his father's death made him King, he was actually guided by a witty, remarkable old politician, philosopher and socialist poet, George Papandreou. He was the father of the present Prime Minister, Andreas Papandreou. The old man had a great following among the left-wing elements, and his name served as a ready passport to his son's election victory.

'I find it bizarre,' King Constantine reminded me. 'A Prime Minister who left Greece, renounced his citizenship to become American and served in the armed forces *as a nurse* – when Greece itself was fighting for her life against the Nazi and Fascist forces. It is bizarre for him to dare claim that my family and I are not Greek!'

Greece is today a troubled country, criticized on three counts: its nationalistic manner during its tenure of the Presidency of the European Union; for being taken to the European Court of Justice for its embargo against Macedonia, and for some of its dealings in the Balkans and neighbouring Albania – though obviously not guilty on all counts, since it won its case in the European Court.

If King Constantine does not receive justice in the Greek courts, his case will be taken to the Court of Human Rights in Strasbourg where few expect Papandreou to be upheld. Now no longer Prime Minister his claims are certainly suspect–that after two visits in twenty-seven years, Constantine is a threat to Greece, and that he and his family are not Greek.

The King has been in Greece since his deportation on only two occasions: to attend his mother's funeral in their family's graveyard (one day was all that was allowed, no more), and in early 1994 when he took his family there for a sailing holiday. They were buzzed by the air force, harassed by gun boats, but welcomed warmly by village people.

As to his Greekness: since 1863 the family history has been Greek. His great-grandfather, King George, came from Denmark but was *elected* and was on the throne for fifty years. His grandfather was born in Greece and led the forces in the liberation of Epirus and Macedonia. His uncle, Alexander I, born in Greece, was its King and saw the liberation of Thrace. Another uncle, George II, born in Greece, was King when the Communist aggression was stopped in 1944–45. Every single man served in the Greek army.

In 1967, he fled from Greece when the Colonels seized power, gathering up his mother and sister and pregnant wife, Anne-Marie, daughter of the King and Queen of Denmark. She has proved to be remarkably calm and dignified for over twenty-five years of enforced exile. I was a guest at their wedding when both were very young, and could hardly have been aware of their difficult future.

Constantine took what little he could carry, and flew as far as the petrol in his plane's tanks would take him – which was to Rome. Between then and now, he has lived in London amid other Greek exiles. Eventually he made a deal with the Greek Government, a tax deal to cover all the money they said he owed. In addition, he also handed back the forests around Tatoi, the family home outside Athens, to be used as a picnic area, a wildlife sanctuary and a parkland for the people. The land was worth much more than the taxes owed. He kept Mon Repos on Corfu, where Prince Philip and his own eldest daughter Alexia were born, but which has since been forcibly taken over by the Mayor of the Municipality, as has their home in Tatoi along with the family graves.

In London, he maintains a dignified political silence, though connected by marriage to cousins everywhere, including Queen Elizabeth II. All royal Europeans are in fact connected – Belgians, English, Luxemburgers, Dutch, Danes, Swedes, Spanish and Norwegian. They frequently come together in royal style, as on Constantine's fiftieth birthday which was celebrated at Spencer House in London. It was a magical feast, where every table (there were seventy) had a royal person as its host; I sat next to the handsome son of the late King of Italy.

Before that, at Elsinore Castle in Denmark, all came together to celebrate the King and Queen's twenty-fifth wedding anniversary.

What is he concerned with now? Education is very much on his mind. Through the friendship and teachings of Dr Kurt Hahn he became a Patron of the Round Square Conference Group of schools – there are twenty-five around the world. The pupils are taught service, adventure and international understanding. With Queen Anne-Marie and other members of the Greek community, he founded the Hellenic College which all his five children attended.

As a sailor, in 1960 he was the first Greek in fifty years to win an Olympic gold medal. He is still involved in the Olympic movement and remains President of Honour of the International Federation of Yachting.

His children give him cause for pride. The oldest, Alexia, now twenty-nine, lives in Barcelona where for three years she has dedicated herself to teaching children with Down's Syndrome – brave work. Crown Prince Pavlov, twenty-seven, lived in Washington with the Crown Prince of Spain; both were students at Georgetown University, studying international relations. He celebrated his marriage to Chantal Miller in a two-day wedding event. They now live in New York City. His next son, Nikolaos, twenty-five, graduated from Brown University in the USA and now lives there as a TV journalist. The two little ones, Theodora, eleven, and Philippos, eight, are still at home.

His exile, he admits, has given him much time with his children. I have observed the same closeness that I used to marvel over when in Greece and saw father, mother and children together. Their London house, not unlike its neighbours, is a red-brick suburban villa with an acre of garden. It is wonderfully compact, chintzed, of course, as in Tatoi. There is no ostentation but family portraits do reveal their royal background. Everything they brought out of Greece was authorized and stamped by Greek Customs officials.

Constantine keeps an office in London where 35,000 items of correspondence arrive each year, many requesting his help. He sees Greek delegations, some from as far away as Melbourne, which has the world's third largest population of Greeks. He worries about the fate of Greeks persecuted in Albania and Macedonia and would dearly like to help alleviate their suffering.

We were close enough for me to be invited to go with him and his

Queen on their 'second honeymoon'. I was in Sussex when my butler announced, 'The King is on the phone.' To this day, I am still being ribbed by guests who were present when I asked, 'Which King?'

They were going off to the infrequently-travelled north, an idea popular with the Greek people, and I was thrilled to receive an invitation to accompany them. We left Athens in a plane piloted by the King, landing at an army base for lunch. Then we drove northwards in the King's green convertible with the army ahead and behind us all the way.

We stopped before each village and walked through it on flower-laden streets, then got back into the car – this procedure was repeated at each stop. We ended up close to the dangerous terrain in the north and this time I swear there were soldiers in the trees. We slept on the floor of churches and halls, little interested in or worried about luxuries. The people of this remote territory were overjoyed by the unique sight of their King and Queen.

I recall another time, while he was on the throne, when we both realized that I was being watched, taped, even followed – because of my closeness to the family. It was agreed, in a moment of hilarity, that it would be a good idea for me to use the code name '007'; from that time, whenever I called him at the palace, I did so. We would then meet and talk as we walked around the palace garden, and I gave him information I thought would be useful to him. His enemies were crudely vocal. Even the CIA wished to see me because they reasoned I might know more than they, and I often did, but I didn't collaborate. When we resorted to the code name, the palace operator always asked who was calling His Majesty. I would give my code name. She then would ring the King to announce, 'Fleur Cowles is on the phone!'

Today, the King refrains from speaking out on political matters; he does not want to become a destabilizing factor during a period when the country faces many problems, but he does feel he deserves the same rights to speak out as any private citizen.

He was invited by both Nelson Mandela and President de Klerk to Mandela's inauguration as President of the new South Africa. On his return, he pronounced to me that both men had put a credo into practice, a great truth: that to build bridges, you have to be unselfish and patient, that it is better to light candles than curse the darkness. He was himself able to light a candle and effect an important mission for both men when he was asked to intervene with Chief Buthelezi of the Zulus.

He had hoped to serve Greece as a modern king in a democratic society, but it was not to be, he told students in a highly popular speech he made at Oxford University in June 1994. But there are those both within and outside Greece who think he could be a potent healer for a troubled country.

His sister, Sophia, the Queen of Spain, had been described to me by her mother, Queen Frederika of Greece, as '. . . the most dignified of the three children'. She grew up in a fairy-tale tradition, marrying a prince who became a king. If Queen Frederika were alive today, she would be full of pride to know that in the opinion of most Spaniards, she is 'the King's secret weapon', popular and loved.

Few men in a position of power today came to it in the way Juan Carlos did. Franco so trusted the young royal he reared him as his successor. He would not have suspected how Juan Carlos's true strength would come to the fore when he succeeded to the throne after Franco's death. He gave Spain democracy after years of dictatorship and oppression. He had concealed his true intentions, even from friends. When we entertained him and Princess Sophia earlier in London, all our guests were charmed by his quiet, modest personality.

Queen Sophia, like her husband, eschews ostentation. She walked her children to their schools, is good to and with her countrywomen, dresses well but not pretentiously, and is considered 'a good sport'. If an 'unembellished' yacht and the King's pet motorbike scarcely accord with the preconceptions attached to royalty, so be it. By the way, it is rumoured that the entire cost of the monarchy in Spain is less than the cost of the Royal Yacht in Britain.

I once enjoyed a remarkable tribute from an exceptional Emperor, Haile Selassie. His eventual brutal death and the continued imprisonment for years of all his family in Addis Ababa under desperate conditions, make it difficult to recall the King in lighthearted terms. Yet meeting him in the early fifties was, in fact, a delightful experience and I shall tell it as it was.

The Emperor's place in history was secured when he bravely denounced Italy to the world for the invasion of Ethiopia in 1935.

Before that, on becoming Emperor in 1930, he was internationally acclaimed for his modernization programmes, including abolishing slavery in 1932. But vanity must have played a part when he began to style himself 'Elect of God', 'King of Kings' and 'Conquering Lion of the Tribe of Judah'.

I remember vividly the sunny day in spring when he was ending a State visit to the US. We met unexpectedly in a highly unconventional way. It followed a weekend in our country house in Weston, Connecticut, to which I had invited the Assistant Secretary for State for the Middle East and Africa, Henry C. Byroade. The weekend bulged with pulchritude: Jean Vanderbilt, Greta Garbo and Lilli Palmer were there, three beautiful women. Tennis, swimming and good talk filled three very merry days. Byroade intended to return to Washington on Sunday but changed his plans in order to remain in New York to pay Haile Selassie the added courtesy of seeing him off to the airport when he left on the Monday.

Driving to New York City Monday morning in my car, I urged him to use my desk, my telephone and my secretaries to check in with Washington. He was in such a rosy mood that I cautioned him to forget the weekend and 'get back to work'. I continually chided him to become businesslike again when we reached my office. At eleven o'clock, after calling Washington, he telephoned Haile Selassie's apartment at the Waldorf Towers Hotel just around the corner. As he left he popped his head in the door once again to wave one more smiling farewell.

'Tell the Emperor I'll take him to lunch,' I joked as he disappeared.

At eleven-thirty, my telephone rang. 'The Emperor accepts your invitation,' Byroade announced.

'You can't be serious,' I replied.

'Oh yes! He will be delighted to lunch with you before leaving for the airport at three o'clock!'

'You must be mad,' I hissed back at him. 'How can anyone possibly give luncheon to an Emperor and his entourage at an hour's notice. My staff would resign!'

'That's your problem! Come over at twelve-thirty to pick us up,' he announced as he hung up.

What could I do? I thought it over, cursing my own idea of humour, until I saw the better side of the situation: in an hour, entirely through a chance remark, I would meet and get to know a great figure of history. I determined to make the most of it.

Giving a meal to about a dozen in a royal party which included the Crown Prince and Princess of Ethiopia, equerries and lady-in-waiting, Mr Byroade and Henry Simmons, head of Protocol at the State Department, was a challenge. How to do it – with valuable minutes ticking away? Nothing is more embarrassing than formality without perfection, so I knew I could not take them to my house in town. Flowers from our weekend home in Connecticut might still be parked everywhere in their buckets, suitcases probably still unpacked, and only cold food sitting on ice for the returning staff's own luncheon.

I decided that the Emperor had probably never been to a fine New York restaurant. It might amuse him and it would certainly be a change from the rigidly-controlled events of a State visit. I turned over in my mind the possibilities between restaurants and settled for the famous '21 Club' where the food, unquestionably, would be superb. I also knew the ambience would be lively, with a probable handful of notables present.

I telephoned my friend, owner Robert Kriendler: 'Bob, don't ask me *who*, but I'm bringing one of the world's most distinguished gentlemen in a party of eleven to lunch today at one o'clock,' I told him. 'You must promise me not to have the press on hand. Promise me we will be left alone at the table. I'd like the following food ... the following wine ... I'd like four waiters detailed exclusively to our table, and I'd like to have the comfortable large round centre table in the first room upstairs. Make it the finest food you've ever served!' I concluded. Robert Kriendler purred in acquiescence and with the meal in hand, so to speak, I went off in a giddy spirit to the hotel to pick up my royal charges.

My mood took a nose-dive as soon as I left the lift on the royal floor of the Waldorf Towers. A double queue of tightly packed Ethiopian citizens lined the halls leading to his apartment. It would take hours, I realized, for such a procession to file by him for even the briefest presentation.

'Henry! How could you do this to me?' I demanded of Mr Byroade as I found him alone inside the drawing room. 'The Emperor can't possibly see all these people waiting outside and fit in a meal at "21" before leaving for the airport.'

'Relax, please,' he insisted, unruffled. 'The Emperor wants to go. He's looking forward to it. Believe me!'

At that moment, the doors suddenly opened and there stood the man officially titled 'The Conquering Lion of the Tribe of Judah; Haile Selassie I, Emperor of Ethiopia'. The fabled five-foot-two royal, then sixty-one, walked toward me with his stiff formal gait, with hand outstretched. How curly his hair, how grey his beard, how wrinkled his brow, I thought.

'It is kind of you to invite us to lunch,' he announced in English in an almost inaudible voice. After a few minutes of polite conversation, he gave me the cue: 'We might go whenever you wish.'

'Now,' I replied.

Other members of the party filed in, introductions were made and we started out in single file, a strange procession led by an Emperor. We passed the queue in an awesome silence, people realizing that this was the only glimpse they'd have of their ruler.

At the kerb was another surprise; a motor cavalcade, headed by motorcycle police. Though we were only going from 50th to 52nd Street, the official escort, complete with sirens, whined and howled to the door of '21'.

The Emperor rode in my car at the head of the procession. When we arrived at the door of the restaurant, he got out first and I followed. Absolutely insistent that I lead the way, the Emperor slipped behind me as we entered the crowded foyer. Behind us, protocol strictly observed, the party moved back into single file. Mouths dropped open in astonishment as Haile Selassie was recognized. Groups parted, an opening was made for us to file through.

We made our way upstairs, leaving silence behind us; all talk had stopped. Everyone on the stairs immediately flattened themselves against the wall, eyes popping, giving us the greatest possible room. When we entered the dining area, the usual hubbub of noise and conversation came to an abrupt stop. I knew there might be friends in the room but I was determined to avoid making contact, counting on a wall of privacy to be provided by a covey of waiters hovering around us with food and wine.

The Lion of Judah was in a wonderfully relaxed mood, I thought, although nothing about that solemn, somewhat sad mien would have suggested it to anyone out of earshot. I spent the time during luncheon discussing the non-political items of the day, the amusing things one could do at that moment in New York City and even told him a funny, somewhat shaggy, story making the rounds at that time.

'Can't you extend your stay, Your Majesty? If you'd remain for a few more days, I'd love to entertain you properly in the same unofficial and informal way at my home!'

'I would like to accept your invitation but I must leave this afternoon to keep an appointment with Tito; I'm making a State visit to Yugo-slavia,' he replied. 'After that, I'm going to Greece for a four-day visit!'

'Greece? How very exciting,' I replied. 'I'm going to be in Athens myself next Monday. Perhaps we can meet again there.'

He seemed intrigued. I explained I would be there on behalf of President Eisenhower to discuss the Cyprus issue with Foreign Minister Stephanopoulos and his assistant, John Sossidis. This also explained my connection with Assistant Secretary of State, Henry Byroade.

'What bad planning,' the Emperor replied simply. 'You'll be getting to Greece one day after I leave.' On the way to the airport, we repeated to each other how sad it was that we would miss each other in Greece.

Coming back to my office, I was pleased by the way things had gone, from a quip to a successful royal luncheon. My guests had enjoyed it and so had everyone else dining at the '21'.

A few irresponsible diners had tried, but failed, to get my eye in an attempt to meet the Emperor. One person did break through the barricade, however, the late Hollywood gossip reporter, Louella Parsons. She crossed the room unswervingly, put one arm around my shoulder, the other on the Emperor's chair and announced in a loud lisp: 'Fleur, you must introduce me to Haile Selassie; Tyrone Power tells me he is a very nice man!' I gently put her off, suggesting as tactfully as possible that it was not the time and the place. Undaunted, she wrote in her column next day that she'd lunched with Haile Selassie, 'who gave her a beautiful gift!'

She did get a gift, but by mistake. During lunch, the Robert Kriend-lers presented themselves to us as owners of the restaurant. A present which Haile Selassie intended for Florence Kriendler, which a security officer went to get from the hotel, arrived after our departure. It was mistakenly presented to Louella Parsons when the man asked, 'Which lady talked to the Emperor?' Louella walked away with a piece of gold jewellery meant for Mrs Kriendler.

The first thing I did when I got to Athens the next Monday was to call the royal palace and ask the Chamberlain of the Court how Haile Selassie's State visit had gone. 'Don't mention that little man to me,' Mr Levidis responded. 'Would you like to know what he actually tried to do when he was in Yugoslavia? For a person who knows perfectly well how much work is involved in a State visit, he had the cheek to call up from Yugoslavia just a few days before he was due to arrive, to ask if his visit could be postponed for a day or two!'

My heart stopped beating. The legendary Selassie had actually tried to re-arrange his visit so our trips would coincide! Although it was patently impossible, I couldn't get over the flattery implied. Few gestures have touched me more.

Haile Selassie was the most respected man in Africa and the most influential. He will always be remembered for his dramatic appeal to the League of Nations when Ethiopia was invaded by Benito Mussolini. The League's impotence against the fascist invasion was its downfall, and Haile Selassie will go down in history as the man whose test of the League of Nations led to its death. His own death was no less dramatic or sad; he was assassinated by his enemies of whom there were many.

I am not going to add to the mainly scurrilous articles and books that have appeared in 1994 about the beautiful Princess Grace, in which one of the loveliest people I have known was headlined and maligned in ways she didn't deserve after her horrifying accidental death. I would just like to pay her my own personal tribute. I had known her very well for almost forty years since Cary Grant brought her to dinner in New York. I can describe her in a few words: she was good, not bad. She was happy about her life, not sad. She loved all her children and they loved her. So did Prince Rainier, and everyone who really knew her (including the population of Monaco). She was fair and open, unlike many of the jealous women who speak badly of her now. Once when I criticized her for giving an appointment to a man I felt was a very unpleasant person, she silenced me with 'but there's something good in everyone'.

Princess Grace would be proud of daughter Caroline's closeness to Prince Rainier since her death and would have enjoyed seeing Caroline's children grow up in such a natural way, shielded from the pomp and ceremony which was never enjoyed by their mother. She was always proud of Caroline's erudition, especially her knowledge of music. She would have been immensely proud of Prince Albert speaking eloquently at the United Nations in New York in 1994 on behalf of serious causes.

As well as acting, Princess Grace had another artistic talent: ignore the critics who called her dried-flower paintings an amateur activity; her painstakingly finished pieces were imaginative and beautiful, each one a tribute to the flowers she loved.

She was able to fulfil a frustrated wish to act again through her poetry readings to raise money for her charities. I listened to many of them in many countries, delighted by her ability to reflect the style of differing poets. She was generous, and gave a large, often tiring amount of her time to needy local projects, in particular the Ballet School. She had kindness in her deeply Catholic heart.

Her death was a terrible tragedy. The image I retain of the tiny family mass in the palace's chapel is one I can't erase; the loss of a great friend and the brokenhearted, almost comatose, husband and children. So overcome was I that I fell down the stairs immediately after, breaking an ankle so badly I couldn't walk without crutches for almost a year. I still reach for the telephone to call her, as I used to do. Time no doubt will cure that sad habit.

Few people think of Prince Rainier as the family man who gave his children first priority, but they always did come first, and do still. I've seen this at firsthand and frequently read of it in his highly confidential letters.

Cary Grant, the 'villain', as he appears in recent accounts of Grace's life, was anything but that. He was always the warmly-welcomed guest who was also in the palace every time we were there. He was, in fact, a favourite of Prince Rainier; they had similar likes and dislikes. He wouldn't have been asked if the Prince had not looked forward to his visits.

Princess Grace did not deserve the current revelations and lies. And what purpose do they serve? She would have hated the sleaze in these stories, as I do, if she were still alive to read them. That she is not is one consolation.

*　　*　　*

The Shah of Iran's death was a tragedy of cruelty and continued indignities heaped on him by many nations. I knew him well enough to be able to judge objectively his last years in power; some good, some not. I shall never forget, for instance, his remarks on British television while being interviewed by Lord Chalfont, when the Shah was still sitting firmly on his throne. All was very circumspect until Chalfont asked him what reason he could give for treating political prisoners cruelly. Angered, the Shah actually replied that if the West would take a lesson from him they would be rid of their own criminals as well.

I saw a fair amount of the Shah over a period of years, enough to recognize his growing notion that he was a mystic. He was a bundle of mysticism, believing that he actually had psychic powers. Decisions and judgements made on such a basis obviously produced enemies, who finally forced him to flee the country, leading to his final downfall.

It is said, though unconfirmed, that the imprisonment of the American Embassy staff in Teheran was prompted by a New York hospital's acceptance of the dying Shah. The even more dreadful rumour is that he was later rejected by a hospital because of the raid.

When he had to flee from Teheran for the second and last time, he discovered he was turned away by one friend after another all over the Western world, to die slowly of leukaemia. He had ruled for forty years, but in the end he saw his country fall to the aged fundamentalist, Ayatollah Khomeini, who had used his asylum in Paris to plot the Shah's downfall.

The Shah replaced his father during the Second World War when the Allies realized the old man's sympathies for the Nazis would allow them to converge on Iran. He had to begin his reign in this treacherous atmosphere, trying to assert his power over the Mullahs, not always with success. Allowing women to dispense with the veil did him no good. For instance. In the years before his death, I also came to know his second wife Soraya very well after two personal visits to them in Teheran and accompanying them on the trip they made at my invitation to America. He later divorced Soraya and married Farah Dibah and had her and himself royally crowned in a lavish ceremony.

He had been exiled briefly in the early fifties. In those days, according to Soraya, they had to sleep with loaded guns by their beds, concerned by threats from Mohammed Mossadeq, the strange, frail old aristocrat who had taken over the government in order to set the stage for a move to bring Iran closer to the Soviet Union.* The foreign oil conflict gave him the opportunity to strike at the Shah, though it was to be a short-lived success. However, the small scar above the Shah's upper lip resulted from a shootout as he fled the country. Haunted by his father's image, he acted as he thought *he* would have done.

Mossadeq denounced the Shah as too kindly disposed towards the Western oil interests, the foreign firms which for a half century had developed Iran's oil industry. The Shah, in turn, had Mossadeq arrested and tried for treason. Hatred for the eccentric old man grew and pro-Shah support was regenerated.

Soraya explained that they had taken little money out when they had fled to Rome. The Shah, worried beforehand, even wondered if the gold wedding presents in the cellar should be sold. Once he thought of buying a farm in the USA where all his brothers and family could live together and the children be well fed. His salary, according to Soraya, was about a quarter of a million pounds, from which he paid all his and his family's expenses, putting little aside.

I asked about the Crown jewels. They were owned by the State and strictly guarded. They could be borrowed, but Soraya was entitled to only one tiara, one necklace, one bracelet, one ring, one pair of earrings and a triple string of pearls. These jewels, redesigned by Harry Winston, were locked up and *this* wife never saw them again.

The palace, not very grand, was then eighty years old, built by a former dynasty. The rooms, I knew, were large and lavishly brocaded, but all may have been altered by Empress Farah Dibah. The Shah's office was the most interesting room of all, and there we talked at length. I did not need to ask who were his heroes, as they were in a photographic line-up on the mantelpiece: Haile Selassie, King George VI, his father Reza Shah, and President Truman; it was too early for Eisenhower's photo.

When I left Teheran after the first visit, he said: 'My best wishes for your country . . . I have seen it before, and hope one day to see it

---

* See Mossadeq, page 144.

again.' That was all I needed and went quickly to see President Eisenhower. The Turkey-Pakistan Pact was very much on his mind, but a State visit for the Shah was not possible at that time when US oil companies were in a struggle to survive there.

The President hoped I could help, and help I could and did. Since the Shah could not be officially invited, I flew out and gave him my personal invitation to come informally to the USA. First he agreed, and then declined: 'Let me first send the Empress. She's never been and I have, in 1948.' I finally persuaded him to come as well and took the trouble to find out what in the United States he wanted most to see and do. Whatever it was, I arranged it, on an interminable trek over the whole of the land, planning entertainment by suitable hosts in advance.

One California visit he talked about with high hopes still looms large in my memory: our hysterical attendance at the Rose Bowl football game, a fixture which traditionally takes place on 1 January. The night before, we were dancing in the ballroom of one of my friends' homes in Hollywood. I had a hard job to persuade the royals to retire at three o'clock to get some rest before leaving our hotel the next morning to attend the game. The Chief of Police instructed me we must leave at seven a.m. to avoid the crush of traffic through Hollywood and on the freeway to Pasadena, where the match was to take place. Governor Goodwin Knight was campaigning for re-election but sent his personal car and chauffeur for the use of the three of us as a gesture of goodwill, although I actually had a hard time persuading the Shah not to travel in his own limousine.

Not only was seven a.m. far, far too early, but the sun suddenly fled and it began to snow, the first time *ever* in January in California. The Queen and I were in suggested pastel linen suits; we nearly froze to death in the grandstand huddled under quickly-requested umbrellas to shield us from the falling snow. We got back to our hotel after continuing crises there and at lunch, amid comical gaffes, at five o'clock, all ill, all with flu, including the Shah. The details of that day would make a comedy film. The Shah was determined to see it through, but the Queen and I left immediately after the luncheon party, entirely missing the game which was played in awful weather, the Shah huddled under newspapers supplied constantly by his equerry.

213

In New York, on our return and before meeting President Eisenhower, I entertained them – including agreeing to the Shah's wish to play poker one night. Not my game! However, beginner's luck struck and although I couldn't have wagered more rashly, or tried harder to lose, I simply *could not be beaten*. I made a fortune that night, despite fruitless attempts to quit, to send the royal party home early. The Shah was to be given an honorary degree at Columbia University in the morning, and I wanted him to have a rest beforehand. It was after three a.m. when he finally, very reluctantly, agreed to stop.

For nearly six weeks, the royal entourage travelled across the United States. The group included a lady-in-waiting, the equerry and eleven 'colonels', his personal guards in disguise who joined us at every meal, often adding females 'found' *en route*! A new car was bought regularly by the Shah. In Iran his favourites were Jaguars and Rolls-Royces and he flew about in his Beechcraft Bonanza.

Queen Soraya and I often went shopping. I paid for everything and later asked the Embassy in Washington to reimburse me. I gave the royal pair two Chinese dogs I had just found for myself, because Soraya so loved them. They became my farewell gifts.

Their long American trip had one endearing aftermath; my friendship with Ardeshir Zahedi, who was then the Shah's equerry who eventually became Ambassador to the United Kingdom and to the United States. This friendship has lasted without interruption for forty years, ten of them caviar-packed. Since the Iranian Revolution, he lives quietly in Switzerland, but not in isolation.

During the visit I saw enough handholding and affectionate glances to feel assured that the Shah and Soraya were in love. So why the divorce? Any Mohammedan man could get a divorce anytime he wished, provided he promised to look after his wife; but why the sudden decision in this case after seven years of seemingly happy life? The reason was that after all those years, Soraya was unable to produce an heir. By law such a marriage is easily dissolved.

When we first met, I marvelled over the recently married bride, her happiness, her green-eyed beauty. Simply dressed, she wore as jewellery only a wedding ring and pearls. Though quite shy, she revealed her intelligent tastes to me. I noted the bedside books of the former student who had been chosen, without her knowledge while at school in Paris, to be the Shah's bride. She read the most serious books of the time, having been educated in French and loving the classics. She was a changed woman the next time I saw her after their divorce when she came to visit us in Sussex; still beautiful, mature, but very subdued.

When I first knew the Shah, he was relaxed and at ease. Later, I saw his eyes harden and become cold when something irritated him. He always looked straight at me, which I liked because it made me feel immediately at ease. He was only twenty-two when he ascended to the throne in 1941, and thirty-two when we met.

The book *Soraya*, written by the former Empress, includes many warm references to me in her account of that American trip in which they saw New York, San Francisco, Hollywood, Sun Valley, Pasadena and Palm Beach. She met the young Senator, Jack Kennedy, and enjoyed endless rounds of parties. Yet, she wrote, she made no other friends but me.

She was greatly appreciative of my help and hospitality, writing: 'On December 4th, 1954, we flew to America and now began for me an unforgettable period of my life. Our guide was Fleur Cowles, who had visited us in Teheran a few months before. Now she more than repaid our hospitality to her . . . apart from officials and Mrs Cowles, we knew for all intents and purposes nobody in America . . . even in Los Angeles she gave us her helping hand . . . The New York editor, Fleur Cowles, was an entertaining and intelligent woman who I always enjoyed meeting.'

Many years later, when the deposed Shah finally fled his country, he was gravely ill, although neither he nor Empress Farah Dibah actually knew how seriously. He soon discovered that his friends were torn between loyalty to him and their wish to work with Ayatollah Khomeini, his successor. Country after country let it be known that he wouldn't be welcome, following President Carter's lead; the United Kingdom, then the Germans, the French and the Swiss. Where he was welcomed, the hospitality did not last long, even in Morocco. He was not wanted on their territory.

Carter relented when the Shah's grim state of health was revealed. He finally granted him the right to come to America – with horrifying repercussions. The US Embassy in Teheran was suddenly attacked and occupied, all the residents becoming prisoners, blindfolded and frog-marched to an uncertain fate. The Shah was already in New York

City's Cornell Medical Center, under an assumed name (this has been arranged with the help of Henry Kissinger, David Rockefeller and John McCloy). It is said these gestures could have provoked the invasion of the Embassy in Teheran.

As a result of the Embassy horror, the Shah was immediately sent to a 'less visual site', this time in Texas. He was already dying, but again had to leave. The cursed traveller spent his last day in the United States in a Texas air force base, lying in the psychiatric ward where windows were barred. Panama was his next stop, but not for long. His wife apparently still hadn't been told he had cancer, learning this only after his death.

In the end, unexpected salvation came from President Sadat of Egypt who gave him a refuge without any strings attached. However, the Shah died after surgery to remove his spleen, dignified to the end, despite bewildering rejection. He died a brave but broken man.

Sadat may have paid with his own life for his loyalty to him, according to William Shawcross, who in his book *The Shah's Last Ride** believes that the Egyptian President was promptly repaid for this kindness by whipped-up fundamentalist fury which led to his assassination.

The medical gossip after the Shah's death was not pleasant. All the eminent doctors apparently disagreed constantly in diagnosing his illness and in deciding on his treatment. The Shah himself could never have been sure of his condition, but somehow must have mustered up adrenalin from time to time to keep alive his hope to return one day to Iran.

He had wanted to turn his country into a huge industrial power, like Japan or Germany. I believe that the man I knew failed because he was such a mix of mysticism and ambition and unwisely confused the two. His son, crowned as his successor in a ceremony far from his country, expects one day to return there to make good his father's dream. That was the Shah's last wish.

On his American visit, Ambassador Ardeshir Zahedi was the Shah's equerry (his ex-wife was the Shah's daughter). Over the weeks in the USA, he and I had so much to discuss and arrange that we got to a 'call me sister and brother' relationship, which in the countless years

* Chatto & Windus, 1989.

since has remained after he became an Ambassador. In 'exile' at the moment in Europe, we continue the friendship each time he visits London.

The only remaining members of the Shah's family whom we still see regularly are the Shah's brother, Prince Gholam Reza Pahlavi, and his beautiful wife, Princess Manigeh, who have now made their lives outside Iran. Princess Manigeh comes from the Jahangani line in Iran, the oldest royal family name in Persia. Their three children have adapted miraculously to changed conditions. All have been superbly educated and all have succeeded in interesting careers. I think of all of them with the greatest affection.

A little story, but a charming one: for the many years that I served on the International Board of the World Wildlife Fund in Geneva, I used to enjoy the dinners which concluded each meeting. At one such gathering, I was seated between Prince Bernhard of the Netherlands, then WWF's President, and the Prince of Nepal, Gyenendra Bir Bikram Shah. His very shy wife insisted on being seated near to her husband. He and I are good friends, so it wasn't difficult to conduct a three-way conversation to include her, sitting next to him at the end of a one-sided table.

Running out of talk, I noticed the vast collection of narrow ruby bracelets that clinked and shone at least nine inches up each arm. I took a moment to admire them and she promptly took one off her left wrist to let me have a closer look. I exclaimed over it as volubly as good manners suggested.

'You must have it,' she said.

I politely refused. 'I simply cannot accept it,' I insisted, to no avail.

'Please,' she continued. 'Keep it. They only cost one dollar each. They're not real!'

I had never before seen a royal Princess in fake jewels, nor have I since. But it certainly endeared her to me.

There are all kinds of royals; one, in particular, the beautiful Ayasha Jaipur, intrigued me so in the mid-sixties that I determined to find out what inspired her extraordinary career. She had been born into royalty and married the Maharajah of Jaipur, an even greater hereditary power than her own family.

But what led one of the most celebrated figures in the international set, totally untrained, to decide to enter the turmoil of Indian politics? Bravely, like a sitting duck, to run against the professional politicians to try to join India's Congress?

We talked it over at that time. She calmly explained that she was tired of hearing royals described as pleasure-loving and money-grabbing; (I know a few who were). She had already been deprived of the right to work with her people because of her position, so she turned to the democratic process, the rough-and-tumble of a political campaign, to seek a national role. She chose the hardest possible route by campaigning against Nehru.

Confounding the critics, she won an opposition seat in the House of Parliament in the first-ever selection of a tiny right-wing party called the *Swatantra*. She chose it because the word itself means 'free'. It was the country's first effective opposition to Nehru's Congress Party other than the Communist who was in the Second House.

I can think of few candidates with so many political handicaps: for one thing, her highly vulnerable 'jet-set internationalism' which her opponents represented to the masses as 'un-Indian'. She was rich *and* royal. And she had chosen to oppose her friend, Nehru, calling him 'too socialistic'. Attacking this father-figure for any reason at all was hardly the wisest platform for a wealthy woman.

Another hurdle was her Western upbringing, although even Prime Minister Gandhi's two sons, Sanjay and Rajiv, were educated in England. Her opponents put a great premium on 'backwoods nationalism' as against her 'foreign internationalism'.

She won the election, in fact, by turning to advantage every one of her supposed handicaps. She never dressed down: instead, she campaigned in elegant gilded chiffon saris, wearing extraordinary jewels without embarrassment and certainly without apology, generally thrilling her audiences of turbaned peasants and village women who thronged to see her, eager to be near and to touch the glamorous princess.

She turned her 'evil internationalism' into an asset by describing what she had seen done for the poor in the world outside India. Such things, she explained, should be made available to Indians. She boasted of her political break with her friend, Nehru, as a badge of courage. If asked a difficult question to which she didn't know the answer she admitted it, a vote-catching display of honesty. Later, she had to support Nehru over the outbreak of fighting with China. 'Being such a central figure in the crisis, we all must support him, give him a hand and do what we can to avert disaster,' she explained.

Summarizing those campaigning days, she told me: 'When I started moving out in the rural areas, I don't think I've ever known such love or felt as much affection in my life as the people gave me.'

Our conversation was taken place in the drawing room of the temporarily-rented home of a friend, Felix Fenston, in London. The ravishing Ayasha, calm and collected, seemed perfectly at home in its atmosphere of trophies from shooting forays, stuffed heads, fully mounted standing tigers and the wildly decorative paintings by Indian artists that punctuated the decor. Soon she would be outraged by mounted tigers when extinction faced them, and she and I fought against this as co-members on the International Board of the World Wildlife Fund.

I found it hard to keep my mind off her own shooting record, off the royal tours, and jewelled elephants, in fact, any of the embarrassing trappings which have become unacceptable in the world today. 'What is your future in politics?' I asked. 'Where can you go? Do you think you are in politics for life?'

'Well, yes, unless something drastic happens,' she replied.

Something drastic did happen in the mid-seventies. Her handsome husband died suddenly, leaving her alone and lonely. The government of India, headed by that very different woman Indira Gandhi, took all royal privileges away from the powerful princes and princesses.

As a widow, she became the Raj Mata of Jaipur, starting a new life. We later talked about the time before her husband died when I had found her on a huge couch, rolled up like a ball, during a Spanish lesson. In a month she would add a fifth home and a fifth city to her list of addresses, this time the Embassy in Madrid. Her husband, Jai, had become the first-ever Ambassador to Spain from India.

Today, almost all has changed. The Pink Palace in which she once lived was taken away to become one of the world's most extraordinary hotels, a tourist mecca. Ayasha Jaipur lives in the grounds, in a small palace. Trials and family feuds abound: jewels, antiques and paintings are squabbled over, court decisions are pending. Her husband died leaving no will.

But a new undertaking interests her in the field of education, and I too get enjoyment from it: I like the notes I now receive from young schoolchildren in India who write to say how much they like the books I have sent them through the Raj Mata. She draws my world and theirs together. So does she every time we meet, whether together in London or when she visits us in Spain.

General George Marshall and I, during the Coronation rounds together in London, had hours and hours of companionship. Between conversations with the other international participants, he managed to get to know a great deal about me and insisted I must meet the vital, brave Queen Frederika of Greece, whom he encountered when the Marshall Plan affected her country.

During our talks, he once took a long handwritten letter from his pocket: 'This is from the remarkable woman I want you to know,' he stated. It was a political document written to him in strict confidence by Queen Frederika. He trusted me and I have kept the political contents secret since.

When back in the United States, he wrote to the Queen, suggesting we meet. We soon did so in Athens, and more than forty years of friendship with the Greek royal family was the rich result. Since then I have seen the family through two deaths, a military coup, the decision of the sad Queen and Princess Irene to make India their new home, and then the exile of the King. I had gone to Greece twelve times a year for twelve years. I had been present, by urgent invitation or by chance, during many of their dramatic moments, some tragic, and some happy. It was expected that I should keep most of them confidential and I always will.

The Queen liked to drive me about the countryside in her bright red sports car telling me her ideas and plans, and I also accompanied her to parts of Greece where she had located gifted people to be contributors to the Queen's Fund she created immediately after her return from South Africa. This gave paid work to women, survivors of the war who had a talent for local handiwork: embroidery, needlepoint pillows, and rugs of many shapes and sizes. In fact, any craft which had sales possibilities was encouraged. She saw that they were supplied with all the necessary equipment and materials. Finished articles were then shipped to Athens to be sold in a shop called the Queen's Fund. It was simple, without overheads, run by lady volunteers, often members of her court. All my homes have beautiful reminders of their efforts, but the original shop no longer exists, alas.

I recall their weddings, and the times I brought them visits by movie stars. Why are royals so impressed by Hollywood?* I remember State occasions, the simple meals *en famille*, and I remember most of all my delight at the closeness of that royal family. I've never seen more affectionate camaraderie, except today in King Constantine's home. I was in their confidence, a fact which once led Queen Frederika when talking in our home in London to the British Foreign Secretary, to say, 'Fleur is my real ambassador everywhere!'

She and I frequently visited the poor, she hatless, in brown slacks and an old raincoat. In one terrible hole of a dwelling she was not even recognized when we walked in and sat down; on the floor lay a woman dying of cancer, a child watching. The Queen took the woman's hand and saw to it she was sent to a hospital to die in peace. The woman was convulsed in sobs when she realized that it was the Queen who'd been involved.

Another child kept pulling at her: 'Come to my house, *please.*' She went and she brought help to them as well. When she finally had to leave she explained that her husband was waiting. 'King Paul? He's a good man, he won't trouble you,' the sick woman replied.

That was his reputation; he was considered a man of steadiness and wisdom. He was courtly and gallant, giving the spotlight to his Queen in public; but in the family councils, he was the leader. His chief concerns were rebuilding schools, reforestation and spiritual education. When the family returned to a ruined home and garden at Tatoi after the war ended, they were without a gardener, and the King took on the job. He also gave up sailing as there was 'no time'.

---

* Garbo once remarked that 'When royals get a smell of greasepaint in their nostrils, they won't let you go' – from *Walking with Garbo* by Raymond Damm, published by HarperCollins, USA.

Frederika became a member of the Greek Orthodox Church after her return from South Africa at the war's end. Politically, she was the quick-witted star of the family, forever judged by her last remarks. Jan Smuts must have contributed a fair share of his political thoughts to her after she had taken refuge in his South African home when the Italians and Germans stormed Greece. Smuts had much to give a budding queen: he had quelled the rebellion against entry on Britain's side in the First World War, played a key role in establishing the League of Nations, became Prime Minister for a short time in 1919 and then again in the Second World War. He took South Africa into the conflict on the side of the Allies. He died a sad figure after he lost the 1948 election to the Nationalists.

When they returned to Greece, the royals went immediately to Tatoi, their ruined home above Athens, a place I learned to love during my frequent visits there. I can still see that house and garden, which would have looked absolutely natural if it had been placed high on a Sussex hill. Large, warm, cosy, book-filled, chintzed and redolent with family sounds.

There I have listened to King Paul playing Bach at his piano, with Princess Irene hovering alongside, eventually also to be taught, as was the King, by Gina Bachauer as I have mentioned earlier. The Princess learned in six short years to become a respected concert pianist but she gave it all up to accompany her mother to live in India after the Colonels' coup. There she continued her studies, specializing finally in the study of comparative religions. She started 'World in Harmony' in Madrid in 1986, following her concern over the EEC's decision to exterminate four million dairy cows to limit milk production. All her studies were abandoned; she dedicated her time to calling attention to unnecessary waste and the slaughter of precious animals.

The very first time I went to Tatoi, I saw the rebuilt drawing room where the temporarily victorious Communists had dug holes in the floor to light fires for their cooking. Today, no one lives in the dark mansion but memory is vivid of visits there, including my last one. I had kissed the Queen and hugged the King to say goodbye, as was our way; my car started out of the circular drive, only to be instantly beckoned back by the Queen. I rolled down my window and the smiling Queen Frederika leaned inside: 'Now the King smells just like you!' referring to my perfume.

The King's love for the Queen was apparent whenever he looked at her in his deferential, romantic way. One evening she and I were sitting before the blazing fire in the big room at Tatoi, waiting to have dinner after the King returned from his daily walk in the woods nearby. He rushed in, apologized, went over to the fireplace and quietly put a small object which was folded in his large hand on the mantelpiece. He then rushed off to dress, but looked back from the doorway. 'Aren't you going to see what I brought you?' he asked the Queen. She bounced to her feet and brought the tiny gift to show me. It was a snowdrop, the first of the season which he always sought to bring to her. I was so moved because my husband has the same kind of loving gestures. He too seeks out and finds the first snowdrop to pop up in our garden through the snow, and brings it to me.

I have since learned how much the tiny white flower meant to Queen Victoria: her bouquet for her marriage to Prince Albert was a tiny bunch of snowdrops, which were Prince Albert's favourite flower. When he died, the same small flowers were placed on his coffin by the sorrowing Victoria, a heartbreaking sight, surrounded by great wreaths from mourners all over the world.

I remembered the romance of the snowdrops* when sending flowers to thank Queen Elizabeth the Queen Mother after lunching at Clarence House. I found six bunches at a florist, tied them in white satin ribbon with a big bow, wrapped them simply in tissue to be delivered with my note. The Queen Mother's pleasure was confirmed in a delightful handwritten reply.

On her ninetieth birthday (she honours us by celebrating birthdays in our home) I had a similar bunch of snowdrops copied, life-size and tied in a similar satin bow – all made of fine bone china. This I presented to her at table after coffee, to her delight.

Another warm memory of Tatoi: I was honoured to receive the Order of Bienfaisance from the King himself at dinner. Without ceremony, he simply held out one hand, took one of mine in his and placed the beautiful medal in it. With his famous broad smile he

---

* The snowdrop of religious stories and festivals is also the flower of my birthday. I cherish the tiny bloom. The snowdrop, according to one legend, symbolizes the pledge of an angel who appeared to Eve in the first winter after the expulsion from Eden as an assurance that spring would follow.

commanded, 'Here, pin it on. You've earned it for your help to us in Cyprus.' When I returned to London, I also received a letter from Lord Colyton at the Colonial Office, commending and thanking me for my efforts. The strife-torn island had been my port-of-call for nearly two years on behalf of President Eisenhower. He knew my closeness to such important officials as General Papagos, who was then Prime Minister, John Sossidis, his ADC, and later, Prime Minister Stephan-opoulos and Prime Minister Kanellopoulos.

I remember Tatoi with nostalgia. The Queen and family had collected completely unimportant little objects which lived at ease with beautiful serious works of art, their treasures. The library shelves were crowded with biographies and historical novels. The cellar was arranged with a bar and a cinema; 'For the children, where they can grow up and feel free and be unnoticed and unreported,' the Queen once explained.

Once I asked her to describe her three children. She began with the eldest, Sophia, born in 1938: 'She is the most dignified of the three . . . always interested in children . . . knows exactly what she wants . . . has very good taste in clothes . . . rides excellently . . . has a very artistic nature . . . is good at singing and painting. All my children love animals,' she concluded. Sophia, now Queen of Spain, still lives up to her mother's description.

Queen Frederika continued with Constantine, born in 1940: 'Tino takes after his grandpa, and he is very like his father, and just as softhearted.'

The youngest, born in 1942, Irene, has a great understanding of metaphysical things, absolutely frightening! But she is very funny. In a letter to me, she once wrote that she was 'riding a horse called Pius. Isn't it funny to call a wild horse after a tame pope?'

In 1953, King Paul and Queen Frederika came on a State visit to the United States. They had an informal stay in New York, coming to us for cocktails before going to the theatre to see *South Pacific*. I invited twenty friends, among them Marlene Dietrich and Noël Coward. (Elsa Maxwell, who invited herself, blurted out to the Queen while in the queue to be presented, that a 'Celebrity Cruise' to the Greek Islands ought to be a great help for Greek tourism. 'It should put Greece on the map,' she added. The Queen's approval was soon treated as if it had been a 'royal command' and a trip was actually organized with a guest list entirely royal, from all of Europe. One great result was that Prince Juan Carlos of Spain met daughter Sophia and they later became engaged.) I worried about the show they were going to see and gently pushed out the guests so I could get the royals on their way to dine. 'Where?' I asked.

'With you! That is if we can take pot luck,' the King answered with his devastating smile. My heart sank; I had told my cook she could take the evening off, and she had disappeared after making the last canapés. But I had reckoned without a golden woman, Andrée Lartigou, my maid, my hairdresser, my 'everything'.

'Andrée, what can we do? They'd like to stay for a quick meal!'

'Don't worry, leave it to me.' She exploded with laughter and rushed to the kitchen.

Half an hour later, dinner was announced, a typical French meal: Andrée's famous lemon chicken, which she later taught me to make, a salad, followed by hot brandied crêpes filled with gingery marmalade. But the table was the real coup – it was laid with solid gold plates. They had been given to me by my mother-in-law, originally a gift to her by her sons on her fiftieth anniversary. Like her, I found them far too pretentious so they were stored away; I had even forgotten where. Andrée not only remembered, but knew that this was the time for them to make an appearance. That simple, delicious meal was suddenly regal.

Because my present husband was once a racing driver, we both love motoring and still tend to wander around Europe. For years we used a very special map given to me under unusual circumstances. I had just got my divorce from Mike Cowles, and my idea of a new life had one particular proviso: *no more large Cadillacs.* I wanted a small fast car instead, to dash around Europe, and asked this new friend, (whom I subsequently married) to design me one as he had so often done for himself. It was ready in three months. I went to Athens to tell the King and Queen of my decision to divorce and to describe the new life I hoped to lead. After they got over the shock of the news, King Paul asked if I really did want a fast car. When he realized I was serious, he took me to the library, Crown Prince Constantine alongside us; the three of us sat on the floor, doubled over a map of Europe on which the King marked up the roads he said were 'safe enough for a hundred miles an hour! And how I wish I could do so myself,' he added sadly. We used that map for years, although my husband already knew the roads intimately from racing events.

In 1963, I was asked by Columbia Broadcasting Company in the United States if I would persuade the King and Queen of Greece to work with me and appear in a film to be called *The Roots of Freedom*, which would examine the age of Pericles. CBS hoped it could be filmed in the royal palace but after discussing the idea, the King and Queen preferred that it be done on the Acropolis instead, since it was the original site and appropriate for such a programme.

The press nitpicked a bit when it was shown in the United States but this letter from Eric Sevareid made the King and Queen and me feel good: 'Let me tell you that I have not had such a good general reaction to a programme in years. Waitresses, cab drivers, strangers in the street, everybody at the long table at the Century Club, all manner of people who found it exhilarating. I have learned to judge how a show goes over, whatever the critics write, and I have no doubts whatsoever that this was a resounding success.'

I went to Athens for King Paul's funeral. His death for me is a sad, sad memory. A few days after the funeral, Queen Frederika asked me if I'd like to come with her to see his grave, a heartbreaking journey as the King had been so good to me.

'You loved him very much. I'm going to give you my favourite photograph of us together,' Queen Frederika said as we parted. Since then, the picture of the delightful laughing pair, in its original silver frame, sits on the open desk in our bedroom; it is the first thing I see every morning, reminding me that the Queen said, in giving it to me: 'This is what I've seen every morning when I opened my eyes. Now it will be with you to do the same.'

She died after exiling herself in India, a fascinating but bitterly sad woman whom I greatly miss.

Eulogies to monarchy seem things of the past now, since the public today has a more questioning approach to royalty, but Queen Beatrix of the Netherlands is patently a modern favourite.

Her father, Prince Bernhard, the Prince of the Netherlands, or PB as all his friends call him, came into my life during Queen Elizabeth's Coronation festivities. Soon after, the Prince came to New York, where we talked over the ideas he brought. I named several members for his planned Bilderberg Conferences, still being held today. I suggested many names, including Mike Cowles and Jack Heinz.

After I came to live in London, the Prince invited me to join another of his remarkable organizations, one that he and Peter Scott planned and had organized, the World Wildlife Fund. I served on its International Board in Geneva for many long years. The Prince had then been a remarkable President, a versatile and hardworking man whose title gave him immediate access to and influence with Heads of State everywhere, useful to the twenty-eight WWF organizations that had been established around the globe. On his departure as President, Jonkheer John Loudon of the Netherlands took his place. He was followed by Prince Philip, now in his second term. After he left the Presidency, Prince Bernhard became WWF's President in the Netherlands, still contributing in his usual effective way.

I also know Prince Bernhard's daughter Beatrix, who is now the Queen of the Netherlands. On coming to the throne, she quickly established herself as a modern monarch. Although she does not cycle around the streets of The Hague, as her mother Queen Juliana did, she rules with a warm dignity and a noticeable sense of fun, but is patently deeply involved in her country's affairs and people and is obviously admired and loved by them.

She has a close Dutch friend in Sussex, Lydia, Lady Stewart-Clark, whom she visits, occasionally detouring with her to our home. There were tears of joy on the face of John Loudon when the Queen astonished him by arriving for the surprise party I gave him on his eightieth birthday at our home in London. We won't forget his face as he saw his Queen come into the room with her husband to pay tribute to their distinguished subject.

The Princess Royal, Princess Anne, is a remarkable individual, a serious royal worker with a genuine sense of responsibility. Compassion, firmly controlled, has taken her to see the starving and dying and they are now part of her lifestyle as the working head of the Save the Children Fund, duties performed *without* the paparazzi at her elbow.

I am a member of the board of the late Gerald Durrell's zoo in Jersey, of which Princess Anne is a very active royal patron. Some years ago, a Canadian donor gave us funds to open a Snake House for endangered species. The Princess was to be guest of honour at its opening, but because of my phobia about snakes, I originally and misguidedly declined to be present, but in the end I thought I should show my responsibility, and attended. I heard her make the most amusing speech, the point of which was that snakes had the wrong name. 'Snakes! give them another name and you'll never fear them,' she announced. I obtained a copy of the speech to give to her proud grandmother, Queen Elizabeth the Queen Mother, who was just as delighted by her humour as I was.

A great moment for any public person is receiving the Order of the Garter. The Princess Royal is one of the few females thus honoured. The ceremony is extraordinarily dignified and beautiful. I sat in the audience when Lord Carrington walked down the aisle of St George's Chapel at Windsor in the awesome ceremony. His normally smiling face became solemn during the ritual although ostrich plumes bounced outrageously over the black hats each participant wears for the highly-costumed pageant. At other times, I have watched Harold Wilson and King Juan Carlos getting the same honour but missed Ted Heath's day in the sun.

An American friend, Margaret Biddle, was also a close friend of the Duke and Duchess of Windsor, and through her introduction I saw a good deal of them, not only while they came to live at the Waldorf Towers in New York City, but in Paris at Rue de la Faisanderie and later in the Bois de Boulogne.

Over the years, it was easy to observe how obsessed the Duke was by Wallis Windsor and how coolly she responded to his insistent attention. Did she ever really forgive him for giving up the throne? Did she fly to Paris *before* he gave up the throne hoping that after her departure he would *stay* and insist that she at least become his morganatic bride, eventually being accepted as Queen? She often gave this impression by her attitude. I also saw at firsthand her considerable skill as a hostess, how interesting she could be – and how right-wing were the politics of both.

A variety of incidents marked our friendship. At their own huge dinner party in New York's Stork Club, I was given the place at the

Duke's right, and lost a few jealous friends. I regularly sat to the Duke's right at other dinner parties for the Windsor's after the word was out how well I knew them. Some unsure hostesses counted on me to make the occasion 'easier' with royals. I soon became irritated by the Duke's habit of letting me do all the talking, responding with merely an 'of course . . .', 'quite so . . .' or 'how interesting'. This isn't the most pleasant way to spend time, so one evening I finally erupted: 'Talk to me! Say something! Do as you always do when otherwise we are together. No more monosyllabic responses, *please!*'

The Duke understood quickly: 'I'm so sorry to be so rude. I do apologize. Ask me a question!'

An unplanned retort from me did the trick: 'What was the best advice your father ever gave you?' was my impromptu question.

'Oh, that is no problem,' he responded immediately, with a broad smile. 'I can see my father as if he is in this room in front of me now. He looked me sternly in the face and said, "My son, pee first".' I almost fell out of my chair. Had I induced the right dinner conversation!

Another more 'important' occasion took place in our townhouse in New York City. The Duke's book *A King's Story* was soon to be published and I decided to 'launch' it by preparing an amusing occasion (the real purpose kept secret from both Windsors). I arranged my own 'Book and Author' luncheon. This was New York's counterpart to Christina Foyle's Book and Author luncheons held in London to announce a new book. I planned the usual ingredients: ten tables for six were set up on the top floor of our house on East 68th Street (the area normally used as our movie theatre), to which I added a raised dais for guests of honour.

Ladies were met at the front door and asked to choose an over-blown hat to wear to caricature the attire of female lunchers. They also had to pin on a dreadful purple orchid corsage nested in too much fern. Men were allowed to be themselves.

'Only short speeches allowed' was a part of my plan and many of them were given by famous authors. All this was to prepare the Duke for what was ahead for him as an author: what to say, how to deal with after-luncheon invitations, how to deal with critics, how to spend the money earned. The Duke tried to rise to his feet to reply but this I gently refused to allow. 'You are here to be instructed, not to make any speeches.' The event was a hilarious success.

A more touching, sad occasion occurred when I flew over to Paris to lunch alone with the Duke and Duchess in their home in the Bois. The Duke was very ill, so frail he was carried down to be placed in a chair at the tiny table set up for three by a window in the drawing room. It was a cold, cold day (it unexpectedly snowed so hard later that all flights out of Paris were cancelled and I had to spend the night in my favourite Lancaster Hotel instead of flying home to London). Inside the Windsors' home, all signs of cold had disappeared. The room was filled with forced lilacs and other spring blooms. A fire glowed and there was good talk.

The Duchess was, as usual, brisk and well-informed. Eventually, since it was one of her favourite interests, we talked of fashion. When I tried to include the Duke she exclaimed, 'Oh, the Duke isn't interested in women's fashions. He never even notices what I've got on!'

'Quite right,' he responded, 'but I do often think of my mother. Fashion held no interest for her. *She* never changed how she looked.' Never before had he mentioned his mother. I shall never forget his sunken, sad face. He died soon after.

An addendum; Margaret Thompson Biddle a royal? Yes, she was, unforgettably, one of the most 'royal' non-royals I've ever known, a modern Renaissance figure.

Her successes were thought by many to be merely financial, because her father, Colonel Boyce-Thompson, ordered his sixteen-year-old only child to come to his office daily to be prepared (like a son) to inherit his goldmining empire. This she did, eventually tripling the enormous fortune, spending the money with giddy abandon. She was far better known in Europe than in America, though born as Margaret Thompson in the Yonkers suburb of New York City. She lived in London throughout the blitz while her husband, Anthony Biddle, was US Ambassador to the Occupied Countries of Europe. Later they were divorced, and Paris became the favoured centre of her social life.

She had everything that money could buy. There were five homes, she wore jewels fit for a monarch, she had dozens of wealthy and influential friends. The Windsors were among her closest, as well as politicians of many countries. She loved best of all the world of French politics.

Her lavish Paris home, like her four others, was ready for her whenever this constant traveller turned up, often without notice. Each house was fully staffed. All her clothes were ordered in sets of five, one set for each home, five of all her fur or cloth coats and dresses, five suits, five hats, five pairs of shoes. One was always available wherever she landed, which made her every couturier's dream, although Balenciaga was her preferred designer. On occasion one of his suits would be such a favourite it would be ordered in three different colours – fifteen copies! Each home had its fill of priceless treasures, though none more than the two in Paris and Versailles.

But what didn't she have that she wanted most? A job on my magazine, *Flair*! We met in an amusing way when her lawyer made an appointment for me to have lunch with them. There she asked me for a job.

I decided to make her European Editor, a decision which shocked my European professionals (for instance, Rosamund Berniere, who was then *Flair*'s Paris Art Editor). What may have seemed to them an odd appointment in fact made good sense. Her name made instant impact in the world of fashion and art for instance; but the greatest benefit accrued from her famous salon, which was a magnet for the most influential members of the government.

King-making took place in Paris; pulling strings was still a woman's accepted role. In 1950, when the woman doing it was *American*, speaking bad French, it was a pleasurable phenomenon. Meeting the Government, top members only, was routine; it was *de rigueur* for France's top politicians to be found at her superb dinner table and both *Flair* and *Look*'s foreign editors benefited.

She and I flew together to and from Europe. In those days she took the four-seat compartment between the pilot and other passengers, on the largest Pan-American planes. Before take-off, her butler would bring aboard a heavy container of food for us, packed in a solid gold box designed by Tiffany. Inside its gold compartments were usually roast game birds, pâtés, breads and beverages. If asked, all she ever wanted from the plane's galley was hot water for tea. If alive today, she would be flying about in a private jet.

Travelling on European trains with her was a very different experience; we would share a conventional double-sleeper compartment where, luckily, she preferred the upper berth. She behaved like a typical tourist, turning the tiny space into a crowded little room. Torn strips of fabric were soon wound round small batches of her hair to curl during the night. The sights and sounds were almost cosy.

She died after I had moved to England. Her death was shrouded in mystery; for years there was gossip about her alleged murder by a disgruntled lover to whom she had denied one of her goldmines. I found it very sad that after her death her son and daughter (who was then married to American pop singer Morton Downey) sold *everything* left them in her will and simply divided the money from the sale of her mansions and their contents, appearing not to want to keep anything.

She gave me many gifts, but one in particular I loved: I had just received Sotheby's catalogue for the sale of King Farouk's treasures. I fancied an exquisitely beautiful little box for my collection as on its cover there was a diamond 'F'. The price was, to me, nonsense. A few days later it arrived, a gift from Margaret Biddle. I shall never forget the pleasure of her friendship, or the usefulness she greatly demonstrated as an employee.

RIGHT: The exhibition, 'The Animal in Art,' part of a project I devised for the International World Wildlife Fund was opened in Glasgow's Museum of Art by HM Queen Elizabeth The Queen Mother. Her obvious and much appreciated glee at the idea of animal art was reflected in her flattering opening remarks, which filled me with pride.

LEFT: Peter (Lord) Carrington, decorated hero of World War II, had his first significant post in Britain's government when, in his early thirties, he became High Commissioner to Australia. After many Cabinet posts, ending as Foreign Secretary, he became Secretary General of NATO and then a thankless mediator in the Yugoslav Civil War.

RIGHT: George Marshall, then the United States' Secretary of State, was President Eisenhower's personal representative at the Coronation of HM Queen Elizabeth. He and I went to the ceremony together (I as American Ambassador). It was the beginning of a great friendship which I've retained to this day as a Trustee of the George C. Marshall Home Preservation Fund in the USA. Mrs Marshall joins us in this photograph.

ABOVE: Pierre Mendes-France, when Prime Minister of France, his wife, Lily (whom I knew when she lived under a false name in New York City during the war), and I were skiing in Switzerland. He was suddenly rushed to detour from the hills to a telephone booth. It was Winston Churchill. I held his skis as he took the urgent confidential call.

RIGHT: Two house-guests – one a sex symbol, the other a saintly old lady: Marilyn Monroe in hiding in my Connecticut home from the movie industry in hope of a better contract, and Bertha Stafford Vester, the American concerned with sick Arab children in Jerusalem. Marilyn dressed like a hobo, confusing the old lady who had expected more glamour. Their affection for each other was almost instantaneous.

LEFT: I wanted America to know a man I'd just met, the brave, honest President of the Phillipines, Ramon Magsaysay, whose nation was considered corrupt. Whilst in the USA on the pretext that he needed medical advice (a ploy which I had suggested to him to make it possible to see the President on an informal basis), he visited me in my office at *Look* magazine. His government preceded the Marcos regime. He died in a suspicious plane crash in 1957.

ABOVE: Jacqueline Auriole, one of the two greatest female pilots of her time (Jacqueline Cochran was the other) crashed her jet airplane headfirst into the Seine in Paris. Her face was so mutilated that she would not allow her sons to see her. New York's gifted Dr John Marquis Converse gave her this miraculous new face. I was a party to the secret rescue operation.

ABOVE: Of my countless photographs, I chose this favourite of Prince Rainier and Princess Grace because it personified their essential characters: the Princess's great, dignified beauty and the Prince's soft, proud style which we grew to know so well after countless years of affectionate friendship and visits made to us and them in England, Spain and Monaco.

LEFT: Sir Stafford and Lady Cripps, our house guests in New York, came to an exhibition of 'Paintings by Famous Amateurs' which I helped launch to benefit the Urban League. The most fascinating exhibit was by President Eisenhower; I had persuaded him to try his hand at painting – he produced the head of an Indian on a canvas which was numbered for colours. It sold for $27,000!

LEFT: Salvador Dali stepping off the train in London after months of persuasion to launch the book he authorised me to write, *The Case of Salvador Dali*, in the late 1950s. The launch was at The Planetarium and he actually demanded that the universe of the sky had to be arranged exactly as it was when he was born.

RIGHT: That wise old American statesman, the advisor to Presidents, Bernard Baruch, described me in an authorised biography by Margaret Coit, as his 'daughter'. He had an enormous influence on me, teaching me to treat facts as a religion and pushing my mind to its fullest. In fact, he helped to mould my adult life.

LEFT: Jung Chang and I at dinner in London. We were already friends, but it was hard to leave her side. This brilliant and amusing woman's book, *Wild Swans*, gave us one of the first glimpses of China under Mao Tse-tung. When visiting us in Spain at Christmas 1995, Jung Chang and her husband reported to us and friends that more than 6,500,000 copies had been sold since publication.

LEFT: Mamie Eisenhower, wife of the President, often felt more at home in the kitchen than in the strictly formal protocol of her White House life. Food and recipes were on her mind when she took me by the hand to taste the tempting soup inside the pot on the stove in their former home outside Paris. It was, of course, delicious.

RIGHT: Here I am in five layers of battledress (it was 27° below zero) on the 'safe' ground in Panmunjon during the Korean war, the dangerous truce conference I was given permission to attend by President Eisenhower. The Truce Conference always took place under gunfire except for a ten minute break to allow conference members to rush and leave by jeep each morning and night.

BELOW: The Shah of Persia and I never lost the opportunity to argue politically. Here, in the Palace in Teheran, we debated the pros and cons of foreign oil rights in Iran which were a dangerous source of trouble with worldwide oil companies. Queen Saroya sat quietly alongside, amused by my temerity.

LEFT: Vivien Leigh and I at *Look* magazine when she was playing in *Antony and Cleopatra* in New York. We continued to see each other after I went to live in London as we were near-neighbours in our weekend homes in Sussex. This glamorous lady and I used to exchange recipes – her sardine soufflé is still a 'must'.

BELOW: Prince Juan Carlos of Spain joined me and Gina Bachauer after the wedding of Crown Prince Constantine of Greece to Princess Anne-Marie of Denmark. The wedding pair are now King and Queen of Greece and Prince Juan Carlos is now King of Spain (his Queen, then Princess Sofia, is King Constantine's sister).

BELOW LEFT: Cary Grant never missed a visit when he was anywhere in Europe. In this photograph in my study in London we are recounting the antics of the great Russian clown, Popoff, whom we watched with delight in Monaco at Prince Rainier's annual Christmas Monte Carlo Circus. Following circus activities is one of the Prince's private loves.

BELOW RIGHT: Maurice Chevalier collected the water troughs from the streets of Paris (they'd been placed there by British horse lover Mr Wallace, of the Wallace Collection). Chevalier then plonked them all over his garden in Paris, planted with roses. Indoors, he hung rose paintings, including fine ones by Impressionists.

ABOVE: At an informal luncheon during George Bush's Vice-Presidency, Russell Train, American Chairman of the World Wildlife Fund, and I met at the Official Residence during the session held in Washington (Mr Train and I were still international Trustees). It became a relaxed time for the 'Veep'.

RIGHT: General Omar Bradley, before I broke the news to him of the sight I'd seen at the Russian meeting in East Germany which I had attended (armed with a false identity). On a two-storey glass wall of the building's staircase they had hung a full-length poster of gentle Bradley bayoneting a baby. We both dissolved in tears as I reported it.

BELOW: Governor Chris Patten and Britain's Prime Minister John Major at Government House in Hong Kong in March 1996. My husband and I visited the Governor twice in 1995.

At my desk as the lady editor at *Look*, *Quick*, and *Flair* magazines in 1950. Forty-seven years later, November 1996 will see the revival of *Flair* in a new book, *The Best of Flair*, which I have edited and re-designed from the pages of the magazine that once made publishing history.

VII

TWO PIONEERS

TWO MEN COULD BE CALLED truly modern pioneers, though in vastly different ways and with vastly different aims: one was my husband's father, Montague Meyer, who had earned his reputation between the World Wars. The other was Dr Armand Hammer, the oil baron who was known for his wealth as well as for his unofficial diplomacy (explaining American interests to the Soviet Union).

My father-in-law's story began when the Panama Canal opened in 1913. The far-sighted young man realized that this highway of water made the great timber resources of Western Canada and Western USA available to the European market. He turned this vision to reality when as timber buyer for the British government during the 1914–18 war, he used Canadian timber to help meet the demand created by trench warfare. The Canadian government's civil servant who helped him mastermind the supply was 'HR' MacMillan, who was later to become British Columbia's greatest timber and tinned-fish entrepreneur.

After the war ended in 1918 HR left the Canadian Civil Service and he and Montague Meyer, this time as business partners, continued to supply Canadian timber across the globe, HR taking responsibility for the organization of the company and the cutting of the timber, Meyer handling the selling and marketing. The enterprise thrived but my father-in-law wanted to widen his interests and set out to conquer new fields. He went south to Los Angeles and, ten years too early, invested in a 'talking picture' company which was a total failure. Not disheartened, he then continued even further south to Peru, where he obtained an emerald concession. While this continued producing for ten years or more, it was never a great success.

Then came a worldwide commodity slump. The price of timber fell below the cost of freighting it to the market. Montague Meyer realized that eventually the situation would change for the better, so with great courage he borrowed as much money as he could and bought and bought against the prospect that demand would rise and make for considerably higher prices. He was right. Seventy years later, the company, still bearing his name, was the largest timber merchant in the United Kingdom, in which for over thirty years my husband played a major role until he decided to retire from business and give his time and talents voluntarily to the service of public health in Britain.

The other pioneer I so quizzically equated with my father-in-law is Dr Armand Hammer, oil tycoon, millionaire, philanthropist, long-time friend of Russia's ruler, and one of the world's most acquisitive art collectors.

Hammer emigrated to New York from Odessa in the Crimea with his family at the end of the last century, to start a new life. His father Julius founded, ironically, the American Communist Party, a political philosophy that obviously did not feature largely in the dreams of his sons Armand, Victor and William. Julius, a doctor, had left behind in Odessa a drug manufacturing company.

Armand, although the eldest son, did not plan to follow his father into medicine. He finished medical school, no doubt to please him, and then Julius and his three sons returned to Russia to do business with Lenin and get the money they claimed was owing to their drug company. The story of what happened, which I heard over and over from Victor, is not the 'official' one later told by Armand. I knew Victor best; he ran the Hammer Galleries on East 57th Street in New York City, where I have had four exhibitions of my paintings over the years. I saw quite a lot of all three brothers. Victor's and Armand's versions soon began to differ.

Armand's story was that they made their fortune by developing, among many deals, an asbestos concession in Russia and an agency for Ford tractors. Victor's story is that they shipped a freight train (rolling stock) filled with pencils to Russia, telling Lenin or Stalin (the name tended to vary) that what Russia needed most was *education*. In exchange for the pencils, which would be desperately needed by the new government, they asked for and got the government's Fabergé jewels taken from the banished Russian nobility and aristocracy! Victor's account is the one I believe tells the true foundation of the

Hammer fortune, because the Hammer Art Galleries originally sold not paintings but the Fabergé collection, those immensely valuable masterpieces by the Czar's official jeweller. It was true that I first met Victor and his brother William when I bought a Fabergé brooch. I later came to know Victor's wife, Irene, of children's television fame, and Armand too.

The tale which follows does, I think, typify Armand Hammer. It concerns his invitation to me to come to tea. The powerful head of the Occidental Oil Company regularly visited London, hoping, gossip had it, to be knighted through his friendship with the Prince of Wales. He telephoned me to say that he and his wife had just arrived and would I come and have a cup of tea with them the next day? I accepted happily, but with one proviso: 'It will be just us, no mob!' I knew he loved to collect an audience but I stay away from crowds.

He always occupied the Royal Suite at Claridge's. When I arrived the next day, I started up the beautiful staircase that leads to it. I once lived at this hotel, and knew all its old hands, so when I turned to the stairs, the concierge beckoned me back. 'Don't bother going upstairs. Dr Hammer is giving cocktails in the private room opposite,' he explained.

My heart sank. He *is* having a big party. I almost turned away but decided to open the door to the room just a crack to be sure. I was right; inside was the sort of mob-scene I detest. I closed the door quietly and backed away – too late. Armand Hammer was just inside the door and had seen me. He rushed out and grabbed me by the arm. 'You lied to me,' I explained, with all the politeness I felt I could muster. 'You said tea would be just us *upstairs* – but look at *this*!'

'I'm sorry I misled you, but I suddenly had something to celebrate, so I immediately asked everyone I know to join me here. Don't go away.'

He pushed me gently into the nearest armchair in the foyer and said, 'Stay. See what it is that I'm celebrating!'

He put a small notebook into my hands. 'Look at this. I bought it last night for £450,000. It's a bargain! I want to celebrate my luck.'

The notebook I held contained Gauguin drawings done in pen, pencil and in paint. His South Sea life was encapsulated in a notebook no larger than 5″ × 8″. I sat there in wonder and delight. Fifteen minutes later, he came out again to collect it from me. 'Now you may go!' he announced with a wide grin. I'd held a beautiful thing in my hands, more precious than any jewels.

After Armand Hammer's death at a ripe old age came controversy: who really owned the huge collection of paintings in his estate? Had it been his or did it belong to the oil company? How did he manage his affairs? Was he really just a 'buccaneer' who had a talent for attracting political friends simply to improve his economic interests? His heirs began to sue.

My father-in-law had only one thing in common with Armand Hammer, an interest in Russia. With his usual courage, he was the first to lead a trade delegation to the Soviet Union in 1920–21 after the Revolution, not for political reasons but because he always said that commerce was a step towards peace.

I, like Armand Hammer, have a notebook. In the late 1870s, Edgar Degas departed from his usual paintings and, with a playful flourish, filled a sketch book with scenes drawn at the home of his friend, Ludovic Halery. Life there must have been lively to judge by the sketches.

In 1947 or '48, a very limited edition was produced, which I bought. Few can believe it isn't a Degas original, so extraordinarily well have both paper and drawings been reproduced. One can almost hear the convivial conversations and imagine and smell the heady aroma of gaslight, cigar smoke and beer. I sometimes see a touch of Goya-like cruelty in the women he portrays, the actresses, the woman alone in a theatre box, an onlooker giving advice over the shoulder of a card-player, chanteuses, vaudevillians, café-concerts, Turkish baths as well as parodies of Cézanne's fat women bathing. Some say he was a better sculptor than a painter. He used to hide his sculptures in the grand piano his parents gave him as a wedding gift, having removed the strings to make room for them. He started his career by painting plates for the Haviland porcelain factory for fifty francs a day. A photograph in Degas's notebook shows him gaily demonstrating to his friends that not only ballerinas could dance. Bearded and aged, he is making a little whirl of his own.

VIII

SHOW BIZ

SHOW BIZ WAS AN ESSENTIAL ingredient for *Look* magazine's viability. A sizeable segment of income came from Hollywood's film advertising, especially after the magazine's image improved. None came easily. *Look* had to find ways to prise money from Hollywood advertising budgets. Trips from New York to the West Coast became routine, but the most effective idea was the yearly *Look* Awards for the best films, winners to be chosen by film distributors on the basis of audience success, then announced at *Look* Award parties and published in the magazine. *Look*'s millions of readers for each issue were the magnet. The *Look* Award was a major idea, but there was still a regular degree of 'kow-towing' needed to movie moguls in the tinsel town. I soon lost my amateur standing by making friends of most of them and the stars.

Tickets were eagerly sought-after for the black-tie ballroom Award ceremonies – which were grand and carried a high publicity value. An issue of *Look* immediately followed the event, giving major space to the films, their stars, producers and directors.

After awards were given and speeches were over, dancers always had to wait for a touch of Hollywood protocol: Louis B. Mayer, the potentate, as he proclaimed himself, had to be the first on the dance floor. So he and I always started out alone in the embarrassing glare of spotlights until other mortals bravely joined us.

Show Biz is the art of entertaining an audience. It can be the vicarious thrill of danger at a circus from trapeze artists, sword-swallowers, fire-eaters, lion-tamers or snake-handlers. Or a matador fighting bulls. Or street-corner performers. Or on stage, Shakespeare superbly spoken. Show Biz involved itself in war when such stars as John Gielgud, Bob Hope, Gertrude Lawrence and Laurence Olivier saw it as their patriotic duty to entertain the troops, often in danger, always as a life-saving boost to morale.

Government assemblies everywhere, particularly the House of Commons and the US Senate, are cynically considered 'the most unlikely Show Biz of all, starred by failed actors'. Regardless, the final bow must go to Hollywood, which provides the biggest slice of Show Biz of all.

I remember Louis B. Mayer, that Napoleonic head of MGM, the self-designated 'royal'. I remember the first time I met Ingrid Bergman and marvelled over her naturalness; apple-cheeked, very little make-up and simple speech. I remember Cary Grant, who became my best friend and who taught Hollywood a thing or two about comedy and 'British Manners'. I remember the Picasso painting which slid up to disappear in the wall to allow a film to be shown in the art-laden drawing room of the William Getzes.

I remember my 'forever friendships' with the Justin Darts – she was once an actress, he the head of the giant Dart conglomerate in whose Bel-Air mountain-top residence Tom Montague Meyer and I were married with Cary Grant as best man. His then wife, Betsy Drake, and Adrian and Janet Gaynor were the other guests. The Darts' beautiful home was soon after burnt down, impossible to save because of its location.

I remember only Cadillacs in those Hollywood days; today, these are replaced by Rolls-Royces, even those stretch limos which are sent free to ferry customers to certain Beverly Hills shops. I remember the Hollywood houses: they were big, yes, but more or less conventional. Today, the fashion is to tear them down and build larger ones, often in the same small area, for millions of extra dollars. In 1992 I saw the house sold by a friend for eight million dollars smashed out of existence by bulldozers to make room for a new one which had already cost, before being furnished, over fifty million dollars *more*. All this must flatter the vanity of a movie mogul whose underground garage has room for a dozen cars, whose wife's dressing room is as big as a shop. The architecture itself reminded me only of a nondescript city hall in a small French town.

Friends like Anne and Kirk Douglas have no place for such nonsense. They still live in the same beautiful art-filled house I knew in the fifties; no face-lift or expansion needed. The Jimmy Stewarts bought the house next door to theirs, tore it down and put in a kitchen garden instead to grow their own food: a smile spreads as I write this.

*   *   *

Hollywood has created dozens of gold-plated stars in its time but it also produced a formidable pair of tycoon-pashas; not only Louis B. Mayer but Sam Goldwyn, who, when alive, *was* Hollywood. L. B. Mayer took himself the *most* seriously and acted exactly as if he were King, expecting, of course, to be treated like a monarch. Sam Goldwyn, the genius who never made anything but great films, had an even greater reputation: *he created a language,* called 'Goldwynism'.

He entered the Cinema's Hall of Fame with such masterpieces as *Walter Mitty, The Little Foxes, The Best Years of Our Lives* and *Wuthering Heights,* but his legendary 'Goldwynisms' carved him another niche in Hollywood's history. Such phrases as 'Gentlemen, include me out', or 'I can answer you in two words – *impossible,* or 'Life on the brink of a great abscess' have become his verbal monuments.

If one didn't know Sam Goldwyn, it would be hard to believe he really made the remarks attributed to him. The famous 'Include me out' was actually said in England under deadly-serious circumstances. He tried to avoid seeing reporters at Oxford University where he was lunching with the Chancellor. World War II had just been announced and Goldwyn was too distressed to relish being interviewed, odd behaviour really for a man to whom publicity was a life-essential. When asked by his host for a statement to hand out to the waiting press, he blurted out the now famous and much-used, 'Tell them to include me out!'

I can vividly recall a wide repertoire of the Goldwynisms attributed to that remarkable movie-maker and master of exploitation, but will concentrate on those he produced while he and I were actually together. Two come immediately to mind. The first occurred after a dinner party hosted in London by Hugh Cudlipp, then editor of the *Daily Mirror.* Sam Goldwyn's comings and goings were never in secret; publicity was too important to his successes, and whenever he and his wife, Frances, were coming to London to launch a new film the city knew it. Mr Cudlipp telephoned me after their arrival on one such visit.

'Fleur, you obviously know Sam Goldwyn. What would you think of my giving a dinner for him? We've never met, but he certainly merits a tribute from our paper. Would you be for the idea and if so, would you and your husband come? You'll probably be the only ones there who will know the man.'

243

I agreed that it was an amusing thing to do; why shouldn't a news-paper honour a great film-maker? I telephoned the Goldwyns to re-commend the dinner to which an impressive cast was gathered from government, publishing and banking in London. All of us gathered in a large private dining room at the Dorchester Hotel. After hours of liquid enjoyment, it became obvious none of the other guests actu-ally knew the guest of honour, but speeches began to flow, somewhat intemperately.

Goldwyn was properly toasted by his host but other surprised gentle-men were suddenly called to their feet to say a few kind words about a film-maker they were meeting for the first time. His exact status in Hollywood's hierarchy was generally unknown and this gave rise to confusion; most actually knew little about him or the film industry. One famous politician stood up, glass in hand, toasting him as 'Mr Goldwyn Mayer', another called him Mr Mayer, his arch-enemy. One also compared him to the huge, bold lion who roared out the MGM logo. What they didn't realize was that Sam Goldwyn had been an independent producer of Goldwyn Films for dozens of years after an explosive break-up of the partnership of Metro-Goldwyn-Mayer. The mere mention of that lion made him mentally roar with rage.

The evening finally drew to a close. Mr and Mrs Goldwyn fled away, rushing to the door. I didn't see or speak to them until a few weeks later in New York, when we were asked to the same dinner party. 'Sam! I'm so sorry I missed you after the Dorchester evening in London. How did you enjoy meeting so many important English gentlemen?'

'Who *met* them?' he answered. 'I never spoke to anyone, not one of all those strangers, but *you* must have had a good time, sitting next to one great guy. You know, the man from the *Communist*.'

'Sam, you've got to be kidding,' I replied. 'There wasn't a single Communist there!'

'There *was*. The man who edits the paper, the *Communist*, sitting on your left. I remember him absolutely.'

'On my left, a Communist? Impossible!' I insisted. Suddenly I saw it, and asked, 'Do you mean Donald Tyerman, the editor of the *Economist*?'

Of course Sam Goldwyn got certain things wrong, but never the essential ingredients. Tyerman was no Communist but he was one of the most interesting men there. I did, in fact, have a fascinating evening.

Another occasion was funnier, especially to anyone who knew the person to whom Sam and I referred in the following story: I was giving a dinner for the Goldwyns in our New York home. Sam and I misbehaved terribly before dinner was announced, having stolen into a corner where both of us shed buckets of laughter over the funny stories exchanged. I could never explain it, but for some reason Sam Goldwyn brought out the humour in me and I always made the sad-faced man laugh a lot as well.

At table, the atmosphere became even more embarrassing as we continued to involve each other in the secret jokes which no one else shared. My former husband and Sam's wife, Frances, sitting opposite, couldn't have liked it.

'Sam, we simply must stop. We are being rude. Let's try to be serious. No more jokes. Let's talk current events, the news, *anything* that won't make us laugh,' I insisted.

'Okay. Ask me something,' he squeaked at me in his rather high-pitched voice, thick with his inimitable accent.

'Well, have you seen any good plays lately?' I asked.

'Nyeh,' he replied.

'What do you mean, no? You've *got* to go to theatre. It is part of your life,' I insisted.

'There's nothing to see,' he complained.

'Come on,' I insisted. 'There's plenty around to interest you.'

'What about yourself?' he retorted. 'Have you seen *America*?'

I could not place the play. 'America' did not immediately sound familiar to me, but suddenly the penny dropped. 'You mean *Miss America*, Bob Sherwood's new play? Yes, I've seen it. I drove all the way to Philadelphia to see it previewed. Of course, you've also seen it, Sam?'

'Nyeh,' he said again, in disgust.

'But Sam, it's impossible! You simply couldn't pass up anything written by Robert Sherwood. You say you love him like a son. He's your favourite writer! He wrote *The Best Years of Our Lives*, your greatest film!'

'Maybe, but he's got no right to write musical comedies. Bob Sherwood's *too tall* for musicals!'

I nearly fell out of my chair. Sam Goldwyn had never made a funnier remark, nor one more profound. Robert Sherwood, height six foot four, was indeed 'too tall' for musicals. His play, *Miss America*, survived about fifteen days, never came to New York and lost a vast fortune for investors. It was Bob Sherwood's only attempt at the genre and his only creative failure. He wasn't cut out for musicals. Too tall.

Many Goldwynisms are classics. A most pertinent one, in my view, was his observation: 'I don't care if it doesn't make a nickel. I just want every man, woman and child in America to see it.' He was talking about Bob Sherwood's *The Best Years of Our Lives*, that big postwar film, a great financial bonanza.

Robert E. Sherwood, best known for *Roosevelt and Hopkins, an Intimate History of the War Years*, and the speeches he wrote for Franklin Delano Roosevelt, got to know Sam Goldwyn in 1945 when he went to Hollywood to write the script of *The Best Years of Our Lives*. The same Bob Sherwood once submitted to Winston Churchill a long questionnaire and Churchill took him seriously enough to reply in fourteen typewritten pages. One of the joys in life was to hear him sing 'The Red, Red Robin Goes Bob, Bob, Bobbin' Along' in full voice, which he used to do after dinner in our home.

The last time I sat in Goldwyn's studio office in Hollywood, he had his top executives there to review his latest film, which was another box-office success. The men had secretly decided beforehand to play their parts modestly by confessing what each could have done to make it even better. Goldwyn was incensed: *make it better?* He thought, as usual, it was the finest *he'd* ever made, it needed no improvements. He jumped up and dismissed them with: 'Gentlemen, if I want your advice, I'll give it to you.' I fell out of my seat.

Here are other Goldwynisms I have collected over the years:

'Any man who goes to a psychiatrist should have his head examined.'

'Throw out everything before 1935, but before you do, make a copy.'

'I read part of it all the way through.'

'I had a monumental idea this morning, but I didn't like it.'

'In this business it's dog eat dog, and nobody's going to eat me.'

'I would be sticking my head in a moose.'

'You've got to take the bull between your teeth.'

'Let's bring it up to date with some snappy nineteenth-century dialogue.'

'There is a statue of limitation.'

'I'll write you a blanket cheque.'

'Our comedians are not to be laughed at.'

'I never put on a pair of shoes until I've worn them at least five years.'

'Next time I send a fool for something I'll go myself.'

To his secretary: 'Take a letter. James Mulvey, 729 Seventh Avenue, New York City, New York. Dear Jim . . . Read that back.'

'Tell me, how did you love the picture?'

He called *Black Narcissus* 'Black Neuroses'.

En route to Europe on the *Queen Mary*, he ran into a friend on board: 'Oh, hello! You going to Europe?'

Goldwyn is also credited with this order to his staff: 'Never let that bastard back in here again – unless we need him!'

When President Woodrow Wilson's administration raised the tax on animal skins it took the profit out of glove-making, which was Sam Goldwyn's profession at the time. He left Gloversville in New York State, went down to New York City and entered the movie business. That event gave the world fifty years of the 'Goldwyn Touch' and many of Hollywood's best movies.

Marilyn Monroe, as of course even the most out-of-touch man on earth knows, was an unsurpassed blonde, a gentle mocker of sex, whose childishly small voice reached out to most men like a siren, but who died in a silent coma. She used that voice to good effect on the press corps in London when she came to star opposite Laurence Olivier in *The Prince and the Showgirl*. It was not the best film either star ever made, but it did earn her and the film millions of newspaper lines.

Her sex appeal worked on *all* men, including very different characters, such as John F. Kennedy and Joe DiMaggio, and a famous intellectual, the grave, craggy icon, Arthur Miller. Did she marry him only to give him maternal protection? In order to do this, as Elizabeth Taylor did for Mike Todd, she became a Jew, but I can never come to terms with the idea of Marilyn studying Judaism seriously.

A most significant though short period of time in her life was spent in the 1950s in my weekend home in Connecticut. She had been brought there to hide by photographer, Milton Greene, whose work she loved. She had learned to trust him and accepted his guidance. He gave her the courage to walk out of her studio in protest at being asked to make bad films, turning her back on the Hollywood system. All America was on the lookout for the sex symbol, who had simply disappeared. The most unlikely place to find her, one, of course, never thought of, was in my luxurious Connecticut country house well away from the world.

While there, she dressed like a Charlie Chaplin hobo – not a trace of the famous anatomy showing. Days were spent with another unlikely visitor, a lovely ninety-year-old, pink-faced lady with a halo of white hair, the First Lady of Jerusalem, Bertha Stafford Vester. She had been taken to Jerusalem from Boston as a tiny baby by her missionary father. She made history later when she accepted the Arab surrender and handed it to General Allenby.

The atmosphere in our Connecticut hideaway was at all times easy and friendly; each woman had a childish admiration for the other. Mrs Vester was overcome by Marilyn; 'How could a movie star be so cuddly?' Marilyn had never seen or been with anyone like her; 'What an innocent old lady!'

A few months before, I had been with Bertha Vester in Jerusalem. We had walked from her front door into her garden, arm in arm, aware of gunfire from hidden snipers. 'Isn't this a dangerous place?' I asked her as we headed for the American Club, which she ran.

'Oh yes. Yes, it is,' she replied with a broad smile. 'My brother and I were on this same path a few weeks ago and he was killed by a bullet.' Meeting Marilyn Monroe was more frightening to her than the shells and gunfire, she confessed to me.

Both women instantly fell in love with each other, Marilyn after hearing of Mrs Vester's bravery and Mrs Vester at the sight of the movie sex-symbol obscured by oversize men's trousers, an old pullover and tennis shoes. We three were an odd assortment.

I had brought Mrs Vester to America as my guest, to help her raise money for sick Arab children, to whom she gave much care. She finally went home to Jerusalem with funds for the hospital, quite overcome by the experience. As a last token, I arranged for her to meet President

Eisenhower in the White House after I had intrigued him by my account of her bravery. She went to the Oval Office wearing white cotton gloves, even though I told her they certainly were not necessary, because she wanted to show her friends in Jerusalem the glove 'that actually shook the hand of the President of the United States'.

Marilyn killed herself (or was it murder?) over thirty years ago, but there is still a Marilyn Club and dedicated Marilyn worshippers who mourn her: never mind the drug-taking and other addictions of her life, or her pathological lack of punctuality. Never mind her untruthfulness. What of it, they ask? Studio problems? Only the studio's fault, they contend.

Marilyn Monroe had no offspring to tell tales, as Marlene Dietrich's daughter Maria, and Joan Crawford's and Nancy Reagan's daughters do. But stories there are and they will persist, because legends die slowly. Many believe the rumour that she meant to remarry Joe DiMaggio. He rescued her body and lovingly buried her after her lonely death. He still adored her – a moving circumstance.

Many tales concern the woman who has become a fabulous legend. How she 'took' London in her stride in 1956 is for me a personal example. Nowhere was readier for a symbol than London when she arrived to make a film with Laurence Olivier on the arm of a new husband, Arthur Miller, who was himself no mean celebrity. One hundred and fifty photographers and fifty reporters and other onlookers shoved and complained behind metal barriers before her plane arrived. In keeping with her normal style, even the plane was an hour late. Three hundred more, ready to embrace her, waited in the airport lounge.

She was on her best behaviour for the huge, chaotic conference held the next day in the Savoy Hotel ballroom. She was dressed, characteristically, in a tight black number with a transparent peek-a-boo net area over her midriff. Three hundred hardened press men and their bosses gave her the sort of newspaper coverage seldom seen in Britain before or since for a film star. For days the headlines belonged to her.

I marvelled over her voice for years; so did the tough press audience; it was so whispery, so vulnerable, a mixture of sensual sex-symbol and earnest girl. But it worked, it helped to reveal a new Marilyn, bringing out her unexpected wit, her warmth and naturalness. The cold sweats, psychosomatic ailments, the rashes, the insecurity? They were absent.

We later attended the party given for her by the Oliviers together with Terence Rattigan in Rattigan's beautiful suburban home. One hundred people watched as Marilyn came down the stairs, late, as usual. She had to move slowly, very slowly, her dress did not allow for anything else. She had been poured into a long white beaded chiffon, tight at the seam and reinforced. Every step had to be a geometric calculation. Down she came, bolted to the side of her new husband. Above, a full moon hung over the garden on what must have been one of her happiest nights.

After that occasion, Marilyn retired from social life, protected by police, but continued to be treated as if sacred. Much of the public's endearing interest in her arose from their identification with the hard life she had once had led. But even this fairy-tale visit ended in bad press; rumours of tension on the film set and personal differences between her and Olivier began to surface.

Her marriage to Miller had brought her new status on many levels. She had captured a man with the kind of face so many New York women coveted, and women in London also liked seeing that craggy face crease into smiles whenever he looked at Marilyn. Embracing the Jewish faith drew further attention to her. Because of her continuing fascination, she even crowded out Suez and Stevenson or the Soho gangs in the daily press.

Whatever she wore, fashionable or not (usually not), was taken up instantly. That first dress in which she was seen photographed, with the transparent midriff, was widely copied. Her shoulder-strap snapped at the very moment press cameras were focused on her to record the signing of her contract with Laurence Olivier. The pleated skirt flying high as she stood on a street corner is one of the most evocative images of the second half of the twentieth century and is reproduced even today. Both these outfits soon adorned the bodies of hundreds of thousands of women in the Western world and made a fortune for the garment industry.

The chic Cecil Beaton wrote of her in British *Vogue* as 'a composite of Alice in Wonderland, a Trilby and a Minsky artist'. Wasn't it all just a build-up to the days of disaster that followed? Few have made more dramatic cinema history and even fewer have matched the Marilyn Monroe legend.

I summarize her this way: a forlorn childhood may explain her air of constant anxiety. Her sensual (wriggly) curvaciousness brought her close to many men but for me, her innocent personality touched me when I got to know her well enough. And her mysterious death compounds the mythology which will always surround her name.

Too many books have been written about the handsome Cary Grant to require any addition from me. I have never agreed, even if asked to contribute to them, nor do I have any intention of writing about him now except in a strictly personal sense. I had known him since 1950 but I began to consider him a genuinely close friend after he married his third wife, actress Betsy Drake.

Her personality must have been a welcome change from wife number one, Virginia Cherrill, the Countess of Jersey, and wife number two, Barbara Hutton, one of the world's richest women.* Betsy Drake had none of their characteristic money-wise habits. She was, and still is, modest enough to get around London, where she now lives, on a bike, and has her own style, her own vocabulary, her own ideas and is a close friend.

Their marriage lasted until the complications of being wife to a world-famous, successful but mixed-up man became obvious – in addition, he decided he did not want the responsibility of marriage after all.

But he changed his mind again to marry for the fourth time. This bride was Dyan Cannon. They spent their honeymoon in our Sussex home. I like to think it was there that his only child, the most constant love of his life, may have been conceived. However, divorce was to follow after interminable squabbles.

Notwithstanding those four previous wives, he married wife number five after he met her in London at the Royal Lancaster Hotel. He had to make regular personal appearances at Fabergé Cosmetics Sales Conferences after he became a member of the company's board. Wife

---

* He never got over the irony that he, though one of the highest-paid cinema stars, had to pay Hutton's enormous taxes in England in the year they were divorced! She had already given the splendid Winfield House to the nation for use as the American Ambassador's residence in London. The Ambassadors who followed must have given many a secret thanks.

number five had been the hotel's press agent. As his widow, she soon remarried.

I cannot forget how he reacted when I telephoned him in Hollywood to tell him I was getting a divorce from my former husband. He replied, 'I'm coming,' hung up the telephone and took the next plane to New York. After lunch at the Pierre Hotel at which I gave him my reasons, we started to walk down Fifth Avenue. The sight of Cary Grant calmly walking down the Avenue hand in hand with a lady created a near riot.

'What are you upset about?' he demanded. 'Look how excited everyone becomes just to see you!'

Two years later he was best man at my marriage, after reassuring himself, somewhat to my future husband's irritation, that the Englishman was the 'right man'.

When he and Sophia Loren* starred in *The Pride and the Passion*, made in Spain outside Madrid, we went to stay with him and Betsy at the Palace Hotel. They couldn't go to the Ritz at that time as the Ritz didn't accept actors as guests! The weather was warm and wonderful. A Sunday arrived without location work on the film, so Cary planned to give the four of us a picnic on a hill overlooking Toledo's wonderful views.

As soon as we'd driven out, a perfect place had been chosen, and preparations to eat concluded, a wild, sudden thunderstorm broke. We rushed back to our Madrid hotel; there, astonished waiters supplied a tablecloth as well as cups, saucers and all other necessities, and we sat ourselves down on the floor to pretend we were having our picnic. In that posh suite, we ate in luxury without the interference of ants, bugs or rain.

Betsy could not stay for the entire filming, but she was frightened of flying back alone. She couldn't face the journey so I finally persuaded her to go by sea instead, on the much-admired new Italian liner, the *Andrea Doria*. She went off, relaxed and happy to face the voyage in unfrightened comfort.

Not far from the United States coast the *Andrea Doria* was involved in a dreadful collision with another ship. Betsy found herself in the cold Atlantic Ocean waiting interminably to be rescued, and found

---

* She turned down his proposal of marriage.

out later that the one unexpected friend she had encountered on board was among several who died in the tragic event. She flies now.

All of Cary's adult life was plagued by psychological problems, some secret, some known. One was his neurotic problem with his mother in England. He constantly tried to assuage this by worrisome visits to her in Bristol, where he was born. Cary, then called Archie Leach, was a former performer in a circus there. Her death years later may have released him. He became very frustrated trying to persuade my husband and me to go to a psychiatrist 'to find out why you're so happy!' – a piece of advice never taken.

His involvement in our lives encompassed many aspects, and provides a host of memories: how he loved Osbert Lancaster's 'Maudie Littlehampton' cartoons in the *Express* . . . how he loved riding about in his Rolls-Royce convertible that he kept in Europe. He drove with the top down in the sun and wind, getting ever more tanned. It was in a similar open car he sat on a cliff above Monaco with Grace Kelly in *How to Catch a Thief* – the exact spot where Grace later met her death by driving over the cliff, some fourteen storeys high.

His telephone calls to me were always brief and to the point. I can still visualize him, feet parked on his desk as he asked: 'What happened to the two kangaroos who jumped into each other's pouches?' or: 'Do you know what one rabbit said to the other one he passed in the park? "Love is wonderful, wasn't it?"' He'd often order me flowers (he would do so from California, Europe or Asia). He loved Hong Kong and went there for his tailoring, and would show his affection and approval of my husband by ordering duplicate suits for him to be sent to London as gifts. He impulsively bought a charming painting of daisies to send me instead of real ones which were out of season. There were so many notes and little gifts, small but enduring remembrances of our 'Best Man'. He had become Hollywood's symbol of romance – debonair, dashing, urbane – but he was also capable of stinginess and paranoia. He took the drug LSD and also begged my husband and me to take the drug, without success, to find out why we were so happy together.

One of Cary Grant's best friends was the mysterious, hermit-like Howard Hughes, who was born to the right father to ensure a billionaire's future, for no oil can be drilled without the little device his father invented. Money on a non-stop oil-well basis from the Hughes Tool Company followed for his son, Howard.

Through Cary Grant I got to know this elusive man, who lived a life which swung between the extremes of mysterious seclusion and avid public attention. He was famous for both his fear-driven behaviour and for the girls who decorated his lifestyle; he liked to have no less than a dozen on hand. Stories about the way he lived and behaved abound, but one I like to recall involved his decision to add the giant RKO film corporation to his collection of companies at a cost of $500 million. It was reported that he bought it by telephone. One day he chose to visit his new baby. On arriving at the RKO studios in his usual attire, crumpled white slacks and shirt and worn tennis shoes, he was ushered around miles of film sets, buildings, equipment, offices and employees at a fast clip, having said not one single word.

When the rounds were complete and he was escorted back to the gated entrance, the studio Head, no doubt almost as speechless as his new employer, asked if there were any instructions for him to carry out in running his new and complicated purchase.

'Paint it,' Hughes murmured in his low, slow voice as he jumped back into his dilapidated car.

Hughes owned TWA Airlines at the time my English husband and I were married in Los Angeles and he was somehow marshalled into the dizzy plans being made for the ceremony. Where and how the wedding would take place were serious worries because I didn't want a gush of publicity. After having had great press attention for years I simply did not want to publicize my remarriage or my decision to go abroad to live, or even to be asked questions. I had recently left hospital after life-saving surgery, and looked gaunt and tired. What I needed desperately was a quiet wedding, a secret honeymoon, and no hassle on the flight to London. Nor did I want reporters to bother my husband-to-be, to whom any press attention was, and still is, anathema. It was his father's strict counsel that 'big business stays *out* of the news'.

Cary Grant's advice was that we could keep it private in Mexico and to help us he enlisted Howard Hughes's aid to ensure that the preparations would go unnoticed. One of Hughes's planes was sent off to Mexico City to see if it would arrive unnoticed. The private plane landed and was immediately surrounded by cameramen; no one could find out how the plan became known – but Mexico was ruled out. Howard Hughes then wanted to fly us to Las Vegas where, 'I have a tame judge who could marry you secretly'. Instead, happily, we were invited to be married in the beautiful Bel-Air garden on a mountain-top overlooking Hollywood, at the home of Jane and Justin Dart, two very close friends.

I had already known Howard Hughes for some time. A year before he had invited me through his front man through Cary Grant (no one ever talked to him directly if he could avoid it), to fly with him to Reno to see the Las Vegas hotel he owned. While in the casino, he insisted on backing me while I played the game called craps, not a game I'd ever played before. He insisted that he would put up the money and we could divide the losses or gains. I won a fortune! It took difficult months to force him to accept half of the winnings, for money seemed of no importance to the man.

One of Hughess' medical problems was his deafness, which embarrassed him. He chose to fly with me for one simple reason: he knew I was a pilot and that we would both be wearing microphones and could thus talk to each other effortlessly. I shall never forget those in-air conversations. He did most of the talking and perhaps in those flights he revealed a Howard Hughes that has never been recorded in the many books and articles about him* A man who broke so many air records, but a man who could expose a hidden soul.

One conversation was all about flying: the beauty of the air, the serenity, the feeling of being in space, the views below, the contrast between life 'down there' and the calm privacy and joy in the sky, the feeling of power, the freedom from other people's curiosity, the luxury of being out of reach and his excitement over launching the airplane he was then building. It was the giant flying boat known as the Spruce Goose that only once got off the water. Today it sits next to the *Queen Mary* liner, the two tourist attractions at Long Beach, California. The failure of this mammoth project could have had something to do with his eventual behaviour. When I described all our talk in the air to Cary Grant later, he exclaimed: 'No one has ever heard him talk so profusely or so poetically!'

---

* A typical tale was of the time he flew his plane under the East River Bridge in New York City – illegal *and* dangerous.

Another of Howard Hughes's acts of friendship was to give my husband and me his private house in the grounds of the Beverly Hills Hotel to use while in Los Angeles on that wedding trip. He later sent us off to my new world, London, as guests in his own plane, a trans-Atlantic plane belonging to the TWA company he'd founded. We were given the entire back section of the plane (and he added an extra chef to cook us whatever we fancied on the then twenty-one hour flight). I still remember the hot creamed spinach served with smoked salmon with iced slibovitch to drink. I gave up all drinking soon after but the memory lingers on.

A sumptuous wedding gift arrived soon after we married, mistakenly coupled with a simply huge customs charge. I refused the package and wrote to Hughes's front man to say I was surprised that it had come via a competitive airline. It didn't take long to arrive again, in the hands of a person who flew via TWA.

Although I never saw him for years before he died in 1976, I knew he'd become a caricature of a human being, his death caused by kidney failure and dehydration. Half-man, he was drugged and frail, as dreadful to see as a dying victim in a concentration camp. His nails were frighteningly long, his matted hair below his shoulders. Surrounded by guards, he lived in hotels that became prison cells, more dead than alive.

The anticipated squabbles over his vast estate when he finally gave up life filled press pages but fortunately, an earlier tax-evasive move settled the argument: the bulk of his millions went to the Hughes Medical Institute. An irony for a man who died starving for the medical help he refused to take.

Louis B. Mayer was a self-appointed 'Mr Important' in Hollywood, and a necessary target for me when there, as his studio's film advertising was worth pandering to him for; pander *was* the operative word, but I did not mind doing it if it benefited *Look* magazine. LB used to give me lunch in the MGM commissary; 'So you can meet my stars there,' he would say. But once, in a moment of vanity, he suggested I have lunch with him in his new home. Would I meet him there at one o'clock?

Everyone was curious about his much-discussed new wife, Lorena Danker. There was a great deal of gossip about her, his new lifestyle and new house, designed by Bill Haines who later decorated the American Embassy in London for the price-no-object Walter Annenbergs when Walter became American Ambassador.

Haines must have been under the impression that L. B. Mayer liked white, something I discovered as I sat waiting in the new library for my late-arriving host. I had forty minutes to survey the effect of an all-white room: walls, ceiling and floor were indeed all dead white. All the furniture was in white leather, and even the pristine new books, all in French, yards and yards of them, were bound in virginal white leather with titles embossed in gold.

When at last my host arrived, my opening gambit was to say that everything I had seen was incredibly glamorous. He glowed with pride.

'But, LB,' I announced, 'I didn't know you spoke French!'

'Who speaks French? Not me!' he replied in his squeaky voice.

'But you must speak French,' I insisted.

'Why *should* I speak French? I don't.'

'Listen, LB, every book in your white library is in French.'

'*Are they?*' he replied, absolutely astonished.

Whenever I see the word faithful, I think back to a racehorse named Be Faithful, and thereby hangs another L. B. Mayer tale. He invited me to the Santa Anita racecourse, an invitation akin to a royal favour. We went in his large black limousine, talking politics. His and mine did not agree: I was a *liberal*, in fact, an independent who voted for *men* not parties, and he was further to the right than General MacArthur. I tried to be polite whenever he cussed anyone as 'too leftish'. I particularly resented his insulting remarks about Paul Hoffman and told him so; few were less left-wing than the distinguished Mr Hoffman, I insisted. He was a citizen's citizen, appointed by George Marshall to direct the Marshall Plan in Europe. He was also a friend whom I didn't wish to hear vilified.

By the time we reached the racecourse we were almost in silence. We were led by officials into the box where he held court. No one was allowed to leave to bet; messengers were provided for that purpose at his order. When I saw that one horse was named Be Faithful, I decided to back it despite his command not to waste money on a nag which, he said, was his horse but wasn't worth a bet. 'Don't bet on it – she can't win,' he insisted.

I left, explaining I was off to powder my nose, which he allowed. I sped to the betting counter instead and bet $100 on the horse, my usual bet being $5. The beautiful horse with such a romantic name *did* win, and as it was expected to lose, the odds were colossal, ninety-to-one, and I made nine thousand dollars. Mayer was so angry that I had ignored his edict, and made thousands by doing so, that he refused to speak to me again in the car. Two silent passengers, one irate, the other with spirits flying, rode home together.

I had an important role in Olivia De Havilland's second marriage to editor Pierre Galente, when she asked me to be her *témoin*, to sign her marriage certificate in France. I obliged happily as neither her mother nor sister Joan Fontaine were then on speaking terms with her. An affectionate substitute for her real family, I have countless photographs commemorating that romantic country tableau.

The delightful French ceremony took place in the *Mairie* of a small French village on the Loire. Friends and villagers paraded through the town to the chateau of the publisher of *Paris Match*, which the bridegroom edited.*

Olivia won two Oscars, one for *To Each His Own*, the other for *The Heiress*. She will also be remembered for *Gone With the Wind* and *The Snake Pit*, for which she won many awards, but another film she made much later showed her telepathic connection with her profession. She still talks about it.

In the early sixties, she was so frustrated when for the third time the exterior of her home in Paris was painted in the wrong colours. She went off to Switzerland to 'sit it out' until the painters got the façade right. She was content to use a small parlour undisturbed, surrounded by out-of-date magazines. She found a year-old copy of the *New Yorker* in which a story caught her trained eye: *The Light in the Piazza*. It related experiences of an American woman sojourning in Florence, and wound on through several issues, all stacked in the room. When the façade and shutters were finally painted as ordered,

---

* I casually mentioned to M. Prouvost at lunch later in his chateau that a news magazine ought to be printed in black and white. *Paris Match* was then principally (and expensively) in colour. 'News doesn't look instant if it appears in colour,' I suggested. *Paris Match* went black and white, looking like today's news.

she returned to resume her Paris life, forgetting the magazine tale which had helped while away her stay in Switzerland.

Months later, Benjamin Thau, a Culver City movie mogul, called her to discuss the studio's decision to star her in a film which there was no time for her to read. She would have to take his word for its qualities.

She declined the offer, saying she wouldn't agree unless she could read the script first. Thau then outlined it; to her delight it was an adaptation of the very story she had read with such pleasure in Switzerland. She made the film in Florence, Rome and then England, where we saw much of each other. Thirty-odd years later, the Dior-designed wardrobe she had worn in the film was auctioned by Christie's in London.

Joan Crawford was another Hollywood legend; high cheekbones, painted lips, exaggerated clothes and oversize shoulder-pads. The capacity to live in the same overblown style helped her become a Hollywood flame and box-office draw with few equals.

At the top as an actress, she moved into a different arena when she married 'Mr Pepsi-Cola'. After his death, she became a director of his company. This suited her oxygen-charged personality in her post-movie-making days when she retired to live in New York. She supported the correct charitable causes, rejecting much of the old razzmatazz but remaining tough, flirtatious and as agile as a cat.

She was eventually trashed by her adopted daughter Christine in a book, *Mommie Dearest*; this received millions of lines of press coverage as a sorry tale of a girl who hated her overbearing and ruthless mother. Did Crawford deserve it? Did Nancy Reagan or Lana Turner deserve like treatment?

She and I used to lunch from time to time. I found her great company after I became accustomed to her exaggerated style. Our conversation was often about the niche she hoped to occupy in New York society – but in the end it was her films that spoke best for her. She was a brilliant and exciting star who brought genuine sexuality to her work, even if her private and social life proved to be of a more doubtful quality.

*   *   *

To anyone who saw her on stage, watched her on screen or had the pleasure, as I had, of knowing her that ravishing actress Vivien Leigh was the opposite of Joan Crawford, a very different kind of legend. Her last few days of life were tragic; chasing joy, though severely ill, possibly drug-addicted.

In the period between divorcing Laurence Olivier (whom she never stopped loving) and her death, she used to spend weekends at her Mill House in Sussex. Every corner was filled with memories: from parts she had played, paintings by those she knew, and odd treasures she had brought back from tours. The last time we met there, the guests raved about the first course at dinner, a sardine soufflé. She purred with pride because it was her own personal recipe. 'I'd love to have it,' I told her when she came to lunch the next day in our nearby home. The recipe arrived the following morning, written in her own hand – a touching legacy as she died a day later.

A photograph of this extraordinarily beautiful woman, taken in the sitting room of my office at *Look* Magazine in New York while she and Laurence Olivier were playing *Antony and Cleopatra* in New York, is a highlight of my Rogue's Gallery of friends.

Spain's Andres Segovia, who died in 1987 aged ninety-four, came to us for a cocktail not many years before, as amusing as a young blade. A virtuoso who internationalized the guitar as a serious musical instrument, not only by playing it exquisitely but by extending its repertoire, Segovia was no stranger to Bach or Brahms or Mendelssohn. His work and prestige led to the recognition of such other guitar geniuses as Julian Bream and John Williams.

On this occasion Segovia came on his own. 'Señor Segovia, if you have a wife, *where* is she? One never sees her with you.'

'I *do* have a wife, but she has to stay home to mind the baby,' the old man replied. Reaching into his inside pocket, he brought out a photograph of his very beautiful young wife holding an infant. 'What a wonderful child,' I responded. 'Have you any other children?'

He quickly assured me, smiling from ear to ear, 'Oh yes, I have another son by my first wife, but he's now over fifty-nine years old!'

*   *   *

The New York theatre in my early days had a 'Mr Broadway', George Abbott. He died aged over 107, actually preparing a new musical. His second wife, Mary Sinclair, is a very close friend who has become a superb painter as well as a beautiful actress. Abbott's true successor is Harold Prince; all agree he is today's Broadway Supremo.

George Abbott was the mentor who allowed Prince as a gifted assistant at a tender age to produce his first musical success, *The Pajama Game*. It was the one with which I started out as a Broadway Angel, a role I have greatly enjoyed. Others followed under Prince's production, such historic successes as *West Side Story*, *Cabaret* and *Fiddler on the Roof*.

My one-time office boy (his first job) is now one of the world's greatest stage directors. *Evita* was the idea of two Londoners, Tim Rice and Andrew Lloyd Webber, who found it far too difficult to stage themselves. It was saved by an SOS to Prince to come to London, where he directed it with resounding success. I was pleased to be asked to those *Evita* rehearsals. Prince knew I was one of the few who actually knew the real Evita, after reading my bestselling book about her. My desire was to prevent any idealization of that dreadful woman.

Prince remained a Broadway producer until costs began to escalate dizzily. Money-raising took up too much of his time; to raise as much as ten million dollars for a musical wasn't a simple task and didn't seem to go hand in hand with creativity. He gave up the task of producing, and took to *directing* plays instead. Such successes as *The Phantom of the Opera*, *Evita*, *A Little Night Music*, *Sweeney Todd* and *Kiss of the Spider Woman* followed, great artistic achievements and money-spinners. Having finished a revival of *Show Boat*, making theatrical history, he is rehearsing *The Petrified Prince*, based on an Ingmar Bergman film, as I write. His record-breaking successes helped change the nature of musicals.

Another theatrical great was the late Londoner, Binkie Beaumont, the friend who produced the history-making *My Fair Lady* among dozens of other great successes of the London theatre. Every production was both a financial and a social event: opening night parties at his North Street house provided great conversation, fine food and superb surroundings in a house filled with wonderful paintings. His death was a loss to British theatre.

Two other master showmen, Luciano Pavarotti and Placido Domingo, learned quickly and gallantly to bring opera show biz to the 'masses' – not only by their visceral performances on stage but with recordings galore – not just opera, but records, featuring, for instance, Pavarotti with country singer John Denver, and Placido Domingo singing 'Steppin' Out with the Ladies', a racy bid for the hearts of ladies who already adored him.

Their concert appearances together with José Carreras, following the last two World Cup football tournaments in Italy and the United States, were seen by tens of millions of viewers worldwide and the spin-off videos and CDs have sold hundreds of thousands of copies. Pavarotti's rendering of 'Nessun Dorma' as the theme music for the 1990 World Cup has made it one of opera's best known arias, loved by people who have never heard of *Turandot*.

Both men must recall occasions at our home in London. I gave Placido Domingo his fiftieth birthday party, to which he and our mutual friends flew in from Madrid. At another party I invited Luciano Pavarotti to lunch when we celebrated the ninetieth birthday of Queen Elizabeth The Queen Mother. Of course, he sang, and all joined in for the obligatory 'Happy Birthday'. He had regaled her at the table with advice on how to make proper spaghetti, a conversational gambit as amusing to the royal guest as to all the others. He spoke with the same passion about pasta as he puts into his singing. At that same luncheon, ballerina Alicia Markova announced, 'I have danced with Nijinsky and now I have sung with Pavarotti!'

The elegant Placido Domingo has to meet back-to-back engagements conducting as well as singing. Maria, his wife, is the all-important key in his life, always at his side. The twenty-stone Pavarotti deals with similar commitments but there is the added problem of his size – beds and doors are simply too small. Flying Concorde across the Atlantic helps with the bulk problem because the three-hour flight time means there is no need to get through the doors to the loo!

*   *   *

My election to the Rabinowitz Society in New York came unexpectedly while attending an Easter celebration at the home of the Russian 'Grand Dame' of couture, Valentina, and her husband George Schlee, the devoted friend of Greta Garbo. Both were ardent members of the club. Rabinowitz was the name given to a mythical man whose life was concocted from the jokes members came together to tell at their gatherings. I got the hang of their game after I heard of the club's history and sampled a few of the jokes.

The thirteen members were mainly from show business and the writing profession. They collected funny stories or jokes heard during the year, each capable of being converted to events that might have happened in the fictional life of a lovable Jewish gentleman, Mr Rabinowitz, who was usually in deep trouble but always came out on top. By the time he 'entered' my life, he had two very stupid wives, two unrewarding sons and a history of rags-to-riches. Sam Behrman, the playwright member, had begun to write his 'biography'. Garbo, usually remote, was like a kitten, whether telling tales or reacting to them.

Unwittingly, I gained membership by telling a story which I thought could be added to the life of the incredible man; I was invited to become the last member of the Rabinowitz Society, which is no longer in existence.

This is a shortened version of the story which made me a member of this exclusive club:

There was once an itinerant rabbi in Russia, who travelled about in a horse-drawn wagon, driven by his simple assistant. They covered a great part of Russia, never returning to the same place more than once a year, where he greeted the same faces and had the same experiences. Women always presented the rabbi with warm gloves, hats and scarves they'd knitted while waiting for his return.

After leading his horse for years, caring for the tired old animal on their way, the driver suddenly became angry. Turning to the rabbi he complained: 'It's not fair. You give the same sermon everywhere. I've heard it so often I could give it in my sleep. You get the gifts and I get nothing!'

'You are absolutely right,' the rabbi reasoned. 'In the next village *you* must be the rabbi. You give the sermon and take the gifts. I'll be happy.'

Nimble-minded and perfectly relaxed, the driver gave the exact sermon. All went well until out of the blue, for the first time even, a man in the tiny crowd asked him a serious rabbinical question. The driver, though no fool, didn't have the answer but he thought fast: 'Such a *stupid* question, I'll ask my driver to answer!'

Club members immediately decided the driver must have been Mr Rabinowitz before he left Russia for America.

No Hollywood kaleidoscope can leave out Kirk Douglas. He remains, like James Stewart, one of my closest ties with yesterday's original, lavish Hollywood of great stars, great films and great memories. Like Stewart, he has remained the same without changing his character or lifestyle, despite the fame that has come his way, and has kept his star rating for over forty years when few other names have lasted long enough to be remembered. Anne, his wife, has been a great partner, having produced many of his successful films. They are close enough friends for us to admire their unique companionship.

A creative turn in Kirk's life came when he wrote his bestselling autobiography; he found writing as compelling a craft as acting. The book is earthy, straightforward and as honest as its author. The reception it received must have given him and Anne great pride.

A remarkable woman died in February 1994. I woke up to see on television that Gloria Stewart was dead. Her husband, James Stewart, according to the rash of stories that followed, was inconsolable, had become a recluse and refused to see or receive visitors. One London paper headlined that he was 'dying of heartbreak'. This brave man, who saw war service as a Brigadier General in the US Air Force, had become a tragic figure. This was believable to us because we had known husband and wife throughout their perfect marriage. After I heard the news I tried constantly to telephone him, but could get no answer. I had to resort to a letter.

Gloria Stewart died of lung cancer, which I believe was kept a secret. Their children took turns to comfort their father and the world reacted instantly.

His life with Gloria was ideal. We saw a good deal of both when Jimmy played the star role in London in the play *Harvey*. When the play ended he sent us a glass rabbit made by Steuben which sits quietly on our country dining table, a sad reminder of other days. Whenever the Stewarts went on camera safari, they visited us in Sussex, *en route* for Africa or homeward bound, and many of our friends there got to know their hearty humour. For years, she had been a volunteer expert on museum collections in the San Diego zoo, and we often compared notes because this zoo and the Jersey zoo, which I serve as a trustee, have similar aims: we have a *purpose*. Two of the Stewart children, twins, are professional anthropologists.

I once took the Stewarts to the Isle of Jersey when I went for a board meeting at the zoo. At a friend's house, Jimmy sang his slow songs, accompanying himself on the piano. He later told an unforgettable hilarious story about his father but, alas, to appreciate it fully you need to be able to enjoy the pleasure of Jimmy Stewart's unique style of telling it. I shall paraphrase it: his father had run a highly profitable general store in a Southern town. One day, the boss of a travelling circus called in. He admitted they were broke until they got paid for their performance. Would he let them have credit? The kind man said, 'Yes, of course.'

The circus was a total failure. No one cared that they were in town. Still with no money to pay their bills, they asked, 'What could we give you as collateral for future payment?'

'Have you a snake?'

Yes, they had a huge python, a circus act. It was brought to the store and carefully placed in one of the windows, with precautions taken to prevent its escape. The senior Stewart was pleased by the increased 'traffic'. Everyone in town came to watch the snake, safely, at close hand. Extra business followed until one day two aged ladies saw it in the window and fainted on the street, and the town erupted in an uproar. The snake must go! But how to get it out of the window? Jimmy's father called the family doctor: would he come with enough anaesthetic to knock out the snake? They made a small hole in the wooden wall and sprayed ether through it. None of it reached the coiled, sleeping snake but both men were instantly anaesthetized and were found later unconscious on the floor.

The end of the story? I never found it out. Jimmy liked to leave it to others to decide what eventually happened to his father, the doctor and the python.

The Stewarts have made me proud by their love of my work. They have a 'Fleur Cowles Room' in their Hollywood home, devoted to eleven of my paintings bought at exhibitions.

I first looked into the large violet eyes of Elizabeth Taylor at the London party celebrating her marriage to the late Mike Todd. After eight marriages (twice to Richard Burton) her capability as a mother to four adopted children remains undiminished.

Lassie was her first co-star in films, soon to be followed by a horse in *National Velvet*. But as the sultry, psychotic Maggie in Tennessee Williams's *Cat on a Hot Tin Roof* she displayed her exceptional skill in a mature and powerful performance.

Despite emotional stress and physical pain, problems of weight and drug abuse, all under the constant scrutiny of the international media, she remains one of the world's most beautiful women, and, for me, the most wonderful company, especially when she is with such close friends as Tessa Kennedy in London. At dinner in private with Liz Taylor the talk is not of films, producers, the usual Hollywood chatter, but of opera, concerts, music and ballet. Fund raising for AIDS charities now occupies a great deal of her time. To date she has raised more than $50 million since 1984 when Rock Hudson, dying of the syndrome, gave her her first donation. Now over sixty, her last marriage, the eighth, was to an 'outsider', the ceremony very much an overblown Hollywood-style extravaganza. Divorce, alas, followed in a short time.

The Tessa Kennedy I write of is someone I call 'daughter' (her real mother smiles understandingly), and she refers to me as 'Mother Fleur'. She is truly beautiful and gifted, a noted interior decorator, one of whose regular clients is Prince Hussein of Jordan. She has five children, one of them is my godson, the brilliant young Cary Elwes with, not only a handsome face and beautiful mind, but heart. He already has a fine career in Hollywood. I am proud of him and even more proud of his mother.

*   *   *

The mysterious Garbo I once knew could also be witty, curious, could exhaust by questions and could be a delight *if* she chose the moment, the situation, and the companion; she loved walking about New York City streets despite her rumoured lumbago, wearing a dowdy cloak, flat shoes, rumpled trousers and no make-up under a face-hiding hat; everyone recognized her but left her alone.

She lived like a queen in her 52nd Street apartment which she allowed me to reveal in 1950 in *Flair* magazine. After her death her accumulated relics were sold by Sotheby's in New York for $20,700,000. The collectors competed avidly, pushing the total raised to twenty times the estimate. A scent bottle fetched $18,000, a Renoir portrait $5,700,000, a Berard portrait of Cecil Beaton, $12,000 (Beaton was the man who asked for but didn't get her in marriage after a somewhat publicized affair; her earliest real love was Hollywood's John Gilbert). Her Duesenberg maroon convertible car had been sold in 1987 for $1,400,000.

Her final companion, until his death, was George Schlee. He had met Garbo in 1948 at his wife Valentina's couture establishment, which he managed. He soon became Garbo's replacement for Mauritz Stiller, who had brought her from her native Sweden to Hollywood in 1925 in a Svengali-like manner.

Schlee looked after her money and her international reputation. A *ménage à trois* resulted, from which Valentina was slowly inched out. The arrangement, though, was never a secret. Schlee bought Garbo a house on the Côte d'Azur and they shared a suite at the Crillon Hotel in Paris, where Schlee died in October 1964. Valentina had the last word, though, flying from New York to Paris to claim his body. Valentina died in September 1989, aged ninety-one.

When my husband and I visited Garbo and Schlee in their Riviera villa, I left him with her while Schlee and I went to see a local painter who had impressed him. (I bought one canvas and still love it.) My husband still talks of Garbo's unbelievable eyes. She sat opposite him on the long veranda in front of the house, the sea behind her, keeping her head down, showing little but the crown of the hat she wore to shade her face. When she raised her head to make a point, she looked straight at him, eyes never wavering. He still says he will never get over that beauty, especially the blue-grey eyes staring at him under those long, long eyelashes. She always registered her thoughts with those eyes; they told it all. Many women still measure their faces by her cheekbones.

Her background remains veiled in mystery, although her father may have been a butcher, Karl Gustafson. She chose her future name from the two offered her by Mauritz Stiller to replace Gustafson. The improbable alternatives are supposed to have been either Greta Garbo or Gussie Berger! Stiller taught her how to eat, to walk, to sit, to stand. I wish I knew *who* the delightful person was who described her as 'the blonde with a brunette voice'.

She often came to dine with us in New York, with varying results. Once the rather frosty British Foreign Minister, Selwyn Lloyd, was seated next to her; the tired man had only just got off a plane from London. He left the dinner a changed man. When I saw him later in London, I admitted I had been mystified by his over-effusive, lingering thank you at the door, which he gave me as I bade him farewell in New York.

'What on earth was that for?' I asked.

'Why? Because you gave me Garbo! I shall never forget you for that,' he exclaimed with renewed euphoria. He never seemed a formidable figure after that. Garbo had apparently been a great listener, always flattering gentlemen.

Another time I seated my fourteen-year-old stepson, Gardner Cowles II, next to Garbo at table. When I asked him how he liked that famous lady he asked 'Who is Garbo?' He and the Foreign Minister had both seen that beautiful face break into an enormous, absolutely devastating smile, but it was lost on the fourteen-year-old.

She died a very sad and lonely woman on Easter Sunday, 1990, aged eighty-four. The public had not seen her on film for nearly fifty years, but there was her legacy of ten silent and fourteen talking films. A beautiful portrait of her, painted by René Gruau of Paris, the artist called by many a modern Toulouse-Lautrec, hangs on our wall in Spain to bewitch every visitor.

In our hallowed Albany chambers, the rules set in very fine print guide our pleasantly ordered lives: no music, no noise after eleven o'clock, no children, no dogs, no cats. The Edwardian atmosphere is maintained with astonishing success. Most of us who live there are grateful for the restrictions, and something happened many years ago to illustrate the rigidity of the rules.

At midnight, a poker-faced porter had to unlock the heavy door to let in a tiny woman. It was the haunted Judy Garland, arriving for a late supper snack – so late she was no longer expected. Tired and totally unglamorous, like a ragamuffin, in rumpled trousers, with tousled hair and careless manner, but with a difference: she was smiling and gay, rare in her neurotic life. Once inside, having proved she was actually expected, she started skipping on her way, and singing. That's not allowed at any time of day – but at midnight!

'I'm sorry, Miss, you simply cannot skip through these halls and certainly you cannot sing here,' the porter announced firmly. Stopping dead in her tracks, she burst into laughter: 'You must be kidding! I'm Judy Garland! Anywhere else, I'd be getting $20,000 for this!'

'There, there now, Miss,' he said, patting her gently on the back. '*Not here.*'

I shall never forget Danny Kaye and Charlie Chaplin acting out for a group of guests how they'd show the difference between comedy and tragedy – sitting on a small parlour bench. Chaplin hardly moved but his version of tragedy produced a number of moist eyes among the audience.

The handsome Basque, Jacques Bergerac, one of France's favourite film stars, now lives in Biarritz. When we are there to stay with him, we see sights no tourist gets to, enhancing our trips with a walking, talking encyclopedic knowledge of the history of the area he loves so much. His life should be told in a book: married to Ginger Rogers, a film star himself, then head of the Revlon cosmetics company and now in luxurious retirement with a lovely wife. To walk with him in Biarritz is never straightforward; he is constantly stopped by fans.

Janet Gaynor, when having drinks with us in London, was joined by one of the world's great authors, the Brazilian Jorge Amado and his wife. Janet Gaynor's presence gave them great pleasure. *Seventh Heaven* was Amado's favourite film. He is still speaking of the meeting. Janet Gaynor died a terrible death in a crash in a taxi in California with Mary Martin, star of the musical *South Pacific*. It was hit sideways by another car, killing Janet. Mary Martin fortunately survived, not only to sing again, but to see her son Larry Hagman become an international TV hero as a star of the soap opera *Dallas*.

My former husband was voted Marshal of his class at Harvard University at its twenty-fifth reunion. As his wife, my job was to look after and amuse the hundred or so other spouses who arrived in Boston – and to find a way to entertain the gentlemen as well for a gala evening. I had the great good fortune to name as my co-chairman the glamorous actress, Gertrude Lawrence, wife of Richard Aldrich of the same graduating class, all of us close friends. For the big evening, we made a mad decision to stage the best moments of the current musical, *South Pacific* – but with a difference; we chose to rewrite the lyrics to reflect the period twenty-five years before, we even rented clothes of that same period, we bravely danced, and, yes, we sang. Despite my inability to carry a tune, Gertrude Lawrence's voice and others in the cast saved the day. We all had a hilarious time (especially the other drafted unprofessionals). In theatrical terms, the evening was a smash hit, far, far away from any serious critics.

A year later, when enchanting Gertrude Lawrence suddenly died of the cancer she didn't know she had, her husband asked if I'd decorate her coffin for the church. I did this with an aching heart.

Peter Cary is a low-key, highly polished gentleman who, though now retired after twenty years, is still 'Mr Paramount' to his friends. Recently he bought the great house in London's Mayfair which once was home to his lifelong hero, Dwight D. Eisenhower, who lived in it during Britain's war years. A totally new image has resulted – it is now the home of an important collector.

One addition made by the Carys in the house they gutted was an amazing creation of a 'Fleur Cowles gallery'. A new glassed-in room, bounded by plants and gardens, is now a magical backdrop for twelve of my most recent paintings. Elsewhere in the house are other signs of my work, the books, porcelain, bone china animal figurines and specially designed rugs I designed for them. A visit there quickens my heartbeat. A new home in New York will also be a Fleur Cowles showpiece. I am proud of their affection.

The reformed hellraiser, Peter O'Toole, frequently dines with us, which is always a thrill for us and other guests. When he published his memoirs in late 1992, I learned how obsessed he was by Adolf Hitler. In 1976 in the film *Rogue Male*, he tries to kill the Führer. In real life, apparently, he would have *loved* to have done so.

The most important thing in his life is his son. At his remarkable performance as a drunk in *Jeffrey Bernard is Unwell*, the boy used to stand in the wings, watching his handsome father. He gave up drinking at least twenty years ago following intensive surgery. It annoys him to think anyone calls *Lawrence of Arabia* his best work. Like his own father, a racetrack bookmaker in Leeds, he could 'charm the birds off the trees'.

Sir John Gielgud once gave us and our guests an unforgettable evening when after dinner I persuaded him to draw up a chair and tell us what he thought were the best stories of his life in the theatre. Timidly the great actor began to take us slowly through years of theatrical encounters. Many stars came to life in new guises, particularly Laurence Olivier, Clifton Webb and his mother. He always said that appearing on stage was a release because he could escape into the identities of his characters.

Sir John Wolfenden, later Lord, belongs, by divine right, in Show Biz, despite his importance in other fields. He was a guest on the above occasion; earlier, Gielgud whispered to me that he would like to speak to Wolfenden, so I brought the two together and turned away. 'Don't go,' said Gielgud: 'I have only one short thing to say to Sir John and it is not a secret.' With that he turned and said simply: 'I want to thank you for saving my life.' He was referring to the then newly-enacted

Wolfenden Report which, for the first time in history made it legal for adult males to have sex together in Britain. At that time a recent grim experience with the law underscored Gielgud's grateful thanks to Sir John.

John Wolfenden, a good friend, had been a scholar, an educator, a law-maker (of historic significance) in his lifetime, and also the Director of the British Museum.

Marlene Dietrich's gift to me of a coffin-sized box of huge red roses as a thank-you for a dinner party left me wondering where she could have found them; they were thirty inches tall. I shall always remember her voice; she gave up her German citizenship but not that accent, which proved a wise decision.

It is hard to forget her on stage, her slim body covered in sheer flesh-coloured fabric, swathed in furs which were always allowed to slip off onto the floor as she stepped slowly across to soak up the audience's delight. Wasn't it perhaps with a measure of disdain, and didn't we sometimes glimpse the same disdain from Laurence Olivier when curtain calls continued too long?

There was also a disdainful air about Rudolf Nureyev, the legendary dancer, many believe the greatest ever. He made ballet history in 1961 when, in Paris with his Russian ballet company, he decided to defect. Margot Fonteyn helped him get to London where he burst on to the Western consciousness with the most captivating and brilliant dancing since Nijinsky. His grand panther-like leaps gave the illusion he was hanging in mid-air.

He adored music, and wanted to create a ballet without a story, just dancing to express Bach or Chopin. He was so self-assured he began trying to improve on the music, the steps and costumes in such classical works as *Giselle* and *The Nutcracker*. He wore his hair unusually long, a fashion soon taken up by other male dancers.

We got to know him well and I decided to give a supper party for Margot and Rudolf after the first night of a gala at Covent Garden. Most of our other guests came home with us from the theatre to await their arrival. I was well aware that they could be late, with make-up to remove and callers to greet before they could leave. However, all of us were too ravenous to wait, so at eleven-fifteen we crowded to the buffet table and the food was soon all eaten.

My panic subsided when I had the table reset for Margot and Rudolf with a fine new baked ham, plenty of salad, a new large round Brie cheese and extra cake, all prepared before they arrived in case of need. I filled a plate for Nureyev and took it to him. 'No!' he announced. 'No. *Steak.*'

'If you want steak, put your coat back on and try to find a restaurant open at this hour to get it!' I announced, walking away.

He laughed loudly, swallowed his supper and rushed to join the guests.

We saw him at other times in a less demanding mood, often at Tessa Kennedy's home as they were such close friends. She went to his funeral in Paris, which was marred for her by his grasping relatives from Russia. He had died of AIDS, a shadow of his real self – a tragedy for his many followers.

Jean Renoir, son of the great painter, chose to write and became a film-maker whose work was revered. We met at a dinner in Paris. I had just finished reading an English translation of his *Stories of Captain George*. We were placed together at table, and I could talk of nothing else; the result was his decision that we should collaborate on a film of the book. He needed an English-speaking writer and decided I was it.

The exciting project took nearly two years to die. The plan was that we could work together, he helping me with the script, for I knew little enough about screen-writing. We both knew enough producers in Hollywood to ensure the best contacts when the work was done. Suddenly, however, he had to leave for Hollywood to direct a film and our collaboration died. I was swamped by other work, having written two books meanwhile. I also had exhibitions of my paintings to prepare for as well as designing porcelain and other artistic commissions. But the book has great possibilities for a film and I would still love to see it done. Renoir and I wrote to each other constantly, comparing ideas. He fell ill and in his last letter from Hollywood wrote: 'Dear Fleur Cowles, I love your lions, I love your tigers, your butterflies and I love you because you are a poet. But for the time being my health doesn't allow me to join you. With my sincere affection, Jean Renoir.'

Maurice Chevalier lived in a Paris suburb, Marnes les Cocottes – what a name. We enjoyed visiting him in the surroundings he had created, first because of his impressionist paintings, but just as importantly, I loved his garden, adorned in an extraordinary way by a strange assortment that had belonged to the Englishman who left the British nation one of its finest museums, the Wallace Collection in London.

Wallace was obsessed by the horses he saw everywhere on the Paris streets. He saw them as overworked, thirsty creatures, so he set about placing stone water-troughs all over the city to help in their working lives. Maurice Chevalier bought not only Wallace's house but also the troughs, peppered his garden with them and filled them with plants, mainly roses. Any of those Impressionist painters whose work so pleased Wallace and Chevalier would have enjoyed painting them.

When I think of adding salt to food, I think of Gloria Swanson. She ate practically nothing on the first day of her first visit to us in Sussex because she wouldn't touch anything which she suspected had been cooked with salt. Our chef thought her less than a satisfying guest after having to spend time the next day trying to produce food without any.

I had known her for many glamorous years in America including the period of her liaison with President Kennedy's father, Joseph Kennedy, but a certain crankiness developed as she began to face oncoming age. I still hesitate before adding salt to anything, shaking on ground black pepper instead because of her threat that it would kill me. She gave me a book to prove it, but I carefully hid it. I *do* like salt.

A terraced rock garden, shaped like an amphitheatre, drops down through our lawns to one of our four lakes. When he saw it, Peter Brook once said he'd like to produce *A Midsummer Night's Dream* there. If only he had: the actors would have had, in spring time, a copse behind them covered with a bright carpet of bluebells. On that same site, we have seen Margot Fonteyn leaping from stone to stone in something akin to a private ballet. It was an early morning and very exciting to watch.

Conversations for posterity are usually of political or historic importance – but what about those that simply make you laugh? Peter Ustinov certainly contributed on this level, intermingling the political, historical and the personal.

I remember a sidewalk event after my husband and I said goodnight to Leslie Caron at her home in London. Ustinov was directly behind us. We were getting into our car when he began with: 'Did you ever hear about the bus load of American tourists who arrived in Nice?' No, we hadn't.

The mad account of every imagined passenger began. Forty minutes later he had given us all their comments on the South of France's tourist attractions. Each was mimicked in native accents, encompassing Brooklynese, Bostonian, deep Southern to Jewish. After tears of laughter, we finally drove away.

I could not end Show Biz without a deep curtsy to Dulcie Gray and Michael Denison, two great treasures who, for me, are the 'royals' of the English theatre. This married pair have been chosen by the best of West End theatre producers for almost half a century; they have starred in at least thirty of the most important plays of our time. They are indestructible. They are masters of the art of acting, who delight us at every experience.

They have been involved in all aspects of the theatre, including Equity and The Arts Council. Both have had an impact on TV. They also write: Michael Denison's *Double Act* describes their lives together in an enthralling mix of personal stories and contemporary theatre history. Dulcie Gray has already written twenty-nine books (between-the-acts activity?) with subjects ranging from butterflies to sinister mysteries.

They are part of our Christmases, always with us on the great day itself, affectionately enlivening conversation with their unique style of anecdotal storytelling, told with gusto and affection.

IX

PERON-ITIS – AFTERMATH

To BE PERSONA NON GRATA in a country, as I am, means that
you don't go there. Since the time of the Perons, I have never
returned to the Argentine, and do not intend to.

I had gone there on a junket which included many other publishers,
but after I insisted on being able to visit President Peron and asked
to meet his First Lady, he unexpectedly invited me to join her on her
regular rounds. I, too, wore jewels. She coveted one of my brooches
but Peron cautioned me, 'Don't give it to her!' Mistakenly taking me
as a possible friend, after I left the Argentine she had no more ardent
enemy.

An amusing anecdote about the aftermath of the publication of my
book, *Bloody Precedent*, was revealed by a stranger sitting next to me
on the plane I had taken to Rio. When the stewardess spoke to me
by name, he was very startled and soon told me why. It was a dramatic
story.

His tale involved my book's account of the Argentine in the nineteenth century, when de Rosas' regime was at its peak. A movement
to oust the cruel Manuel and his wife Encarnación was started by a
group of intellectuals who secretly plotted in the basement of a certain
bookshop in Buenos Aires. A little more than one hundred years later,
my companion on the plane had become one of a group who met and
plotted in the very same basement to rid the country of Evita and Juan
Peron. The shop was owned by a brave Jewish refugee, a woman who
had escaped from the Nazis and established the cellar for secret political
purposes. Down there, my book was being read by all, cut apart page
by page to avoid the crime of being found with the book itself – one
page each night. It made me very proud to hear about it from the
elegant lawyer on the plane, a man who couldn't have looked less like
a revolutionary. He was very, very grateful; 'Come and let us give you
our thanks and pay our respects,' he pleaded.

279

'I can't do that. I'm *persona non grata*,' and how proud I was of that, 'and the edict still stands,' I explained. 'I have never gone back. I am still *persona non grata* because the edict must remain, in spirit even if it is not now official.' Proof that it is came not too many years ago at a dinner in my honour in New York when an Argentine cabinet minister, an Army officer, was placed next to me. My place card had been hurriedly rewritten by the host, changed from *Fleur Cowles* to *Mrs Tom Montague Meyer*. I spent the dinner asking my companion stupid questions to put him off the track: 'What is the Argentine like? Is its capital as beautiful as I hear? What about the countryside?' I asked anything that might suggest I'd never been there. He answered questions politely.

The minister had to leave before coffee was served. 'I must work on my speech for my UN address tomorrow,' he said apologetically as he rose to go. Then he took my hand and announced, 'I am delighted to meet you, Fleur Cowles. However, don't come to my country. We cannot guarantee your safety!' How did he know I was Fleur Cowles?

Nearly fifty years later, the 'Evita-influence' still haunts Argentina. I never planned to write my book about the Perons, but an incident impelled me to do so. I was staying at the American Embassy in Buenos Aires as a guest of Ambassador Stanton Griffis. On 4 July, the usual 'open house' for Americans took place.

I had gone to a country rendezvous but returned to attend the Embassy party after meeting a distinguished publisher, Sr Tito Gainza Paz, to whom I later dedicated my book. The brave man attempted to keep his distinguished anti-Peronist newspaper alive in the face of intimidation, threats and arrests. His son was still in jail. We had to meet far outside the city in cloak-and-dagger fashion in the country cottage of an American friend, one which surely wouldn't be bugged. We were free to discuss the harassment of his family and of his newspaper by the government. I suggested well-intended intervention but this was quickly rejected on the grounds that it would certainly worsen matters for him and his family if I even tried.

To change the subject he told me about a 'White Paper' which had been written by a token opposition Congressman now locked up in an unknown jail for sponsoring an unacceptable legislative bill. Supposedly it was on educational reform but after it had been routinely printed, distributed and 'buried', the harmless pages were suddenly read by a Senator who went on to discover that the document's real purpose was to expose in detail Juan and Evita Peron's manipulation of the law, their corrupt finances and political activities. Copies were immediately confiscated and, in true totalitarian tradition, burned. A few were rumoured to have been saved from the fire.

'I assume you have a copy?' I asked Gainza Paz.

'Yes, I have, but don't ask me to pass it on to you. Think of my family and what that might cost them.'

'No, I won't ask for it,' I replied, 'but the Congressman will obviously disappear without trace, and no one will know why he risked his life.'

I returned to the crowded Embassy celebration, saddened by the story. As I was swallowed up in the crowd, a hysterical woman grabbed my arm, handing me her card. 'You must come with me at once. We must go to the jail. You can save the politician! We all know that if Evita finds out you are interested you could save his life,' she whispered frantically.

I took her into an outer hall to calm her down. 'Listen to reason,' I begged. 'If a foreigner acts on his behalf it will surely cost him his life. He will instantly disappear. I am also in the awkward position of being an American in the American Embassy on American soil. You are asking me to involve the Embassy in internal Argentinian matters. I cannot do that,' I whispered back, gently ushering her out. I was numb with concern. Did I do right or wrong about the poor man in jeopardy?

Ambassador Griffis soon approached to ask if I would agree to dine later that night in a nightclub with other diplomats. 'In the noise there, bugging would be useless and we can talk openly. Fleur, they all know you've spent a lot of time with Evita and they want to ask questions because not one of them has ever been received by her.' The upper classes foolishly never accepted her as First Lady and in return she refused to recognize *their* existence.

Though exhausted (it was ten o'clock and dinner would be at midnight), I agreed to the invitation. Amid the noise and music in the nightclub we talked freely about my experiences in and outside Peron's Casa Rosada. I somehow managed to come up with the answers although the only thing on my mind was the unfortunate man in jail.

I was seated next to the British Ambassador, Sir John Balfour, who talked of Britain's sensitive position at that moment and of the insurmountable commercial problems over wheat and beef. My mind wandered. Realizing how upset I was about the Perons, he said quietly: 'If you think the Perons are so terrible, you should examine the history of their predecessors, Manuel and Encarnación de Rosas. Read history and you'll see where the Perons get all their ideas. The de Rosas were the couple who tried everything first. The Perons are poor copies!'

After I absorbed that piece of revealing information, I suddenly turned to him to ask rather wildly: 'Have you got a copy of the famous "White Paper"?'

'Yes, I have. How could you possibly know?'

'Never mind *how*,' I responded. 'I must read it. Will you let me have your copy?'

'Certainly not. I cannot risk it.'

I pointed out the author would probably die in anonymity. 'What a tragedy,' were my last words to the Ambassador.

I left for the United States the next morning, pleased to see the back of the country. However, I had my last taste of 'Peronism' at the airport where a farewell crowd had been organized. Evita had also sent what seemed like hundreds of orchids. I saw a lean figure suddenly appear, a man walking swiftly towards me across the tarmac. It was the British Ambassador. Under his arm was a slim package.

'Here! You have a long trip ahead of you and I've brought you some interesting reading,' he hastily explained as he tucked the package under one arm, nudging me up the stairs. In the air, doors safely locked, I opened the package to find the 'White Paper' inside. In it, a note explaining why he had to bring it to the airport himself. 'My chauffeur is an Argentinian and I couldn't dare send him.'

The document was a short-lived obsession. I wanted to expose the man behind Juan's oily smile, and the woman behind Evita's glittering showmanship. Thanks to the Ambassador, the idea for a book had been put in my lap, placing the Perons against their forgotten counterparts, the two de Rosas.

I had the 'White Paper' copied and sent to every member of the American Congress to try and whet their and the public's interest in Latin American problems, because at that time attention concentrated on the stories of Peron's virility and Evita's jewels.

When Random House announced the forthcoming publication of my book, my life began to be punctuated with threats of death unless I withdrew it. The FBI came to my rescue, gave me protection, and finally located the man involved. He was actually the son of a pro-Peron newspaper publisher, a competitor to my publisher friend, who had been sent to threaten me and stop publication. The culprit was expelled from the USA and I relaxed.

When the book did appear, in the absence of any other literature about the pair I became the ally of the anti-Peronistas. Endless data began to pour into my office. Front page pro-Peron controlled articles in the press (containing the most glaring lies) were cut out daily, translated and coded in red and sent to me after brave men and women secretly swam with them each night across the River Plate to Montevideo. I used to send them regularly to Allen Dulles, then head of the CIA.

The Peronistas must have kept me on a card file because they knew when to make life difficult for me even after I moved to England. On one occasion there was a bad experience with the captain and crew of an Argentine liner which we had chosen to ferry our car as far as Lisbon. Because of my husband's contacts with the Port Authority, we had the pleasure of being escorted aboard in London by the harbour police. They attended to the formalities, handing in both our passports.

Not long after we left port, the ship's Tannoy began announcing: 'Would Fleur Cowles please bring her passport to the purser?' No amount of insisting that the police had handed it in could stop the loudspeaker continuing to demand my passport.

We wrote out a cable to send to Jock Whitney, the American Ambassador in London, giving all details and asking to be met at Lisbon so we could leave ship without a passport. The captain refused to send it until my husband recited the law of the sea to him. I never got that passport back, although a new one was issued to me *en route*. Before we landed in Lisbon, the purser actually admitted to us, smiling broadly, that he was a Peronista. They still have my passport.

Evita had never been received in Argentine society. She was treated as a common intruder and she knew it and threatened revenge. The second-rate actress whose mother, Juana Ibarqurea Dorita, kept a brothel, really did her best. She tried, and succeeded, mercilessly. After she died of cancer, her body was taken from pillar to post but was finally put to rest in the cemetery called La Rocoleta, the special burial ground of the rich oligarchs who hated her as much as she hated them, holding each other in total contempt. If a dead woman could sneer, she would.

Carlos Fuentes described the cemetery as 'a Polemkin Village of afterlife, a Disneyland of death, where all good Argentinian oligarchs are buried and where it seems they believed you *could* take it with you. One wonders how many head of cattle, pails of milk and packs of hide it took to build some of those extravagant funeral monuments . . .'

The Perons were pale copies of the de Rosas. Peron researched their lives during the time he spent in Rome as Argentina's Military Attaché, also gleaning much from Mussolini's tactics. On returning, when Evita captured him as husband, the parallel began. At de Rosas' end, he fled for his life to England. Peron was overthrown by a coup in 1955 and fled to Madrid. Both wives died of cancer, but Evita's meticulously embalmed body journeyed from Buenos Aires to a spare bedroom in Peron's Madrid flat while he was there in exile. After he went back to Buenos Aires he married cabaret singer, Isabel, who then became Argentina's First Lady before the Peronistas were finally ousted a second time. Gossip has it that Peron's body, buried in yet another cemetery, was exhumed and his hands cut off.

Herbert Herring, Executive Director of the Committee on Cultural Relations with Latin America, reviewed my book in the *New York Herald Tribune* on 22 January 1952. His review only led to future trouble with Peronistas.

He wrote: 'Fleur Cowles has hit upon the fantastic parallel between the Argentine dictator Juan Manuel de Rosas and the present incumbent, Juan Domingo Peron, and told a most readable story . . . She has placed in vivid juxtaposition the two first ladies of these strong men. No historian, no matter how he might argue with Mrs Cowles on some details of facts and interpretation, has done a sounder job of explaining the current embarrassment of good Argentinians.'

My own final view is that where Evita lies buried, many are still fond of her, but a new Argentina is now making a remarkable recovery.

X

DIPLOMATIC COUNT

IN THE NEARLY FORTY YEARS that I've lived in Great Britain, I have seen Ambassadors from the United States come and go. Only one in two hundred years of history ever got the plum appointment to the Court of St James's as a *professional* Foreign Service Officer of the State Department. That man was Raymond Seitz. With a great knowledge of European affairs, few have been better prepared, and in a short time he became a most widely known and popular diplomat. He was no stranger to the country; years before, he had served as American Minister and got to know the British countryside and its people before returning to Washington as Under-Secretary of State for Europe. In that position he put together an impressive network of political and social contacts, great assets for Ambassadors.

If asked, my advice to newly-arrived American Ambassadors has always been 'to get out of London to let the rest of the British Isles know who the Ambassador is'. Ambassador Seitz needed no such advice. By the time he retired in the spring of 1994, he had become known in most cities, towns and villages by personal visits, or through television. He was quick off the mark, succinctly discussing America's action whenever it hit the headlines. This he did in a charming and non-aggressive manner, no matter how barbed the question or sensitive the subject.

Each incoming American President always chooses his own Ambassador, so all on post must automatically resign after any election. Some remain, others prepare to go. When Bill Clinton won the election, there arose an amazing opposition in London to the removal of Ambassador Seitz and his remarkable wife, his 'assistant Ambassador'. It became quite a voluble appeal from men and women in all walks of life. An impressive list of admirers even wrote to President Clinton to persuade him not to remove Raymond Seitz.

The message became a chant, and it was taken up by the press. The

Ambassador's close friends, including myself, were worried that the chorus could harm him, even hasten his departure. In spite of the support for Mr Seitz, Admiral William Crowe was suddenly announced by the press as his successor, although Seitz was never officially notified. Ever gallant, he spoke highly of his successor in the speech he gave to the Pilgrim Club at their farewell dinner for him, one of the most memorable valedictory addresses ever heard by members.

In it, he showed his skills, deftly discussing the established relationships between Great Britain and the United States. It was reprinted almost in full the following morning in the London *Times* and other papers, a rare mark of recognition. With his typical simplicity he discussed the causes, present tensions and concerns that face the West after the Cold War, and stressed what it is that keeps the interests of the United States and Britain mutually advantageous.

His address was interrupted with constant applause. There were a few moist eyes as he pointed out the unforgettable talents and charm of his wife, Caroline. His remarks came from the heart, providing a human and personal touch not usually found on such formal occasions.

He ended up explaining one of the reasons why he regretted leaving his post – he would be gone before the fiftieth anniversary commemorations of the Allied landings in Normandy on D-Day in June 1944, an event which had personal overtones. His father, at thirty-six, had commanded an American regiment that went ashore on Omaha Beach on that harrowing morning. He described how his mother and he had later gone back to the little French village in 1960, standing at the top of a shallow hill that ran down to the Channel while watching his father stride alone slowly across the empty beaches.

He had already told this anecdote on *Desert Island Discs*, the famous long-running BBC radio programme. It had been heard by a woman who wrote to say that she was the widow of a Brigadier Sewell with whom his father had been friends. Long before, the seven-year-old Seitz had met the Sewell family when they visited the United States staying at First Army Headquarters on Governor's Island in New York. When they bid the Seitz family goodbye, a young Sewell son gave the young Raymond Seitz a silver dollar coin as a souvenir of their friendship.

Following his *Desert Island Discs* broadcast, Seitz also received a letter from Major-General Toyne-Sewell himself, then Commandant of the Royal Military Academy at Sandhurst, informing him that he was that English boy who had given him the coin. Pausing, Seitz held the shining coin up to the light and announced, '*And here it is.*' The audience's response was a loud sigh of pleasure.

He ended the speech thus: 'I see many reflections in this coin, some bright, some dim, some happy, some sad. I see history and I see hope. I see youth and age and the timeless rhythm of generations. And I see chapter after chapter of friendship between two great peoples who continue to write their own fine Book of Nations.'

With that, he paused, looked out at the audience and quietly said, 'Goodnight and goodbye.'

He will be missed as Ambassador despite the quality of his successor, but he does at least remain in London as Senior Managing Director of Lehman Brothers.

He was replaced by a tough, strategically sound sea-warrior, Admiral William J. Crowe, the man who was regularly turned to by President Clinton when he needed help to solve an intransigent security problem. He finally chose him personally to go to the Court of St James's.

The genial new Ambassador had a difficult mission; he arrived at a time when the popularity of the USA in Great Britain had suffered a blow. The 'special relationship' was strained by the welcome given in America to the President of Sinn Fein, Gerry Adams, which appalled most of the British population and enraged the British government. Nor had it been very pleasing to see Britain's Prime Minister so coolly received on his visit to Washington. The Reagan-Bush love affair with Margaret Thatcher had been too well publicized for coolness to go unnoticed, and the diplomatic flak was costly to relations.

Could the new, sixty-nine-year-old Ambassador do as well as Ambassador Seitz? And why had Seitz received such cavalier treatment despite his unique record, prompting him to resign from the State Department? People continue to ask.

My resentment evaporated when I got to know the jovial, intellectual new Ambassador. To his credit, though never a career diplomat, the Admiral is a man who hasn't paid a penny for the post. In fact, he may be one of the first ever to have turned down offers from President

Clinton to serve as Ambassador to three different countries. He obviously saw the value of the appointment in Britain, a country he admires. He is the first naval officer to hold the position of Ambassador to London.

After a distinguished career with the US Navy, he was appointed by President Reagan as the eleventh Chairman of the Joint Chiefs of Staff, Department of Defence. He served as a counsellor to Washington's Center for Strategic and International Studies, and then became professor of geopolitics at the University of Oklahoma. He has written two books on military and foreign policy and co-authored two others. He can even be fun!

Though important Ambassadorial posts seem mainly to go to those with financial backing, another Foreign Service professional, like Raymond Seitz, broke the mould after years spent in other significant positions in the State Department. Reginald Bartholomew's first Ambassadorial post was in the Lebanon, a dangerous appointment, during the civil wars there.

He saw his Embassy in Beirut blown up while he was inside. The bomb had been delivered into the guarded compound in a truck driven by a suicide driver who smashed his way in. The Ambassador's facial scar is the only noticeable evidence of a terrible event which he handled with such courage.

Another of Bartholomew's delicate posts had been in Athens. There were other tough assignments; for example, the heavy security required during his Spanish posting wasn't easy. He and his wife, Rose Anne, often visited us in Spain during this time so we know how well he dealt with the sensitive problem of removing US Army and Air Force bases after Spain insisted that they must go.

That it was accomplished with amity, not anger, was exemplified later during the Gulf War when the Spanish government gave priority in landing rights to American Air Force planes *en route* to the fighting zones. Madrid's busy airport was cleared of civilian flights whenever necessary to give space to US war planes. Reginald Bartholomew's diplomatic skills must be given the credit for the speed and ease with which this was arranged.

Eventually these activities and those in the past in areas of defence at the State Department and the National Security Council made Bartholomew a natural appointment as US Ambassador to NATO. This posting immediately gave us a reason to visit the Bartholomews in Brussels, a city we know well.

We had an unforgettable weekend at their Residence, and enjoyed a trip to Bruges, guided by the knowledge of the popular Belgian Ambassador to Britain, Jean-Paul Van Bellingher.

The Bartholomews were soon to make yet another move, leaving the beautiful residence they had so recently occupied for him to take up a newly-created post in the former Yugoslavia. More anger, just for a change! His job was to liaise between Russia and the warring Serbs, Croats and Bosnians to counteract Russia's influence in that devastated region. We were once in Washington after he landed from the Balkans. He gave us an unforgettable insight into civil war, one that only personal experience could reveal. In such circumstances, service for one's country has to be total.

The Bartholomew musical chair came to a stop in late 1993 when he was made Ambassador in Rome, a post he deserves. One of their first jobs was to welcome President and Mrs Clinton to the beautiful Embassy. We later stayed in the same Presidential suite in early 1995, and learned more about Rome's great history than any ordinary visit could have given us. I had been in the Villa Taverna was as a guest of Clare Boothe Luce, whose Ambassadorship ended with her account of arsenic falling from her bedroom ceiling, dubbed by the world press as 'Arsenic and old Luce'.* It has been fabulously restored.

The courtly, civilized Virginian, David E. K. Bruce, remains the most urbane holder of the rank of Ambassador to Great Britain. We got to know each other in Paris in the late forties, when he was on post there to help overlook the reconstruction of Europe. His wife, Evangeline Bruce, wrote an essay on the city which appeared in a special edition on Paris in my magazine *Flair*. He had also served in Bonn and after London he became the United States first liaison officer to Peking before formalized relations with China began.

China's cultural impact on Evangeline Bruce was obvious in the

* See 'Woman Achievers', p. 27.

house in Brussels which became theirs during the NATO position that followed. Her flair turned an ordinary suburban villa into a magical place, something she does wherever she lives. The flower-laden Winfield House in London's Regent's Park gave full scope to her talent as a hostess and diplomatic spouse.

She recently published her first book, *Napoleon and Josephine: The Improbable Marriage*.* Her editor, Ion Trewin, called it 'a successful balance of political and military affairs, personalities and relationships'. Tragically, she died soon after, following a brain tumour in December 1995, but she lived to see the success of her book.

David Bruce brought his charm, humour and skills on visits to us in Spain, which he loved. We never gave up teasing him, however, about a luncheon he attended in London which we were giving for a certain French gentleman. After he returned to the Embassy, he telephoned me to ask: 'Who was your guest of honour, he looked terribly familiar?' Such beguiling honesty!

'Oh, that famous face belonged to a man called Maurice Chevalier,' I replied with a smile on my face.

He had set high Ambassadorial standards and London was sad to lose him. He died soon after in his home in Washington, honoured by all who knew him.

David Bruce was European head of OSS (Office of Strategic Services) during World War II. 'Wild Bill' Donovan was the overall head of the organization, the precursor to the CIA which was established later. An anecdote involving the two men is one to share: it was told to us on a hilarious occasion in Spain during Bruce's visit. Both men had found themselves together in London. Both champed at the bit after D-Day. The call was too great and after D-plus-4 they both embarked for France.

Things were still fairly chaotic on the other side, but they got ashore and moved ahead. They hadn't gotten very far when they found themselves pinned down by machine gun fire.

Donovan said to Bruce: 'You know much too much to fall into enemy hands. I hope you've got your suicide pills with you.'

Bruce felt all his pockets and replied: 'No, I haven't, Bill.'

Donovan then said: 'It's a good thing I brought mine,' and pro-

* Published in the USA by Macmillan, in the UK by Weidenfeld and Nicolson, 1995.

ceeded to search his own pockets. 'David, I haven't got mine either! I left them behind at Claridge's. If anything happens to me, will you tell Brooks, the Head Porter, that my two suicide pills are just behind the tooth mug in my bathroom?'

Although we became close friends after Sir Antony Acland became Britain's Ambassador to the United States, I originally knew him at the time he was on post in Spain when I began to restore and rebuild our castle there. Later in London, he returned to direct the Foreign Office.

Not long after, he was appointed to Washington. Raymond Seitz, then the American Minister, gave him a farewell dinner with a typically amusing and imaginative guest list: only Americans were invited, without spouses. The twenty-odd guests included bankers, brokers, businessmen, writers, a Catholic priest from Oxford, a publisher and myself.

We were there for a purpose. After the last course at dinner, Seitz announced he would ask all of us for our advice to the departing diplomat. One by one, starting at his left and ending with me at his right (Ambassador Acland was on my right), we were expected to produce a pearl or two.

Sir Antony went home with a few sore ribs from my elbow during certain suggestions. Advice dealt with the American stock market, press, geography, religion and banking. Since few diplomats worth their salt go off to Washington (the *numero uno* of Ambassadorial assignments) without exhaustive advance briefing, it was an interesting exercise.

The elegant Acland was then newly widowed, having sadly lost his wife just before being asked to tackle the heady climate of Washington. He would arrive as that rare creature, a man alone. I knew Washington well enough to foresee how women would welcome such a distinguished single male.

I decided on humour that night, especially as I was the last of the advice-givers, so I turned to Sir Antony with: 'My advice will be short, sweet and to the point: *take a suit of armour!*'

I had given the right advice. Antony Acland was quickly lionized by Washington's hostesses, but the picture soon changed when he had the good sense to remarry. The new Lady Acland had already been the friend of his late wife and the Acland family. Both Aclands became a great credit to Britain. Today, they are at Eton where Sir Antony is presently its Provost, yet another perfect appointment.

At the Embassy in Washington, the tall, spare man used to look out from the upper floors at America's capital city with pride in the success he and his wife achieved. They had an important position during the Reagan-Bush-Thatcher regimes. I stayed many times while they were there. The diplomatic atmosphere was delicate because of trading differences: would Britain put Europe ahead of the USA in view of EEC obligations? Acland's patent fondness for Americans was useful in keeping alive the 'special relationship' at a tricky time.

They lived elegantly. The Washington Embassy has a ballroom, a vast dining room and several floors of rooms worthy of its visitors, including the Royal Family. It was home away from home to me while the Aclands were there. A warmer, more beautiful port-of-call would be hard to find. I had originally been introduced to its comforts as a house guest during the time that Prime Minister James Callaghan's son-in-law, Peter Jay, was British Ambassador. His wife, Margaret Jay, is now Baroness Jay and Peter is economic correspondent for the BBC News. They have both remarried.

Sir Nicholas Henderson came out of retirement to become Ambassador to Washington again after previously serving in Warsaw, Bonn, and lastly Paris. Few are recalled to such a final assignment. The only other person in my time was Lord Trevelyan, who though retired after serving in Moscow and Bonn, was sent to troubled Aden. After Edward Heath had predictably and tersely declined Margaret Thatcher's offer to send him as Ambassador to Washington, Sir Nicholas was beckoned back to take up the post at the very moment the Falklands crisis began.

He had started his career when one quarter of the world comprised the British Empire, but Britain's prestige had fallen low enough since then for Argentina's military government to think it would strike a blow with impunity. I was pleased, as an American, to hear television reports from Washington in which he acknowledged America's significant aid to Britain during this crisis.

His brilliant wife, Mary Barker, had been in Greece in 1944 for

Time magazine. She personified the romantic image of the brave woman reporter during the bloody civil war in her book about it. She redecorated the Washington Embassy by giving it a 'Laura Ashley' look.

A very different sort of American Ambassador was Walter Annenberg, a non-professional who came to London after David Bruce.

Ambassador Annenberg survived a period of painful criticism before striking a more successful note, leaving London with a profile very different from the one that accompanied his arrival. The British public have a way of taking the side of the underdog; tired of criticism of Annenberg, they came to his rescue. He and Lee, his wife, left England in a glow of popularity.

Soon after his arrival, the use of one word produced press criticism. The occasion was his televised official presentation to the Queen. The Queen asked if they had yet moved into the Embassy. He replied: 'We *are* in the Embassy Residence, subject of course to some of the discomfiture as a result of the need for elements of refurbishment and rehabilitation.' Somehow, that one sentence and the use of the word 'refurbishment' to describe the situation produced a reaction of derision. It must be said that the word eventually found its way into daily, common usage. It can now be regularly heard without one's brain registering 'Walter Annenberg'.

The Embassy they were 'refurbishing' was originally given to the American nation by Barbara Hutton when she was married to Cary Grant. Before the Annenbergs, it had been kept flower-laden and elegant by Evangeline Bruce. The wealthy Annenbergs spent a fortune on redoing it, donating many of the fine objects and some of the furniture to the residence when they left. Going to parties there, I was always interested to see what kind of cornucopia of blooms was on display. The flowers were often flown over from their California residence.

On one such occasion the luncheon was in honour of the aged mother of the murdered John and Robert Kennedy, a visit to remember. Whether or not Rose Kennedy did actually once say that Embassies were perfect places for verbal *faux pas*, she certainly chose this Embassy luncheon to make one of her own.

She was seated next to a prominent English peer, who found talking to the tactiturn Rose somewhat difficult. Edward Kennedy, her third son, had just made news by removing himself as a candidate for the Presidency of the United States, his reputation still tarnished after the dreadful Chappaquiddick tragedy. Lost for other subjects, her luncheon companion asked Mrs Kennedy if she wasn't happy he had withdrawn from the race.

'Why should I be?' she responded sharply. 'Anyway, it isn't permanent. He'll run later. And why *should* I be happy?'

'Well, you have already lost two sons,' he whispered in surprise.

'If my sons are born to be murdered, they might as well be President first,' she angrily pointed out, and got up to leave. Coffee had been announced. Turning to the table, she retorted: 'I am an old lady. I must go now.'

The Annenbergs' wealth had come from his numerous communication companies, two Philadelphia newspapers, a television guide and two New York newspapers, a racing guide, a magazine and a chain of television stations, making the family extremely rich.

Their home in Palm Desert in California is a museum with spectacular grounds, regularly visited by President Reagan and all the California mafia, the Justin Darts, the Charles Prices and Homer Tuttles, to name a few. There is always a certain welcome for their British friends.

Another diplomat, Edward Streator, was Minister and Deputy Chief of Mission when Annenberg was Ambassador, and between 1977 and 1984 he served several Ambassadors. We got to know him and we have become close, as did most members of the main British political parties, because he so quickly made friends everywhere.

America's reputation was high in his time. Those who knew him expected him finally to be named an Ambassador in London, but because of the vagaries of the State Department, that never took place. He was, instead, named Ambassador to the OECD (Organization for Economic Cooperation and Development) in Paris. After that, his promised next post was to be Ambassador to NATO; this he relished as he had been Deputy to David Bruce when he was Ambassador from 1969 to 1975, and he knew and loved Belgium. He was packed and ready to leave within a few days, when his plum post simply slipped away at the very last moment. Reagan inexplicably gave it to another man to fulfil an obligation.

Streator's life has nevertheless been a parade of fascinating appointments, from technological projects to the theatre; President of American Chamber of Commerce, consultant to banks and also involved in strategic studies with communication companies, with Think-Tanks and Anglo-American institutions. Yet he never appears too busy to be interested in the art of friendship, a talent he shares with Priscilla, his wife. The Streators and ourselves take trips together; one which was especially memorable was a cruise on the Rhine. We docked every night to enjoy the pleasures on both French and German sides of the river, particularly the night spent with my friends, Prince and Princess Metternich at their Johannesberg estate. On another night in Strasbourg we drove an hour away to Colmar to revisit a monastery and see *The Life of Christ*, the huge many-panelled masterpiece painted by Grünewald. This was our second visit to see the work, which took sixteen years to finish. It is, for us, one of the most remarkable paintings in the world.

Jacques Beaumarchais, France's Ambassador in London, had a successful posting until he was suddenly, almost brutally, removed. President Giscard d'Estaing of France apparently needed to place someone quickly in a top job and impulsively chose to give the London Embassy to a cabinet minister he wished to remove. Beaumarchais had just returned from Paris after calling on his President, where he had been firmly assured he was secure in the post which he loved. To be replaced immediately was a blow that certainly contributed to his death soon after.

Our friendship blossomed with his widow Marie-Alice after his death. On our way to Spain we still like to drive to her home in a village in the French foothills of the Pyrenees near St Jean de Luz, where we lunch together.

She always leads us from her ancient hillside chalet to a tiny mountain pass so we can drive through a sleepy one-man border post instead of waiting in the crowded tourist jam at the regular crossing point. This was the route her husband had to take to escape the Nazis. We imagine his courage and his hardships as we pass through the difficult, dangerous terrain.

The Brazilian Embassy in London has been home twice to my adopted relatives, the family of Osvaldo Aranha*, Zazi and Sergio Correa da Costa. It was a luxury to have them so near for many years of a long posting. Their son-in-law, Rubens Barboza, who married their daughter Maria Ignez, carried out the family tradition of service by coming to London as Ambassador some years after the da Costas.

It was not the first time other generations of the same family followed each other. Zazi da Costa's father, Osvaldo Aranha, had gone as Ambassador to Washington in Franklin D. Roosevelt's time. Some years later the da Costas were posted there after leaving the United Nations. Whichever and wherever, all Aranha relatives leave their mark on the arts, politics and society while on post, as the Barbozas continue to do today with great political skill and imagination and popularity.

One of the several other Brazilian Ambassadors in London was the cultivated Mario Gibson Barboza, who soon became a favourite. It was another bad day when he was retired. However, a promise was made by the Ambassador: he has kept me regularly informed in letters which tell me in detail what is going on politically, economically and otherwise in Brazil. I like to know what happens in a country that has honoured me in so many ways. He remains an affectionate collaborator.

Spanish diplomats, the Marquis and Marquesa de Santa Cruz enriched lives in England – and especially ours. They actually stretched the normal stay for diplomats into fourteen years in their Embassy in London, leaving a permanent impact.

The Marquesa gave one of her family palaces in our own village of Trujillo in Spain to be used as a convent, keeping a corner area for a weekend flat which she usually uses when we are there. A special

* See Aranha, page 91.

pleasure is the use of her well-placed corner balcony on Easter Sundays, to watch thousands in national dress dance in the Plaza Mayor below.

The Marquesa is still in touch with British politics, knowing most people involved. her affection is genuine and priceless; it is her opinion that friendship should be treated like a religion. This she does – and I have inherited that luxury, repaying it in kind. By the way, she is still a Manchester United supporter!

After the Santa Cruzes left, their successors have continued as friends. The closest were Jose Joaquim Puig de la Bellacasa and his wife, Paz. After a short stay in the royal palace in Madrid (following his London post) as the King of Spain's private assistant, Ambassador de la Bellacasa returned to diplomacy as Ambassador to Portugal. After he had brought the King and Queen of Spain to London for the first time and then the Queen of England to Spain, iciness between Spain and Britain melted. His magical touch deserves the post in Washington. I had once impulsively suggested a name for an Ambassador to Washington to Getulio Vargas, Brazil's President, while talking to him and Oswaldo Aranha, then Minister of Finance, about the financial practices of the American businesses who started up there after the last war. Turning to the Washington scene, President Vargas mentioned that the Brazilian Ambassador, Dean of Ambassadors there, would soon be retiring. As a possible successor, I impulsively named the man who was appointed. How I wish I could do the same for Bellacasa for Washington. His talent deserves it.

XI

GALLANTS
(MALE AND FEMALE)

GALLANTRY TAKES MANY FORMS and takes no account of gender. Both women and men have offered me examples; some are gallant by nature, others have astonished me by stepping out of conventional boots to reveal it. Courage can often be involved, and affection is more or less obligatory – no matter in what degree. All have enhanced my life (as have others not mentioned here).

In Portugal, the remarkable and very gallant Dr Antonio Judice Bustorff Silva was an unusual memory-maker. At more than eighty years old this Hogarthian figure, now dead, was Portugal's premier banker and philanthropic business magnate, a friend we often visited in his museum-like Lisbon home. Possessions crowded every available space – he collected everything. A Holbein sat casually on an easel by his bed, defining the measure of his wealth and artistic taste. When his interest in painting and sculpture had been sated, he chose to collect Roman jewels, his last enthusiasm before Portugal's Civil War entirely changed his life.

During the Second World War, he made it an obligation as a banker to safeguard the property of French nationals, even the property of the French government, refusing payment for his services. President de Gaulle invited him to France in order to thank him personally. There the tall French authoritarian and the equally tall banker walked slowly around the beautiful Versailles gardens discussing the matter.

De Gaulle stopped suddenly, and turned to him to ask: 'What can the French possibly do for you in return for your gallant, enormous help? Choose anything you like. France will gladly give it to you!'

Dr Bustorff looked around as they stood at the edge of a lovely lily-pond, filled with gleaming fish. Turning back to de Gaulle, he smiled and replied: 'I'd like one Chinese carp from this pond to be sent to Portugal.'

The General sent two, adding one to the 'price' after all other offers

303

of payment were refused. The last time my husband and I were in Portugal visiting Dr Bustorff, we saw the fish, larger and fatter, swimming in his own lily-pond in Setubal. He walked around with us, holding the hand of his pet chimpanzee, who always accompanied him when he strolled through the garden he loved.

We were already living in our Trujillo home in Spain at holiday times, close to Portugal's borders, when in spring 1974 a left-wing military coup disrupted life in Portugal. We decided to drive into the mountains to find one of my husband's associates who disappeared after his extensive business, substantial home and land were confiscated by the Communist-inspired Armed Force movement. We finally found him, living in a small hut like a peasant, having been accepted back by the Communists after 'becoming poor'. He had managed to get his wife and children to safety over unguarded mountains into Spain and then returned alone to see by what means his possessions might be salvaged. Everywhere, hammer and sickle signs were posted on the roads we drove through. Our friend refused to leave but his possessions were eventually returned when the Communists were defeated in 1976. British licence plates had given us temporary safety as we drove our powerful car through the unfriendly atmosphere but we were very glad indeed to get across the border back to Spain.

Very soon after, I was sadly brought back to the coup when I answered a telephone call from Dr Bustorff Silva calling me from Portugal. 'Fleur,' the deaf man shouted, 'you must come and save me!'

'Of course! Of course, I'll come – but *where* are you?' I demanded, in great distress.

'I'm right here, *in the middle of the road*!' he yelled back.

'What road? Where? In Setubal or Lisbon or Cascais – or where? *Where?*' I shouted back to the old man.

'It doesn't matter where,' he replied. 'Just come anywhere.'

'*Of course* I will come,' I replied, dismayed. He had already hung up.

No one allowed me to try to find him though I wouldn't necessarily have been in very much danger, although bullets were flying about in every direction in any of the areas where he might be found. With depressing difficulty I finally got in touch with a friend in Lisbon who agreed to look for the temporarily unbalanced man. Soon after, he fled to Brazil, aged and very sad. He was eventually able to return home after the Communists lost the elections in 1976. The persecution had ended but the great, good man died soon after.

In 1956 he had introduced us to one of his contributions to the preservation of Portugal's heritage, the Hotel Seteais Palace in Cascais, which had once been a summer palace. When Prime Minister Antonio Salazar ordered him to take over Portugal's monuments, he turned the residence into a hotel, leaving much of its original decor, painted walls, garden and maze intact. We visited the hotel every summer, leaving every morning with the well-filled picnic hamper the manager always arranged for us. We sought one of the lovely beaches on the Atlantic coast to spend the day in the sun, keeping cool in the cold water. I painted and my husband read.

We stayed there for many summers but gave up the idyllic place for a special invitation from our Greek friend, John Carras, to borrow his three-masted schooner for a holiday cruise in the Greek and Turkish waters of the Mediterranean. We jumped at the chance to live on this splendid boat, with more than a hundred feet of sail and a twenty-two man crew and, more importantly, to enjoy barefooted life on a sleek vessel (not a Renoir in sight), eating food caught daily from the sea.

I wrote to the affable manager of the Seteais Palace in Portugal to say how sorry we were that we couldn't make our expected visit that year, and why. I framed his reply and hung it on my office wall. The four-word message reads: 'Dear Madame, We have been robbed'. Soon we became wedded to Spanish life in the castle I have since restored in Trujillo and so we never went back. But we send every friend to the Seteais Palace in our place.

Another special gentleman I have known from Portugal is Duarte Pinto-Coelho. He, like me, was constantly drawn to Paris in the early fifties, when we met in Elsa Schiaparelli's garden; her great house and garden on the Rue de Berri was a mecca for artists, writers and all manner of interesting people. Her chaotic and dramatic decor is as unforgettable as she was herself. Not an inch was free from her surrealist accumulation, her eclectic discoveries of paintings, furniture, fabrics and rugs. Periods didn't count, neither did colour, nor, perhaps, price. The resulting crowded ambience had the same quirky flair we associate with her Schiaparelli Couture Collection.

It certainly appealed to me and to the young but already established Duarte Pinto-Coelho who has since become one of Europe's busiest and most respected interior decorators. Though born in Portugal, he now lives in Spain where he has two palatial homes. One is in old Madrid, a district which in many ways is the city's architectural jewel; the other is next to ours in the Extramadura, in Trujillo. There, twenty years after we met in Paris, fate drew us together again. I like the fact that he gathers around him people who count and others who may not but are still good value. I like the concerts by talented musicians that this ardent music-lover gives in his twin-pianoed drawing room. We regularly share meals and guests as we are generally in Trujillo together.

Having decorated both palaces of the former President of Malawi and helped to start an industry there, he was rewarded by being made their Consul in Madrid. He is a good neighbour and a great friend.

Sir Peter Scott was a conservationist beyond compare. He founded and supported so many causes, and saved the lives of too many creatures to list. Sadly, he died in 1989. He championed conservation of wildlife and co-founded with Prince Bernhard the World Wildlife Fund in Geneva. The Prince was its first President at a time when neither fashion, fad or money abounded for the cause. Scott designed its Panda logo.

He also opened his own Wildfowl Wetlands Trust at Slimbridge in Gloucestershire, which every year draws thousands of tourists to see the hundreds of species he loved and protected. He pioneered natural history on television, using the medium to reveal both the plight and pleasures of wildlife, and his paintings and sketches of wild birds are widely respected. His death saddened all his international admirers.

Of the over fifty exhibitions, world-wide, of my own paintings, none was more lavishly launched than that by my friend David Tang at a dinner in my honour at his China Club in Hong Kong in November 1995. For sheer drama, beauty, opulence and *success*, other exhibitions tend to pall in insignificance. Another has just opened in Beijing.

Twenty-eight paintings were chosen and bought by the evening's end; the rest went next morning to Alice King's Alisan Gallery, tended further by her remarkable staff who had hung them so well in the

Club. But it was David Tang's reputation as an event-maker and a giver which gave so much panache to the start of my exhibition. People, in New York and London I'm told, talked of the coming event in ripples of far-flung publicity.

His talent as an auctioneer was the next surprise. I had given my two best paintings to be auctioned off for two charities, the Society for the Promotion of Hospice Care and the Hong Kong Marrow Match Foundation. Much advance work by Alice King and the committee women helped create the interest in my work, for which I am grateful. Alice King and I each added 10% of the sales to their organizations. Tang's skill was such that he practically winkled money out of rich hands: the result was an incredible HK$2,200,000 for those two paintings and an additional HK$1,700,000 for the charities by famous Hong Kong bidders!

David Tang is a symbol of Hong Kong's economic excellence. Of an old family, and though still young, he is now chairman or director of twelve important companies which include television, bus, oil, banking and development corporations. He has a smart London address, so activities afoot in England may be involved – especially in the newly opened department store of Tang-designed fashions and accessories which may eventually go global.

How can I try to thank him for his generosity to me? When I tried, he replied in writing: 'My sponsorship is cockroach compared to your friendship!'

A very different kind of personal impact was made by the beautiful white-haired Madame Banac, mother of the former United Kingdom Consul for Morocco, our friend, Vane Ivanovic. She was often called the uncrowned Queen of Monaco before Princess Grace's arrival.

Madame Banac had a mind of her own, proving it in her own way by marrying *both* of Yugoslavia's great shipowners, who were famous rivals. Her advice to her grandchildren, particularly her favourite, Tessa Kennedy, whom I love and treat as if she were my daughter, was to develop a strong and independent mind.

Madame Banac had a distinguished style of clothes. It was a 'look' Balenciaga had designed for her, a simple shirtwaist which fell to the floor, a superb sweep of luxurious silk in pale Jordan-almond colours which she punctuated with her famous Banac jewels. The look was elegant and very *personal*. I learned the lesson: ignore fashion, dress to suit yourself.

I have taken her advice and developed a style of my own, ably assisted by the brilliant designer, Philippe Lempriere. Hardly a uniform, it has no slavish connection with what's in fashion. I have the luxury of being his one and only couturier client. We enjoy mutual creativity and the resulting family friendship. He and his wife Mina, and daughter, are as important as his highly original designing – they are like family. I am interested in all their lives. One daughter is called Fleur after me.

When it comes to the world of *haute couture* I think of Coco Chanel. I can still see her as she used to sit, in particular above us on the stairs leading up from the atelier to her private flat. Suited, hatted and silent, she kept her eyes riveted on the audience, especially the press, as models slowly strode by to present each new creation.

After her death, her home 'above the shop' became a shrine, almost intact. Not long ago, my husband and I were invited, while viewing a collection there, by the amazing creator who took over her design realm, Karl Lagerfeld, to go upstairs to see her apartment again. When lunching with her there, which always meant eating *well*, I had always enjoyed her extraordinarily eclectic surroundings, and this time, I found the same untouched beauty. Her inimitable sense of decor still had the magic touch. As we reached the top of the stairs, the very first thing I noticed was the portrait of a lion's head I had painted. It was still in its antique gold leaf frame, sitting as it always sat on a table in the drawing room. Coco loved lions as much as I do, but with more reason. She was a Leo.

To dress 'à la Chanel' is still how many women want to look. Whatever she did, women followed; they cropped their skirts, then their hair, and became as suntanned as she did (she was the first to use the tanned look as a fashion accessory). She also wore costume jewellery as if it were royal jewellery. Her No. 5 Chanel scent remains a classic, possibly the world's bestselling perfume.

She opened her first shop in Paris over half a century ago. Her story, told in a number of books, and in a recent television documentary, is exhilarating. She snobbishly refused to marry one of her lovers, one of England's premier dukes, but was less discriminating when she formed a liaison with a German general in wartime Paris. She was ostracized for a long time for this after the Liberation. Chanel's fashion magic still shows through Lagerfeld's genius.

Another gallant, an American in Paris (in the film industry), Edward Pope, married the Turkish Princess Niloufer and they lived happily ever after – except for the last years of grim illness before she died. He returned to America, where he lived with his new wife, Evelyn, in the midst of Virginia's rolling hills and horse country before he died in 1995. Having become involved in pharmacy-related activities. He was preparing to show the late Princess's saris and jewels at the Fashion Institute of Technology in New York City before he died suddenly of cancer. The display in June 1997 in New York will complement exhibits in the Louvre and others in Paris, as well as the Nizam Museum and the Niloufer Hospital she built in India.

Women in all walks of life touched mine. Andrée Lartigou, my former personal maid, did so by making my busy, complicated American life possible. Later she came to London to live with me when I moved there after my re-marriage.

I had found this remarkable woman by accident, the result of an impulsive remark to the proprietor of the restaurant where I frequently dined. We shook hands as I left: 'How are things, Madame?' he asked. Without thinking, I blurted out: 'Just fine, but I do need a personal maid.'

'Good!' he replied. 'I have a great friend who is the perfect person for you, my former mistress. She's looking for an interesting job. She's a great lady.'

I liked her so much I hired her instantly; she was soon friend and confidante as well as a matchless maid. In emergencies, she was a jack of all trades, and secretly a fine French cook. She was a great strength when divorce loomed up. It had been painful, despite the care we both took in not letting anyone know in advance. (We acted in such a civilized manner two newspapers describing it as unique behaviour for a famous pair.) There had been provocations for divorce and I regretted the failures, but nothing whatsoever could persuade me to turn back after discovering Mike Cowles had a mistress. Andrée gave the divorce a wry French touch when one morning she saw me having a private weep. 'What *are* you crying about?'

'I'm sorry to tell you that I am getting a divorce. *I hate change*,' I replied.

'So why do you weep?' she asked. 'Now you can have all the onions you want!' Onions, a favourite of mine, were not popular with Mike Cowles. Roars of laughter put paid to any sadness over the divorce.

After a year or two with us in London, Andrée finally retired to a family farm in France. Before she died, we always paid her a visit when driving in southern Europe. She was unforgettably gallant.

A quite simple comment can often linger in the memory. Lord Widgery, then Lord Chief Justice of England, made such a memorable remark when we were present at the annual induction of new members of the bar, a ceremony which takes place once a year at Westminster Abbey. We waited with Lady Widgery for his arrival, standing just outside the entrance to the Abbey so we could observe everyone in the procession as it approached.

The most important person was the last in the parade. It began with Justices of the Peace and progressed up the ladder into the High Court. All wore wigs, and the robes appropriate to their station, some of black cotton, others of black silk; some added purple and scarlet ribbons to identify their rank, a wonderful sight seen nowhere else in the world.

Finally, Lord Widgery greeted us in the doorway and we readied ourselves to follow behind him to our seats. Just as we were going through the door, my husband announced to him: 'I've just had a startling thought. No court is sitting today. No justice of any kind is being meted out!'

'And no injustice either,' was the Lord Chief Justice's instant response.

What better clue to a lawyer's sense of purpose.

*   *   *

When it comes to erudition, Isaiah Berlin's reputation as the 'big brain of Britain' precedes him and has done so for thirty-odd years, especially after our first encounter.

The BBC had asked me to appear on a radio broadcast to America. With a new husband, a new life and a new land, it was exciting to be asked to go 'live' to my own country. I hadn't enquired what the broadcast would be about, and I was thrown when I realized the programme was like a Brains Trust, a discussion on matters of the day. When I saw who my companions were to be, my heart sank: there sat Bernard Levin, Diana Trilling and Isaiah Berlin.

I was placed next to Isaiah Berlin, of whose substantial reputation I was so well aware. To debate with Bernard Levin seemed daunting enough, and Diana Trilling's fame as an intellectual was also formidable. For an American newcomer to match words with such a group was an awesome challenge.

However, just before going on the air, I blurted out to Isaiah Berlin: 'If I'd known *you'd* be here, I'd never have come!'

To which he replied, with a broad grin: 'Oh, I knew *you* were coming – and I *almost* didn't come either!'

When has a man been more gallant or given more comfort to an uncertain companion? His warm remark saved my nerves. He and Bernard Levin eventually became great friends.

A number of admired and respected women achievers have given steadfast support to the Fleur Cowles Award for Excellence which I donated to London's Royal College of Art for many years. The jury needed to be both prestigious and knowledgeable. Elizabeth Esteve-Coll, at the time Director of the Victoria and Albert Museum, Jean Muir, Britain's internationally acclaimed couturier, Beatrix Miller, one of the best of all British magazine editors and Elizabeth Gage, who brought about a renaissance in British jewellery design, were four women who came to my rescue and joined the award jury. Each woman has become a genuine friend. Lord Snowdon also was in the original group.

For almost forty years I had been an *aficionado* of the college, eventually becoming an Honorary Fellow. My interest began when I first came to live in London. I regularly visited the college, lunching with the Rector and walking round the classes and the departments –

painting, computers, engineering design, architecture and fashion – seeking budding new talent to encourage and support financially. My Award has provided the best overall graduate each year with a sum averaging about £9000, a considerable help in furthering the careers of a number of brilliant young graduates.

Beatrix Miller, when editor of *Queen* magazine, published as a book feature inside an issue my *The Hidden World of the Hadhramaut*. Later at *Vogue* she kept an editor's eye on all of my many activities as a writer, painter and designer.

Jean Muir's sudden death from cancer in 1995 shocked and saddened everyone. Her couturier skills ranked her with the best in the world. Her hallmark was designing elegant, classic clothes which paid no attention to the fads of the day, or indeed of the past. She designed how she thought *today*'s woman of taste wants to look, ignoring fantasies and historic revivals. She had been an 'engineer in fabric', her own description. My husband and I and she and her wonderful husband enjoyed untold pleasures together on holidays at their Scottish border home or in all our homes.

Elizabeth Gage has made me beautiful jewels and has given me much good advice at the Royal College of Art, because we share similar views on art, decor and politics. Her jewellery is easily recognizable (and so are the copies!). Both her homes reflect her art and mind.

Two very, very different women lit up the New York scene while I lived there; one was writer Anita Loos; the other, who happily is still alive, aged over ninety, is Eleanor Lambert.

Anita Loos gave blondes the world over a historic definition of their status when her book *Gentlemen Prefer Blondes* was published and became a bestseller; when the archetypal blonde, unforgettable Marilyn Monroe, made such a hit in the film, the hairdressing industry positively glowed.

I am in debt to Anita Loos for a serious literary idea. In 1950 she made it easy for me to begin to write my first book (about Juan and Evita Peron). After personal experiences in Argentina, I had the substance of a worthwhile biography; but how could I, an editor, jump from being a critical judge of others' writing to produce a publishable manuscript of my own? It was a daunting leap.

I asked her to lunch. She rolled about with laughter when I confessed that I wanted to know how to write a book. 'Why not? Why not?' she replied. 'It's terribly simple. All you need to do is have a lined yellow pad. Choose your favourite pen. Write your first sentence. The book will rush after you!' The yellow pad is now an imperative ally in my writing life. The Perons became the subject of a bestseller, widely praised and published in several languages.

Eleanor Lambert, high priestess of fashion publicity, was affectionately and glamorously fêted by New York City when she reached her nine-tieth birthday in 1993. Her hundreds of celebrated friends came from all strata of the fashion world, the press and politics, from *everywhere* in fact. Her age is of no consequence: she doesn't look it or even begin to act it. Although she has a New York office and staff, I some-times think her real office must be a seat on a plane jetting from country to country. If a boast can be made I would like to make it: *she is the fashion industry.* She brought it to prominence in the 1930s. Most big names in the industry owe their fame to her, and charities benefit from her ideas and support.

I've been her friend since the late 1940s, when her husband and mine were both publishing chiefs (he was head of Universal and International News Services and later the *New York Journal*). I know that if I ever, ever needed her, this unique woman would want to be there.

A real life-enhancer appeared when I first met Toni Tomita, who looked after me for years while she worked for the Spanish couturier, Elio Berhanyer. 'Take care of Fleur,' was his edict. That meant more than arranging fittings – she gradually moved into my life. After more than twenty years of knowing each other and being together she has fulfilled the difficult role of a substitute sister after mine sadly died in San Francisco.

Whenever we are in Spain, Toni Tomita always comes to stay from wherever her husband's engineering activities have taken her. This means Korea, Texas, Thailand, Argentina or Japan – three times a year! She is loved by everyone; 'Is Toni there?' I'm always asked when inviting guests. Spain would never be the same without her calm and loving friendship.

Bonnie Angelo also 'fell into the family' after countless years admiration heightened while she served as *Time* magazine's Bureau Chief in London. Her astonishing talent and charm gave her immediate access to those of influence in high places, whether in government or other circles. She later became head of *Time*'s bureau in New York City, before 'retiring' but continuing to write for them. A woman as Bureau Chief is hardly a common occurrence in *Time* magazine's corporate structure, and rarely found in the tough press world. We see her regularly in England and Spain.

Nancy Holmes worked on my life when we were at *Look* and has remained there since. She defines the meaning of friendship.

Trudy Sundberg of Seattle is not a women's libber – gender means nothing to her. We originally met when her husband, Captain John Sundberg, was Military Attaché at the American Embassy in London. I know no other person who appreciated and absorbed more of the British way of life in so short a time as she did – more than any other foreigner I have ever come across.

She epitomizes the true nature of friendship. As long as we have known each other, over thirty years, I have had her affection, which continued after her husband was posted to the US Embassy in The Netherlands, where I frequently visited. An extraordinary measure of goodwill was created by them for America wherever they served abroad. In The Hague she, of course, learned to speak Dutch. Her talents are now obvious in Seattle teaching and giving needy young children her constant concern. She lectures on Dutch art and literature, but when asked she can, and does, speak on a dozen other subjects. The work 'given' exactly describes her.

A gallant in the French sense of the word was the late Baron Philippe de Rothschild of Mouton, France, creator and purveyor of some of the world's great wines. He lived in a style commensurate with his wealth and, one might even say, his eccentricity. The luxurious ambience one found in his château had also been contributed to by his American wife, Pauline, who left her mark everywhere before her untimely death. His first wife died in Ravensbrück, a victim of the Nazis.

She created a museum at the vineyard to display their rare collection of objects from the world of wine. One of her idiosyncrasies was her dislike of plants in porcelain containers; all hers sat instead not on the finest French antiques but in clay pots, looking just right. The vineyard, directly outside the glass wall of the drawing room, was lit by night to produce a theatrical backdrop, the creation of the Baron. In daylight one marvelled over the meticulously organized planting.

Not only did the decor reflect his very personal tastes, so did the food and of course the wine, including some one-hundred-year-old vintages. My husband and I annoyed the Baron because neither of us takes any alcohol, ever.

We knew Pauline before she died, but on a later visit to Mouton we met the Baron's platonic consort, Joan Littlewood. This equally odd lady is famous for her genuine anarchism and as one of the most inspired theatre directors of her time, mainly at the Theatre Royal, Stratford East for many years from 1953. Always inspired by contemporary events, *Fings Ain't Wot They Used T'be* and *Oh, What a Lovely War!* were among her outstanding successes which she produced with raffish independence. She has been called 'The Conscience of the British Theatre', having helped formulate it after the last war.

It was a shock to find her in the lavish Rothschild setting. How did this happen? Baron Rothschild was mourning Pauline's death; his first wife had died in a Nazi concentration camp. Joan Littlewood was, at the same time, mourning the death of her manager and lover, Jerry Raffles. She was persuaded to come to Mouton after the imaginatively dressed baron had been completely intrigued by the tiny woman in man's clothing with hair hidden under a Brechtian cap – almost the most incongruous sight one could meet in the luxurious Mouton château.

The final word on this improbable liaison was written by Baron de Rothschild in his autobiography, though rumour has it that it was written by her. He ended the preface with: 'Joan, my love to you. Iris Mouton, your home for ever, if you wish, which begs you to carry on, not to stray too far from the one you call "the Guv". Never stop being the Joan I met in Vienne on the Rhône.'

His daughter, Baroness Philippine de Rothschild, has the vineyard and the famous name in her formidable hands these days. No eccentricities!

An amazing act of appreciation and friendship was recently shown to me in an unexpected and extravagant way, touching me deeply, by the gallant Richard Martin, Curator of the Costume Institute at the Metropolitan Museum of Modern Art in New York City. He greatly admired my magazine, *Flair*. We had never met but when he read the announcement of my forthcoming exhibition in October 1993 at the National Museum of Women in the Arts in Washington, he flew down to see the paintings and to discuss the possibility of his giving a talk about *Flair* magazine. My paintings were still unhung and he reacted by writing the following unsolicited review. It was instantly blown up and hung on the walls of the Museum during the exhibition. I have never been more proud.

My husband later had it reprinted on parchment as a Christmas gift to hang in my office, where it is a constant inspiration. It will always be a revealing explanation of my work for friends and/or collectors.

> *I will be the gladdest thing under the sun!*
> *I will touch a hundred flowers and not pick one.*
>
> Edna St Vincent Millay
> *Afternoon on a Hill*, 1917

Fleur Cowles has found a place for art within her extraordinary life. In fact, she has placed the creation of art at the center of her busy, effective life.

Journalist, editor and Presidential representative, Fleur Cowles has tended her own garden, a proliferation of flowers enchanted by a nature rich and benevolent. Other artists have created gardens in verse and in image; some have created peaceable kingdoms; some have even realized that nature emulates us. But Cowles, influenced by her friendships, patronage and deep engagement with Surrealist artists as well as by a lifetime commitment to painting, imbues each mushroom, flower, or fictive jungle with the properties of enchantment. We are drawn into the mystery of nature as a child might be. We may even be uncertain about scale when a friendly leopard, industrious bird, or fanciful unicorn appears amidst the petals.

It is commonplace to believe that the appearances of nature can be beautiful. What Cowles does is to transform nature, turning it from a perceived grace into a mysterious beauty that surpasses perception and invokes the imagination. At the same time, she practices a detached science: her flora and fauna are depicted with an apparently cool scientific (with the exception of the unicorn) objectivity, but they reveal subterranean strata that are as inhabited and as fanciful as any Lewis Carroll or Kenneth Grahame world. Like her friends, the Surrealists, Cowles invites us to dream. In a tranquil and busy bower of nature, she has invented a microcosm, a little world known to us in every rational taxonomy of flower and life form, but ultimately exotic to us in elegant perfection.

In entering into the world of Cowles's lyrical imagination, we share her delight and invention in offering an alternative to the real. We see where magic ameliorates even nature; we see where we dwell even more contentedly than in our own world; and we realize the thrill that art gives when it transports us beyond ourselves to a very, very special place, the interior of a dream. In exposing her enthralling images, Cowles beckons every one of us to enter our own secret garden.

Gallantry exists in many differing forms. Yehudi Menuhin is in a class of his own, not only as the child prodigy who became a world citizen, but because a more caring man is hard to name. Few have been more articulate, not only when making his beloved violin talk, but in his defence of justice. We have been friends for *years*, sharing close ties to the Greek royal family, but the first time he and I talked seriously together was on a television programme which I was chairing. Lord Cecil was the other lucid companion.

One early morning, I looked out at the soft hills rising above the lakes on our land in Sussex, and I heard gentle music. It was coming from Menuhin's violin as he walked among the grass and wild flowers. The sun was just up. The dew had not dried. A beautiful vestigial memory.

*   *   *

I first met two gallant friends in the late sixties while in Seville staying with the American Consul, Robert Tyler. He asked if I would see Robert Vavra and his fellow American, John Fulton; both hoped for help.

Fulton had read what I had written about bullfighting. He was already fighting in local arenas, longing to be *officially* accepted as a matador, and he asked if I could intercede and ask the great Ordonez to give him the 'cape'. This is the *alternative* graduation ceremony which bullfighting at a serious level requires of every matador. At that time, no other North American had become an official *matador de toros* in Spain; even Sidney Franklin had to get his in Mexico.

'I'm afraid not,' I had to explain. 'You are American. I am American. Any foreigner who tries to fight bulls in Spain is unwelcome and to be spoken for by an American woman could actually be harmful.'

Fulton then went to Ernest Hemingway, asking for the same favour. Hemingway later told Fulton that Ordonez did agree to do it as a personal gesture to him, a fact the bullfighter later confirmed to Fulton, but for two or three years, Ordonez continued to put him off, intimating 'Later, later.'

It was a valueless promise. However, it was made good by another friend, the rancher Felix Moreno de la Cova, then Mayor of Seville. He arranged for Fulton to get that ephemeral honour in the bullring in Seville; it is called the *La Scala* of bullfighting. Fulton performed with distinction and even confirmed that *alternativa* in Madrid later. He is the only American ever to take it in Spain.

He officially retired in 1994 in a corrida in San Miguel de Allende in Mexico, the scene of his debut as a bullfighter years before. The first bull in the ring was a bad one and Fulton, aged sixty-two, didn't do too well. The second animal was a decent one and he performed magnificently. The crowd, who minutes before were booing, then began to cheer and throw flowers. He was carried from the ring shoulder-high. A *Don Quixote* dream ended happily.

Today, he has taken up painting, illustrating a book by James Michener. He has become an artist-matador, painting pictures of bulls, often using the blood of the vanquished animals, many of which hang in the homes of the famous.

By way of a postscript on bullfighting: although I once followed the bulls in order to write about them, the ritual in a bullring has always deeply disturbed me: the atmosphere of fear (even the bull is scared) is in the air itself, insidious and unyielding. The matador's fear is born with him, it is in his blood, a fear which gives him the devoted audience he wants. He courts death, arrogantly exposing himself to it, feeling more male, macho, than any star on the cinema screen – braver, certainly.

I never want to see another bullfight. I have given up trying to judge how abject the fear must be, or how deep the matador's secret admiration of the bull's indomitable sense of power. I can believe that to conquer such an animal makes a man feel very much a man.

The bullfight is not a sport. It is a ritual, a contest with the bravest animal on earth; every lion, tiger or elephant matched against a bull has lost. Professional bullfighting can make men rich; those at the top are millionaires – but perhaps it is the fame more than the money they enjoy. In any case, I am glad that John Fulton has retired from the ring.

Both Americans loved Spain, but Robert Vavra's profession was photography, not bullfighting. Could I help him find a publisher for a book he had compiled of hundreds of photographs of a young African girl who had brought up a baby gorilla? Yes, I said I could and did by talking to my publisher, Sir William Collins, whose interest in animals and African life was well established. He saw Vavra and his photographs and provisionally bought the book rights but it was never to be published; the cost of reproducing such a myriad of photographs proved uncommercial. Vavra came to London to discuss the book's future and was told that he could keep his advance but that the book couldn't be printed. He came to my office to pass on the sad news, and there he saw a collection of my animal and flower paintings being readied for shipment to an exhibition in a New York gallery.

A touchingly beautiful bestseller was born instead. Vavra loved those paintings so much I gave him packets of colour films, ektachromes, to take to Spain to do with as he wished. There, after studying them, he designed and wrote the book called *Tiger Flower*, using about forty. This is an allegorical story written around my paintings. More than a quarter of a million copies were sold.

Four more similar books followed – again allegories written around my already finished paintings: *Lion and Blue*, *Romany Free*, *The Love* *of Tiger Flower* and *To be a Unicorn.** Enchantingly ambiguous, they are written for adults but they are equally loved by children, selling in incredible numbers in many parts of Europe and America. The ACA and ABA United States book societies voted for a list of children's books with all-time adult appeal. Their list of ten included *The Little Prince* by Saint-Exupéry and *Tiger Flower* and *Lion and Blue* by Vavra and Cowles.

Vavra and my husband and I have become very close friends and see each other often in Spain where he still has a home. His first real international recognition had come from collaboration with James Michener when he was writing *Iberia*. Vavra, so well suited to the challenge, became its camera eye and guide. In the last few years his expertise in portraying the beauty and behaviour of horses has given thousands of readers extraordinary pleasure. There is no one who can catch the magnificence of the horse on film better. His photographic work is now much sought after by collectors.

His love of Africa has led him to live there from time to time with his favourite people, the statuesque Masai tribes. The book he wrote about them is illustrated with breathtaking photographs. He never stops; he has already written thirty-two books and there is always another on the way. He is just like his work, a magical man.

One of my most extraordinary gallant friends was Baroness Renée Lippens, who must be described as a heroic lady.

Somehow she managed to reach London from Brussels during the Second World War to join MI5, the Intelligence Service. This was amazing: she was built like a ship's figurehead – someone whose presence was difficult to conceal. My guests tended to melt in hysterical laughter whenever I persuaded her to talk about having been a spy; the image of such a large lady, well over six feet tall, being parachuted on to German territory seemed comical until she explained her rationale: 'How could the Germans suspect me, a giant lady, of being a spy? I just walked about as if I was another oversized German!' Brave.

She took up a very different sort of heroic activity after the war ended, as Director of Belgium's National Theatre, much involved in

* Collins, England; Morrow, USA and elsewhere in the world.

its financial problems, using her influence with government and pro-
moting her eccentric notions of the kind of plays to be produced.

One of the last conversations I had with her before she died took
place in Brussels, sitting beside her in her car, en route for her home,
my husband following in ours. We passed the home of two mutual
friends, and as we did she turned to ask: 'Which of the two – the
husband or the wife – do you consider the *better* friend?'

'I couldn't begin to decide,' I replied. 'They are *both* very dear to
me, just like family, both very close.'

'Well,' she said, 'I find it easier to decide. I'm sure *he* would do
anything for you, but *she* would die for you!'

So this was her evaluation of amity. It made me realize the special
quality of her own gift of friendship.

Still a young man, the ever-gallant James Rosebush goes through life
wondering what he can do for others. I can think of several examples:
when the Challenger space ship so tragically went down, the President
of the United States chose him to visit the surviving family members,
to give solace, to console and deal with the problems, resulting in
memorials to those who died which he helped design. Most importantly, he created the Challenger Space Centres for children. There
they fly in space simulators, feel the thrill of adventure and learn to
appreciate the past and future of the space age.

Rosebush also set up the model programme for the aged which
became the inspiration for the nationwide programme which we now
know as 'Mobile Meals': 'Meals on Wheels' for the United States.

He created President Reagan's Private Sector Initiatives programme
(PSI) to engender private business solutions for public problems when
he convened the first nationwide White House task force of top corporate executives to recognize and deal with the issues.

He helped Nancy Reagan boost her failing public opinion rating
when he became the White House's Special Assistant to the President
and Chief of Staff to the First Lady. He took her name from the
lowest-ever for an American First Lady to one of the highest ratings,
before the issues of astrology and extravagance again took their toll.

After leaving the White House, he became head of his own company,
which now has a record of counselling US and foreign corporations,

governments and start-up ventures, and organizing global marketing, finance and communications.

When I asked him how he would describe his life, he wrote 'the richness of one's life is in proportion to the degree in which one serves another, the community and the world.'

Another businessman who correctly balances his professional and personal life with a measure of gallantry and commitment is John Studzinski. He has access to heads of government and financial high flyers but keeps a low profile himself, combining business with fundraising for 'The Passage', the largest centre for the homeless in London. He actually works in the night shelter in order not to lose touch. A typical Saturday includes a morning business meeting with the head of a company, followed by a private spiritual discussion with Cardinal Hume and an evening in the night shelter. On my last birthday, a man arrived at our door completely hidden behind a huge collection of flower-painted balloons, a gift from John. They almost took over an entire room for weeks until the helium inside them slowly dissipated. Not only gallant, but imaginative.

At his home, I found one night a writer from India whom I had first met in Delhi at the High Commissioner's dinner, Vikram Seth. At age forty-one, he has already been called the best writer of his generation after the publication in 1994 of his incredible novel *A Suitable Boy*. Impressive as it is, a tiny book four inches by six inches called *Beastly Tales* captured my heart as much. It has been described as the modern Aesop's Fables. It takes a new look at storytelling *in verse*, a poetic look at the good and bad creatures of the animal world: how a greedy crocodile outwits a monkey, a mouse outwits a snake, a frog and a nightingale sing together. Vikram Seth read the book aloud to us one night at John Studzinski's dinner for him. A charming memorable occasion.

One of the bravest and most delightful men I shall ever know was Louis Camu, a Belgium and a former head of the Banque du Brussels.

322

He had survived unbearable treatment and imprisonment by the Nazis after his capture as head of Belgium's Resistance Movement. He emerged a living skeleton and it took three years of hospital treatment to repair the damage, but the recovery he finally made astounded everyone.

He was given a knighthood on his deathbed by Queen Elizabeth II. It was almost a lifetime away from the events that merited it, but all his friends were glad he lived to be honoured and recognized. Nisette, his wife, deserved a medal too, for her own wartime bravery in the Underground.

We were always delighted with our frequent visits to their homes in Brussels and Alost. I recall a memorable occasion when on leaving their Russell Paige garden we entered the neighbouring forest planted with millions of lilies of the valley. We walked on this 'carpet of snow' trying not to harm a flower while nightingales sang around us. It remains a vivid painting in my mind's eye.

Equally enjoyable were the wide-ranging conversations around a log fire, grilling sausages and bread, usually at two o'clock in the morning.

Enrico Donati and his wife Del are among my closest friends. He is a painter living in New York who started in Paris as a Surrealist, creating an important place for himself within the movement. He eventually left Surrealism behind to paint dimensionally in marble dust, becoming one of the most respected and successful artists in the New York School with work now hanging in important collections everywhere. A few years ago, he added sculpture to his work, producing shining molten abstract pieces like stones and ancient primitive objects. I have collected his works through every change in style.

Enrico Donati neither lives nor works like any other artist. He paints and sculpts in his vast studio overlooking New York's Central Park from one to seven o'clock daily, unless, on rare occasions, he lunches elsewhere. In the morning, he used to run his business. From a wealthy Milanese background, he is a self-made millionaire, chairman of the elegant and highly successful perfume company, the House of Houbigant. He is that rare hybrid: an accomplished artist and successful industrialist.

Being rich, he never liked other less fortunate artists to know how elegantly he lived; on the other hand, he took a real interest in how *they* did. No struggling painter friend whose work he admired went without his help in selling their work to his own collectors.

As a typical act of gallantry, in 1994 he gave his entire Houbigant Company to his associates when he retired, conceding that the company's success was also due to their efforts. A rare event in big business.

Jeffrey Selznick, son of David and Irene Selznick and grandson of L. B. Mayer, enhances the family reputation by his generosity as a giver and a gallant gentleman, particularly by his donation some years ago of the enormously valuable David Selznick Film Library of 5,000 cases to Texas University's Harry Ransom Humanities Research Center. There's no larger library for film research anywhere for students of the industry. His profession, if he'd allow me to call it that, is *giving*.

Of many women gallants, one American living in London of whom I am particularly proud works in the inner circle of Queen Elizabeth's court, Virginia Ryan Airlie. She is the daughter of the late Mrs John Barry Ryan ('Nin' to her friends) who regularly visited London to give her annual party which drew government, society and the famous together.

Virginia ('Ginny') is married to old Etonian ex-banker the Earl of Airlie, now Lord Chamberlain to the Queen. His brother, Sir Angus Ogilvy, is married to one of Britain's most beloved royals, Princess Alexandra. Lord Airlie's royal connection is an old one; his grandmother was lady-in-waiting to Queen Mary.

Years ago Ginny Airlie began her amazing work on behalf of the American Museum at Bath (she is a member of its Board, as I am). She still manages to give it many ideas and much of her time, despite her life as lady-in-waiting to Queen Elizabeth, normally accompanying her on overseas journeys. Nothing changes her direct, honest and lovable manner.

One irrepressible friend, the Lebanese Lady Elsa Bowker, is always on our minds in this same context of lovableness. She cares about us, over-rates us, and treats us as if a part of her family, a luxury. Now a Londoner, the widow of an important former British Ambassador, she brought an amazing middle-eastern brand of warmth to his important posts, with resultant friendships wherever the gifted pair operated, as she still does in England.

There is one man who absolutely symbolizes gallantry. He is our great friend Jorge Rius, the heart specialist in Spain who must end this chapter on gallants. He not only saved my life, but other friends's. To improve the quality of all his patients' lives is his saint-like motivation. To ensure that his skill and dedication to both surgery and patient care are passed on he has trained one of his talented daughters to work with him. She will become not only his medical successor, but also his heiress in humanity.

All of his patients, including myself, admire him and are deeply proud of his friendship and place in our lives.

XII

FLAIR MAGAZINE:
ITS LIFE
AND CELEBRATION

Q UIXOTICALLY, ONE OF my best friend-makers over the last forty-five years has been not a person but my magazine, *Flair*. It has made friends for me in many parts of the world, year after year, since it died in January 1951.

It has brought me multiple honours from the great University of Texas. It has newly delighted my soul by the international publication of the handsome volume to be called *The Best of Flair** – to which collectors of the original magazine have already responded with excitement. It will be my longed-for 'obit' – one that I am gratified to be able to live to enjoy.

There are facts about the birth, death and ultimate celebration many years later of *Flair* magazine, which I created, edited and published in 1950 in the United States. Some of the facts are better left *said* – the magazine has never been repeated, copied or equalled, and its name and fame are still alive today.

To explain this I must go back to when I married Gardner (Mike) Cowles and 'inherited' his three wonderful children, Lois, Kate and Gardner II. He had recently launched the money-spinning photographic magazine called *Look*. Unfortunately, although it was earning a million dollars yearly, it had also earned the dismal tag of a 'man's barber-shop magazine'.

I refused to marry the divorced Mike Cowles unless he agreed to move from Iowa to New York. He was at that time Domestic Chief of the Office of War Information (OWI), living temporarily in Washington. Also, I insisted he must give up absentee management and actually edit the magazine he had personally created, rather than leaving others in sole control. Most important, he had to change *Look*'s image.

He agreed. Soon after our marriage, after filling his pockets daily

* HarperCollins, 1996.

with suggestions, I agreed to accept his invitation to become *Look*'s Associate Editor and to plunge into the tricky role of being the boss's wife while working on the staff. Joining that all-male arena was hardly a comfortable move, especially when a few male heads had to roll in turning *Look* into a *family* magazine.

It was a difficult, though excitingly creative time. Using kid gloves, I worked hard to build a growing sense of quality, and to add women's interest to its pages. Our husband-and-wife rescue operation ultimately changed mere money-making into publishing pride by lifting *Look* from its tawdry barber-shop circulation to an influential family magazine. Until we were able to guarantee an *equal* female readership – they were the real decision-makers in buying goods – national advertisers stayed away in droves. *Look* was *very* slim at the beginning.

The changed general editorial content, together with finer paper and better printing and new family appeal, led eventually to the *Look* magazine now remembered for its powerful presentation of human events and its *equal* appeal to men and women, massive advertising revenue, and a final circulation of seven million copies.

I remember well not only the glamour but the pain involved in helping it to change. Men who lost their jobs in the magazine's restructuring found it easy to blame it on 'the boss's wife', an unpleasantness which I had to take in my stride. It wasn't until years later that I was able to say what I should have said much earlier.

The occasion was on American television, and happened after a New York call from Mike Wallace. My authorized biography of Salvador Dali was being published: would I be a guest on his coming TV show?

Why does an overseas call always seem important? I replied yes, that I had to be in New York in a week anyway to promote the book. At that time Mike Wallace had a terrifying reputation as an interviewer, but I decided to brave the experience anyway. By staying calm, I won out, to such an extent that at the finish he pointed his finger angrily at me to say: 'I couldn't *get* you.'

On the programme, he had asked sneeringly if I hadn't been the 'hatchet woman' at *Look*. 'How silly!' I replied. 'You simply shouldn't underestimate Mike Cowles. After all, *he* was supposed to be running *Look*.'

To make the necessary changes to *Look*, time was needed. Endless 'board meetings' between the two of us took place daily in our library at home at the day's end, often between 11.30 p.m. and 1.30 a.m. We knew that a flash-flood of changes would drive away current readers and that attracting new ones could take years. But *how* to bring an end to the current avoidance of *Look* by advertisers? A far-thinking decision was taken to launch a *class* magazine to prove to the advertising world that *Look* management knew perfectly well how to edit for *all* groups of readers.

Mike Cowles, despite what he said later in a privately printed inaccurate book about his life, ghost-written just before his death, had been totally enthusiastic, full of expectation, completely supportive in every way and in all discussions. 'Would *I* do it? Could I create such a magazine overnight?' he asked. Most women married to rich men hope for a yacht or racehorses or more jewels, but what *I* secretly longed for was the opportunity to create a 'magazine-jewel' which would reflect the *real* me. When the chance came, I jumped at the challenge.

There was no point in creating yet another magazine frozen to the format of competitors who specialized either in literature, fashion, travel, art, decor or entertainment. Why not put these *all* in one magazine? This I decided to do. I knew where I needed to look for guidance, so I made a beeline for Europe to see the finest book and magazine publishers who were producing the kind of adventures in paper and print that I dreamed of for a genuinely new magazine. Their production in Europe was done mainly *by hand*. The problem was to see if this could be done *by machine* in the United States.

With delight, in Paris, Rome and Milan I studied the techniques and presses, sought out handmade papers, talked with designers. I returned enriched by their expertise and genuine helpfulness. I found and brought with me Prince Pallavicini, a gifted artist-designer escapee from Hungary whom I found in Milan, and for whom I arranged a stateless person's passport.*

In my mind's eye, I was finally able to form a picture of the future magazine. I gave it the name *Flair* because no other word better embodied tasteful originality. *Roget's Thesaurus* has nearly one

---

* His real name was Prince Bercoviczy; eventually he became an American citizen and changed his name to Prince Pallavicini, the name of the Austrian aristocrat he married, Princess Pallavicini.

hundred synonyms for the word. We intended *Flair* to be the most beautiful monthly publication anywhere, a new dimension in magazine publishing for the five classic fields that concern human activity: art, literature, entertainment, travel and fashion. In doing so, we introduced to the magazine such names as Jean Cocteau, Tennessee Williams, W. H. Auden, Christopher Sykes, Barbara Ward, François Mauriac, Dr Margaret Mead, Hoyingen-Huene, René Gruau, Saul Steinberg, Lucian Freud, Tamayo and Simone de Beauvoir.

The big question was: would it be possible to introduce such innovations in the United States, where even available commercial production methods would certainly be cost-prohibitive? Yes. A few far-seeing printers, engravers and binders found the way to do by machine what was done expensively by hand in Europe, each hoping to make their own contribution to printing history. A magazine giving readers such a completely new editorial content would be testimony to their skills.

Finally, there was the question of staff; quite a queue stood by as rumours fuelled excitement and curiosity. Young men and women sought jobs on every level. Those hired were skilful and dedicated, the best creative talents I had ever seen – for which I shall be ever thankful.

What was *Flair*? I had to answer these questions regularly. I would say, if the dimension of a feature could be enhanced by fold-in half-paper, why not do it that way? If a feature was particularly significant, why not bind it as a 'little book' into each issue to give it special focus? If a feature was better 'translated' on *textured* paper, why use glossy paper? Why not follow glossy paper with dull matt finish? If hand-fed offset printing or hand-fed gravure suited a photographic essay better than letterpress, why not use it? If a painting was good enough to frame, why not print it on heavy cut stock? Why not bind in little accordion-folders to add a little fun?

Why not an element of surprise in every issue? Why not a magazine with cross-gender appeal? And in the age of television's newly-acquired allure, why not a magazine of *visual* excitement?

Working twelve-hour days, our first issue was produced in September 1949 – but not for the public. It was a limited edition preview to show the advertising world how *Flair*'s promised ingredients would be presented in future issues. It caused a stir, indeed it aroused violent passions, *instantly* galvanizing our competitors into great retaliation.

Who was I to make the other magazines seem too conventional?

Magazine executives seemed to have banded together to fight us, with the advertising agencies. They uttered not a word of praise, sneering at the hole in *Flair*'s two-part cover, that has since become the personal trademark I use for all my own printing. Differing page sizes were ridiculed, so were the differing types and colours of paper in each issue, as well as the little book bound inside its centrefold. They ignored *Flair*'s contributors, those future celebrities for whom *Flair* provided new ways to present what they had written or designed; *many have become legends.*

Advertisers and agencies were warned to 'stay away from that rich woman's *toy*' . . . 'Fleur Cowles's folly' . . . 'her short-term plaything'. Despicable personal gossip insinuated that *Flair* could only be short-lived. This, once, was denied to Walter Winchell by Mike Cowles himself.

In my introduction, I invited the advertising community, not foreseeing how coolly they would react, to see that *Flair* 'extended' an opportunity to advertisers to design uniquely, to give editorial and advertising pages an uncluttered continuity of expression. I hadn't bargained for laziness; to design special copy for just one publication was too much work because of the extra time involved.

Despite such unfriendliness, the readers' fan mail and press applause swelled my heart and I ignored the flak. *But the enemies won.* On a sad Saturday morning less than a year after its birth, *Flair*'s advertising and other non-editorial executives were called to a sudden meeting at the Waldorf Towers Hotel, to hear Mike Cowles announce *Flair*'s demise: despite his promised very generous three-year budget, he was closing *Flair*! Advertisers had sat on their hands to see how long *Flair* would last, *meanwhile sentencing it to death.* I was too shocked to speak. I sat on the sidelines, emotionally drained, in tears.

It was an undeserved murder. It had sold 265,000 copies monthly from the news-stands. It cost readers a mere fifty cents a copy. The difference between the thirty-three cents we received from news-dealers and its actual cost to us was never made up by the expected advertising revenue.

Somehow, on the following Monday morning, I broke the news to my shell-shocked staff. I tried to console myself with the fact that if the perilous Berlin airlift, at that time jittery news, did lead to war, I would want to be flying an airplane again, not sitting at an elegant magazine's desk. Khrushchev had told Secretary of State Rusk that Berlin was the testicles of the West, implying that he could squeeze them at will. War, fortunately, didn't follow, but *Flair* was gone.

In its last issue I published briefly a 'Smile and Farewell', explaining that after most of the issue had already gone to press, a decision had suddenly been made to suspend *Flair*'s publication. Reasons given: 'due to the foreign situation, rising costs and the imminent shortage of paper . . .'

Ironically, *Look* was the beneficiary. *Flair* had definitely helped to influence big-time advertisers, who compared the creativeness of *Flair* with the changing concept of *Look*'s editorial direction, and saw *Look* in a new light. Advertising began to flow in. Even so, tragedy overtook *Look* in 1972 when it, too, expired. I was living abroad, listed as *Look*'s Foreign Correspondent, when Mike Cowles told me that mailing and circulation costs and its own, new unreasonably high advertising rates made it impossible to continue. *Life* magazine had already ceased publication, its death caused by similar ailments.

At the time *Flair* ended, I decided to revive it as a new hardbound book, *The Flair Annual*, to continue the magical experience. Only one edition was published before I left the United States. This book, a work of pride, was turned out by just three of us: a superb writer, Robert Offergeld, art director Federico Pallavicini (both enormously gifted men from the original staff) and me. The pale, often paranoic genius, George Davies, had sadly gone – he had fallen on the magazine like a last drink of water, helping to give it an eclectic content.

Back in 1953, important White House assignments began to come my way (for example as Ambassador to Queen Elizabeth's Coronation, followed by other assignments for the President personally). *Look* editing also continued. My time and mind were fully absorbed until November 1955, when I divorced Gardner Cowles to marry Tom Montague Meyer, to live in London, to enter a splendid new world.

Hindsight is a luxury but it *does* exist. To me, it's obvious that *Flair* had the right *rich parents* but the wrong *nanny* – it was born to a family which was a master at news-stand selling, and thought news-stands were the only outlets for *Flair*. But wouldn't it have been wiser to sell it by *mail*, at a profit-making price, rather than for fifty cents? Would it then have *lasted*? It would have sold for a competitive, probably profitable, price instead of the 285,000 copies sold at a loss. A new American magazine did start in 1991, to sell for $45 for six copies a year ($7.50 a copy). It refuses advertising and *is* a success.

Flair never really died. For me it continues to be a lifetime passport to recognition: I am still regularly asked: 'Isn't Fleur *Flair*?' Copies still arrive at every personal appearance I make, which is *often*, considering nineteen books and fifty-one openings of one-man exhibitions of my paintings around the world. I am constantly brought copies to sign; they are now more than forty-three years old. When I travel, *Flair* is a calling card; from painters to writers, to intellectuals, to designers, doors are opened wide.

Students who hadn't been born in *Flair*'s time have come to know the copies their parents *bound, cared for, read*, and *re-read* before passing them down to succeeding generations. Hence *Flair* is cherished and discussed by new youth, which makes me the happiest. It will soon be nearly half a century since it appeared, yet to some it was only yesterday. Whatever it lacked in longevity was made up in publishing immortality.

I meet people who recall for me what *Flair* had in its first February 1950 issue: *The New Bohemian* by Charles J. Rolo; no word need be changed today – the first presentation in the United States of Lucian Freud, who was twenty-eight then and is now called Britain's greatest living painter. Angus Wilson's short story, *Real Politik*, is still superb reading. He was an ex-member of the British Foreign Office. The first book bound inside was Jean Cocteau's *A Letter to America*, 'edited' in the same issue by W. H. Auden. I am stunned by its current perspicuity. Cocteau had written this essay for *Flair* on the airplane which flew him home from his first journey to America.

Tennessee Williams's fame as a playwright arguably obscured his great gift as a short story writer. *Flair* repaired this in his first, *The Resemblance between a Violin Case and a Coffin*. The Paris home of the Duke and Duchess of Windsor was detailed in four pages. Morocco is not so changed that reading nine pages on '*Flair* travels to Morocco' would be wasted today.

That *Flair* is still alive is proven in countless ways. Not too long ago I was in the customs area of Seattle Airport, standing in a long queue, unfortunately behind hippies whose baggage was being very carefully subjected to painstaking searches. I slipped up to ask politely if I might be taken next, 'because a distinguished elder man was waiting for me'. It was the distinguished John McCone. 'Certainly not!' the burly officer replied.

I went back to my place prepared for a long wait. When I finally reached the unfriendly man, I handed over my declaration. '*You're* Fleur Cowles?' he almost shouted. 'You're *Flair*! Welcome to Seattle, I'm sorry I kept you waiting.'

Two days later, more evidence: I was the guest of honour at the opening night of the Seattle Opera Company. My paintings hung on the Opera House walls, before going to the Seattle Art Museum the next day for their first modern exhibition in that handsome building. All the music that evening was dedicated to my paintings; every item concerned with animals and flowers, played by the Seattle Symphony Orchestra.

At the first intermission, a spotlight focused on me as the chairman took the stage to announce that the exhibition would move the next day to the museum and to suggest that I might be willing to stay behind in the Opera House later to meet any who wanted to meet me. More than fifty did, and each brought copies of *Flair* they hoped somehow I would sign.

In South Africa, *Flair* saved me from jail. I was warned that I would be arrested for having Father Huddleston and a black man in my car. A journalist who had just become engaged had given three rare copies of *Flair* to his bride as an engagement present. He felt he had to warn me, and *did*. He has become the famed theatre critic and author of plays, opulent and admired in London, Herbert Kretchmer. I just had time to fly out of South Africa.

My most poignant *Flair* experience came from a young man who had been drafted and was about to be shipped to Vietnam. He wrote to me to say he didn't want to go, that he disapproved of all war, and was pretty sure to be killed in action. 'Who'd want to survive?' he asked. 'I'll probably stand up and let it happen.' He concluded: 'I have nothing left in this world to give anyone other than my complete set of *Flair*. They are now on their way to you.'

Where is he now, if he *is* alive? I have given him the distinction he deserves in *The Best of Flair*, using actual pages from his set, *his* pages – posterity for a brave, elegant, anonymous young man, in my introduction.

I recently discovered a letter from Mike Cowles, dated 9 September

1971. He had written: 'Dear Fleur, *Flair* was so completely your "baby" that I think anything you ever want to say about *Flair* can be said without any suggested editing on my part. Affectionately, Mike.'

If any sort of post-mortem on *Flair* is in order, I would say: what money was lost will probably never again be available on the same scale. It would cost many, many more millions. It was put in my hands by Mike Cowles because he and I *both* thought it would be commercial, but, for the good and bad reasons I have mentioned, it was not. In any case, where could one find those fresh, untapped talents who filled the cubby-holes of *Flair*, or their seven-day-a-week dedication and enthusiasm? Could this emulsion be re-stirred?

Am I heartbroken that the magazine only lasted for twelve issues? Certainly not. *Flair wasn't* just a dream, it *did* exist, it *still* does. It *was* the first magazine to be called an art form in its own right. It had a noticeable, acknowledged effect on graphic design. It *was* genuinely loved by its readers. In fact, it is one of the proudest episodes of my versatile life.

As a living monument, one of America's greatest universities has honoured me and *Flair*. The University of Texas at Austin, the amazing seat of learning populated by men and women of imaginative skills, announced on 17 September 1992 a unique event.

The invitation itself was a replica of *Flair*'s first cover, the same golden pin, shaped like a swallow's wing, which I had bought in a Paris flea market in 1944. This inaugurated the opening of the Fleur Cowles Room in the Harry Ransom Humanities Research Center as well as the inception of the Fleur Cowles Fellowships worldwide and in perpetuity for post-graduate students to study art, literature and journalism in my name.

I now lecture to students each year. Every other year, starting in 1994, an international *Flair* Symposium will be held and the world's best brains will be invited to attend. No other honour I have received could outshine this recognition or make me more proud, although I have already been decorated by five countries, two with their highest awards.

These academic honours came from the Institute's Director, Dr Thomas F. Staley,* a hallowed figure on the world's literary stage.

* See Thomas F. Staley, page 112.

Under his exciting direction, the largest collection anywhere on earth of twentieth-century literature and the arts is now available for research.

The Fleur Cowles Room in the Institute is the exact replica of my own study in London: the same colour, the same furniture, carpet, books, *objets d'art*, and my own paintings, all faithfully reproduced in Texas. It is a miracle of reproduction through the efforts of lovely Sue Murphy, the Center's erudite Director of Art who is also Tom Staley's assistant. I lecture in this, my own room, in my own ambience. There is a satellite connection and fibre-optics cable transmission.

There is also an audio-visual film about *Flair*, the books I have written and a filmed close-up, 'Fleur Cowles', by former Hollywood award winners, Roy Flukinger, Curator of Photography, Theatre and Film, and Charles Bell. The Fleur Cowles Fellowships have furthered the study of the humanities, having already provided fellowships for post-graduate scholars engaged in post-doctoral research on twentieth-century topics and internships for students in the humanities from many parts of the world.

It is a wonderful thought that this takes place in one of the world's greatest institutions for literary and cultural research where they proudly boast that they have an unparalleled collection of twentieth-century British, American and French literature.

Postscript: *Flair* Magazine and my own paintings:

Throughout my life, I have been in love with paintings; I've sought out the painters and their friendship. This became a source of pleasure which finally led to my becoming a painter myself. I have just had my fifty-first one-man show in Hong Kong; others have been in Japan, Brazil, France, Germany, Holland, Britain, Hong Kong and the United States.

My own painting began with the help of the painter I sought out to help, a handsome twenty-two-year-old Florentine, Dominic Gnoli. I bought his work from his first gallery show in London, introduced him to my friends and then invited him to Sussex for a weekend. He wanted to paint as soon as he arrived, so I put him in a room where he would not be disturbed.

Watching him, I longed to try my hand at painting; I borrowed a board, paints and brushes from him and arranged a Dutch-like still-life of walnuts, roses and a golden apple. Seeing it, he was enraged: 'You simply cannot paint anything so banal!'

'Young man, if you know so much,' I replied, 'tell me what I am supposed to paint!'

'It's quite simple,' he replied. 'You are the woman who created *Flair* magazine. I know it well, as my mother loved it and bound all her copies. If you could accomplish that beautiful object, you must have imagination and memories. *Paint them!*'

I pushed aside those objects and, gathering my inspiration, I began anew. This time I simply painted an image, in a style later described as Magic Realism, of a floating island of pink cyclamens embedded in soil with hanging roots, flying through a deep pink sky. When the owner of Gnoli's gallery picked him up on Sunday to take him to London, he inspected it.

'Go on. Go on. You are good enough to warrant an exhibition,' he ordered as he left.

The young Gnoli, who instilled *Flair* in my mind as an inspiration, died twelve years later, in 1970, recognized as a genius. To me, he still exists in everything I paint.

XIII

PERILS OF FRIENDSHIP

FRIENDS HAVE OFTEN brought peril into my life by being collaborators on journeys that sometimes ended in dangerous situations. I had never heard of the Hadhramaut until the bountiful and beautiful friend invited me to go there. Going to the war in Korea only happened when President Eisenhower responded to a smiling but urgent plea for permission. Taking a suite in a hotel I had never visited before led to a dreadful mugging in the night. The hotel, and in particular the suite, were chosen by a devoted friend. My possible death, along with the Brazil government's entire Cabinet, resulted from the impulse of a distinguished friend who thought I should be included in the group going to watch an army's dawn manoeuvres. A trip into Russian-occupied German territory at a dangerous time was the idea of a friendly official who certainly meant well.

Fourteen other situations were caused by friends who probably overestimated my heroism or underestimated the dangers. Still, I am thankful to everyone. Each has prevented a dull life, though. Peril, whether real or imagined, makes little difference to my adrenalin or heart or mind. I do not claim a penchant for flirting with danger but I accept it.

Dictionaries are no help in attempting to describe *peril* which is given scant prominence, in fact very little space. But whatever the source, all agree that peril *is* a condition of imminent danger. 'A condition exposed to harm or loss or serious risk' is the definition which helps me most.

Both real and imagined peril have regularly left their imprint on me. An experience of genuine danger occurred unexpectedly in a very grand New York City hotel. I had arrived from London in a merry mood after selling the option on an allegorical book written about my paintings by Robert Vavra, *Tiger Flower*, to a Hollywood film company. The invitation for me to come to a story-conference in their

New York offices was to be the first step in a fascinating future in films.

I decided to go to the hotel just around the corner from the film company's offices on Madison Avenue rather than my usual hotel. Discussions taking place on *my* territory would give me more control of the situation than on theirs, and I would be more relaxed. The hotel had been recommended by a musical friend who pointed out to me that its location was close to the film company's offices. She immediately telephoned the hotel manager, whom she knew well after years of repeated visits, and reserved her usual suite for me. Just under the roof, where she used to practise her music for hours without complaint, it also had a luxurious atmosphere to please the Hollywood gentlemen.

On arrival, I telephoned the film executives to invite them to have a drink. Three gentlemen arrived for cocktails an hour later and we talked for two hours, debating the choice of director, the final script, and so on. By my watch, still on London time, it was already well after midnight, and I was weary enough to call a halt, but things had gone so well that instinct told me to press on, so I invited them to dine. By the time we had seen the waiter, selected the menu and been served with the food, it was one o'clock in the morning for me, eight o'clock for them.

The table was set in the oval dining area between sitting room and entrance door. I sat with my back barely a foot away from the door. We were having coffee when there was a sharp rap and I merely leaned back in my chair to open the door.

I didn't recognize the man standing there. 'I am the house detective,' he said threateningly. 'And you have opened your door without latching it or using either of the other two safety locks. I'm here to warn you not to do this in future.'

I stared in amazement. 'I feel quite safe with these three gentlemen here.'

'That may be, but get into the habit, lady,' he warned as he turned away, leaving all four of us completely nonplussed.

At ten-thirty (three-thirty in the morning to me) I suddenly began to feel so flakey it was decided we would meet again the next day. After the guests left, I craved sleep. I did all that the detective demanded: I closed the door chain, pushed across the latch and rolled back the knob on the door. Then I shut the door between living room and bedroom, too tired to turn off the living room lights. Ignoring my unopened luggage, I switched off the bedroom lights and fell on the bed, fully clothed, in a weary coma.

Some hours later, I heard a faint, faraway scream. Was it from the street below or was I dreaming? I slowly forced my eyes open in fear and trembling, to discover it was not a scream but the creak of the door from the sitting room into my bedroom as it was being slowly opened by two men. The light from the room behind them showed their silhouettes although their faces were in blackness. They were masked; one very tall, the other very short.

They lunged at me, trying to prevent me from screaming. I kicked and fought them off, knocking over the telephone as I yelled for help. I kept on screaming despite attempts to silence me and started pounding on the wall behind my bed to wake the occupant of the next room, making so much noise the two men fled, having accomplished nothing. Whatever they were after, they left empty-handed.

A small square hole had been cut out of the door, just large enough for a hand to push inside to reach and open all the locks; this had been easily done by a laser, the detective explained.

Gathering the threads of my mind, I announced, 'If anyone dares to call the police, I'll sue the hotel for a million dollars. I don't want to be publicly identified as a target for thieves. All I want to do is to get out of here, and *at once*! Order a car to take me to the airport. I am going back to London.'

No time was lost. After half an hour, still dressed in my rumpled clothes, bags unopened, feeling weak and shaken, I slowly walked to the waiting car. But before I sat inside, I turned back to the house detective who had escorted me with heavily plied sympathy.

'I have something to say to you,' I said, looking straight at him. 'Only someone on the staff could have known it was safe to touch my door. Who else would know that everyone on my floor was already inside, in bed? My door faced the elevator; *no one would dare stand directly opposite it in the hall to cut a hole if there was any chance of being caught by a guest.* And, by the way, I am a painter as well as a writer. I couldn't see the faces of the two men who attacked me, but I have a professional eye and absorbed the exact shape of each man. *You were the tall man!*'

I slammed the door in the detective's ashen face and drove off. I finally reached London, after hours of waiting in a not-yet operative Kennedy airport. There I had yet another shock. My musician friend telephoned the hotel manager to demand how such an outrageous attack could have occurred.

'What did you say was her name?' he coolly asked.

'How can you ask? I personally talked to you to make the reservation for Fleur Cowles. How can you *now* ask me her name?' she demanded.

'Because,' he answered, 'Fleur Cowles never showed up! She hasn't yet registered!' With that lie, he hung up.

The sequel continued on its dizzying way. My friend never again went back to the hotel she once loved. And, in Hollywood fashion, the film of our book was never made. The President of the company, who loved the book and paid money to Robert Vavra and myself to option it, suddenly lost his job. As usual in Hollywood, his successor vetoed all of his predecessor's commitments.

Another time, without doubt, I was absolutely uncertain of what was going to happen to me. It was in Germany immediately after the war. While staying with friends, the John McCloys, an invitation came to visit West Berlin. The city was then divided like a pie. One quarter was America's responsibility, Russia had the East Berlin sector and Britain and France each of the remaining two areas, and John McCloy was the *overall* Commander of the conquered city. Being his guest was fascinating, for it was an interesting time to be in Berlin. A few pleasures did manage to mix with the horrors of the destroyed, impoverished, unhappy city.

The drama occurred suddenly when the Russians called an unauthorized conference on the Unification of Germany, something that was certainly not in their authority to do without total agreement and collaboration of the Allies. The United States declined to send anyone to attend, as did the other governments. On second thoughts, McCloy asked me if I would be interested in going as an American 'observer', if provided with a false passport? I was.

The day before I left, a disapproving general in Intelligence concluded his briefing by warning: 'You know you are going into dangerous territory. Yesterday we sent ten senators into East Berlin in a bus with huge American flags painted on each side. *They were shot at*, so be careful. If you put a foot wrong we may never be able to locate you again.'

It was too late to withdraw so without saying another word, I was soon in the car driven by one of John McCloy's drivers in civilian clothes. After we passed through the great Brandenburg Gate into East Berlin, my nerves were showing; what a journey to be taking!

My concern was further underlined when the car was stopped and another car provided with a non-English-speaking Russian driver. I had no choice but to go with him.

Arriving at a newly-built, modernistic cement horror, my heart jumped: two soldiers with machine guns stood at the entrance. After being ushered in, I was asked for my pass, or so I gathered, as they spoke only Russian. I didn't have one. Whispering at great length, they probably decided that having arrived in the 'right' Russian car and with the right driver, it was safe to pass me on. On the way to the end of the long hallway leading to a flight of stairs, every step resounded. Then my heart really sank as I looked ahead. There, hanging the full length of a wall of glass, was a narrow two-storey-high poster on which General Omar Bradley was painted, *bayoneting a baby*!

At the top of the stairs, high doors opened into the Conference, which had already begun. The room was meant for no more than fifty, but at least one hundred or more delegates had crowded in. High on a ladder-platform, a man sat with a movie camera to record the proceedings. After my late arrival, I nervously decided the camera was focusing on me.

In the US Intelligence briefing I had been warned to dress inconspicuously. It was a very cold winter so I wore my simplest choice, a grey flannel suit and warm jersey sweater far from inconspicuous (no other woman in Europe seemed to own a matching jacket, skirt and a warm pullover). I had brought a fur coat to Europe but I never once wore it, not wishing to be cruel enough to flaunt such an example of our sheltered life in the United States.

Instead of the fur, I wore my only substitute, a black topcoat lined in a bright satin. I could not dare open it for that nonsense to be seen. The room was unexpectedly hot; the men had left their outer garments elsewhere in the hall and women wore only odds and ends of clothing.

Few even had stockings, the rarest of all possessions. I was embarrassed by mine.

The proceedings were being conducted in German, which I don't understand. I controlled my nerves until a man arrived, *late*, and took the empty chair at the official horseshoe table. I immediately recognized him as the Russian spy who had been jailed in America during the war until, in a much publicized recent event, he had been exchanged for an American prisoner-of-war held in Russia.

We at *Look*, as well as most of the American press, had carried the story of the spy prominently photographed. *But could he possibly recognize me, someone who had so often been publicized in the American press?* What excuse could I possibly give for a false name and passport? Would I be able to contact anyone for help?

The heat in the room was unbearable but I could not unbutton my coat. Was it better to faint and be taken away, to disappear in some mysterious hospital, or casually stand up and leave? I chose the latter, trying to do it as if it was the most natural thing in the world to walk out before the end of the session.

Nothing much happened; heads turned, that was all. Perhaps I wasn't recognized. However, I knew the walk down the stairs could be crucial. Who would follow me for the arrest? The walk across the cement floors from stairway to door was worse; what would the guards at the door do? Would I be taken into oblivion, a fate which in those days regularly overtook anyone who displeased the Russians? Would I just disappear, like others who had fallen foul of Russian security? Relations with the West were very tense in those days. But nothing happened. The same car was still waiting. Once again, I realized, I was at the driver's mercy. To my considerable relief he went straight to the place where our cars had been exchanged. There, waiting, was John McCloy's car. Once inside West Berlin, I knew the danger was over but it took a very long time for my heart and pulse to accept the fact.

When I got back to the United States, I told Omar Bradley about the poster I'd seen hanging in East Germany. The gentle general was appalled. The man who Eisenhower said deserved credit for winning the war against the Nazis cried. So did I.

*　　*　　*

Beirut, which at that time was as yet unshelled and unbloodied, still glamorous, wealthy, cosmopolitan and sophisticated, was to present me unexpectedly with a potentially very unpleasant situation. I had arrived relaxed and intrigued by the famous city *en route* for my second personal visit to the Shah in Teheran.

At dinner one evening I sat next to Ambassador Hare of the United States, who urged me to make a detour via Israel. I declined because I hadn't brought the 'special passport' issued to anyone going to and from Israel through any Arab country. I couldn't risk going to Israel and having them stamp my regular passport, since I had to return through Beirut and proceed to Iran. The extra 'special passport' would have avoided any problems.

Ambassador Hare charmingly said he would make arrangements for me. 'You won't need to use your passport or have it stamped. I will speak to my opposite number in Tel Aviv and he can meet you personally at Tel Aviv's airport. Ambassador Taylor will drive his American diplomatic car right to the plane on the tarmac. You will then cross the border with him, right into Tel Aviv, and will not need to go through Immigration formalities.'

Although worried, I went, grateful for such special favours. The plot worked perfectly, up to a point. We were not stopped and went straight to the Ambassador's residence in Tel Aviv, where I stayed the night. He and his wife had hurriedly arranged a dinner party for me, to which they invited several members of the Israeli government. Dinner was delightful, conversation lively and worthwhile for me. When the evening came to an end, the hosts and I lined up in the front hall to bid all goodbye. Suddenly, the Minister of the Interior stood before me. 'May I have the honour of stamping your passport?' In one quick gesture my passport had the potentially dangerous stamp boldly imprinted on it.

His friendly act was an unpleasant omen of what was to follow, for serious trouble did occur the next night when I returned to Beirut. There I would have to wait late at night in the airport for an incoming plane to Teheran. Going through their Immigration formalities I was questioned interminably and the Israeli stamp became a nasty problem. I was eventually surrounded by police and escorted away.

A man dressed as an Arab fellahin perched in a corner of the airport, watching what was taking place. He sprang to his feet. 'Don't touch that woman,' he shouted. 'She's a guest of American Ambassador Hare.' He was actually a disguised security man from our Embassy. I was taken aside, surrounded by police, to wait for the Ambassador's arrival. He had been awakened by telephone, rushed to the airport and rescued me.

Instead of a cell I was taken back to the Embassy. The plane I had intended to take to Teheran had by then gone. President Chamoun, father of the more recent assassinated President, invited me to breakfast with him and his wife to make an unnecessary apology. I took the next plane, arriving in Teheran a day late, peril behind me.

Peril can also be physically beautiful, as it *was* when I went to the Korean War front. The word, ironically, is the best one to describe the site where men in tents attempted, for years, to establish peace between the North Koreans and Allies while the seemingly un-stoppable conflict went on, right over their heads.

The war began at 4.00 a.m. on 25 June 1950. One hundred and fifty thousand Communist North Koreans (ROKs), equipped by the Russians, ruthlessly invaded South Korea, crossing the 38th Parallel to do so. Even General MacArthur, then Pro-consul of Japan, hadn't expected it.

Author John Gunther was then in Japan on an assignment for our magazine, *Look*, to write a feature, 'Inside Japan', while it was still under General MacArthur's command. His confidential account (not then for publication), after he returned to New York, was dramatic. General MacArthur had suggested Gunther and his wife visit Kyoto and offered them his own private train for the journey. At the last minute, keen on publicity as ever, MacArthur decided to join them. On the train on that fatal night, they were stunned to hear the news that fighting had just broken out on South Korea's northern boundary. The train turned back quickly to Tokyo where MacArthur had to face up to the fact that the CIA's reports, which he tended to ignore anyway, had been accurate and that his own Intelligence operation had not.

Two and a half years later in January 1953, having been given permission by President Eisenhower to go, not as a journalist but as an observer, I attended the Korean Truce Conference in Panmunjon.

It had already been moved there from Kaisong to protect it from Communist fire. The casualty toll was tremendous in the cross-fire between the armies before truce proceedings began.

Going through no-man's-land morning and night to attend the Truce Conference was dangerous. The brave Kate Adies of our time must smile wryly. In today's wars, women regularly go to the front lines; not so then, I was a rare sight.

It was while flying from Tokyo to Korea that I felt the first grip of fear. The approval to go, which had been so enthusiastically given, lay heavily on my mind after the classified briefing arranged beforehand by General Matt Ridgway, General MacArthur's successor at Command Headquarters in Tokyo. I was fitted out in five layers of battle dress (it was twenty degrees below zero at the front) and instructed how to behave if I was captured.

Ridgway gallantly lent his own personal plane for the trip to Korea. It was far from comfortable in the freezing aircraft, where ice-cold cocoa was served 'to keep you warm', the comment of a kind young airman. The Air Force pilot in charge soon made it clear to me that he thought any woman was an idiot who asked to go up to the front, and that probably Eisenhower was an even bigger one to allow it. He threw a parachute into my lap, barking out: 'Here. Put it on!'

'I don't jump,' I replied.

'Do as I say. Put it on. I'm in command here and you are under orders. We may have to push you out,' he retorted. For a fleeting moment I yearned to turn back to Tokyo. The frightening parachute didn't fit, it doubled me up, adding cramp to other problems. My stomach turned over when the plane apparently began to be fired upon. Were we being shot at? No. Pellets of ice, not bullets, were hitting the wings, but each sharp crack sounded like enemy fire to me. I didn't stop to rationalize a fact I knew well, that enemy fire was actually safer than icing up. The open terrain of mountainous peaks below was the actual war zone; it was terrifying to think of arriving on it by parachute. *This was not just imagined peril.*

After landing I was to be bivouacked with officers in Seoul, on bunks in an all-male dormitory, which brought up obvious difficulties. I was simply the 'new person', so covered in layers of clothing I was hardly recognizable as a female. I was driven daily to Panmunjon's truce area, to the tiny tent city directly under enemy fire. The drive to and from

351

those conference tables to Seoul was made by jeep at heaven-bent-for-hell speed, morning and night.

The two armies faced each other on opposite sides of two facing mountains on the 38th Parallel. The Conference itself took place on Panmunjon's low flat plain. A cease-fire by mutual consent stopped the guns for ten minutes every morning and again each night to allow Allies and North Korean peace participants to scurry up or down each mountain. Jeeps and helicopters descended like bugs for men to take up daily their monotonous positions in the war of nerves across Conference tables. Haste was essential, to be safe from the guns which instantly re-started at the end of six hundred seconds.

War fronts are always nightmarish, so how could I call this perilous place beautiful? Yet it was, in its dreadful way. The puce-coloured plain, as dry as pottery between the two armies, looked just like a Braque palette. On all four sides of the Conference zone narrow strips of Schiaparelli-pink plastic fabric had been laid down on the ground. At each corner of the zone, to mark the area from attack, silver helium-filled barrage balloons were anchored to float aloft. Lit at night by searchlight beams, it looked like a stage.

The black Russian and khaki-coloured ROK tents mingled with the tents of the Allies in brown and white, all contributing to the impressive Braque canvas which you saw as you sped down the hill in jeeps. The black, brown, khaki and white tents became Cubist blobs.

The press corps was a little UN in itself. From the Communist side were two well-known faces; Wilfred Burchett, the freelance reporter, easily spotted by his Russian fur cap, and Alan Winnington, representing London's Communist newspaper, the *Daily Worker*. Fraternization was frowned on, but Winnington's job seemed to be handing out whatever Communist propaganda was delivered at Conference tables. At night, about thirty journalists went back to the parked trains they called home, and official observers jeeped bumpily back to bivouacs in Seoul, my destination.

Once inside the truce tent, my place was behind the negotiators where I marvelled at the patience and civility of the Allied delegates facing the stony-eyed, taciturn North Koreans and Chinese. Only the keenest eyes would suspect that a woman heavily camouflaged in battle dress was among them.

In a small gap to the south-east of the horseshoe-shaped no-man's-land, five decrepit huts still remained. Women and children still lived there, ignoring the war! When I asked if I could walk closer, promising to stay *inside* the truce area, an armed soldier was ordered to take me. I made the mistake of stepping over the pink plastic line which defined the 'safe' area. Instantly bullets whizzed past, and I could actually see the machine guns of North Korean soldiers dug in on the nearby low hills. I knew I was an easy target, but it was only by mistake that I disobeyed the rules of placing just one foot outside the permitted line. I was a fair target, but what bad marksmen!

Another day, I went behind the Allied trenches to see the wounded being treated and readied to be helicoptered out for further medical care in Tokyo, shells falling all around. Frank Pace, the American Secretary of War, was comforting a man seriously wounded. 'Don't worry. We'll soon get you to the hospital in Tokyo,' Pace soothingly explained. The soldier grabbed the doctor's needle, with which he intended to close a smaller wound, and stabbed it into the palm of his own left hand. Looking up, he said: 'Me Turk. Me no hurt. Go away.'

When I got back to Tokyo, I went to see the men in a special ward where those with head injuries were treated – laid out with feet to the walls and heads on the corridor side for doctors to read without disturbances. I was distraught for days after that experience.

In July 1953, a sigh of relief was heard around the world: the truce was formally signed. The UN, as in the Gulf War, had proved the virtue of an international force.

Panmunjon was just below the 38th Parallel, the area made famous by MacArthur's foiled attempt to cross it against Truman's and the UN's orders. It was once a small farming town, and a favoured jousting-place, on a centuries-old traditional invasion route. Samurai, Mongolians and Manchurians fought there, and more recently the guerrillas fought against the Communists to the north.

It is still the place where the North meets the South, where military, economic and political problems are discussed. As I write, the Red Cross, Olympic officials and the military still gather there to keep the peace. Thousands of tourists wind their way there regularly for eye-witness views of the former war zone, only an hour and a half from Seoul on the newly built Freedom Road, in bumper-to-bumper traffic. It took twenty minutes to race there in 1953.

The tented Panmunjon city had been constructed in 1951 as a

neutral area to negotiate the armistice. Sixteen nations provided combat forces. The war had begun with fifty US military advisers, but the Soviets gave hundreds of jet planes and tanks to the North, and also 2500 advisers for the 175,000 Communist troops.

Not long ago, the first of three tunnels was discovered; dug by North Korea in solid granite fifty to one hundred metres below ground. All are directed towards Seoul. It is said there is a total of twenty. Their purpose? To mount a surprise attack on the South. The truce has apparently ended the shooting war, but has it prevented a new one? South Korea is again faced with the same enemy after more than forty years. In the late-nineties, a tense level of readiness exists in case of a new war on the same border, although former-President Jimmy Carter's 'missionary' visit ended that immediate threat of a nuclear conflict. But days are still uneasy.

Another unpleasant episode, not easy to cope with (not really perilous, but extremely disturbing) occurred after a friend asked me to appear on BBC television in London, one of four guests of Lord Boothby. This man, with a rich voice and bulky frame, was as usual elegantly suited and wearing a bright pink carnation. Winston Churchill once sneeringly called him in the House of Commons, 'The member for television.'

Unexpected trouble surfaced. Boothby was hosting a new television programme, *Dinner Talk*, which consisted of dinner conversations in a studio decorated as a dining room. Three walls were actually oak-panelled, but the fourth, through which cameras focused, was a transparent screen painted so skilfully it looked like panelling. We felt as if we were in a fine old room.

The three other guests were friends, and we were all at ease. I looked forward to good talk and a fine meal, which it was. We would be given plenty of time to reach the right degree of relaxed naturalness before being given a signal that we were on the air.

Instructions from the director were simple: 'Chatter away. When you are in "top form", I will give Lord Boothby my signal. He will then place his finger at the side of his nose to tell you that you are about to be on air.'

Boothby, obviously aglow after fine wines and good food, simply forgot, and we were actually on the air much of the time without knowing it. When I got home and watched the programme (it had been taped before it went on the air), I realized that a serious mistake had been made. Boothby had turned sharply to me to ask: 'Fleur, would you agree the British public should put up millions of pounds to prevent an American buyer from taking the Madonna masterpiece by Michelangelo from Britain to America?' My answer was quick: 'I dislike nationalism in art; why not let others in the world enjoy the painting's beauty?' I pointed out that very few had ever seen this work because it was gathering dust in the Royal Academy's basement, only to be seen by appointment.

The debate about the sale to an American had already been widely aired in countless newspaper columns and editorials, and the matter had even been discussed in the House of Commons. But the Royal Academy thought these comments didn't count as much as millions of viewers who watched us and heard me on that prime-time BBC programme.

Legally, the fault was the BBC's, not mine. It was actually Boothby's – but it was I, not he or they, who was immediately sued by the angry Royal Academy for 'implying' their housekeeping was bad. The suit was eventually withdrawn, but it was a painful experience – perilous, as I dreaded any court appearance.

I have since become the Royal Academy's good friend, even to the extent of bringing it one of its greatest successes, 'Four Thousand Years of Nigerian Art', an exhibition which had just been refused to the museum by the donor country. I was graciously thanked for getting it for them. The Royal Academy and I are close again.

In November 1968, I was in Brazil for the opening of the Bonino Gallery exhibition of my paintings. I had to make a quick return to England to open Durham University's Surrealist exhibition. This became a Surrealist experience, a nasty one.

Because I had momentarily forgotten about the commitment while in Brazil, I quickly refocused my mind and wrote a speech on the plane. Some of the world's best-known Surrealist work had been collected by Durham University's Student Committee. I was delighted to be asked to contribute one of my own paintings.

On the day, sudden fog cancelled the plane I meant to take to the north, leaving me just enough time to catch a train instead. The heating on the coach had broken down but fortunately I had taken the rug from my car as a precaution. The only other person in my carriage was a woman sitting opposite. She seemed to turn blue with cold. Feeling guilty, wrapped in my rug, I impulsively offered her the only thing I could part with – my stockings! As if it was the most obvious suggestion in the world, she thanked me and rolled them over her own.

Durham's fabled beauty lived up to its reputation. I was met by Professor Louis Allen, who had extended the original invitation, and we crossed the bridge to the town and passed its remarkable ancient cathedral. My fears about the speech slowly faded, for I was totally unaware of what lay ahead.

In the University's hall, Vice-Chancellor Christopherson introduced me to a vast student body, masses of faces. I had been asked to speak because I had written *The Case of Salvador Dali*, the authorized biography of the Surrealist painter.

Nothing prepared me for the fate the students had in mind. At my first word, someone fired off a pop-gun; others followed. More danced noisily in the aisles. Then 'music' rang out; fifty men had been hired to sit outside right alongside the wall of the hall, and each had been given an instrument they'd never seen or played before. The noise was deafening. Neither they nor the students could be stopped by anyone or anything. My first instinct was simply to walk out. My next was to ignore them completely and go on through the din with my speech. They might have liked it.

I finished and then yelled for silence, which I got. Though very angry, I smiled and coldly announced: 'You students have made a stupid mistake. You should have invited Salvador Dali, who would have enjoyed your nonsense. *I didn't*. And may I make a second point? Some students think that by taking drugs they are on a shortcut to Surrealism. They are *not*. It is simply cheating.'

Later that night, at the home of the embarrassed Louis Allen, we dined superbly with other university dons, trying to overlook what had happened. Suddenly the doorbell rang – a delegation of students had arrived 'to apologize to Fleur Cowles'.

Three were deputized to come inside to Professor Allen's tiny book-crowded library. Two boys held up an ashen-faced girl standing rigidly between them. Her pallor changed to yellow-green as she fell flat on her face. 'Send me what you intended to say,' I announced as I walked away and Professor Allen ushered them out of the door.

Real adventure came in the rarely travelled Arabian region called the Hadhramaut. It began unwittingly at dinner at the home of Lord and Lady Shawcross in Sussex. A tiny blonde woman ran excitedly towards me as we arrived. She was someone I hadn't seen for at least ten years, but I recognized her as the brilliant French reporter to whom I had given a welcome at *Look* magazine at the suggestion of her Paris newspaper's editor.

Since then she had married Antonin Besse, the man called by many 'the King of the Middle East'. His 'empire' in Aden was eventually confiscated when the English were turned out, and he now operates in Paris. Years before, his father had generously given five million pounds to Oxford University to found the Besse College, and he continues a family tradition of interest in education.

From that Sussex meeting and the resulting friendship came a remarkable journey in 1962. It took me, as the first American woman ever to do so, across the Hadhramaut, that vast, little-known incense and slave route which cuts across the Southern Arabian peninsula, by the warm waters of the Arabian Gulf.

Permissions for the trip had to be obtained by Antonin Besse for me and his wife, Christiane and a bodyguard. We flew in his twin-engined Aero Commander plane, which I co-piloted at times, especially when hot thermal updraughts were rough enough to require two sets of hands to keep the plane under control. One saw no people – only sand and sun, apart from the occasional plodding camel-trains (today they are probably four-wheel-drive trucks). At that time the rulers in the area were not interested in the lure of oil wealth; they needed water before oil, and kept oil interests out.

Life was feudal and medieval. In one small Sultanate, I was stoned by women who were outraged to see a woman in trousers. Many women were still shut away in harems and led separate or secluded lives.

England's legendary explorer, Dame Freya Stark, had made the very same trip many years before, thanks to Antonin Besse's own father.

She did it the hard way; there were no planes then. Instead, she was given space on a dhow going eastward from Aden, one of the work-horses of the sea which were the traditional trading craft, uncomfort-able and slow, the sort of conditions Freya Stark took in her stride. She never minded having to travel or live rough, to eat strange food, to be in discomfort, despite the sciatica which often plagued her.

She had disembarked at the port of Makulla, which was also our first stop. Transportation from then for her was by donkey to the first Sultanate in Salem, but we flew directly into the desert, there to be transferred to jeeps. Our escorts were slaves, nearly naked, carrying machine guns to protect the jeeps from marauding tribesmen in camel caravans. From Aden we flew without the benefit of navigational equip-ment, hoping that our ultimate destination would be the port of Muscat, where desert meets the sea. The city of Muscat faces Bombay across the Arabian Sea.

Mrs Besse brought along sheets for sleeping on the floor of the palaces of the three Sultans we visited; inside each palace were hundreds of rooms but not a piece of furniture. Exteriors in the desert city of Tarum were absolutely beautiful, like sugar-coated candy. Each build-ing had been painted in brilliant pastel paint mixed with date-sugar, shining in the sun like a toy village.

As guests, we estimated our importance in all palaces by judging the rugs strewn about the rooms the Sultans gave us; some were fine, some terrible. Sanitation was primitive – deep, wide-open pipes laid into floors, stretching out through the palace's outer walls to flow on to the streets below.

Food was indigestible and never-changing. Always a whole goat, slightly, *very* slightly, cooked, oozing with grease. Alongside it, the ubiquitous huge mound of rice containing not raisins but dead flies. Fingers were used, not cutlery, as we crouched on the floor alongside the long narrow carpet which served as the table. Food was laid out every ten feet. The Sultan sat anywhere, ignoring protocol, often next to whoever happened to be the last to come in from the desert to see him.

To avoid touching the goat, especially the animal's penis and testicles which were always offered to me as the guest of honour, I pretended to be a vegetarian. I lived on the rice, carefully waiting until other dirty hands had opened up the pile. For dessert, I ate dates which had fallen and gathered up enough sugar to become sticky mounds. These, too, had to be eaten with care to avoid dead flies.

Leaving the Hadhramaut to fly to Muscat would have been fascinating but we couldn't proceed as planned. The despotic Sultan, Said bin Taimur, made it impossible by continuing to refuse access to me. Americans were the lowest on his popularity list and, being a woman, I was even more unwelcome.

However, Antonin Besse's magic unexpectedly worked after we returned to Aden. He had decided we should visit Haile Selassie in Addis Ababa in Abyssinia rather than wait any longer to get to Muscat, when suddenly the Sultan's permission arrived, just as we were about to leave from Aden's airport. Minutes before taking off in the opposite direction, a man ran to us with the necessary papers.

He had relented; I could come, but on strict terms. First, I must agree never to write about Muscat. I did agree, but I did write as soon as he was replaced by his modern-minded son. Secondly, I must never go outside the walled city into the desert.

After a council of war on the plane, I accepted the terms since the royal dispensation was obviously a rare gift. Turning the plane's nose from the west we took off to the east for ten hours of rough flying over johls whose height varied from a thousand feet to ten thousand or more, with constant down draughts to contend with.

Peril appeared as we reached the Muscat of the early sixties, where landing was highly dangerous. The little airport has since been replaced by a superb landing strip and new buildings, but at that time the port and town sat inside a deep bowl with high mountains on three sides and the Arabian Sea on the fourth. We had to circle and re-circle many times to make a landing, descending dangerously from 12,000 feet in a nose-dive to zero feet, and abrupt braking.

All of it became complicated by the sudden arrival of night. Day disappeared. A few minutes later, we would not have made it. I still shudder when I realize we could have crashed on that tiny airstrip. The Sultan's civil and military Air Force would only have attempted it in broad daylight; it was as close as I ever came to death.

We were met at the airport by the Sultan's Minister of Defence, the tall, handsome English mercenary soldier, Brigadier Waterfield MBE, a native of Devon and typical of the best British soldiering in the Arab world. He was delighted by rare visitors, and with the unwanted me on board, ours was an exceptional invasion. I quickly demanded to know why the Sultan had refused for so long to give me the royal consent.

His answer was simple. The Sultan had announced wearily: 'The terrible American lady must not come here. She's going to get killed!'

I turned pale. 'How am I going to get killed?'

'Well, guerrilla warfare is going on in the desert now. It is mined, it's more or less a battlefield. It's dangerous out there.'

Waterfield continued with his account of the royal refusal: that the Sultan had complained that after I was killed he simply didn't want the bother involved. 'Then the trouble begins for us,' the Sultan contended. 'She's an American, so I'll have to *find* an assassin just to satisfy the American government. I'll have to take hostages from all my sheikdoms. I'll have to put them in the dungeon. Feed them, not too much, until someone confesses.

'Because she's an American, we'll have to worry about justice, a trial and all that nonsense, and put the man to death painlessly because the American will be watching. It will be a long and costly affair, *and what for?* She doesn't even offer to pay me!' he concluded.

Despite the Sultan's decree, the Brigadier took me secretly to the dangerous outside: but we always made sure to be inside the giant gates before the Sultan commanded they be locked, at differing times, according to his whim!

In Muscat we slept in the only comfort available, on the roof of a British official's flat because it was too hot inside. The present Sultan has created a wonderful Arab city. There are no high-rises, there is no ostentation, no fear. There is a glorious beach, people look happy, including neighbouring desert people. The war atmosphere existing elsewhere in the Arab world is absent and, apparently, so are the causes. Muscat is an example of the right kind of modernism. The present Sultan was twenty-eight when he started his Sandhurst education. In 1970 he instantly changed his father's savage policies to bring the modern world and greater democratization to Oman, after bloodlessly forcing his ailing father to retire. Muscat is no longer a backwater but a modern Arab society.

*   *   *

Back in 1953, when it was time to leave the Korean War front to return to the United States, the only way to do it without more fuss and bother to General Ridgway in Tokyo was by hitching a lift on any outgoing troop carrier. The first chance came from a pilot of an empty hulk of an Army plane. Sitting on the floor without heat was uncomfortable, but I was at least leaving. His destination was Taipei in Taiwan, where Madame Chiang Kai-Shek lived.

She obviously hated living in modest circumstances after exile from China, and even more being discovered in them. Her warm welcome must have required a lot of acting. Given an option, she would surely have postponed this unexpected visit but, having no choice, she put on her best behaviour.

'We haven't any extra bedrooms here, but I shall put you up in our official guest house outside the city until you leave,' Mme Chiang announced, without a discussion. Not knowing what was in store, the prospect was actually an interesting one; the quiet house had originally been built as a 'reward' house for Japan's kamikaze pilots in the last war and was unchanged in any way.

What was awaiting me soon became obvious. Her limousine had driven halfway out of the driveway when she beckoned it back to say something that chilled my blood. I wound down the window and she said sharply: 'Don't worry about rats, Fleur. My housekeeper keeps a boa constrictor.'   ·

Now, this *was* peril! Even *thinking* of a snake makes me ill. To suspect that a giant one could be slithering around, perhaps sleeping under the low pad which was my bed, made me want to scream. The Korean War front had been much less terrifying.

The President's guest house was 'home' until the next army plane heading out in the direction of the United States could offer further transport. I had to wait four days and nights. Days were spent in Taipei, nights in the guest house on the mountain overlooking the bay. It would have been impossible to ask the American Ambassador to provide a rescue, and leaving the official residence might have been considered an insult to the Head of State. The 'rest' house certainly didn't rest my nerves. Its rear wall clung to the upper side of a cliff; the front façade was of open-work cement in a lace pattern. At night, the fog floated up from the bay below, slipping slowly through the lattice of the cement, right into the rooms. Bedrooms were reached by climbing down, down, down to a low level, in itself frightening. I never slept, ever on the alert for the snake. Sanitation was a hole in the floor, hideously primitive, another horror.

One of the unforgettable 'entertainments' arranged by Mme Chiang was an invitation for me to be the guest of honour at the wedding feast of an important local girl. Her father, sitting at my left, paid me the compliment of not eating anything, the traditional gesture to the principal guest. He just 'fed' me, which involved slowly filling my small bowl with each of the twenty-eight different courses, one at a time, most of them unrecognizable. When we got to monkeys' brains, I held my hands up and carefully explained why I couldn't touch them, pretending to be a vegetarian. The pretence was a life-saver by the tenth course.

Neither the promised housekeeper nor the threatened serpent ever materialized in the guest house, but the worry never ended. When I went down to the safety of the city in daylight, I used to reason that, in all likelihood, neither snake nor housekeeper really existed, that the snake had been conjured up as a mischievous form of revenge by Mme Chiang for 'dropping in' on her, but at night I didn't dare take a chance. I just couldn't sleep. By the time I left, I had decided that insects, whether flying or crawling, and the hole in the floor for sanitation, were horrible enough to make the snake merely another ingredient in a nightmare. Mme Chiang's gift to me of one of her paintings was hardly a *quid pro quo*.

Not only the boa constrictor lived on in my mind; real snakes also spoiled the week I spent at Spain's Coto Danana. Driving there beside the Director of the Reservation (my husband, Tom, and Robert Vavra were in our car behind) I sought to make conversation with this man, who was still a stranger.

'What's new in the Coto?' I asked.

'Not much,' he answered, 'except snakes are having babies at this time.'

My heart stopped. 'Could you wait a moment? I want to remind my husband of something important.'

Both cars stopped. I ran back to tell my husband that we couldn't possibly go on because of the snakes. He grinned, suggesting the

Director was probably only joking. The journey continued in silence.

At the main house, the former hunting preserve of King Alfonso, I walked inside gingerly to find my worst fear realized. There on both sides of the big hall that divided the building were huge posters, warning everyone to beware the poisonous snakes. I somehow swallowed rising hysteria.

Days were spent in a mixture of pleasure and dread. The Reservation was a research station, unequalled in Europe. Inside the huge acreage is a lake, inlets, twenty miles of beaches, all happy areas for baby snakes and parents. Once, our jeep broke down and we had to walk back through tall grass to the lodge; I could only manage by slipping into my husband's footsteps to feel vaguely safe. He is a brave man, and had once been bitten by a cobra, one of few humans ever to survive such an attack. Everywhere around us in the sand and grass were the swirling outlines of snakes in passage.

I was there by invitation to design a wildlife trademark for the Reserve. I couldn't sleep until beds, floors and tops of curtains were carefully examined. I even tried to sleep with eyes open in case a snake might somehow slide inside.

Another time, another danger: while in Rio, a friend arranged for us to join Brazil's Cabinet ministers and their wives for a dramatic view of military manoeuvres taking place south of Rio de Janeiro, two hours by car, on the Atlantic Ocean. We left Rio at five o'clock in the morning and once arrived we settled down on the beach for sandwiches and hot drinks, and watched the sunrise. Without warning, the blast from a large artillery piece barely missed all of us – it would have struck us if we had chosen to enjoy that early meal inside the temporary hut built for our protection on the beach: it was demolished. I suddenly realized that the shell could have knocked out or killed all of Brazil's government other than President Vargas, who had chosen not to join the party.

On another occasion of 'near peril' I was assumed dead. It occurred when I was on my way back from South Africa. I stopped in Nairobi intending to go into the interior to meet Ernest Hemingway who was there, piloting his own plane, to work on his article for *Look* magazine on the state of Kenya at the time of the Mau Mau insurrection.

When I arrived at Nairobi airport, officials met me to explain that I would not be allowed to take the contemplated journey into the interior: there was *too much increased danger from the Mau Mau*. While talking to the officials about Hemingway's own dangerous position under such conditions, a message arrived from up country that *Hemingway had been killed after crashing his plane*. I realized that to my family and others it would appear that I too must have died, as I was expected to be with Hemingway. I had in fact overstayed a day or two in Johannesburg because of a meeting with the Minister of Education. I wanted to see him to discuss his quoted comment, headlined in the morning papers, in which he had announced that the blacks must understand that they would never get the same education as was given to whites. I managed to get the news out that I hadn't joined Hemingway and that I was very much alive. The party that finally rescued Hemingway found him barely alive, terribly injured internally. It was many months before he was well again, but in the meantime news of his death had been widely published. He was one of the few men who ever lived to read his own obituary.

As I've already written, I always wanted the re-incarnation of *Flair* to be my own obituary. This is now taking place with *The Best of Flair* – the best of Fleur – which is about to be launched by HarperCollins in New York in the autumn of 1996.

INDEX